D0957004

To Patricia Goedicke
1931 to 2006

CONTENTS

PLAINS

MONTANA WOMEN WRITERS

A Geography of the Heart

MONTANA WOMEN WRITERS

 *A Geography of the Heart*

Edited by Caroline Patterson

Introduction by Sue Hart

FARCOUNTRY
PRESS
Helena, Montana

COVER PHOTO: Fra Dana, *On the Window Seat*, oil on canvas, undated.

Used by permission of the Montana Museum of Art & Culture
at the University of Montana, gift of Fra Dana.

Softbound
ISBN-13: 978-1-56037-379-7
ISBN-10: 1-56037-379-2

Hardbound
ISBN-13: 978-1-56037-405-3
ISBN-10: 1-56037-405-5

© 2006 Farcountry Press

This book may not be reproduced in whole or in part by any means
(with the exception of short quotes for the purpose of review)
without the permission of the publisher.

For more information on our books, write Farcountry Press,
P.O. Box 5630, Helena, MT 59604; call (800) 821-3874; or visit
www.farcountrypress.com.

Cataloging-in-Publication data on file at the Library of Congress.

Created, produced, and designed in the United States.
Printed in United States.

CONTENTS

MOUNTAINS

CONTENTS

TOWNS

CONTENTS

EDITOR'S PREFACE

I MAGINE STANDING IN A ROOM, talking with forty other women, women who are fiery, soft-spoken, sad, vivacious, intelligent, hilarious, all telling you their stories, one after another. Stories about loss. About love. About loneliness. About the furious neediness of small children. About the despair of entrapment. About wrenching loss. About the widening of oneself that happens when women seek community with other women. Stories about the fearsome loneliness of the plains, the snow-filled isolation of the mountains, and the intense scrutiny in small towns.

This has been my experience in editing this anthology: that of one long, ongoing, fascinating discussion with forty women whose work is as varied and compelling as the state itself. It has been a tremendous pleasure from start to finish.

This book was born, I believe, because I simply wanted to read it. There are fine women writers from Montana and I wanted to see how the place looked as it was reflected through the work of their widely varied minds and sensibilities. I chose to group the writers by place, rather than isolating poetry and prose in the ghettos of "past" and "present," because I wanted the different pieces to speak to one another, regardless of time.

This book was born, too, because I didn't want my daughter to experience the history of Montana as I did. When I was ten, as Phoebe now is, my lessons about the state's history and literature were from what seemed to me tired litanies about fur trappers, explorers, cowboys, copper barons, and governors, with Jeannette Rankin thrown in as the lone woman. They were dry and dusty to me because—I realized later—there was no one person through which I could enter the past. There was no one in those old texts who could take me there. This is my attempt to give Phoebe a history and literature of the state that takes place in a community of women, all speaking, all intelligent, all soulful, with whom she can converse for the rest of her life.

I wish to thank the following individuals for their tireless help. I am deeply grateful to Sue Hart for providing the excellent introduction and helping acquaint me with many historical women writers. Kim Anderson offered me tremendous assistance in identifying and locating contemporary writers. Also, I was able to find several historical women poets with the guidance of Tami Haaland and Sandra Alcosser. I am enormously indebted to Gretchen Rangitsch, who cheerfully helped me locate writers and fine-tune selections, and spent hours on the scanner—without her help this book would not have happened. Designer Eric P. Hanson and editors Jessica Solberg and Ann Seifert helped turn a vision into a book. And I wish to thank Barbara Koostra, of the Montana Museum of Art and Culture at the University of Montana, for arranging for the use of the Fra Dana painting of the woman reading the newspaper—one of my favorites—on the cover. Finally, I wish to thank all of the fine women writers in this book—alive or dead—whose work I have had the honor to read and collect.

Caroline Patterson is an editor at Farcountry Press in Helena. She has published fiction and nonfiction in publications including Alaska Quarterly Review, Epoch, Outside, Seventeen, Southwest Review, Sunset, *and* Via. *She has an undergraduate degree from Amherst College and an M.F.A. in creative writing from the University of Montana–Missoula. She was a 1990-1992 Stegner Fellow in Fiction at Stanford University and has received fellowships from the Henfield Foundation, the Montana Arts Council, and the San Francisco Foundation. She lives in Missoula with her husband, writer Fred Haefele, and their two children.*

Sue Hart

INTRODUCTION

L IFE IN MONTANA HAS NEVER been easy, even for those who
live in the cities and in the small communities that have matured
since the early days of original settlement. There are the vagaries of
weather to contend with, the open—some would say desolate—stretches
between towns, and, for some, especially "transplants," the sense of
being disconnected from important centers of intellectual stimulation,
professional entertainment, and social interaction on a grander scale than
Saturday night at the local watering hole. For men, the transition from the
known to the unknown has almost always been easier than it was—and
often still is—for women, many of whom, like the characters in several
stories and poems in this wonderful collection, left the homes they had
known all of their lives to follow not their dreams, but those of a husband
or father. And this setting off for Montana is not a thing of the past; it
continues to this day.

My own family experienced the first great wave of western migration
in the late 1870s. One of my uncles told me about my great-grandmother's
reaction when she finally arrived at the family's destination. "The shock
that Grandmother experienced at the sight of her new home, a sod hut, was
so great that she sat on the wagon tongue and cried in disappointment,"
he said. No doubt a good share of those tears were shed for the family and
community she had left behind in Iowa as well as over the hard future that
was forecast by that humble sod hut. How desolate and lonely the West
must have seemed to many, many women—the early women settlers as
well as the native women whose lives were changed forever by the white
settlement of what had been their home ground for generations.

Every woman represented in this amazing—and long overdue—

collection of Montana women's short stories, novel excerpts, and nonfiction books, poems, and personal accounts has a tale to tell or a poetic statement to make about the experience of Montana. Whether it is a cry of frustration over the loneliness imposed by distance, or a joy in the freedom offered by those same vast expanses, a protest against the hardships of life on the land, or an acceptance of the blessing that same land bestowed, it's all here. The words of these women from different generations, different parts of the state, and different life experiences, all tell a part of the Montana story.

These are not the stories of gunslingers, outlaws, and other colorful—and often fanciful—characters so many who do not live here associate with the West. This is a woman's West, not just a geographical location on a map, but a spot in the hearts and minds of both writers and readers.

Three of the earliest accounts in this collection come from women whose Montana experiences were vastly different from their fellow storytellers. Elizabeth "Libby" Custer, Nannie Alderson, whose *A Bride Goes West* was written with Helena Huntington Smith, and Mary Ronan all wrote of life in this state in the 1800s. Libby Custer—while technically not a Montanan—lost her husband, George Armstrong Custer, when he and his Seventh Cavalry soldiers were killed in the Battle of the Little Bighorn, not far from where Nannie Alderson and her husband took up ranching in the Birney area just a few years later.

Nannie's story is one of both hardship and hope. "Raising cattle never was like working on a farm," she says. "There was more freedom to it. Even we women felt that, *though the freedom wasn't ours.*" (Emphasis added.) That thought echoes through many of the pieces in this collection, even those written by contemporary authors. In many ways, the West of both imagination and reality remains a territory dominated by the myth and the reality of the Western male.

Mary Ronan kept journals about her experience in western Montana with her husband, Peter Ronan, who served as the Indian agent on the Flathead reservation for many years. In her memoir of those years, she writes, "I was delighted with the beauty of the place. There I spent twenty years, *the most interesting and difficult of my life.* (Emphasis added.) Something stirring, exciting, dangerous was always pending, threatening, happening." At least one of the difficulties was the heavy demand on her time to entertain guests at the agency, which involved frontier hospitality such as feeding a visitor upon his or her arrival at any time of the day or night—a duty Alderson and other writers of that time period refer to frequently. As the female narrator of Diane Smith's *Pictures from an Expedition* realizes, she (and other female newcomers) "had much to learn while in Montana."

Perhaps tellingly, the stories in this collection by the three Montana women writers best known for their fictional representations of life in the West—B. M. Bower, Dorothy M. Johnson, and Mildred Walker—all revolve around women and ranch life. In Bower's "Cold Spring Ranch," a wife of three years' duration is arriving for the first time at her new home in the West. The very name of the ranch, Cold Spring, and Manley's description of the home he has built—what he modestly calls "a shack," but which his bride has thought of as a "cottage"—sets up the conflict necessary to a good story: Can this marriage be saved? (And how about the husband's name? That certainly lets us know that he's a true Western hero.) Bower, by the way, wrote a number of screenplays for early Western films—the silents— but the men who flocked to see these gun-and-gallop Westerns might have been shocked to meet the female scriptwriter.

Dorothy M. Johnson's "Prairie Kid" is set in the 1800s, when the West was still a dangerous place to be, and the question to be answered in the story is two-fold: whether or not the young woman who is visiting her brother will stay after she and the "kid," eleven-year-old Elmer Merrick, have a brush with an outlaw, and whether Elmer can or will remain on the family's land after the death of his father. The characters "Miss" Johnson (she abhorred the newspaper convention of referring to a woman by her last name only) introduced in this story must have been favorites; she wrote several other stories/episodes about Elmer, leading me to believe she might have planned a novel built on the boy's adventures as he grew to manhood. Johnson never had children of her own, and Steve Smith, her biographer, suggests that "her stories were her children." Her fondness for the young hero of this story, and her continuing to write about him, may well have grown out of a "maternal instinct" for her own invented characters. (She did confess to having fallen in love with one of the male characters in her last, and unfinished, novel—she couldn't bear to give him up to the female character he was supposed to marry!)

It is interesting that the author has the visiting woman character make the important pronouncement that the West will become a safe and civilized place, a good place to live and raise families—even though she credits this transformation to the cowboy who has captured her fancy. This is just one of several places in her body of work where women characters make important contributions and comments instead of standing around wringing their hands or screaming for help, as they so often did in pulp novels and early Western movies. While Miss Johnson often noted that "the women wanted everything in their new western communities to be the way it was back in Iowa, and so did the good men, the fathers of families," she created strong women characters who were capable of bringing about the changes they wanted on their own.

In Walker's "Rancher's Wife," Bella Myers is indeed a rancher's wife, but she's always lived in town (despite the fact that her husband has to commute sixty-seven miles each way to work his ranch). Bella likes the social life of town living and her lovely home, but in this story she has to face the realities of being a rancher's wife when drought is on the land and cash is in short supply.

Another woman writer from approximately the same period as Mildred Walker and Dorothy M. Johnson, although not as well-known, was Frieda Fligelman, a delightful woman who lived in Helena—in two apartments. She needed two, she explained to me, because she had so many books, manuscripts, and papers that she couldn't fit everything into a single apartment. She also had an organ, which she loved to play; she'd often invite me over for tea and treat me to a recital of what she called her "space music." One of her poems chosen for inclusion in this collection reminds me very much of the pleasant clutter of her home. When you read "Hall Bedroom Scholar," you'll see why.

One time when Frieda visited Billings for a conference, she was in the lunch line when her hat—she always wore a hat, as women of that period did—was set on fire by a careless smoker. It didn't faze her, even when a glass of water was thrown on her hat to douse the flames. (Frieda and her sister Belle were cousins of Butte novelist and screenwriter Myron Brinig.)

Butte's Mary MacLane created quite a stir worldwide when *The Story of Mary MacLane By Herself* was published in 1902. Readers were shocked by

Mary's infatuation with the Devil and by her characterization of Butte and its citizens. Mary had a brief period of popularity, even starring in a film based on an article she wrote, "Men Who Have Made Love to Me." After being such a sensation, however, she died at an early age, penniless, in a Chicago hotel.

The thrill of risk that runs through this selection of prose and poetry is identified by two contemporary writers, Deirdre McNamer and Maile Meloy. Jerry Malone, in Deirdre's *One Sweet Quarrel*, needs to "feel [him]self to be at real risk...chancing something." And Maile's female character notes the lack of the "giddiness of adventure" she encounters at a truck stop during a blizzard in "Garrison Junction." "Chancing something"—seeking that "giddiness of adventure"—is surely part of what brought early settlers to Montana, and it is still a part of life throughout the West.

M. L. Smoker writes of "chancing" on a very personal level in her poem "Winter again": "My mother was alive then/and I made my way toward the temptation of finally/getting things right between us." Mary Clearman Blew's "Paranoia" certainly demonstrates that opportunities for "chancing" are still available when she tells of a bizarre academic year during her first college teaching job in Havre. On top of her academic duties, she was trying to resume her successful writing career, while all around her, both at home and on campus, her life was in chaos: "The other thing that happened that spring, besides the end of my marriage, was that the dean called me down to his office and offered me the chairmanship of the English department, thus confirming—what?—whose paranoia?"

The lament and celebration in Melissa Kwasny's "Common Blue"— "Even the most/beautiful days always seem to have death in them"—is a common thread in this book. There is frequent-enough cause for lament— failed marriages (Annick Smith's "Virtue,": "I love trees, these days, more than I love men."; and Mary Clearman Blew's "Paranoia," for example) and lost loves, lost hopes, lost identities, lost dear ones, lost innocence. In Frances Kuffel's "First Love," the rape of a young girl by a neighbor boy is avenged by her brother and his friends, and in Kate Gadbow's "Buffalo Jump," another schoolgirl and her family face disillusionment over events that take place in a Catholic school; all three of Gwendolen Haste's poems, "Ranch in the Coulee," "The Reason," and "The Solitary," focus on the loneliness and despair felt by wives of homesteaders. (Gwenna, however, also wrote of rural women who loved their lives and their land, although she admitted that her doctor, having read "Ranch in the Coulee," told her that he saw patients every day like the woman she described and mostly could do nothing for them. They were, he explained, worn out by loneliness, hard work, and "excessive childbearing.")

In Debra Magpie Earling's moving story "Bad Ways," we read a lament of the Flathead nation over the loss of a way of life, of the Indians' lands and their traditions: "We have lost ourselves when we let the white man come too close, when we gave ourselves away." In Patricia Henley's touching "The Secret of Cartwheels," her young narrator realizes the extent of her losses and tells the reader: "I held my breath to keep from crying...I was worn out with the knowledge that life would be different, but not in the way I had imagined or hoped...The new spring leaves were so bright they hurt my eyes."

Ruth McLaughlin, in her memoir, "Destiny," writes, "Our family had a ninety-seven-year fling here; now we are gone. Ten of us were left behind, six of them children, planted in two cemeteries." This piece certainly resonated with me, as just this past May, I visited the spot where my great-grandparents buried two of their young daughters, Maud and Ellen, on the land they were farming.

In Melanie Rae Thon's gripping "Heavenly Creatures," a heart-wrenching story of homeless children and a woman who, in her own childlike way, tries to help them, a character who has been aware of several such youngsters reflects on one of them: "Sometimes in the early dark of winter I feel Holly at my window watching my daughters and me as we eat our dinner. She won't come in. The cold no longer feels cold to her. The cold to her is familiar."

Patricia Goedicke's "At the Center" also speaks of loss: "Six feet by three feet patch/swells upward, slightly/greener toward the chest...But now you are nowhere in evidence, down there/dressed in the green sweater I knitted for you/when we first met."

Judy Blunt's "Salvage" revisits another kind of loss—the heavy toll on her family's cattle during a terrible blizzard in the 1960s. Her father tells her: "'I guess if you had another lifetime to live, you would have learned

something anyway,' my father tells me now. 'One thing I learned and that's
for godsake don't ever…' He pauses, searching words, his eyes grim and
sad, then starts over. 'If you have a froze up critter, shoot 'em or haul them
off or something. Get rid of them. It's cruel.'" Joanna Klink laments the loss
of eighty-five antelope drowned in Fort Peck Lake in "Antelope": "They
came/because they believed they would be held,/as in each moment there
is no hint of future pain."

Grace Stone Coates writes of another type of loss—the loss of self, or
is it escape?—in "Hardness of Women": "And a woman can leave a man,
without quitting his dwelling,/To loneliness deeper than night with no star-
spawn;/The dearth he has of her is beyond his telling./In the crook of his
arm she is gone from him, she is gone." More can be learned about Grace in
Lee Rostad's informative selection from "An Alien Land."

Ripley Schemm Hugo, in a loving tribute to her son in "Building
Fence," recalls that he could "catch fish in the clearest/waters, enough to
feed the whole bunch/hunkered down to plates and forks. Early,/he built
a whole from parts—heard people's/scattered stories, wove the fragments/
together…And very young, he wanted to know of earth,/of lives lived on
it…I don't know the reason my son should die/a young man before he
could get done/what he wanted.…"

There's even a tribute by Ellen Baumler to Dorothy Baker, one of
Helena's best-known madams, whose "door was without a doubt the best-
known door in town" and whose passing signaled the end of an era. Finally,
Madeline DeFrees's "Climbing the Sky Bridge Stair" provides a rueful
comment about healing: "How better/to salvage one's grief/as body slowly
turns/stone, already tied to/a drowning spirit, than by putting a flat/hat on
one's sorrow, making/the soul and its body dance in ambiguous balance?"

But all is not woe. In this work there is cause for celebration, also, as in
Sandra Alcosser's playful challenge in "What Makes the Grizzlies Dance":
"Have you never wanted/to spin like that/on hairy, leathered feet,/amid
swelling berries/as you tasted a language/of early summer—shaping/lazy
operatic vowels,/cracking hard-shelled/consonants like speckled/insects

between your teeth,/have you never wanted/to waltz the hills/like a beast?" The music of celebration is also in Bonnie Buckley Maldonado's "Blarney Castle Ranch": "Stories and piano tunes swirl/around the stove in winter,/and on the summer verandah/voices carry stories to the stars." One of my all-time favorite stories, May Vontver's "The Kiskis," also falls into this category, ending on a triumphant note for the young teacher of homesteaders' children in a one-room schoolhouse: "The Kiskis ate candy, too. They beamed on everybody. They had had something to give and everybody thought their gift wonderful. . . That noon the Kiskis ate lunch in the school-house."

Tami Haaland's delightful "Scout Meeting at Mayflower Congregational" depicts a wonderful vision of mothers and children in a local church: "One mother nudges her child away,/another grabs an arm. 'Stay/away from there,' she says. 'A church/is no place to play.' I watch the/remaining three, my young son/among them, dancing on toes/toward darkness, whispering into/the center where Jesus waits,/pretending not to notice their approach." The whole scene just makes the reader smile. Janet Zupan's "Plunge" suggests comfort of intimacy when she writes "Your bed is warm, a beach for me...." Cyra McFadden's excerpt from her lively *Rain or Shine: A Family Memoir* ends on a jubilant note: "Meanwhile we rolled along in the Packard, hell-bent for Dallas, Fort Worth, Baton Rouge and Alabama City. We had our classy car, and gas money. We could sing three-part harmony to 'San Antonio Rose.' We had the Brahma bull by the tail."

Nature is often the source of celebration, whether it is a source of bounty, as in Geraldine Connolly's "Morel Hunting": "How sure you are that you must/have them—devils' thumbs, like foreign cities, or new love," or a source of grace as Sheryl Noethe makes clear in "God's Riffling Touch": "A stand of trees stood behind me./The birds launched themselves at it, wings brushing my face,/their wind blowing back my hair,/they rushed and thrummed around and through me/as if I was just vertical wilderness./My scarf flew away with them./I turned and looked at several people gathering to watch./'My friend,' one said, 'You have received a blessing.'"

This celebration, too, includes humor. This scene from Sara Vogan's *In Shelly's Leg* portrays a women's fastpitch softball game: "At second, the woman with her hair in rollers pounds her glove while the shortstop moves out to where the ball is lying in the grass. She fires it off to first and straightens the hem on her sweatshirt, making it even across her hips. It reads: A WOMAN'S PLACE IS IN THE HOUSE AND THE SENATE.

And, we might add, as a major part of the Montana literary landscape.

An English professor at Montana State University–Billings for more than forty years, Sue Hart was an associate producer for a documentary on Ernest Hemingway in Montana, Paradise & Purgatory: Hemingway at the L Bar T and St. Vincent Hospital *and was the scriptwriter and co-producer of* Gravel in the Her Gut & Spit in Her Eye, *a documentary about Dorothy M. Johnson. The winner of a PEN Syndicated Fiction Award for her short story "Star Pattern," Hart publishes frequently on Montana literary subjects in journals and magazines. She has written a book,* Call to Care, *about the centennial history of St. Vincent Hospital, and a book on the history of MSU–Billings,* Yellow-Stone & Blue. *Hart is the recipient of a Governor's HIV/AIDS Recognition Award, a Governor's Award for the Humanities, and the Montana Historical Society's Trustees' Educator's Award—and she was one of two queens chosen for the Billings St. Patrick's Day parade. She has four grown children and is married to novelist Richard S. Wheeler.*

PLAINS

Judy Blunt

From *Breaking Clean*
SALVAGE

T HE REGION WE CALL THE HI-LINE stretches the length of northern Montana from the foothills of the Rocky Mountains to the North Dakota border. Winter along the Hi-Line is all about wind, a cycle of wind. Cold wind brings the snow, whips it into place; warm chinook winds crust the snow, anchoring it until spring thaw. Between chinooks, wind levels the landscape, sweeping ridges bare, filling the low spots until creek beds and long, forked drainages seem to rise, exposed like a network of white veins against the wind-stripped hills. Ground blizzards shut down travel more often than fresh snow, dry winter storms, all variations on a theme: clear, cold nights with snow blowing knee-high, like a low fog streaming over the ground; cloudy days when the horizon disappears and wind pours sky and earth together into one seamless bowl; bright days you go blind trying to find the shadow-white of tire tracks under the continuous slither and glitter of moving white. In chinook country there is no snow pack. Instead, we talk about snow "on the level," a way of imagining a few inches spread out to an even depth. Only the drifts are measured in feet.

Winter mornings of my childhood take on a sameness in my memory, every day a repetition of chores done the day before. The livestock waited, as hungry on Christmas as they were on everyday mornings, and our lives revolved around the responsibility of them. Every evening we had bum calves to feed, water and bed, a milk cow to be tended and milked, water tanks wanting cleared of ice and hay bunks pitched full for the yearling heifers in the feedlot, and two or three dozen chickens to separate from their eggs. As we children were broken in to the evening chores, our supper table took on the farm kid's version of *think of all the starving kids in China*. Fried round steak and gravy, boiled potatoes and home canned green beans piled on my plate, I would lift my fork and center the first mouthful.

"Did you take care of the chickens?" my mother would ask, pointed in her tone, for she would know whether I had trailed through the kitchen for the pail of warm water. Like all our outbuildings, our chicken house was neither heated nor insulated, and in winter only warm water would stay liquid long enough for each hen to drink. The few times I had to admit I hadn't done chores were enough to cure me. How could I fill my face while the chickens that depended on me went to roost empty, trapped inside, unable to fend for themselves? "No, finish your supper first," Mom would say as I clambered up from the table, and I would have to settle back and clean my plate, chewing every bite, finishing my milk, asking to be excused, her silence a reproach, an accusation. No excuse covered the sin, no apology wiped it away. It was a small, small person who bellied up to the table while his livestock stood hungry, and in that lesson we were offered the best of role models.

I suppose there were ranchers who slept in on Sunday mornings after a night in town, or took winter vacations and let their cattle make do for a few days, but my father wasn't one of them. Every morning after barn chores Dad drove to the hay yard adjoining the winter pasture and pulled the pitchfork from its seat deep in the side of a stack. First cutting, second cutting, on rare wet years, a third crop of alfalfa grew in the meadows along the creek, each fragrant forkful cut, raked and stacked by his own hand. Standing knee deep in a stack, he pitched the wooden hayrack full, stabbed the fork into the mound and jumped down to hitch the tongue of the rack to the pickup. Some of the cattle bedded down on the feed ground, and these rose and stretched as the pickup pulled toward them. Others broke into a lumbering trot, bawling in chorus as the honk of the pickup horn called them in from the shelter of coulees. A hundred-yard path cut across the prairie north to south, the snow trampled flat and hard, colored with the residue of yesterday's hay, and here Dad stopped, rolling down the window as the cows crowded around him.

The first times I beat out my older brother as feed assistant, I was small enough to have to kneel on the seat to steer the pickup across the frozen ground, young enough to believe my father talked to his cows in their own language. *Come boss, comeboss, c'mbaaws,* his call melted into syllables bawled out the open window, and the cows answered in long, urgent drones, tipping up their chins and lofting streams of smoke into the bitter air. Planting the stick shift into compound gear, he would ease the clutch and push against their milling bodies to get the door open, jumping out as the pickup began to crawl forward.

Days we had school, the pickup made its own way across the feed ground, Dad keeping one eye on its direction as he pitched a trail of hay. The first forkfuls lit on the backs of the greediest cows, but as the feed stretched out along the path, the animals lined out alongside, and at the end it came out even—a thick line of green with red cattle, head down on either side, a Christmas ribbon unfurled on a field of brilliant white. Swinging down from the rack, Dad trotted to catch the pickup, reaching out to grab the door handle and jump into the cab, settling behind the wheel in a gust of cold air, a flurry of fine chaff. He lingered after feeding, driving back slowly along the row of broad backs, stabbing the air with two fingers, lips moving silently as he counted the tally, squinting against the snow glare for sign of lameness, hocks cut on the sharp crusted snow, a joint sprained in a slide on the ice. He judged health by their eagerness to shoulder and shove together, stopping to study any cow that held herself apart.

It's a luxury of the small rancher to look at a herd of uniform white-faced Herefords and see individuals, to know the old swing-bag cow from the Murphy heifer, or one 1,200-pound animal as the daughter of another, mother of a third. My father's cattle were not pets, but he knew them all, fifty big Hereford cows, the bulk of them descended from his father's herd. Each fall they lined up along the fence at the first sign of cold weather, bawling to be let into the winter pasture. "Spoiled old bitches," he'd grumble as we opened the gate and drove them in, all of them waddling fat, one calf weaned from their side that fall, another growing large in their bellies. It was good business to keep the cattle fed up, healthy, he would say, lest anyone accuse him of sentimentality. A person takes care of what's his. But his cows were far more than property, his connection to them more complex than the desire for heavy steer calves to sell and fine quality heifers to keep. Their contentment was a measure of his own, their wellbeing a source of pride. Cattle that wore his brand spend their summers on good grass, their winters wallowing in hay, nursed their calves with sun rippling over sleek hides. They grazed fence lines along the county road, lifting their heads to gaze after passing cars, visible as any finely tended field.

The winter I was ten I would see my father as beaten as he ever got, though my recognition is one of hindsight. Children tend to observe catastrophe at their own level, maintaining a sort of cheerful indifference to those things outside their control. The blizzard of 1964 and its aftermath were adult problems, ones I assumed my parents qualified to handle. For my part, the hard-packed drifts made great sledding. The snow could be chopped into blocks to make igloos, banks could be tunneled into or skated upon as the mood took me. Plugged roads made school attendance an every morning judgement call, and I went to bed each night in the thrill of uncertainty.

There was a lot of talk about death that winter, a lot of coming and going between neighbors as the community shoveled out and tried to piece together what was left. Though both of vital interest to me, stories of birth and death had always differed in the telling. Birth happened, and whatever initiated the event was never discussed. Death, on the other hand, was caused. When animals died out of turn, the stories focused on exploring the reasons for it and assigning blame, either human error or that of the victim. As a cause of death, stupidity beat out old age by a wide margin. That winter the stories had a new twist—death just happened. "Sonuvabitch just tipped over and died," a note of wonder leveling the voice, leaving the rest hanging in midair. By the end of January, birth and death ran together in a new combination as sick cows aborted, emptying their wombs months early. Calves born dead. In the telling, these births took on a nasty sound, both in the words used and in the bitter tone that spoke of betrayal: "That old red-necked cow sloughed her calf," they would say, or, "She slunk a set of twins the size of jack rabbits."

That spring as the weather faired, Gail, Gary and I played around a deep trench gouged into the prairie a quarter mile from the house. We made games around the bloating carcasses it held, daring each other to cut pieces away with our jackknives, holding our breath against the sweetish stench as we jumped from one set of ribs to the other, playing hopscotch on the bodies of half my father's cattle. We shivered with naughtiness, dancing on the dead. Some we recognized. The new Angus bull, Bellboy, was in there, and Inky, our milk cow. The rest were anonymous—at one end a dozen feeder calves dead of coccidiosis, the bloody scours, their eyes sunk deep in their skulls from the fever and dehydration, at the other, a layer of range cows, bigger animals that seemed sealed in death, eyes and mouths clamped tight.

Their loss was of passing interest to me, an event too large to grasp, perhaps, or simply dismissed because cows were not my job. My memories would have faded with spring thaw but for the community who got past the winter and kept the stories alive until children grew into them. They come down to me whole, stories of a blizzard that took the measure of any man, that became the measure of all storms to come.

DECEMBER 14, 1964. JACKRABBITS GATHER nervously at the edge of the feed ground, the first line moving in low to the ground, those behind rocking up on their hindquarters, ears flipping to the bedded cows and away, registering the stillness. A bad night for rabbits, twenty below zero under a sharp moon, every movement a shadow, every noise brittle, explosive. A good night for owls. But it's the flash of a spotlight the rabbits fear more than the shadow of silent flight. Their bodies are worth a quarter, and the men come hunting most every night. Every rancher has his pile of jackrabbits, his mountain of mad money, stashed in an outbuilding, frozen whole. Every couple of weeks, buyers arrive in Malta, collect the stiff corpses by the semi-truck load, and sell them to mink farms.

Fifty Hereford cows and two bulls doze in the waste of morning feed, and the rabbits work around them, pulling alfalfa stems from the packed snow with nervous jerks, noses working the sharp air as they chew. The atmospheric pressure has fallen rapidly since dark. Strung tight, they scour the trampled ground, erupting in exaggerated leaps at the chalky crunch of snow under a cow's hoof. They've come on trails, hundreds of rabbits single file, and they leave the same way, following the paths beaten by cows coming to water, by pickups checking on cows. Off the trails, they leave body prints in the loose powder, no crust to support their weight. Scattering out of sight of the buildings, they settle in the shelter of cutbanks, under willows along the creek, in snow domes roofed by the spread of tall sagebrush, digging into the drifts and turning to face south. It's twenty-five below zero now and quiet, but something is coming. They can smell it.

Midnight turns with a sigh. A faint breeze eddies along the ruts of the county road, softening the channels cut by four-wheel drives. Over a foot has fallen since Thanksgiving and it lies in loose gathers across the fields, restless where the breeze touches it. Slack drifts taper across the grade, deepest where the road crosses a coulee. Where the lane is plugged, drifted straight across, it's been cleared by hand, a mother or a father with scoop shovel and a pickup load of kids heading for school. The snow shovels like sand or wheat, spilling off the sides of the scoop as it's tossed toward the ditch. The county plows come by every few days, kicking through drifts, shoving it all to one side, to the south or east, so the track will fill more slowly. Fifty miles west, a chinook has cleared the prairie at the base of the Little Rocky Mountains, but here the forecast remains cold, the warm spell overdue, and the ranchers grumble and shovel.

Past midnight, lights wink out to the northwest and the line spreads toward the moon, half the sky gone smooth as wet slate, half still rough with the jitter of starlight. The wind picks up, strong enough to scalp drifts and chase snow across the flats. There the land pitches rough, snow streams flat off the ridge tops like foam spraying from white caps. On the lee side of the cutbanks, jackrabbits flatten their ears as snow fans over their bodies. The claws on their front feet are sharp enough to dig roots from dry sod. Those with full bellies may survive. But the prairie birds, the ring-necked pheasants and sage hens dug their graves at dusk, burrowing under blankets of snow, insulated and invisible as the wind rises around them.

Within hours an inner alarm clock will rouse the birds, and they will shift and push against the solid roof overhead. Some will peck ineffectually at the snow until they tire, until they sleep from suffocation or starvation. Months later they surface untouched, head still tucked under a wing. The strongest die quickly, at daybreak. These manage to crack their sealed coffin like an eggshell and burst upward into the jaws of the storm. They drop within seconds, gaping, the air too thick to pull through the slim nares at the top of their beaks, too cold to breathe directly into the lungs for very long. These will be found first, in the top layers of the drifts, necks outstretched, wings spread as if for balance, or flight.

The big animals have nowhere to hide. The largest population of mule deer winter in the Missouri River breaks, browsing where scrub pine and juniper mute the worst of the wind, but the pronghorn antelope live by their eyes. Winter and summer, they stick to the bench land where they can see what's coming, sheltered by distance rather than trees. This night, they gather in groups of twenty or thirty, pressing into draws and coulees. They are toughened to the cold, plush with winter hair, and still they stamp and shift against the bite. Well before dawn, the snow billows far over their heads, clogging the air, chilling their blood. They begin to move with the wind, walking to stay warm. The late fawns, a few wet does drawn thin from a summer of nursing, grow stiff and stop before morning, but the rest keep going, blinded by snow, pushed by the wind. They walk like machines, heads lowered to breathe in the shelter of their own bodies, slow and steady, a night and a day, another night. There's nothing to eat. Wind-packed drifts pave the prairie, sealing the grass like concrete. Where ramps of snow bridge the fences, they step over the wire, walking south. Hundreds cross the Missouri River on the ice forty or fifty miles from where they started, arriving at the edge of the storm front gaunt and hollow-eyed.

By two in the morning, the stars are gone, whether blotted by clouds or blowing snow there's no telling. On the feed ground, cows begin to rise, silent and miserable. They are range animals, bred for stamina, reared on the unsheltered prairie, and they weather storms on herd instinct. Guarded by layers of fat, thick hide, a dense coat of winter hair, they close ranks, shoulder to shoulder and turn tail to the wind. Those in the center of the herd stand quietly, heads lowered, surrounded by heat. Snow softens and re-freezes in layers on their exposed backs, but inside where the bodies touch, they are warm. The outside ring is less content. Snow lodges under hair, sticks to the skin and builds outward. They clamp their tails and hump their backs against the sting of it until something gives, and they can push toward the shelter inside, stirring the group like a slow spoon. Warm flanks shoved to the outside turn white; cold ones entering the circle of condensed breath collect frost like magnets in a pile of metal shavings.

As the weather worsens, the cattle endure it as best they can, butts to the wind, aiming south like the arrow on a weather vane. With every change of the rear guard, the group shifts a few feet forward, away from the minimal windbreak of the stack yard, toward the open prairie. Icicles dangle from the guard hairs on their chins and bellies, from eyelash and ear fringe. A mile to the east antelope drift by on a twenty-mile wind, coated white, invisible but for the dark slits of their eyes. The air chill is some seventy degrees below zero, already cold enough to focus every creature on survival, domestic or wild. At three, the blizzard hits like a freight train.

THIRTY YEARS AFTER THE STORM I quiz my father about the wind, what does he guess? Forty, fifty miles an hour? Sixty, seventy? "Sixty," he says, "seventy." Shrugging. No one knows how hard the wind blew. Temperatures were a fact, measurable, recordable, though they varied a few degrees from ranch to ranch. Some reported twenty-seven below zero that first morning, others insist it was colder, thirty or thirty-five below. But the wind was a guess. They could only compare it to other winds, gales that hit with summer storms, times someone lost the roof off a shed or watched windrows of green hay roll like cigars across the meadow. All my father knows for sure is he never saw anything like it in winter.

I study the almanac open between us on the kitchen table. "Wind chill charts stop at forty-five miles per hour. Says here anything stronger than that doesn't change the temperature much."

That draws a snort. He tips his head sideways, stubborn, thinking on it. "Matters if you're in it," he says finally. But I'm already testing my meager math skills, looking for a conservative estimate—let's say, thirty below zero with a forty-five mph wind. "That makes it one hundred sixteen degrees below zero," I say quietly, mentally refiguring the numbers: *minus 116?*

He's looking at his hands while I figure out loud, fingers as big around as a baby's wrist, opening and closing a fist as if limbering it up. "Hunerd n' sixteen," he muses, "Hell, it had to be at least that. Had to be." He studies at it a second, clenching, releasing, clenching, then shoves back in his chair, ready to get up and do something.

WHEN IT HIT, THE HOUSE bent and shrieked, a sound like nails pulled from damp wood. In their bedroom on the northwest corner of the house, my father woke, his breath visible in the air over his head. Cold enough to freeze pipes. He turned on the light long enough to find his jeans and socks. The window on the north wall rattled steadily, the curtains trembling, panes plastered with snow. The stove in the living room ran on fuel oil, #2 diesel, but there were no thermostats to kick on when the temperature dropped. In the dark, he made his way to the kitchen to hit the overhead light switch, then back to the oil heater. He turned the dial to "high" and pawed the litter of mittens and boots to one side. High meant cherry red. The stove in the kitchen ran on cottonwood, a couple of logs ready on the floor beside it, a couple of days' worth stacked in the porch. He fed fires, turned on faucets, opened bedroom doors, made the necessary rounds with tense efficiency. The noise seemed impossible. Stove pipes hummed, beams creaked, snow blasted against the north windows like birdshot. Overriding it all was the wind, an urgent moaning under the eaves that rose in sustained shrieks, like a cat fight.

He turned off the light, leaned over the cook stove and rested a hand against the kitchen window, trying to see movement in the wall of solid gray outside. Was the house drifted under? The frigid draft leaking through the frame said not, but there was no light, no shape of trees by the house, no way to judge the speed of the blowing snow. The illusion was one of stillness, a dark blanket held up to the glass. The window looked south, toward the feedground, the stack yard. He stood a moment with the sound of the storm settling in his gut, trying to imagine his cows huddled against the fence, sheltered by the long row of haystacks. He might get them into the lot by the barn. He reached for the coffeepot, lifted the basket of used grounds then stopped and leaned against the stove again. The wind was all wrong, north and west. The cattle were gone. He found his way back to bed in the dark. My mother's voice lifted in a question, and he answered her, "tougher than hell out there." He lay back, listening to the roar. Nothing he could do until daylight.

As what passed for dawn approached, only the prairie birds and children slept on unaware of the storm. Inside our house nine people curled closer to bedmates, drawing quilts over their noses against the chill. The boys had camped out on the living room floor, their bed given over to Granddad, our mother's father. Two neighbor girls were crowded into the cot-sized bunk beds with Gail and me, stranded at our house since school let out the day before. Their mom had buried her pickup in a drift trying to get them and had to dig out and turn back.

My parents rose early, before true light. The smells of bacon and coffee and backdraft smoke drifted through the house, sharpened by the nip of frost. Cold radiated from the bedrooms where the outside walls sandwiched a thin insulation of tar paper, old newspapers and Depression era *Saturday Evening Posts*, and the household gathered as it woke, driven toward the roar of the wood stove. Outside the windows the air turned white as the sun rose, lighter but no less dense, no quieter. Breakfast occurred in shifts as places cleared at the table, adults tense, preoccupied, children hushed with excitement. As we planned our unexpected vacation from school, Dad dressed for morning chores in layers of long johns, coveralls, lined buckskin mitts, his cap pulled low over his eyes, earflaps secured by a wool scarf. Another scarf covered the back of his neck, a third wrapped the bottom of his face. He tucked his coveralls into the tops of his overshoes and buckled them down, finishing as Mom filled the milk pail with hot water for the chickens.

The barn lay a hundred yards south of the house, the low, red granary and chicken house a bit west of there, all of it lost in blowing snow. Stepping away from the porch, Dad aimed east for the yard gate, and then south, guided by the built-in compass of a man who has walked the same path at least twice a day for ten years. A big man, over six feet tall, over two hundred pounds centered in his chest and shoulders, and still it was difficult to stay grounded. The wind cut through the back of his coat as he braced against the storm and fought to keep his feet in the unfamiliar sea of hard drifts, digging in with his heels at every step.

The chickens met the cold by roosting with their feet drawn up, their feathers fluffed like chickadees. Dad fed them, poured water in their bucket. He left the eggs in one nest, their shells split lengthwise, the frozen whites bulging through like scar tissue. The milk cow, a thin-skinned Guernsey/Angus cross could stay in the barn until the storm let up, he decided. The lack of water wouldn't kill her for one day. She was almost dry anyway, set to calve in March. The feeder calves would be huddled in the open-faced shed, safer there than if he tried to lure them out for grain. He saw no sign of the range cows. He could do no more.

Coming home meant walking into the storm, and within minutes his compass failed in the face of the wind. Eyes slitted against the stab of ice crystals, he breathed in shallow grunts, his airway clamping down as it would for a draught of pure ammonia. He couldn't get enough air. Every few yards, he swung his back to the blizzard and stopped to catch his breath then turned into it again, walking blind for what seemed like too long. He corrected to the right and back to the left, trying to find northwest by feel, knowing he might have passed arm's length from the yard fence without seeing it. Sweat chilled on his ribs. A few more minutes and he would let the wind carry him south again. The windbreak or corrals would stop him and guide him back to the barn.

As he blundered left a last time, a single strand of No. 9 wire caught him across the chest and sprang him back in his tracks. He'd stumbled into the clothesline. He was halfway home. Keeping the wire in his left mitt, he bent his head into the wind and followed it until the end of the old house trailer, our bunkhouse, loomed out of white air in front of him. From there, another giant step west to the yard fence, the woven wire buried half way to the top. Down wind from the house, he stopped a last time to strain air through a cupped mitten, then walked toward the light in the kitchen window.

Mom took the pail from his hand and set it hissing on the wood stove to thaw out. The milk had slopped up and stuck to the sides, coating the inside with a thick rime, white ice on stainless steel. Above the scarf, Dad's face had turned the same blue-gray shade. The headgear had frozen together and came off in one piece. Under the scarf, the skin had stiffened in deep furrows that reddened quickly in the heat of the kitchen. I watched him as he thawed out, ice dripping from lashes and brows, his lips limbering to sip coffee. But his cheeks stayed rigid for a long time, stuck in a grimace or a scream. Over the course of the afternoon, the welts softened into frown lines as he passed from window to window, stepping around the card table where Granddad tried to keep us settled to a game of pinochle. They reappeared as he bared his teeth and squinted through the glass into the storm. We stayed out of his way.

Mom rattled pots and peeled potatoes, working at the logistics of three meals, nine mouths, descending with swift justice whenever our quarrels overrode the drone of the wind. Cramped up in the living room to stay warm, we six children grew quickly tired of cards, tired of board games, tired of each other. As a last resort, she hauled boxes of ornaments from their hiding spot and let us squabble over decorating the Christmas tree we'd hauled from the breaks over the weekend. When the water pipes froze in the middle of the day, Dad grabbed the torch and headed for the basement like a man bent on tunneling out of prison.

That evening, he kept to his place at the table, drinking more coffee, feeding the wood stove, while Mom worked after supper. Their voices circled the kitchen, undercurrents of worry. The cattle were over twenty-four hours from their last full stomach, their last drink of water. They were heading into their second night of trying to breathe in the godawful wind, their metabolism kicked into full gear, burning on high like the fuel oil stove. When the tanks ran dry, then what? My parents knew.

⌒

IN THE YEARS THAT FOLLOWED, the ranchers in the path of the blizzard endured the second-guessing of those who were not, those on the edge of the storm, those favored by the early chinook. Where the snow had melted off, the wind and cold were fierce, but visibility remained good enough to see where you were going. The ones who weathered that version of the storm still insist my father and his neighbors might have tried riding out and bringing the cattle in. Why didn't they haul hay to them, or cut the fences to keep them moving like the antelope, keep the blood circulating? Half question, half accusation. The wound of them shows on my father's face, his defense arranging itself quietly across his features. The ferocity of the storm defies description, beggars the imagination of those who were not there. A part of him still wonders if he might have done something, the part that refuses to admit helplessness, refuses to be beaten. The rest of him sags with the burden of reality. It was just flat impossible.

The wind battered through the afternoon and into the night, and we rose the second morning nearly immune to it, voices pitched a notch louder to be heard over the steady scream. Midmorning, the air brightened and the gray shadow of cottonwood trunks appeared outside the kitchen window, then the fence posts further out. By noon, we could see the blurred outlines of the barn and outbuildings. Our voices rang loud in our own ears. In another hour the wind lifted and was gone like a curtain rising on an empty stage. Outside, the temperature held at a crystal thirty-five degrees below zero. Nothing moved in the silence. Nothing showed above the hazy peaks of snow, no horizon appeared where the transformed landscape met the sky under a white December sun.

Dad organized with the urgency of someone held down too long. The shop door, a wide steel panel hung on rollers, had to be shoveled free to get the four-wheel drive pickup. He picked his way around the worst of it getting to the stack yard for hay, but where the gates had plugged bumper deep, he hacked the drifts with a spade, breaking the solid pack into chunks he could lift to one side with the bigger scoop shove. The haystacks had made a perfect snow fence, capturing ten feet of snow on the downwind side, so he shoveled and floundered his way to the upwind side. The pitchfork crunched into the stack. In later years he would have a tractor with a hydraulic grapple fork, and perhaps those huge steel jaws could have taken a bite from the north side of the stack. But the wind had pounded snow so deeply into the hay and frozen it so solidly that one man heaving at a pitchfork could not free a wisp of it. It would take all day to shovel in from the drifted side. Climbing a stack of small square bales, he wrenched a few free and loosed them like toboggans down the steep slope toward the pickup.

Sound carries for miles in still air. He stood atop the stack and looked south, calling his cows, listening for the answering bawl. Silence snapped shut behind his voice. The winter pasture is relatively small, half a mile wide and a mile long, really more of a holding pasture than a grazing pasture, but rolling hills hide the south half from view. The county road borders the east fence line, and from the stack he could see the darker stripe of the raised grade, blown clear in some spots, covered in others.

Mom and twelve-year-old Kenny were bundled and waiting when he pulled up at the house, and they struck off for the county lane. Low drifts held the weight of the pickup; the deep ones tapering toward the ditch could be avoided. Within minutes they spotted the first of them, four cows pressed against the east fence, just across the ditch. All four were down and drifted over, two dead and frozen stiff, the other two only half dead, unable to rise. They grabbed shovels to scoop the snow pack away from their heads, broke a bale and tucked squares of hay within reach, temporary measures. A minute later, they piled back in the pickup, fueled by a new sense of urgency.

Topping a low rise, the pickup slowed as the herd came into view. The cab was silent except for the warm blast of the defroster against the windshield. The fence corner was drifted full. One cow hung dead near the corner post, her hind legs twisted in the brace wires where she had walked up a drift and fallen through over the fence line. A few had made it out, pushing forward and stepping over the bodies of cows that had fallen and been buried against the wire. Some stood belly deep in the ditch, others on the road. One had floundered on across, walking with the wind until her front feet slipped through the grate of a cattle guard.

She had frozen standing up, still heading southeast. Forty head were still alive, the bulk of them gathered in the vee of the fence corner.

Dad turned the pickup around so it faced toward home and stepped out, his face flat and unreadable. Leaning back in to grab the fencing pliers from behind the seat, he started across the ditch, walking easily over the drifts. At the fence, he cut top wires and dug under the snow to get the rest, coiling the loose ends like a lariat and hanging them to the posts, out of the way. He needed a gate to get them to the road where they could follow the pickup home, a longer route, but faster than breaking trail across the dunes. At the sound of the engine revving, the horn blast, the cattle sheltered by the road shifted slowly, testing their strength against the drifts. Those in the pasture stood like a wedge of plaster statues, still posed as the storm had left them, heads low, backs humped, tails to the wind.

Snow had frozen a crust across each back, down each side, smoothing away evidence of the dark hair beneath. Pounds of ice sheathed their heads and hung in cones from their noses to the ground, breath grown solid in the bitter cold. What scant air they could draw whistled and puffed from slim vent holes half a foot from the tips of their noses. It was the only noise the cows made as Dad walked among them, struggling to find his own, some feature he recognized under the white cast. They stood motionless, though his steps creaked and squawked against the snow inches from their lowered heads. Eyes sealed tight under an inch of milky ice, they waited, blind and dumb, rigid with shock.

There was, he would say later, nothing to be done but what they did, an act both vicious and loving, desperate and calm. Pain, their pain, his pain, had reached the cold plateau that allows no more. The cattle couldn't hurt any worse. He could no longer do nothing. Raising the pliers in a wide arc, he swung them flat across a cow's face, shattering the ice that sealed her eyes, again across the bridge of her nose. Now there was motion, noise, as the animals fought to escape the crack of steel against their heads, grunting as their nostrils broke free and air rushed into their lungs. Mom stepped across the ditch where the fence was opened, a piece of board she had wrenched from the pickup bed clenched in both hands. Together they moved through the herd, the forty head of cows and both bulls still alive, and beat away the ice that was killing them, battering against the shields until the eyes jarred open, and again, until the whites rolled in fear and tongues hung from gaping mouths, until the cows began to struggle and live.

As the pickup crept home, my parents and my brother took turns driving, two following behind the staggering herd. Cows straggling to the side bogged down in the drifted ditches, and the procession would stop while someone fastened the log chain around the cow's neck and hooked it to the bumper of the pickup. The pickup eased the slack from the chain and kept going, dragging one after the other out where they could stand again. They lined out behind the hay, blood pumping warmth through their chilled muscles. The weakest formed a line to the rear where shouts and the slap of buckskin gloves kept them moving. These were animals whose eyes were glazed with something deeper than cold, the cows whose brittle hocks clattered like dry sticks as they swung their feet to keep up, the bulls walking gingerly, straddling the strange bulk of their frozen testicles.

Trailed to the buildings, the cattle spent their first day crammed together in the shed connected to the barn, the combined heat of their bodies melting the ice pack and revealing the gaunt frames beneath. Half a dozen went down as their feet thawed and began to swell. With the help of a neighbor, Dad drove back to rescue the two along the fence line still lying in their untouched hay. They winched them onto a stoneboat and dragged them home. They died that night, the Angus bull the next day. It took my father and two neighbors all of that afternoon to shovel out the calves, forty head of feeder steers and replacement heifers trapped in a straw-covered shed in the feedlot, another day to drag out the dead and treat the sick.

School started up and ran for a few days, but before Christmas vacation, another storm dumped six inches of fresh snow atop the old drifts, and the wind had something new to play with. Once a week, plows cleared fifty miles of county roads from Highway 191 south, then cleared them again coming back north the next day. The Christmas play at the school was canceled. No company came for Christmas Eve dinner. On Christmas Day, the milk cow died.

TECHNICALLY, THE BLIZZARD BLEW ITSELF out in thirty-six hours. The immediate marks were made in those first hours, while ranchers paced behind the vibrating windows of their houses and listened to it happening. But the worst of the storm lay hidden for weeks and months. The ranchers shoveled and fed and chopped water. They hacked trails into the haystacks, piled warm beds of straw on the prairie beside the feed, tending the sick and lame with single-minded intensity, as if making up for those hours of helplessness. Dad counted ten dead the first week. When the ground thawed, he would bury over thirty.

Some of the stories that come down from that storm are framed in black humor, the polite way of stating something painful or horrible without burdening the listener. Even the cattle that regained their health turned black around the edges, as if scorched by fire instead of ice, and for months the dead pieces curled and dropped off. Made for extra chores, Gene Barnard remarked dryly, having to shovel the ears out of the feed bunks before he poured the grain every morning. And they found humor in the stories of neighbors like Sandford Barrett, blind-sided by his own cleverness as he picked his way cross country with a load of hay looking for live cattle, counting fifty head of dead. Wise to the ways of wind, he stuck to the high spots, breaking trail along the ridges where grass and sage showed above the drifts like a yardstick, going along fine until he mistook the tips of some four-foot willows for grass and sank his pickup to the windows.

The more delicate irony is found in the other stories, like the fate of the antelope, the hundreds that walked over the Missouri and lived to drop their fawns in new country. The river is a mile wide where the antelope crossed, on the tail of Fort Peck Lake, and the break up of ice left them stranded. For years, the sight of a pronghorn was a rare privilege on our side of the river. The other side was crawling with them. But only for a few months. Antelope with the wit to outrun the storm died in a hail of fire that fall when the Fish and Game gave in to pressure from the landowners and staged a special hunting season to get rid of the surplus.

And there's the double-whammy stories, the farmer-rancher kind of storm that kills the cattle all winter, then washes gullies through the fields when it melts. April staged the spring thaw like a magic show, whipping the white cover to one side with a flourish. Water roared through dikes, washed out culverts and channeled across roads. Water stood in the meadows with nowhere to go as the alfalfa grew pale and greasy beneath it. Cactus bloomed red and yellow around the bloated remains of birds and antelope, fence corners sagged under the weight of dead cattle, corrals and sheds swam in a stew of decay and manure. The fields lay saturated, too wet to hold a plow. By June, only shallow puddles dotted the hardpan, all of them squirming with mosquito larvae. Until frost returned the next fall, the air hummed with a misery of flies and blood sucking insects. Cattle submerged themselves in reservoirs or gathered on the hilltops where the wind could sweep their backs, twisting the useless pink stubs where their tails had been.

The stories are tempered by time, now, the drifts of dead cattle too deep to forget, the loss of faith too profound to call up in words. They talk about luck now, how lucky we were the storm hit when it did, no one caught out on the road, no kids stranded at school. Lucky the electricity stayed on, the phone lines up, still salvaging what they can three decades later. But there is wonder, still, in the facts, in circumstances somehow unreasonable, beyond the logic we lived by. How could it be that a man did everything he knew to do, and it wasn't enough, wasn't even close? What happens when good intentions fail, and the work that makes the man becomes worthless—not just wrong, but simply meaningless, without effect? The old-timers would squint through Bull Durham smoke and shrug: "Well, hell, every so often it's nature's turn." And so it was.

Like every other rancher in the path of the storm, my father kept badly frozen cows alive through the winter, trying to salvage the calves in their bellies. His decision was practical rather than humane, for the animals suffered for weeks as the flesh below their hocks swelled and turned black, and their hooves dropped off. On the surface, it seemed a sensible business decision. If they could get a calf, if they could save the cow for hamburger, at least they'd have something. But he knew them, these cows that lay in their own waste and panted with pain, and I believe that part of him simply refused to give in, refused to turn loose. Saving them was the only way left of beating the storm.

"I guess if you had another lifetime to live, you would have learned something, anyway," my father tells me now. "One thing I learned, and that's for godsake don't ever...." He pauses, searching words, his eyes grim or sad, then starts over. "If you have a froze up critter, shoot 'em or haul them off or something. Get rid of them. It's cruel." He speaks the last word carefully, then lifts his head, steady, resigned to the fact of it. "They got a cruel deal to go through and they're not going to make it anyway."

The range cows gave birth that spring in the stench of decay, their tails gone, ear tips dried crisp, ready to fall. A few stood to wash their calves, murmuring and anxious, with milk pouring from them, milk streaming down their hocks, pooling around their feet, draining from holes in their udders where the teats had been. The calves were put on nurse cows, and the price of a good milk cow skyrocketed. Their mothers went to market, the milk still leaking, replenishing, no way to dry them up. The price of canner cows plummeted. Others were less fortunate still. All winter, in the gloom of outbuildings, those with no feet rose to their knees and fell back when men came to tend them, unable to stand on their raw clubs, unable to halt the poison that dripped from dead flesh to the straw, that crept upward through the blood. Penicillin kept the fever down, the rot slow.

The men tended them gently, expectantly, patient as drones around a gravid queen. We had four or five, bigger places twenty or thirty head plumping in rows in sheds, hours of hauling buckets in and manure out, betting on the get. Every morning they were turned, rolled out of their own muck onto clean straw, pans of grain and water, the best alfalfa hay shoved under their peeling noses. As spring drew near, one by one these cows lay back in the soured straw and strained, their bodies bent on self-preservation, and cast away fetuses that never drew breath. Downwind of the sheds, you could smell their progress, the ones who spent the winter dying.

For years, reminders of the storm lingered at the edge of our vision like the glint of new wire splicing the old along the east fence. Scraps of stiff hide, darkened with age, turned up in manure as we dressed the garden, maybe an ear, maybe one of the buckskin boots Mom sewed to fit that crippled yearling, the one who kept trying to stand on his missing feet. At roundup and branding, we rode in the dust of survivors, cows with healed stumps for ears and tails, cows that grew old grazing lush grass over the mass grave of their sisters. The most lasting reminders were felt in the absence of things we had come to expect, the silence of summers without hearing the crow of a cock pheasant, years without the harmony of pronghorns, the way they swerve and dodge over the cured grass like a school of fish.

Over time the artifacts went back to earth and the wildlife returned, nurtured and guarded by landowners who came to see the prairie as empty without them. Only stories survive, and a restlessness when wind rises on winter evenings. Every generation relearns the rules its fathers have forgotten. One rule is awareness, the need to see past the power of human hands on the land, to the power beneath it. Those who forget have the wind to jog their memory, wind slipping evenly through the sage, dusting across the fields. *Watch your back*, it's whispering, *this land owes you nothing.*

Judy Blunt spent more than thirty years on wheat and cattle ranches in north-central Montana before leaving in 1986 to attend the University of Montana–Missoula, where she received an M.F.A. in creative writing. Her bestselling memoir, Breaking Clean *(Knopf, 2002), won the 1997 PEN/Jerard Fund Award for a work in progress, as well as a 2001 Whiting Writers' Award, the 2003 Mountains and Plains Book Award, and the 2003 Willa Award for memoir/nonfiction. More recently, she received a 2004 National Endowment for the Arts Fellowship and a 2006 Guggenheim Fellowship. Her poems and essays have appeared in numerous journals and anthologies. She is an associate creative writing professor at the University of Montana–Missoula, where she teaches courses in creative nonfiction and Western women's memoirs.*

M. L. Smoker

FROM THE RIVER'S EDGE

Is it poetry to say that each time I cross over a
certain bridge on the Yellowstone I remember the way
green vinyl felt on the back of my legs instead of how
my own mother's feet, stiff from death, felt in my hands.
I did not know that a poet could feel words rising from
drops of sweat around her knees. Or that what my palms
pressed against was only silence. Can a poet speak of a
second version of her mother? The one who lives in a
silent cave where she allows no visitors, gives no interviews.
Her memoir is being written there by a shadow seven feet
tall that can hold no pen or pencil, both hands missing.
My living mother dreams of new waters that have no
adequate translation.

WINTER AGAIN

Once I drove long winter hours alone, snow swirling in
Drifts from one half of the covered plain
to the other. My mother was alive then
and I made my way toward the temptation of finally
getting things right between us.
No matter what size the storm outside
I drove on because I could not live with anything else.

When I arrived it was late and I crawled into the bed
next to her and somehow the distance
between our lives had made our breathing,
our hands indistinguishable.
Now she has been gone for some time
and again I am searching for evidence
that we are more than just blood.

In summer there is the quiet of new leaves settling
and resettling upon one another,
to remind me of how the fragile edges overlap.
But this time of year the trees are leafless and as I find
myself settling and resettling into the very place
she is still tied to, I think of creases
across our knuckles, the palm's winding rivers
reaching out toward the fingertips.

There is no easy explanation, no sudden burst of
I see now or some things must remain lost,
only the unwoven lifelines of two women.
I muddle through the fragments, none of which

can tell me why the reflected light from snow
outside my window seem like a better,
more perfect sort of light. Or why it is

I have gone to her grave only twice
since returning home for good.
After all, she is what brought me here.
But I am not clever enough to discern
those patterns she and I revolve around, let alone
why I have taken to ashing my cigarettes in a shell
from some unremembered ocean,
thinking of gods I fail to pray to.

Now would seem like an appropriate time, but all
I can consider are the formations of new frost
on the trees, just before midday strips
each thin branch bare again.

BORROWING BLUE

I'm not the painter here. I leave that to you, but blue
is the color of my father's camping cup, left tonight
on the Formica counter. This pen I am writing with.
And the beaded moccasins and belt I danced in.
My grandmother made these for her as a child—
spelling out in blue beads on blue beads
each of our names, our collective history
in an invisible pattern only we would recognize.
Not the blue of Montana sky either,
not that at all, but the pulse of lake water lapping
at your ankles, the temperature rising
as a storm gathers on the plains.
The push and pull of forgiveness.
I'm already thinking of leaving again.
Did I tell you this? How can I speak of this wind,
how it has no color, no sense,
no guilt. It makes me feel even more lonely
than I would ever let on.
I'm guessing you figured this much already.
(We will never stop missing them, will we,
the parent each of us has lost.)
I'll be honest, I have no idea what I would see
in the paintings if I were to visit you.
I like to think there would be some kind of end
to the blue, a visual end to what is never
adequate: blue flame, blue bead, blue ovary,
blue lung. See how easily we fail?
How can we believe that our secrets are in good hands—
yours resting at the bottom of Flathead Lake, mine held

in a small leather suitcase beneath the stairs.
I have not worn those moccasins or belt for over
six years now. We should both be ashamed.
Look at us. Look, as the grey fog
settles into your streets outside, how the near-white,
canvases wait. You almost didn't notice again.
Just like I almost didn't notice the wind
dying down for evening.
So yes, let's call it Montana blue, the vanishing point.
Maybe this is the real reason I have never learned
to trust in color. How can you take back
the kind of blue you've been dreaming—trust
it will make something unhappen—
if it is the same blue you're made of?

⌒

M. L. Smoker, an enrolled member of the Assiniboine and Sioux tribes, calls the Fort Peck Reservation in northeastern Montana home. She spent three years working as an administrator at an all-Indian school in Frazer and currently works for the Office of Public Instruction in Helena in the Indian Education Division. Her work focuses on Indian student achievement issues in Montana. A graduate of the University of Montana's M.F.A. program, where she was the recipient of the Richard Hugo Memorial Scholarship, Smoker has published poems in Hanging Loose, Shenandoah, *and* South Dakota Review *as well as various anthologies. Several of her poems have been translated into Italian and appear in* Acoma, *a literary journal from the University of Rome.* Another Attempt at Rescue *(Hanging Loose Press, 2006) is her first book of poems.*

Grace Stone Coates

HARDNESS OF WOMEN

There is a hardness in woman like the hardness of falling water
  That repulses what it compels; her life is barred
To man by her moving purpose. Who has caught her?
  Though she curve to him like a wave her strength is hard.

And a woman can leave a man, without quitting his dwelling,
  To loneliness deeper than night with no star-spawn;
The dearth he has of her is beyond his telling.
  In the crook of his arm she is gone from him, she is gone.

PORTULACAS IN THE WHEAT

My mother was a woman rich in life
Wisely controlled, renewed abundantly
For others; vivid till subdued
To her surroundings; limpid, loving Truth,
Worshiping Right, a living loyalty!
She gave me all I know of honor, faith,
Hatred of lying, scorn of littleness;
She gave me all I cherish, save two things:
A sensuous joy in life that she half feared
For me, and pagan gladness in the sun
Even when I sinned—most, when I sinned, I think!

One hot, late morning, sun high overhead,
(Having sinned and being well rebuked,
Closeted, sentence served, and so, relaxed)
I watched the binders drop their yellow loads;
And, pushing farther in the wheat, achieved
The shivering ecstasy of mimic fear,
Pretending I must hunt all day, all night,
A thousand, thousand miles to find my home!
The wheat was higher than my head, that year;
It caught my hair, I know, and tangled it;
So, bending to avoid the tugging stalks,
I came upon a wonder at my feet.
I looked and held my breath, and looked again,
Then raced to find my mother!

　　　　Past the hedge
The panting path had never seemed so long,
Till crowded to her skirts, and looking up,
Ankle in hand—a much-corrected trick
That deep excitement always reinvoked—
When breath came back, the words came tumbling, too:
A miracle! A marvel in the wheat,
That she must see!
　　　　She answered, not unkindly,
(For she was courteous even when she spanked)
"I have no time to listen, child. Sit down!"
—She held a heavy platter in her hand—
"Now keep from under foot till I have served
The dinner, for the teams are turning in!"

I sat and swallowed tears—not bitter ones;
Mine lay behind the lashes, quick to ease
Grown-up rebuff or happiness that hurt.
The men came streaming in, and last, my father.
He bent to wash; so, slipping down beside him,
Confident here at least, with breath restored,
Both feet on floor, and words more ordered; eyes—
Who doubts?—as wide and eager as before,
I told him of the marvel I had found.
Without a word he leaned to take my hand,
And went to read my riddle of the wheat.
Blossoms! A myriad of them, flaming silk,
Of colors flaunted by the Sun! They glowed
Clear yellow, red, and splashed and blended orange,
Massed till we dare not step, then scattered out,
Each one a passionate discovery!
How long he shared them—minute, hour,
Who shall gauge delight!—a brief eternity
He gave my gladness perfect right of way
While men and harvest waited. Turning home

He talked of leaves so modified to meet
Our arid climate, reservoirs to hold
The moisture, little surface to the sun;
I trotting by him, deeply satisfied.

My mother told me they were portulacas
Gone wild, once planted by an earlier tenant.
No! They were rich enchantment, silken flame,
A whole new continent in Fairyland!
That timeless, golden afternoon I held
Grave converse with my Fellows of the Sun,
Companionship beyond the need of words.
Deep in the sun-drenched wheat, content, I heard
The whirring binders drop their tawny loads
Nearer and nearer, clanking nearer still;
A pause, a question, then my father's voice,
Abrupt, imperative, "Swing out, I say!
The child shall have her flowers! Swing around!"
So past my seignory the shining swathes
Whose mile-long straightness was my father's pride
Veered suddenly, and made a vexing end.
While drivers muttered, brothers jested, gay
Unstricken blossoms bravely cupped the sun.

THE CLIFF

Peace has left my heart,
Driven by dull chatter
On dingy street
To a place apart;
But I know where she is hiding.
There's a cliff where pines are riding,
And exultant winds confiding
Strange intentions of their own.

I shall make my way alone
Past the green alfalfa tillage
At the far end of the village,
Skirt the coulee, dropping down
Till the rounded knolls behind me
Hide the chimneys of the town
With their small insistency,
And no curious eye can find me;
Only then shall I be free
For the prairie and the foothills
And the cliff that summons me.

Free! To run, and free to loiter,
Free to follow out of sight
Startled rabbits' headlong dash
And the screaming curlew's flight
As they wheel and reconnoiter
And protestingly retreat
I shall climb the lichened boulders,
Studying red and black and orange

Mantling their aggressive shoulders;
Lean against their warmth to trace
Lovely gray-green lichen lace
Edging every scarlet splash;
Throw myself full-length to drink
Icy, bubbling springs that wink
From the shaley hill.

Leading upward from the rill
Is a deer trail hunters follow,
That winds high above a hollow
Where the bluebells are a lake.
One quick, stinging breath I take
Coming near.
I shall stand there long, and gaze,
And go softer on my ways
From that passion of blue flame.
Once so quietly I came
That I glimpsed a wary deer
Marshalling her baby fawn;
They were there—and they were gone.
I shall climb the steepening ledge
With its fern and cedar scent
Into timber; almost blind
To the painted cups and lovage
For the bluebells in my mind.

On the cliff's sheer eastern edge,
With the valley wide below it,
Stands a tree that loves the granite
And the cloud-sweep and the wind.
Its grim roots to me are kind.
I shall so sit so quietly
Chipmunks think I do not matter,
Scampering like mad across my feet.

I shall neither feel nor think,
Nor with teasing values reckon;
If I sleep I shall not know it.
I shall rest; and cease to be
All that people know of me—
Idly glad of gay beletus
Netted curious underneath,
Of the drifting vapor wreath,
And the pine cones' deadened patter
On the needles and detritus.
If shy orioles reappear,
Patridges resume their drumming,
Glowing cedar birds flash free,
I shall smile, for peace is near;
But I shall not look or beckon
Or entreat her swifter coming.

When the wind has hushed its story,
And the rounded moon swims pale
To confound the western glory—
When her mysteries prevail,
And squirrels quit their firs,
And haunted birds fall dumb,
Peace will know that I am hers;
Peace will touch my breast, and whisper,
        "Come!"

Grace Stone Coates was best known for her novel Black Cherries *(Bison Books, 2003) but she also published two books of poetry:* Portulacas in the Wheat *(The Caxton Printers, 1932) and* Mead and Mangel-Wurzel *(The Caxton Printers, 1931). During the 1920s, her work appeared in various publications, including* Poetry, *the* Christian Science Monitor, *and the* New York Times. *From 1929 to 1939, she served as assistant editor of the University of Montana's* The Frontier *under H. G. Merriam. In 1929 her story "Wild Plums" appeared in the* Anthology of the American Short Story. *Coates's story "Black Cherries" was included in* The Last Best Place: A Montana Anthology, *and John Updike chose her story "Wild Plums" to represent 1929 in his* Best American Short Stories of the Twentieth Century *in 1999. Coates died in 1976 at age ninety-four in Bozeman, Montana, where she had gone to live in a retirement home in 1962.*

Lee Rostad

AN ALIEN LAND

WHEN SHE FIRST MARRIED HENDERSON Coates and moved with him to the little town of Martinsdale, Grace Stone wrote her father that she had come into an alien land. For the next half century, she lived the life of a shopkeeper's wife in this land, but there was another life in writing. After twenty years of marriage, she wrote of herself, "Her occupation is housewifery: her delight, writing; her passion, music. All she has learned in 20 years of housekeeping drops from her in one half-hour's intense writing, so that she has to learn her business of housewifery each morning anew; and all she knows of anything is drowned in one half-hour of music.

"Fortunately, her husband is sane. He keeps her outdoors, fishing, duck hunting, and deer hunting; and when she is away from her Martinsdale home, she remembers, never the dingy meanness of a western village but the tremendous sweep of valley from the Belt mountains to the Crazies; or the Musselshell [River], swimming in moonlight, below Gordon Butte."

In the 1920s and early half of the 1930s, Coates had over a hundred poems and short stories published, edited seven books for Caxton Press, wrote the local news for the county newspapers, wrote historical essays for state-wide papers and had a novel and two books of poetry published. She also served as the Assistant Editor for *The Frontier*, a regional magazine started and edited by H.G. Merriam of the University of Montana. And she wrote letters. She corresponded with William Saroyan, Frank Linderman, James Rankin, and many other authors and writers, with many friends.

During these years, she had periods of deep depression and periods of unbounded energy, possibly indicative of manic depression—a condition shared by many people who created the great paintings and literature over the years. In about 1935, Coates stopped writing—except for the local news and historical pieces. There were no more revealing glimpses into her soul and events that shaped her work.

Grace Stone was born in Kansas on May 20, 1881, the youngest child of the Henry Stone family. She said of her parents, "My mother was of the blessed company of martyrs; my father, in her eyes, the devil's advocate. She bore her children in the fear of the Lord, and the more immediate fear that they might be like their father." Memories of growing up in this contentious household resulted in her book *Black Cherries,* published in 1932.

In 1900, Grace and her sister Helen were in Montana teaching in Hamilton, although Grace was teaching in Butte from 1904 until 1910 when she married Henderson Coates and moved with him to the little town of Martinsdale where he and his brother built a general store.

Although *Black Cherries* was published as a novel, it is a series of short stories about her childhood. Through a child's eyes, she tells of her parents and their marriage. In an article in *Contempo,* Grace explained her book. "*Black Cherries* falls between two stools. It is more than a collection of stories; it is less than a novel. The book grew around a single situation, whose crux is of two, married, "held in a globe of darkness, yet separated by a deeper darkness at their feet, wherein hid all that later rose between them." When the parts of the story fell into a more or less inevitable alignment, the resultant book became more than the sum of its parts, and was exposed to (just) criticism as a novel...

"...Whatever worth the book has lies precisely in the thing I didn't know I had put into it. One reviewer only, Guy Holt, clarified my own mind, when he characterized the book as the story of a family 'whose common happiness is defeated by the father's immersion in grief for his dead first wife.' Some creative reviewers even have the mother die an unauthorized death; and one suggests that *Black Cherries* is a study of the race problem. Critical comment, unexpectedly generous in the east, has varied in the west from that of a publisher's God bless him, who maintains that Mr. Knopf will be overlooking a lot of money on establishing *Black Cherries,* not as a best seller but as a classic, to that of a department store book clerk in Great Falls, Mont., who lifted an eyebrow at me when I inquired for the book. *Black Cherries.* 'That hooey! A bunch of spinach, lady, if you ask me!'"

WHEN *MEAD AND MANGEL-WURZEL*—honey-wine and hunger-root—was published in 1931, the publishers said "Grace Stone Coates offers love, the food of gods and starvelings. To what thirst the wine was poured, to what famine the coarse beets offered, is any reader's guess; but here *entre vous,* you will find all the calories you can digest…"

Although most of her writing was in the 1920s and 1930s, Coates' poetry can still offer today the "love and the food of gods and starvelings." Grace herself explained, "Mead was the honey wine the gods of Olympus were soused on and mangel-wurzel were the coarse beets without much sugar content, that my German ancestors fed their cattle in good times, and themselves in time of famine. But it isn't verse that is honey wine and hunger root; it is love, which is mead when you are falling in, and mangel-wurzel when you are falling out."

Coates insisted that *Mead and Mangel-Wurzel* was a hilarious book. One eastern critic said, "There is a knife-twist in much of it—into the author, I mean—that makes of life's thrust an irony armour." Still, Grace insisted that the book was good fun—that such poems as "Village Satiety" made her wake up in the night laughing. She maintained the purpose of all poetry is to give one a chance to say, in verse, what would otherwise be said with flowers—or kisses—or a rolling pin.

When Caxton brought out Grace's book with "certain poems of appalling frankness," it was a shock to the local paper in Idaho. As Montanan historian Richard B. Roeder later wrote: "Even Grace herself was shocked by what the collection revealed about herself. While she felt the book 'was a fairly coherent thing,' it was also 'a shocking (I mean that) revelation to me of what I'm like—the concentrated picture wasn't very pleasing.' Later she wrote that the 'general tone of the book is an edgy woman getting it out of her system.' She regarded this as her best piece of work, but she also admitted that it was 'the most annoying to nice persons.'"

Harriet Monroe of *Poetry: A Magazine of Verse,* thought many of the poems were less than memorable, and those that were tended to be the expressions of the wrath of an embittered woman. Understandably, the review hurt Coates. She wrote to Merriam, "…There is a natural antipathy…between Harriet Monroe and me. I asked her to mention me only as an assistant editor of *The Frontier,* and to omit any name other that GSC if you see *Poetry* you will see how charmingly she conformed to the suggestion, the sour old antediluvian…"

A New Jersey reviewer said, "One scarcely looks for great literature from Idaho, but Mrs. Coates is a poet of creative power and this volume includes several dozen titles followed by appropriate verse that is never dull and sparkles with humor and fresh sentiment."

Harold Vinal in *Voices: A Journal of Verse:* "Her poems are irresistible, poignant and authentic."

Robert Lesseur Jones in *Bozart and Contemporary Verse:* "The author is a unique and interesting poet. Her crisp, bitter diction, her originality and perspicacity, and a philosophy that arrives at something definite, give Mrs. Coates an ample place under the sun."

The *Oregon Sunday Journal,* Portland, Oregon: "*Mead and Mangel-Wurzel* is a sophisticated volume of poetry which sparkles with zest and sustains with understanding. It is far superior to the ordinary collection of verse as the fountain of youth is proverbially superior to the ordinary collection of verse as the fountain of youth is proverbially superior to the coarse bread of mortal existence."

The reviewer for *The Frontier* said the poems were "written with energy and craft. They are a genuine contribution to modern psychological poetry."

Mary Brennan Clapp, a poet and the wife of the University of Montana president, was taken by the volume itself.

"It comes in a gay, green holiday jacket carrying a design made by a co-ed of Idaho State University. And under the flapper jacket the little volume wears a strictly tailored gown of elegant simplicity. One loves the binding, black of fine texture, with clear gold printing of title, author, and publisher…you will be surprised, maybe a bit shocked that one small volume can hold such variations of ecstasy and pain, sardonic facing of impossible situations, and absolute and perfect surrender to love that is worthy of trust. You will wish that there might have been more songs of happiness in it and yet you will know after reading them all that this road to happiness had to be a way of pain."

Another reviewer wrote: "To much of her poetry there is an acrid flavor, she sings as if she had found life's bitterness and love's promises delusive, the god himself a thief and cheat." This is her 'Rebuke':

> This is bitterness
> Make no lie that it is sweet.
> Be my one success
> To accept defeat.
>
> Spare me the last gall,
> Your pretense that all is well;
> Only truth should fall
> On the damned in hell.

Throughout the book one finds striking imagery, as in "Fracture," or "The Hardness of Women," or in such lyric phrases as "Go, love the girl whose name is rain against a garden," and the delightful figure of "Reverants":

> My visitants…
> But dead desires keeping tryst
> Beneath remembered cedar trees.

At times the expression seems to lack clarity, and one needs to dig deep to bare a meaning open to the initiate in spirit, but the reader is always stimulated to the search. Here is a simpler loveliness in "Tang":

> I know a harsh berry growing on a hill
>   That never tastes lonely and never leaves me sad;
> Though its tang wrys my lips and my crimped lids fill,
>   I eat the bitter berry and am glad.
>
> Bland fruit of comfort was never to my choosing,
>   The low lying valley and the narrow bed;
> Here, if you hold me, I shall be losing
>   The berry of adventure shining red.

Grace recognized herself that the book was a single poem with many parts.

Roeder said, "This coherence comes from the fact that the poems are examinations of her inner life, her passions which range from ecstasy to anger. Most of the emotions, in turn, arise from her relationship with her husband Henderson to whom the book is dedicated. While the poems express a wide gamut of emotions, they are also united by a common theme of futile attempts to bridge the separation between Grace and Henderson, between woman and man."

However, the poems speak of relationships other than her husband. Grace seemed to have carried on many love affairs, if love and passion through letters can be considered an affair. After the book of poems came out, she wrote to a distant cousin in Michigan:

"I am sending *Mead & Manglewurzel*. Don't jump to the conclusion the poems are about Henderson—some of them are—the first one. The last sonnets are all about a N.E. poet and otherwise writer. I say this because all semi-literate friends of mine assume I'm razzing Henderson straight thru. I'll tell you something nobody else knows but me: One page says "To Henderson" the next has a quatrain. Put the two together:

To Henderson the story tells how one struck water from *his* rock. He fosters and forsakes his flock, and is the shepherd of two dells. In other words: rock is a pun for Stone. The shepherd of two dells is a man named *Twadell Shipley*; and Shipley married and divorced quite a few women. This is a bit of esoterica for you alone—and keep it to yourself, things travel in queer ways, and I don't want to be getting any boxes of poisoned candy from any irate wives. The "bouton he had taken in his head to own, extravagantly priced, he knew" is (was) I. The sonnets from "Ice-bound" to "Recovery" cover the one situation. The last one is not of that group. "Cadence" was more about a drunken brother-in-law than anything else…"

Instransigeant

His secret passion was collecting pearls
(Not perfect ones, which lay beyond the scope
Of purse and personality. His hope

Involved irregularity that curls
The exacting lip). He smoothes his modest strand
Of blemished beauties, draped them so, and so;
Clustered them; liked them better in a row;
And blessed the flaws that brought them to his hand.
One bouton he had taken in his head
To own, extravagantly priced he knew,
Uneven with the rest in shape and hue
Defied alignment, twisting on its thread.
He could not pierce its central humor clean,
Or fluorate its glow to common sheep.

"Beyond Answer" seems to speak to other loves.

Do I love you? I cannot give you answer.
 I know if a great wind sweeps over the brink
Of a gorge, and I am borne like a madcap dancer,
 Or if a hush falls, it is of you I think.

When the empty-minded baffle me with chatter;
 Or a creator's golden thought shines through
His craft, and delicate ways are all that matters.
 To life; if I am alone—my thoughts are of you.

When my lips are quiet under another's token,
 And my craven limbs are bared to another's embrace,
It is your name my shuddering has not spoken,
 And to your darkness I turn away my face.

Grace wrote to a friend about the funding for the book. "Usually I can keep enough checks coming in so that I have all the things that no one knows I need but me. The things that are essential because unnecessary. But now I have to slip this manna to him—but hurrah for God, I have never seen the righteous forsaken nor his seed begging bread. I'll not worry about paying for books for which the contract is not yet signed. And when

Henderson sees my book with my name full of poems that sound like chop feed to him his eyes will be so proud of me that his hand won't notice it's signing a check. I'll rub his arm with liniment! He and I are enormously good friends. This is his sonnet that closed the book:

> Only to the simple, or the very wise,
> Or those who having hungered long, are fed,
> Does Heaven open this side paradise
> And give its glory to their daily bread.
> O these am I: never wise; my candor gone;
> But one long hungered, now in you content;
> And we have seen God moving in the dawn
> When our communion was His sacrament.
>
> My silence would more fitly meet your own
> But the words press, that you will leave unread
> But not unsmiled at. Never am I alone
> When you are him I seek; Uncomforted
> You do not thrust me off. If nights are deep
> I care no longer. On your arm I sleep...[1]

In 1932, Grace published a second book of verse, *Portulacas in the Wheat*. One reviewer suggested that at first glance the new book seemed entirely unlike the intense and passionate lyrics of her *Mead and Mangel-Wurzel*. But it wasn't unlike the earlier book.

"It's all a matter of selection," Mrs. Coates explains. "The character of the writer hasn't changed—anymore than a man's character has changed because he smiles when he meets a friend, and swears a little when the wind whisks his hat off.

"Books of verse are not deliberately planned—they grow. No verse maker decides to write a book, and then sits down and writes the poems for the volume. He writes because something exciting touches off a poem in his head, that fizzers there and demands to be let out. After a while he

---

[1] Grace Stone Coates to J. Powers, Undated, Grace Stone Coates papers, MSS 422, Box 1 Folder 1, K Ross Toole Archives, Mansfield Library, The University of Montana, Missoula

finds he has a lot of poems in manuscript—too many, probably, and they're a nuisance. He wants to get some of them packed away between the covers of a book—if he can find a publisher to undertake the job..."

Coates' electrifying poetry often caused readers to become enamored of the writing and on occasion imagine a personage other than the demure middle-aged wife of the local store keeper. She told of an incident:

"A young Chicago University man, now selling tea, visited in Martinsdale. He sat for hours reading my verse—I could see him from the house—and at last came across the street to look at the animals. He analyzed the various poems, and asked pointblank questions like whether I was really sick of Henderson, and then he analyzed the stories. He was impressed with the astonishing fact that I didn't mind making myself ridiculous in print; and secondly remarked that my characters showed their nature in even the smallest matters—for instance the child had used her remaining nickel to buy a hatpin, not to TIP THE WAITRESS. The suggestion was so novel to me I pass it on. Every man, writes Shipley, recites his age (generation). This was the poem he left to last, and pinned my domestic unhappiness (?) onto.

>
> Turnstile
>
> After Rabelaisian shaft
>   And a kiss in mockery
> To my crazy room, as daft
>   Comes my body, troubling me.
>
> Must the turnstile of my hell
>   Click its worn, accustomed way
> Past the dolt who can not spell
>   One bright word of Rabelais?

Another time, Grace chided an admirer who had gone through Martinsdale on the train and seeing a svelte, young woman playing tennis, was quite sure this was the Grace of verse.

Cherish your dreams,

I waddle when I walk,
To stoop must straddle,
Druel when I talk.

With years came care;
My hair first lost its glint
And then I lost my hair—
And acquired a squint.

Fallen arches fret my feet,
My chins are terraced;
We'll likely when we meet
Both be embarrassed.

But keep your dreams
For dreams alone are real;
In yours, it seems,
I bounce with sex appeal.

We are not all undone
The time's agen' us
While stock trains run
And lither girls play tennis.

Grace stopped writing poetry in the mid-thirties, except for an occasional "ditty." The fire and passion were gone, and she was forgotten. But when the anthology, *The Last Best Place,* was published, Grace Stone Coates was included as one of Montana's noted authors. In 1999, John Updike chose her short story "Wild Plums" to represent 1929 in his *Best American Short Stories of the Twentieth Century.*

In the 1990s, a copy of Margaret Bell's memoir appeared in one of the boxes of Grace's jumbled papers and letters. Margaret Bell's book. *When Montana and I Were Young,* was published by the University of Nebraska Press, edited by Mary Clearman Blew. *Black Cherries* was reprinted by the Nebraska press in 2003 and reviewers found it as moving as when first published. A reader from Oregon declared *Black Cherries* "a work of genius, written in vital fluids, illuminated by lightning, quivering with the truth."

Her story is also told through her letters in *Grace Stone Coates, Her Life in Letters*. Seventy years later, readers again enjoy the passion and love written by the storekeeper's wife in Martinsdale.

⌒

Lee Rostad was born in Roundup, Montana, graduated from the University of Montana, and spent a year in London as a Fulbright Scholar before marrying Phil Rostad, a rancher in the Musselshell Valley. Like Grace Stone Coates, she took her turn at writing the local news for the weekly newspapers and took time from her ranching chores to write magazine articles. She is the author of Grace Stone Coates: Her Life in Letters *(Riverbend, 2004),* Honey-Wine and Hunger Root *(Falcon, 1985),* Fourteen Cents and Seven Green Apples *(1993),* Mountains of Gold, Hills of Grass: A History of Meagher County *(Bozeman Fork Publishing, 1994). She received an honorary doctorate of letters from Rocky Mountain College and the Governor's Award in Humanities in 2001. She served eight years as a member of the Montana Committee for the Humanities and is currently on the Montana Historical Society Board of Trustees.*

❦ Diane Smith

From *Pictures from an Expedition*
LANDSCAPE, RIVER WITH
THREE ENCAMPMENTS

MERIWETHER LEWIS DESCRIBED THAT STRETCH of the Missouri River where we first camped that summer as an endless scene of visionary enchantment, with multi-colored sandstone walls carved by wind and river and rain into strange and fanciful shapes, pelicans and geese soaring overhead, and grizzly bears roaming along the steep ravines. Had Captain Lewis taken the time to venture inland, however, his reports might have been more in sympathy with how fellow explorer, Sergeant Gass, described the scene. According to this explorer, the land was barren and desolate, without encouraging prospects. This is most certainly how it appeared to me.

To my untrained eye, both the Missouri and the land through which it coursed were indeed bleak. Unlike the fresh-flowing mountain river that carved away canyons outside of Helena, the water here was gray, flat, and turbid, and the landscape was devoid of any discernible sign of life except for occasional patches of cottonwood, scrubby pine trees, yellow-blooming cactus, and bursts of grass. The cottonwoods and pine trees provided little in the way of shelter or fuel, although the birds seemed to enjoy them, and the cactus, in spite of its unexpected beauty when in flower, made travel as difficult and sometimes as dangerous as the snakes which slithered out to warm themselves in the heat of the day.

"River with Three Encampments" must have been completed not too long after we arrived, since at that time a Crow Indian hunting camp was situated just to the north and west of us. In the painting, you can see the hundred or so Indian lodges across the river, along with Patrick Lear's campsite with its three wall tents, two wagons, and about a dozen horses picketed next to a stand of cottonwood trees. Our lone tent was pitched off to one side, next to two paltry chokecherry bushes. Augustus even added the large boulder he used as a backrest and the simple wooden table and chair that served as my workspace that summer.

As you have noted, this particular landscape was painted in short, bright lines of color, uncharacteristic of Augustus' previous work, as if he had awakened overnight to a new vision of the world. When I asked him why he had chosen to paint our campsite in such quick, bright brushstrokes, he explained that too much attention to detail would obscure the true nature of the subject. Or worse, capture it permanently, artificially setting it in stone.

What Augustus' landscape with all its sunshine and light has failed to depict, however, was how ill-equipped the Captain's camp was for the conduct of science or art, much less for the basic necessities of living. There were no facilities for bathing or other forms of basic hygiene, no privacy of which to speak, and certainly no accommodations for a woman traveling on her own. The field crew went about their personal business as if I did not exist, and even Patrick Lear was unable or unwilling to acknowledge my sex.

When I pictured my promised employment with the museum at Yale College, I was naive enough in spite of my years to envision it as something like the best of the times I spent in Philadelphia. As the man in black had suggested, I had been nothing more than a hired hand while at the Academy. Still, I had an opportunity to learn from educated men, men outside of the arts who regularly reviewed and critiqued my work. Like the Captain, these men were gentlemen from families of wealth if not prestige. They treated me with a courtesy befitting their rank, and were grateful in an offhanded way for what I did, since I was helping them document and bring to life their discoveries before they were put on public display. And even though I often worked in the back of poorly ventilated rooms, I was never too far removed from the excitement of their discoveries. Shipments of bones and other fossils arrived regularly from the field, and men would talk into the night, smoking, sipping whiskey and tea, and discussing where the new finds might fit into a von Baerian view of the world. In the morning, they would often still be sitting there, arguing about Darwin, Lamarckian inheritance, and God, rewriting science and history as they talked.

While I was never much concerned with the minutiae of their discussions, I had great hopes that by being witness to them I might better understand how the bones of a creature could form the framework for an animal's survival, and that by capturing the basic architecture of these beasts I, too, might in some small way contribute to a new history of the world. I was even hopeful, in a way that I would never have admitted at the time, that once at Yale College my contributions might be recognized and the overall conditions of my employment might improve.

As Augustus would tell me later that summer, I had much to learn while in Montana.

Diane Smith, who worked for years as a writer specializing in science and the environment, published Letters from Yellowstone *(Viking/Penguin, 1999). The novel, currently in its fourteenth edition, won the Pacific Northwest Booksellers Association Award for fiction, was the One Book Montana statewide read in 2005–2006. Her second novel,* Pictures from an Expedition, *(Viking/Penguin, 2002) won the first Montana Book Award and was featured on National Public Radio's "Theme and Variation." Both books are part of the Smithsonian Institution's permanent collection. She makes her home in Livingston.*

Mildred Walker

RANCHER'S WIFE

B ELLA MYERS HAD JUST COME from the women's luncheon at
the Country Club. A whole afternoon's bridge had tired her some
way, or perhaps it was the heat. The lunch had been too hearty
for a hot day like this. She wouldn't want a thing for dinner now, and that
always irritated Will. She sank down on the porch glider to wait for Will,
and picked up her knitting. But she sat idly, moving a little with the side-
long motion of the swing; her toes just touched the floor, her hands lay
quietly over her knitting bag. She leaned her head back against the swing
and looked out across the lawn.

Even with the hose going every day, as much as the city would allow, the
grass was brown in spots and the zinnias that usually did so well in front
of the hedge were stalky and withered looking. It had been a dry summer,
even for Montana.

Mina Gates had said out at the club today that it was hard on a body's
skin. Bella felt the skin of her face that, in spite of her fifty-two years, was
still fresh and smooth. Against her softly waved gray hair her face looked
more youthful than many a woman's whose hair was still dark. Since the
children were gone she took very good care of herself. Annie scarcely
needed any supervision about the house and Will was away so much out at
the ranch her days moved tranquilly along of themselves.

She saw Will's car turn the corner. Will never could keep the car washed
because of the trips out to the ranch. It was certainly dusty enough now.
Will drove up to the curb and got out. He looked more tired tonight, more
stooped, it seemed to her. Maybe it was just that he was in his ranch clothes
and the trousers were always out of press. Bella smoothed her lips between
her thumb and forefinger in a nervous little gesture she had. She shoved

forward to the edge of the swing and then stood up.

"Hello, Will."

"Hello! Hot enough, isn't it?" -Will Myers took off his felt hat and rubbed his hand across the red line the hatband had left across his forehead.

"Brush your hair back. Will. It makes you look so old when it's mussed," Bella said instinctively. She always wanted to fix him up a little. That was the worst of having a rancher for a husband she felt; he never looked real slick like the men who had positions in town. Most of the time, she forgot he was a rancher, the ranch was so far in the background, providing the comfortable income back of the pleasant life on Elm Street, keeping Lucy in summer school this minute.

"Dinner's waiting, Will." Bella touched his arm affectionately as she went into the house ahead of him. Will did look so old and tired tonight. He looked a great deal older than she did even though there was only a few months difference in their ages.

"Did you just get in from the ranch?" she asked when they were sitting in their familiar places across the dining table from each other.

"No, I came in after lunch. I've been downtown," Will answered slowly.

Bella had only a vague idea of her husband's business. She knew he was in town part of the time, selling wheat and cattle, and he had things to attend to besides managing the ranch. She had never lived on the ranch. When they were first married they had taken a house in town because it would be so lonely there and, of course, she was used to living right in town in Iowa. Then the children had come along and it was more convenient in town near to a doctor, and there was school. And so she had always lived in the pleasant, two-story frame house on Elm Street.

Bella let Will serve her to some part of the steak and potatoes and peas and pretended to eat. Afterwards she would say to Annie, "I didn't touch my steak. You just save it for me tomorrow."

But even Will didn't seem to have much appetite tonight.

It was close in the dining room. The Virginia creeper that reached down in long green fingers outside the window hung as still as though it had been nailed to the air. Will never was talkative, but tonight he seemed more quiet than usual. Bella kept track of what Annie was doing by the sounds from the kitchen: now she was getting the cooking dishes out of the way; now she had gone out to put the milk bottles on the back step; now she was reading the paper till they were through. It was so still Bella could hear the rattle of the pages. Bella came back to Will abruptly. She wondered if he would like to go to a movie tonight. Then Will spoke, without looking across at her, buttering his bread, the whole slice at once. He ate at the ranch so much he got into careless habits, but she didn't remind him tonight.

"Bella, I …"

There was something odd about his voice. She waited.

"This is the worst year we've had at the ranch since '33."

Oh, that was all, then. The men who had ranches were always pessimistic. Mina Gates said today that Ben was down in the mouth over the lack of rain. Bella felt relieved.

She nodded. "I was noticing the lawn tonight. With all the water I've put on it, it's dry as a bone."

"We started to plow under all the wheat we put in west of the creek," Will went on slowly as though it were an effort to speak. Bella wondered if he were feeling well. Maybe he ought to stop and see Dr. Blaine while he was in town this time.

"Mhmm," she murmured vaguely. Then she asked pleasantly, "I imagine the wheat isn't as good as usual?"

Will laid down his knife and the piece of bread he had buttered from edge to edge. He looked across the table at her so keenly Bella smoothed her lips nervously.

"There wasn't a spear of wheat worth threshing." His voice was harsh. He spoke in a whisper. "It wasn't even worth saving for seed."

"Gracious!" Bella said softly, feeling it inadequate. Her face was troubled. Annie changed the dishes and they sat quietly until she had brought the cake and peaches and gone heavily back to the kitchen. "More coffee. Will?"

Will shook his head. He laid his napkin on the table; without putting it in the ring. As though by common consent they went out to the porch. There must be something wrong with Will, more than the bad weather and crops, to take his appetite like that, Bella thought.

"I believe it is cooler out on the porch," she said finally, wondering why Will didn't smoke. After a moment or two she leaned forward from the glider and said gently, "What's the matter, Will? Don't you feel well?"

"Bella, I know how you don't like the ranch. . . ." Will began in that careful, slow voice that sounded so queerly, "and how you set such store by living here in town and having your friends and going-around and all that, but this drought's just been one too many for us this year...."

Bella set the glider moving slightly, nervously, yet feeling reassured. It was just Will's talk about the drought. In a dry year people always went on like that. It didn't mean so much actually. Will always found money for the children, and now that John was out of school and working and there were only Lucy and...of course, she might have to put off a trip East to see John and his new bride, but that was all. She did wish guiltily that she hadn't ordered that new Bradley knit for fall, but then the bill wouldn't come in till October.

"Anderson asked me the other day if I'd consider renting the house here; said he had a party that'd give seventy-five dollars a month for it...." Will's voice went on so slowly she could scarcely believe what he was saying. Had he used to speak so slowly? He wasn't looking at her but out across the porch railing to the hedge. Bella stopped the glider with her toe. Will was talking of renting the house here! Will liked to tease her. Only his face looked too sober for teasing.

"I know it'll be hard on you, Bella. I was going to ask you first, but I knew what you'd say. I can't raise any more money at the bank and that rent'll help. I ... I felt we had to do it." He stopped again.

Bella leaned forward. "You mean you've already...."

"I rented it from the first of next month. I thought you could put up with a year on the ranch, till spring anyway....After all, Bella, you're a rancher's wife."

She couldn't believe her ears. Will never went ahead without asking her. She could never rent this house with all her things in it. She wouldn't think of it. But Will's last words stayed grimly in her ears. Her thoughts swung crazily around them. She opened her mouth to protest, but she could only rub nervously at her lips. "After all, Bella, you're a rancher's wife."

A long time after Will had gone to sleep she lay looking around the dark bedroom, thinking of arguments she might have brought to bear on Will, seeing the bare, cheerless bedrooms at the ranch, wondering what it would really be like living out there miles from any kind of town. She hadn't even been out there since spring and then she'd only sat on the porch while Will was off looking at some new calves. She tried to think of leaving the town and dropping out of all the life: the bridge club and the Guild and not even being able to go downtown to shop.

They only had stoves at the ranch; a big range and a base burner and a small, air-tight affair in the upstairs bedroom. She was used to the gas furnace and the thermostat. She was too old now to be uncomfortable.

The ranch house was better than most, Will had said tonight, apologetically. His mother and father had built it and lived there for years before they moved into town, but it was so ugly. Bella closed her eyes and saw it as plain as day. There was not a tree around it, only a gangling row of cottonwood saplings planted along the road. She turned softly in the bed to get away from the picture of the red and white ranch house and the corral and the big barn and silo and windmill standing out so nakedly on the plain. Lots of her friends owned ranches, but they didn't live on them. They lived in town and their husbands went back and forth.

Will said she could take out a few things ... "a truck load ought to be enough; we might take out the 'Beauty Rest' mattresses. The beds at the ranch aren't anything to boast about." And he had smiled for the first time since he got home.

In a couple of weeks she would be lying on this same mattress but in one of those flimsy looking bedrooms at the ranch. She grew panicky thinking about it. Her thoughts fluttered about unimportant objects until the objects themselves became vital, impossible to live without. There was the telephone by the bed. She reached out and touched it in the dark. She had always felt luxurious having one of the French phones, even if it did cost fifty cents more. Now the surface of the phone felt sweaty, almost clammy, but it was reassuring. She wished it were daytime and she could call Mina up this minute. At the ranch there was only one of those phones with a crank and all the other ranches around were on the same line.

Would Will let her take the petit point stool to her dressing table? It had taken her all last year to work it, but how silly it would look out at the ranch! The walls of the ranch bedrooms were plain white plaster, cracked in places. Of course, there were ranches where people really *lived;* smart places done in Spanish style, but there were none like that in this county.

How could Will do this to her? He hadn't looked at her when he told her and his voice had sounded hard, not like Will's voice, when he said, "After all, you're a rancher's wife." It made him seem like a stranger.

The next morning Will didn't start right off to the ranch. He was even slow going downtown. There was something apologetic in his silence. It made Bella uneasy. She stopped in the doorway of the dining room to say,

"I'll lock up all my good china, you better believe, and we'll take the silver with us, no matter what!"

"Of course, Bella, I wouldn't have rented the house to just anybody; I'm fond of it myself." Will's voice was irritated. He was just touchy she told herself as she went up to make the beds. Then she thought about Annie and went down to ask Will what they'd do about Annie.

"The Millers'll be out at the ranch a good deal this winter," he told her, her eyes on the spice boxes along the shelf, "and it would be so lonely for me here in town I'm going out to stay with him." The falsity of her own words smote her as she said them. Will was away so much she had grown used to his absence.

Annie's evident pity irritated her at the same time that it made her feel the bleakness of her own lot.

"And you're going to live out there on that ranch all winter! You'll die!"

"I hear that Mrs. Springer is looking for someone to help her, I'll mention you," Bella said stiffly.

"Oh, I guess there's plenty of places," Annie answered with equal stiffness. Bella went upstairs feeling uncomfortable.

At lunch Will said he had to go back to the ranch and she might go out with him and spend the night and that would give her a chance to see what she wanted to take out.

As they drove down the street Bella thought the house had never looked so good to her. The porch was so shady with the awning and her new bedroom curtains looked so well in the upstairs windows. Just the thought of renting it to other folks gave her a sinking feeling in her stomach. It was as hard as leaving her father's home when she and Will were married. Only then she had sat close to Will with her hand in his arm. Now Will seemed so old and silent and wrapped up in his own thoughts.

Every block of the town seemed dear to her, even the park and the municipal pool that was closed because of the water shortage, and the bridge that led away from town. The signboard pointing out to the open country took on sudden ominous importance. They wouldn't be staying till next month she told herself, but it might as well have been today from the way she felt. She couldn't think of anything to say to Will. They drove silently along out through the ugly fringes of the town, past signboards and gasoline stations and the road to the Country Club.

Then the road to the ranch stretched straight ahead of them, dusty, bare, unrelieved. For miles there wasn't a tree or shrub except for gray clumps of sagebrush and patches of cactus. Far over to the side the rimrock thrust itself up from the plain, the edge against the sky like crustings left in a bake dish. People said they looked like the ruins of old castles but they were nothing so romantic in the naked glare of the sun.

Bella wished she had brought some dark glasses. The sun made her squint. She never had been one to go out in it much. Usually this time of day, if she wasn't at a luncheon somewhere, she darkened the house and went upstairs with a magazine to lie on her bed till it cooled off a little. It hurt her now to think of her bedroom.

Grasshoppers came in through the open car window so fast she had to screw up the glass. Then the heat from the engine rose from the car floor in waves. The smell of gasoline and dust made her a little sick.

"See that!" Will jerked his thumb at the land on her side of the road. "Not worth cutting."

Bella stared almost curiously at the bronze colored field, wondering. She didn't know much about wheat. What did Will mean? It looked all right. Then she saw: wheat should stand three feet tall, yellowed at the top as cornbread. This was no more than five inches from the ground and was more brown than yellow.

"Burned to a cinder!" Will muttered.

As far as Bella could see the brown field stretched away to the sky. "Dear, what a waste!" she murmured.

Will snorted. The sound had bitterness in it.

It was a relief to pass fields that had been cut down to a stubble of bristling stalks. Farther on the wheat had been already plowed under and the sun-baked clods of dirt, specked with stubble like tweed yarn, were restful. At least, the pitiful, good-for-nothing wheat was buried under where you didn't have to look at it.

Bella had never looked so hard at the countryside. Usually, when they drove out to the ranch, she knit. She had her knitting today, but she was almost afraid it would bother Will. She stared at every ranch house they passed, wincing at the ugliness, wondering how women stood it living way out. The water tank on the roof of a ranch house they passed exposed the grim fact that all the water the dwellers there had at one time was contained in that tank. But the women who lived on these ranches weren't like her, Bella told herself; they were used to this sort of life. They liked it. She saw them in town or at the State Fair. She had never thought of herself in the same breath as a rancher's wife.

They passed an irrigation ditch. Between high banks of dirt ran a measly stream of water. It gave back a smiling reflection of bright blue sky. A clump of Black-eyed Susans grew ridiculously out of a clod of dirt along the top.

"But, Will, some of our land is irrigated, isn't it? I thought all that expense you went to the year Lucy couldn't go to Europe…"

"Most of it is, but you couldn't get the water to the land quick enough this year," Will muttered. "The dirt's like gunpowder, Bella, only it hasn't got anything to it." Then he relapsed again into complete silence against which the throb of the motor was deafening and the sound of the grasshoppers a loud aching rasp.

A car passed them at infrequent intervals, leaving them again to the loneliness of the flat, empty country with the dusty road across it. Bella had never felt so forlorn before. Usually she had things to tell Will about: the house or how Annie tried her or about folks in town. Today she felt dried up inside. She felt things wouldn't interest Will anyway. She wished they would get there. How did Will stand this grind every time he came to town? And yet it wasn't far as distance went in Montana, sixty-seven miles to town was all.

She screwed down the window in spite of the grasshoppers and let the hot air blow through the car. It was no wonder the weeds along the road were withered and turned the color of dust. And always there was the sun in the blue enameled sky making her squint because of its brightness. The country didn't seem real in this silence and heat. It was gray with dust as though it were turning to ash. It even looked tired, beat out, the way Will had looked yesterday. She saw the cattle standing beside the road and wondered what they ate. Around them the ground was brown, worn off like old leather. She remembered; Will had said they had to buy feed to keep the stock, but it hadn't meant much to her then.

There was the high gate that marked the road into the ranch. Will got out and swung the gate so they could drive through. The ranch house, looking more barren and flimsy than she had remembered reared up from the ground without a shrub around it. Some of the spindling cottonwood trees had died this summer. The curtain in the front window was torn.

"You can see the mountains from here, anyway," Will said with a kind of heavy jocularity. Back of the ranch there was an indistinct blue line that marked the mountains, to be sure, but even that looked faded from the sun. The mountains might be part of the Rockies but they weren't half the comfort a line of good green trees would be. She had never been one for looking at mountains.

Mrs. Miller, whose husband was Will's head man, came to the door to meet them, wiping her hands on a dirty apron. Will seemed embarrassed and went off to find Ed, leaving Bella there to make difficult talk with this gaunt, stringy woman.

"My, it's hot! I've been over the stove canning chickens," the woman offered. She talked in a loud voice but as though she were glad to talk, almost like Mina Gates when she had a piece of news to tell. "Hawks is gettin' 'em something fierce," she explained.

"You go right ahead. I'll just walk around," Bella suggested.

"Oh, I don't mind sitting a spell. You haven't been out but once this year, have you?"

"No," Bella answered. "I've been pretty busy."

At last the woman went back to the kitchen to get supper, saying so heartily as she went, "My, it'll be nice to get a meal for company for a change," that Bella felt lacking that she hadn't been more entertaining company.

The house was terrible. She couldn't imagine herself living here.

She fled out to the long narrow porch.

Now at five-thirty the sun had lost its glare. The hard outlines of the ruts in the road, the rails of the corral fence, the piece of farm machinery deserted in the dooryard were less blatant. Now the color of the mountains had deepened, turned to lavender. The worn, shabby look of the earth had changed to green, almost the shade of new sage plants. The heat was no less suffocating, but there was a smell of clover or alfalfa or perhaps only sage in the dust. Bella sniffed. She could look without squinting. But it was lonely even if it wasn't so ugly. And the loneliness would be stronger with dusk. It made her afraid.

Then she saw Will, riding slowly along on horseback, coming over the rise of ground back of the house. She could tell it was Will by his hat and the droop of his shoulders. He looked younger on a horse. She had forgotten that he rode much out here. She watched him coming nearer. He was bigger some way against his land than coming up the walk on Elm Street. The sight of him drew her queerly, as it had used to when she was young. He swung off the horse more easily than he got out of the car and came up on the porch. He took off his hat and rubbed his hand back across his hair.

"I believe it's a bit cooler," he said.

"I believe it is," Bella agreed. "It's not bad when the sun gets down a little." The loneliness of the wide earth fading into the mountains had disappeared with Will there or changed to something else.

Will laid his hand on her shoulder a moment before they went in to supper in the ranch house.

Mildred Walker was born in 1905 in Philadelphia, the daughter of a Baptist minister and a schoolteacher. After graduating magna cum laude from Wells College, Walker met and married a young Michigan doctor named Ferdinand Ripley Schemm. They moved to Big Bay, Michigan, on the Upper Peninsula, where Walker wrote her first novel, Fireweed. *From 1933 to 1950, she wrote nine of her thirteen novels in Great Falls, where she lived with her husband and their three children. After her husband's death in 1950, she returned east and taught literature at Wells College, making her home in Vermont. Walker is best known for her novel* Winter Wheat, *which was selected for the One Book Montana program by the Montana Center for the Book. Her third and sixth novels won Literary Guild awards; her eleventh novel was nominated for*

the National Book Award in 1960. Bison Books of the University of Nebraska Press has reprinted all of her novels and will publish a fourteenth novel post-humously in 2006. Walker died in 1998.

Ripley Schemm Hugo

From *Writing for Her Life: The Novelist Mildred Walker*

MOTHER'S SIXTH NOVEL, *WINTER WHEAT*, published in 1944, would be wholly concerned with Montana characters surviving and triumphing in that country. And it has the "drama" that De Voto insists must be present. Natural events surrounding her characters are also essential to *Winter Wheat*. Recently, I found it helpful to read Mother's short story "Rancher's Wife," published in 1940 in the *Junior League Magazine*, because it reads like a rehearsal for this sixth novel. It takes up those Montanans who live in what Mother first saw as barrenness. The short story is a kind of query into who a woman living in the West might be, and it is told entirely from the point of view of Bella Meyers, the wife of Will Meyers, who grows wheat on land sixty-seven miles out of town. As the story opens, Bella, waiting in the front porch swing for Will to come in from the ranch, notices that "he looked more tired tonight, more stooped, it seemed to her." Before his arrival, she has been thinking back to her luncheon at the country club and an afternoon of playing bridge. Now, as he approaches, she thinks: "He never looked real slick like the men who had positions in town. Most of the time, she forgot he was a rancher, the ranch was so far in the background, providing the comfortable income back of the pleasant life on Elm Street." After a silent supper, Will explains the discouragement that Bella has seen in him. The drought has been so bad this summer that there is no wheat to cut, and so, he says slowly, he has had to rent the house in town: "I rented it from the first of next month. I thought you could put up with a year on the ranch, till spring, anyway....After all, Bella, you're a rancher's wife."

The rest of the story is of Bella's disbelief, expressed only in her thoughts, that she must give up her town activities, must endure the ugliness of the ranch house way out there with no trees, "only a gangling row of cottonwood saplings planted along the road." She panics at the thought of not being surrounded by her fine china, her kitchen conveniences, her shady porch. As they drive toward the ranch, Will's assurance that they can bring out "maybe a truck load of things" she will want to have, including the "Beauty Rest" mattresses, is not enough: "But the women who lived on these ranches weren't like her, Bella told herself; they were used to this sort of life. They liked it. She saw them in town or at the State Fair. She had never thought of herself in the same breath as a rancher's wife." Will tells her, "You can see the mountains from here, anyway," but she knows that she has "never been one for looking at mountains." Once there, she feels even more strongly her dread of the wide bare hot land surrounding her. Only when the sun has begun to go down and the dry country seems less harsh can she appreciate the sight of the mountains. The story ends with Bella's reluctant discovery that when she sees Will riding in on his horse after the long hot afternoon, the country doesn't make her so lonely.

Mother's short stories written during the Great Falls years (1933–44) seem sharp glimpses into lives that "said something" to her. Now they seem almost autobiographical descriptions of her interests. The plot of "Rancher's Wife," for instance, depends on the depiction of how a woman of what Mother called "shallow interests" (chiefly interested in her luncheon at the country club or the view from her front porch) might respond to the crisis of having to move to the ranch. I can see how this heroine might not have been a character who would be complicated enough for Mother's sense of what she would want to accomplish in a novel. But a Bella or a Miriam would continue to be present as minor characters in other's Montana novels.

As a writer she could imagine the feelings these women had, depict them with what seemed to me pitying accuracy. But in the world she inhabited as a nonwriter, they were of little interest to her. She took pains to dismiss them from her vibrant life with her husband and friends. And in the years that followed, she would wonder aloud at her children's association with and affection for men and women who struck her as being "of that sort," of less value in her eyes than those she felt to be vital and accomplished. Such remarks of hers would cause wild resentment in me, but also leave me defenseless. This reaction on my part was beside the point to her; she made clear all through her life that she made such a statement "for your own good." No wonder my reading of her novels, not until my thirties and forties, brought me up short: Which perception of human beings was hers? Why could she empathize with them on the page and not in her own life?

I admit that my resentments were my own problem. I still relive a rainy afternoon in the car with Mother on Great Falls's Central Avenue. I must have been about thirteen. As she stopped for a traffic light at the intersection, a tall young woman in a long bright red raincoat wearing high black heels crossed in front of us. I exclaimed at the wonderful air of the woman, the raincoat sweeping out behind her and the rain glittering off her black heels. As the light changed and Mother started up the car, she said in a dismissive tone of voice, "I don't think that. I think the red makes her look quite common." Of course, I have remembered the scene all these years, even the smell of the rain, because I was so shocked, and chagrined, at what seemed to me Mother's dismissal of this woman for the clothes she wore. It didn't occur to me that I was really resenting her disapproval of my delight. I raged silently that Mother was unfair. And yet I would realize years later, reading her novels, that she used an observation like this to evoke the personality of a minor character.

LESSONS ITINERANT TEACHERS LEARN

This side of town looms
warehouse big—the elevator
tall for grain the trains will haul.
Closed machine shop, open
turnaround. One low building
across the alley with one back door
takes up space others meant
to swallow.

Down the road some fifteen miles
Goldenridge School stands white,
one story high on Fairfield Bench
where farmers work their irrigated
fields. A saying goes it takes six kids
to make those farms secure.

Each hardship, failure, removal—so
many words for tough breaks here—
are grownup words that name
a farm kid's road to school.

The boy who's lived three farms,
up and down the same five miles
of road, it's the way it is to him.
His name is Clint, he's fifth grade.
His poem explains how irrigation
ditches tell his time of day, his name
as Schneider's youngest, his hopes
as fields of grain.

RETELLING THE STORY

The moon rides fast
these new black nights
and walking's cold. You can
click your teeth and head home
or stalk your shadow the length
of its legs backward—to mornings
you've already loved, to a story
you've already told.

You tell it again:
you're taking the trail
that climbs to the Pass.
An early morning. A two-year-old
rides your shoulders, an elf
in her dark blue hood.
A five-year-old's tawny thatch
bobs before you, the only warm color
in a low autumn sky of gray cloud.

There's bounce to the sturdy trudge
of the boy up ahead. The mountains
take shape as you climb, step after step
on the trail's gray rock, rock broken
by wind and by cold. You're nearing
those clouds with their promise
of storm when a flutter
in the boy's thatch blurs orange,
is red, is black: A butterfly clings
to the gold of his hair, the only
warm color riding the mountain.

You call out, "Son, a butterfly's
resting in your hair!" He stops,
turns back to you slowly, wonder
blue in his eyes, his smile sly
with caution. He turns again
to the Pass, his head held still
so his stride won't jostle
his lovely burden. And the last
long mile to the wind at the top
the butterfly clings to the boy's
gold thatch, to the only warm
color rising.

BUILDING FENCE

My brother, my son, they're setting
jack posts, stringing wire in high wind.
I come after, pounding staples in good
pine wood. We follow the edge of the jack pine
where the foothill opens out to long drop
after drop of tough grass sliding down
the Front Range. We know it's a fine day,
a rare day, our banter raucous, intent,
tossed to the wind. We're cold, hungry,
but set to get the work done.

My brother could always get something
done. Rebuilt that old Chevy he'd
broke down right to the screws. First
day he had it working, he gave our dad
a ride on the chassis, scattered gravel
as they chugged the road. Then my brother
learned to put people back in their bones
whole, when before they'd only been
painful parts. And his fishing is legend.
He taught that to my son.

My son could catch fish in the clearest
waters, enough to feed the whole bunch
hunkered down to plates and forks. Early,
he built a whole from parts—heard people's
scattered stories, wove the fragments
together. Then, his listeners could hold
their present in the hands of their history.

And very young, he wanted to know of earth,
of lives lived on it.

When I drive the old road in sight of
that fence, now, I know that another
fine day, rare day, there'll just be
my brother ahead of me setting posts.
I don't know the reason my son should die
a young man before he could get done
what he wanted. I only know to thread
that day's green needles through me,
bring back what we all got done together
one wind-loud day on the Front Range
looking east, never worrying west. More than
two hundred staples that day to my credit. No count
for my loss to grass.

Ripley Schemm was born in 1929 and raised in Great Falls, Montana. She earned degrees in literature from Swarthmore College and the University of Montana. After teaching English and American literature at universities across the country, she returned to Montana in 1973 to raise her two children and marry the poet Richard Hugo. She taught creative writing, and especially enjoyed teaching poetry in the schools for the Montana Arts Council. She wrote Writing for Her Life: The Novelist Mildred Walker, *(University of Nebraska Press, 2003), drawing on her memories of her mother and her mother's papers. Her earlier poems were published in a chapbook,* Mapping My Father *in 1981. Hugo lives in Missoula and is a poet and a faculty affiliate in the English Department at the University of Montana.*

Dorothy M. Johnson

PRAIRIE KID

WHEN ELMER MERRICK WAS ELEVEN years old, he marched an outlaw off the Ainsworth place at the point of a gun.

They still talk about it in Montana, telling the story with a proud chuckle, implying that in the old days all the boys were men, and all the men were tough as saddle leather. After Elmer grew up, he was as tough as he needed to be, but when he held a gun on Buck Saddler on that summer night in 1888, he was a frightened, desperate child.

Except for size, he didn't look like a child. He walked like a tired old man, with his shoulders drooping; when he rested, he sagged with patient weariness, not fidgeting. He looked sullen and puzzled and hostile, and he felt hostile toward just about everybody except Lute Kimball. Lute was his idol, for two good reasons: Lute treated him like an equal, and Lute could do well everything that Elmer was still learning. But Lute lived up in Miles City in those days, close to two days' ride on a good horse, so they did not meet often.

In one respect only, Elmer doubted Lute's judgment. Lute was courting Charlotte Ainsworth, and Elmer considered her a fool and a tenderfoot. A tenderfoot she certainly was, for she had come out from the East only that summer to keep house for her brother, Steve. She had to be told the most elementary things, such as the rule that all comers had to be offered food, unless they were Indians.

More visitors came to Steve's place during her first month there than ordinarily passed in a year, so pretty Charlotte Ainsworth spent a great deal of her time cooking quick meals for staring, bashful cowboys, who pretended they hadn't known she was there.

That summer, while Charlotte Ainsworth was enjoying the privileges of being the only single white girl in almost a hundred miles, Elmer Merrick, on his father's ranch three hours' ride to the westward, was learning to live with fear. Waking or sleeping, it stalked him, and sometimes it leaped and took his breath away, and a jeering voice in his own mind demanded. If your pa dies, what are you going to do about Varina?

His sister Varina was six years old, sunny and carefree, unreliable and perverse. She did not know she was lonely, because she had always lived on the prairie. She played with a stick doll and sang to herself and carried on long, murmured conversations with a couple of entirely imaginary girls named Beauty and Rose. Varina was of no use to anyone, and she worried about nothing except her chances of getting over to Steve's place fairly often to visit Miss Charlotte.

Miss Charlotte, she said, had a rosewood melodeon that she had brought out in a trunk; Miss Charlotte was teaching her to play it; Miss Charlotte washed Varina's fair hair and made it hang in curls. Elmer, sick with his own worries, sometimes shouted, "Aw, shut up about Miss Charlotte!" but Varina would answer smugly, "Miss Charlotte likes me."

Once Elmer snapped, "Aw, she pretends to like everybody," and then was ashamed of himself because Varina cried so hard.

He had enough to worry him. More than half his father's cattle starved in the snow in the winter of 1887, his mother died the following fall, and his father, old Slope Merrick, was crippled with a gnawing pain in his belly. Slope had arranged with three cowboys, who were following the roundups for other outfits, to brand and tally his remaining scattered cattle, and sell them if anyone wanted to buy, but that meant putting a lot of trust in frail human nature. He and Elmer, between them, had found and branded only twenty head of calves.

If Slope had any plans for the future, he did not confide in his son, and Elmer confided in nobody. He wanted to talk to Lute Kimball, but Lute spent his time shining up to Miss Charlotte.

The fear pounced at Elmer more than once that summer; he sent it slinking back by ignoring it. He could forget about it if he worked hard enough, and there was work enough to do, with Slope lying in his bunk a good share of the time. Even when Slope decided, one morning before dawn, that he had to get to a doctor, the boy still did not quite face his problem. He was too busy to think about it for a while, after his father groaned, "Elmer! Elmer, git up! We're going to Steve's."

The boy sat up in his bunk, demanding with numb lips, "You want the wagon?"

Slope turned his head back and forth and groaned, "Of course! Of course!" as if they had discussed the whole matter in detail, and his son had forgotten.

Elmer woke his sister by giving her tangled blonde hair a jerk. Varina whimpered and slapped at him blindly.

"We're going to Steve's place for a while," he snapped. "You want to go along, you pile out and git ready!" He was wide awake now, and planning. "You're going over ahead of us, by yourself."

Slope groaned, "No! Not alone."

But Elmer had his first taste of mastery. "She kin do it," he answered, and his father did not argue.

Elmer pulled on his pants and the boots he had outgrown, wrapped his moccasins in his other shirt, and grabbed his throw-rope off its peg by the door. By the time Varina was dressed and had her extra dress rolled up, Elmer had roped and saddled three horses and tied a rope halter on the cow. It did not occur to him to help his sister mount her horse; she scrambled on with what Lute Kimball, smiling, had called a flying clamber. It was the same system Elmer used himself.

"Hurry up!" Elmer barked. "Tell 'em to git the team and wagon ready to take Pa up to town. We'll be coming along directly."

It was midmorning when Steve Ainsworth helped Slope down from the saddle and into the hay-filled wagon bed.

"I'll take good care of the children, Mr. Merrick," Miss Charlotte promised. "Don't you worry about them for a minute." She held Varina by the hand.

Slope lay back on the blankets and the hay. "Elmer," he said. "Look after the women."

Elmer answered, "Yuh, sure." He stood with his hands in his pockets, his shoulders hunched.

"My old Colt," Slope said between his teeth. "You can carry it."

Elmer said, "All right," as calmly as if a dream had not suddenly come true. The old cap-and-ball .44 was in Pa's saddle bag with its belt and powder flask and the leather sacks of lead bullets and caps.

Steve Ainsworth let go the brake on the wagon. "You'll be all right," he told his sister with what he hoped sounded like conviction. "We'll be back as soon as we can make it. Maybe I can send Lute Kimball down ahead."

"Take good care of Mr. Merrick," she cautioned. "Children, don't you want to wave good-bye?"

Varina obediently waved, but Elmer stood with his hands in his pockets, thinking. Children, huh!

The cow lowed, recalling him to duty.

"I gotta milk," he announced, turning his back as the wagon dropped out of sight beyond the first low bridge. "You could cook us some breakfast. We ain't et yet."

Miss Charlotte was off in a flurry of skirts, exclaiming, "Oh, dear, when will I remember that visitors have to be fed! Come, Varina—you may play the melodeon."

Elmer scowled. "Don't you let her fool around with that!" he ordered. "Make her do something useful. She's got a lot of things to learn."

Miss Charlotte turned, looking puzzled and amused. "She's just a little girl, Elmer. What should she be learning at her age?"

"If I knowed," he burst out in exasperation, "I'd learn her myself. Start her off with cooking. She won't pay no attention to me."

As he plodded with the bucket toward the cow, the fear came right up to meet him, and for the first time he faced it. It said, What you going to do about Varina if your pa dies? and he answered, I'm gonna leave Miss Charlotte look after her.

And what for would Miss Charlotte or anybody want to have her around? How you going to fix that, eh?

He answered honestly, I ain't got that quite figured out yet.

Then he milked the cow and started looking after the women, as he had been told to do.

Three days up by wagon, a day to see the doctor, and three days back, if all went well. A week before Steve could get back to the cabin. But Lute could make the return trip in less time: If Steve located him, he might get back late on the fifth day. If Steve met a rider, someone he could trust, there would be a man on the place sooner than that. But the wagon was not likely to meet anyone, because riders came by the horse trail.

The first day Elmer kept busy cutting firewood down by the river, annoyed because Miss Charlotte was pampering Varina, letting her waste time playing the melodeon, although when he came in for meals, Varina industriously peeled potatoes and wiped dishes. Varina helped Miss Charlotte spread the blankets smooth in the bunks. The two of them slept in the lean-to, and Elmer had Steve's bunk in the main room, the kitchen.

The second day, seven Indians came by. Elmer sent them on their way— an old buck, four squaws, a young girl, and a boy about his own age—but he was embarrassed at having let them get clear to the cabin. He did not go back to cutting wood by the river.

After that, when the water buckets needed filling, he made the women go with him down to the river. Miss Charlotte obviously thought he wanted her for protection and made quite a show of being gay to let him know she wasn't scared. Elmer didn't tell her any different. He was learning the patience a man has to have with women.

When she wanted to help carry water, he growled, "I'd ruther carry the both buckets. It's easier." Even Varina knew that. One bucket pulled you down sideways. The old Cavalry Colt, sagging along his right leg, already did that.

Miss Charlotte was slightly amused about his wearing the Colt. With what Miss Charlotte didn't know about guns, you could win battles. She didn't even suspect the Colt was loaded; the bright copper caps were plain to see, but she didn't notice. Elmer felt a little guilty about having all six chambers charged; Lute played safer than that, and he had a Frontier model—a Peacemaker—that took regular cartridges. Lute kept the hammer on an empty chamber. But Elmer Merrick preferred to take chances on shooting himself in the foot accidentally, as long as he could convince himself that he was ready for six kinds of trouble. Reloading took a lot of time; many a man had been killed and scalped, in the old days, while he fumbled with powder and ball.

The third day, Elmer chopped the wood into stove lengths, and on the day after that he started to dig post holes for Steve's horse corral. Steve planned to drive a bunch of horses in from Oregon the following spring.

When Miss Charlotte saw what he was doing, she came flying out, exclaiming, "Elmer, now you stop that!"

Everything she said or did annoyed him, so he answered. "Digging's got to be done, don't it? Steve wants a corral, don't he?"

"Let him go on building it himself, then. I don't want you working so hard as you've been doing, Elmer Merrick. I want you to settle down. My goodness, don't you ever play?"

He had not played for a long time; his spare time he had usually spent in practicing things he needed to learn, like roping, or pulling his gun fast. But while he was affronted by her insistence that he was a child, he was pleased that she had noticed how hard he worked.

"When there's things to be done, someone's got to do 'em," he told her.

"But not heavy work like that!" she insisted. "You're liable to stunt your growth."

That was enough to stop him. Maybe, he thought, she was right. But he could not admit that he was going to take her seriously. He said doubtfully, "Well, I'll find something else."

He set out to chink the cracks of the lean-to, built that spring for Miss Charlotte's bedroom. While he worked at it, he solved part of his problem: What he was going to do if his father did not come back. Somewhere there must be an outfit that needed a wrangler on the home place, a helper to bring in the cavy for the cowboys and chore around for the cook. He dreamed about an imaginary boss saying, "That boy ain't very big for what I had in mind," and Miss Charlotte assuring him, "Oh, but he's a very hard worker. Elmer just works all the time."

And what are you going to do about Varina? his conscience nagged.

I'm figuring about that, he answered patiently. I'm figuring how to get Miss Charlotte to keep her.

That was on the fourth day. On the fifth, Lute Kimball might have come, but a fair-haired stranger got there first, a wary man with quick-darting gray eyes. It was Miss Charlotte's fault that he stayed instead of riding on. She convinced Elmer all over again that she was a tenderfoot and a fool. But it was Elmer's fault that the stranger ever had a chance to feel so much at home.

When the man came, Elmer was in sight, but he was down at the edge of the river grove, with Steve's deer rifle, scouting around where he had seen deer signs. In the back of his mind was the thought, If she was to tell it around, "That Elmer is a good hunter; he got us venison," that would sound good to the boss, I guess.

He did not hear the stranger's horse, but a tingling on the back of his neck made him aware that something was going on. When he saw the buckskin horse and the buckskin-shirted rider, he set out for the cabin at a run.

But Miss Charlotte was already making the stranger welcome. And the man was saying, "Well, now, if you're sure it ain't too much trouble, I could eat all right, and that's a fact."

He whirled when he heard Elmer's pounding feet on the hard earth but the steel-spring tension went out of him when he saw only a boy and not a man. He turned back to Miss Charlotte and took off his dusty hat with a flourish.

"Buck Saddler, ma'am, and pleased to make your acquaintance."

"I am Miss Charlotte Ainsworth," she answered, smiling, "and these are the Merrick children, Elmer and Varina. If you'd like to wash up, Mr. Saddler, there's the basin."

The man hesitated for just a moment. "Thank you kindly. I'll just look after my horse first." He loosened the saddle cinch and walked around the horse, frowning and shaking his head. "Poor boy" he murmured, slapping the animal's shoulder. "Plumb beat, ain't you?" Then he turned to Elmer and commented, grinning, "You sure carry a lot of artillery."

Elmer glanced at the man's sagging gunbelt and loaded saddle and answered, "So do you." Buck Saddler carried a rifle and a shotgun on the saddle, and two belts of cartridges slung over the horn—not unreasonable armament for a long journey, but impressive.

The stranger glanced at the hog leg that pulled Elmer's belt down and smiled with unwise condescension. "By gollies, one of them old cap-and-ball Colts! Let's look at it, kid."

Elmer backed off, scowling. "Nobody touches my gun but me."

"If you was to show it to me," the stranger offered, teasing, "I might let you see mine."

"I kin see it," Elmer informed him. "It's a Peacemaker." In the old days before he had so many other things to worry about, he had dreamed of owning a Peacemaker himself, and money enough to buy all the ammunition he wanted, and hands big enough to handle a man-sized gun easily.

Miss Charlotte called, "I've got the griddle heating for pancakes. It's close to suppertime, so we'll all eat."

"You'll be wanting to go on before dark," Elmer told the stranger, hinting strongly. "We better git in there and eat, so's you won't be delayed."

Buck Saddler looked down at him through half-shut eyes. "I might have to delay anyway," he said deliberately. He walked toward the cabin and left Elmer worrying.

Miss Charlotte worried him more. She fussed as if Buck Saddler were a welcome guest. "Now, if you'll sit here, Mr. Saddler. You prefer the other side of the table? Of course, of course. Varina, Elmer, did you wash?"

Buck Saddler, Elmer noted, preferred to sit facing the window. You got some good reason for that, Elmer decided. And there's nothing wrong with that horse you're so cut up about.

Miss Charlotte raised her eyebrows at Elmer. "Young man, you can't come to the table with that gun on." Elmer kept his mouth shut, but it required effort. Never before in his life had he wanted so much to have a gun handy. But Buck Saddler stood up, grinning, unbuckled his own belt and hung it ostentatiously on a peg on the wall. Elmer did the same and sat down at the table without appetite.

Where's Lute? he fretted. It's time you come, Lute Kimball!

LUTE KIMBALL WAS RIDING AS hard as he dared on a spent horse, but he was also dreaming, as he often did, of being a hero for Miss Charlotte. No one would have suspected so stern-faced a man of dreaming about anything. He was a dark and silent man, thoughtful and practical. He had never stayed very long in any territory or on any job, but he had never quit any job so long as the boss needed him. He had made two trail drives up from Texas, and for most of his life had been looking for greener pastures. When Steve Ainsworth's sister came West, he saw them for the first time— green pastures, full of flowers, wherever Miss Charlotte was. Lute Kimball was twenty-seven years old that summer, and ready to settle down.

He missed his chance to be a hero for Steve's pretty sister, after all. He reached the cabin a few minutes too late.

Elmer had to admit that Miss Charlotte didn't make any more fuss over Buck Saddler than she did over anybody else; she always seemed delighted to see anyone who happened to come. But the stranger, following her quick movements with his darting eyes, assumed that he was a favored guest. He turned courtly and affable.

"That there pretty little organ," he commented; "that's a mighty nice thing to have. I bet you play it mighty pretty, Miss Charlotte."

"Only a few tunes," Miss Charlotte fibbed modestly. "But Varina, my goodness, Varina is learning to play it very nicely." To Elmer's disgust his little sister piped up, "I sure do play it good."

Charlotte beamed and did not reprimand her for boasting.

If Miss Charlotte wanted to bring the little girl into the conversation, the stranger was willing to play along. He said fatuously to Varina, "You're a real smart little girl, ain't you? And all fixed up with your hair in curls, anybody'd think it was your birthday, maybe."

"When is your birthday, dear?" Charlotte inquired.

Varina looked puzzled. Elmer answered, "Fifteenth of August. She don't know nothing."

Miss Charlotte glanced up at the calendar. "I declare," she cried, "that's today! If I'd known, I'd have baked a cake!"

Birthdays had never been of much account in the Merrick cabin; Varina would never have thought of making a fuss it she hadn't been encouraged. But Buck Saddler encouraged her.

"By George, a nice bright little girl like that, and she ain't got no cake or no presents! Now that sure is a shame!"

Varina's eyes flooded with tears. She began to cry, with her face in Miss Charlotte's lap.

Elmer growled, "Shut up, Foolish!" Embarrassed, he explained, "She don't howl like that when she falls off a horse."

Miss Charlotte patted the child's shoulder. "We'll have a present for Varina. I know just the thing—a pretty ribbon I brought in my trunk. Would you like a ribbon for your hair, Varina?"

Varina heard that, in spite of her squalling, and nodded emphatically.

The stranger said, "I can't have a lady beating my time with this here little girl. I'm gonna give her a present, too." He dug in his pocket, fished around a little, and brought out a coin. He opened Varina's hand and closed her fingers over the gift. Tear-stained, she stared at it.

Miss Charlotte cried, "Mr. Saddler, you can't do that! Why, it's a double eagle!"

He said with reproach, "Wouldn't want me to take back what I give her, would you, Miss Charlotte? No sir, that's for the little lady." He looked so smug that Elmer wanted to hit him.

And then he said the thing that scared Elmer: "Plenty more where that came from," said Buck Saddler.

For a few seconds Elmer forgot to breathe. A man might possibly have one gold piece or a couple. But if there's plenty more where that come from, Elmer realized, he never earned it. Was it a bank or a stage?

Miss Charlotte's face had colored, and she looked even a little scared, Elmer thought. Glowering at her, he could suddenly tell what she was thinking: Go away, you man! We don't want you here!

Never before had he been able to see so clearly what was in an adult's mind. The revelation startled him so much that, for a moment, he was dazed by his own cleverness. And then, with desperate cunning, he arrived at the answer to that dismal question: What are you going to do about Varina?

If it was so Miss Charlotte owed me a debt, he thought, might be she'd take Foolish and raise her. Might be she'd be that grateful. Well, how can I get rid of this man?

THAT WAS HOW ELMER GOT ON the track of saving Miss Charlotte—for cold, calculating reasons of his own. Lute Kimball, who had another reason for wanting to do the same thing if he ever had a chance—no less selfish a reason, but very different—still had nine miles to ride.

Miss Charlotte was not one to depend on someone else if she could do a thing herself. She started in a business-like way to pick up the dirty dishes. Pointedly she remarked, "It'll be dark in no time. You'll be wanting to go on, Mr. Saddler."

The stranger frowned. "I don't rightly like to leave you all here without no menfolks," he objected. "No telling what might come along."

"How true," Miss Charlotte murmured. "Don't give it a thought, Mr. Saddler. Elmer is our menfolks, and we are entirely confident that he will look after everything."

Elmer stared, for the first time thinking that Charlotte Ainsworth was, though still a tenderfoot, not actually a fool.

He began to figure: If I do this, he'll do that, but maybe he won't. Well, if I do that, what'll he do? Elmer was eleven years old and scared silly. But he was a prairie boy, and if he had not been self-reliant, he would not have lived to be eleven years old. He would have drowned at ten, when his horse threw him while fording a river, or he would have frozen in the blizzard that got him lost the year before that.

Buck Saddler gave him time to think. Buck wiped his mustache on his sleeve and strolled over to look at the melodeon. To the entranced Varina he suggested, "How'd you like to play me a little tune, girlie?"

Miss Charlotte said, "Varina is going to help me with the dishes," but Varina did no such thing. She started to pump the melodeon; she had to stand up to reach the keyboard, and pump the little metal pedal with one foot. Looking very well pleased with herself, she began picking out notes, making soft, pale-colored tones that you could almost see—silken ribbons of sound.

In the midst of figuring about Buck, Elmer thought, Oh, Lord, how would Miss Charlotte or anybody want to raise her, when she don't mind no better than that?

But he got his problem solved. If I do that, he will do this. There were only a few maybe's this time. Almost everything depended on: If I do that.

When he reached up to get his gun belt, Buck Saddler was instantly alert, but he only watched. He was within reaching distance of his Peacemaker. Elmer removed the old .44 from its holster, but left the belt and holster hanging on the peg. He walked over to Steve's small box of tools on the window sill and began to rummage.

Charlotte, scraping plates, asked tensely, "What are you looking for?"

"Worm," he muttered. "Think Steve's got a worm here. I want to unload my gun."

She looked so sick and helpless Elmer was afraid she would cry out and give everything away.

"This'll do it," Elmer remarked.

Buck watched him, slit-eyed, not moving. Elmer took his own sweet time. Never once did he move quickly; he kept the old Cavalry Colt carefully pointed at the wall while he worked, with the casual carefulness of one who had always handled firearms and had not pointed a gun at anyone since he got his ears boxed for it at the age of four. Delicately, he pried five caps off their nipples and let them lay on the table in plain sight. Painstakingly he reamed the powder and ball from five chambers, and Buck could count if he chose.

Buck relaxed enough to comment, "Mighty pretty tune you're playing, girlie." Miss Charlotte did not relax at all.

Elmer, on the far side of the table, put the gun down on the bench where he sat, with enough force to make it sound believable—and almost enough force to make his heart stop, because one chamber was still charged, and the cap was on the nipple. He sat for a little while, yawning, while he slid the long weapon down through his torn pocket and along his leg. The hole in his pocket was just right to catch and hold the hammer. When he stood up, yawning, Buck Saddler demanded, "Where you think you're going?"

"A person can go outside, can't they?" Elmer answered with elaborate dignity. "Maybe I'm gonna hunt rabbits."

Buck grinned. Hunting rabbits was what gentlemen passengers were invited to do when stage coaches with lady passengers made a comfort stop. Ladies "picked flowers."

When Elmer Merrick went outside to start to rescue Miss Charlotte, Lute Kimball was still two miles away.

"You was gone quite a while," Buck commented a little later.

"I come back," Elmer pointed out. "Your horse is down," he announced, as if he didn't care one way or the other. "I'll get the lantern if you'd like to take a look."

Buck scowled. "There wasn't nothing wrong with that horse!"

He was cornered and puzzled. But how could he be cornered by a small boy who had just unloaded his gun in plain sight? Buck Saddler relaxed and grinned.

"We'll be right back," he promised Miss Charlotte. "And the little girl can play me another tune." So complete was his disdain that he did not even reach up to the peg for his gun belt. Elmer came close to choking, because he wanted to draw a deep breath of relief and could not. That had been one of the maybe's.

He lighted the lantern and held it in front of him so that his shadow was in Buck Saddler's path. Buck grunted and snatched the lantern. Beyond the saddle shed he held the lantern high.

"There's nothing wrong with that horse!" he growled.

"Not a thing," agreed Elmer. "He's all cinched up and ready to travel."

Saddler laughed. "I ain't traveling nowhere. Not till I get ready."

"You're ready now," Elmer told him softly. "And this gun says so."

Saddler sneered. "I seen you unload it."

"You seen me unload five chambers. I got one charge left—and that's all it takes. You want to find out for sure, mister?" he demanded with tense urgency. "You ever get hit with a ball from a .44 not ten feet away from you?" Buck glanced toward his saddle. "Your other artillery is on my saddle," Elmer told him. "You'll get it back, but not just yet. Hold the lantern nice and steady, Buck."

Getting on his horse was another of the maybe's, but Saddler was wise enough to make no false moves. Elmer went up to his saddle like a flying bird, and when he got there, he cocked the hammer.

He heard Buck's grunt at the triple click, as the stranger realized that the gun had not been ready for action until that moment. Buck had been a man for too many years; he had forgotten that a boy's hand might not be big enough to cock and fire a single-action revolver with one quick motion.

"Git on your horse, mister," Elmer told him.

They rode away from the cabin. And Lute Kimball, coming over a hill, saw the lantern on the ground.

Half an hour later, several hills away, Elmer said, "You kin stop now. I'm gonna drop your guns and cartridge belts. You can pick 'em up, and I'll be watching, still with my gun in my hand, Buck. Still with my gun in my hand. Your rifle and shotgun are plumb empty."

The cabin was dark when Elmer got back to it. He could feel the waiting silence. Lute Kimball called, "Elmer, anybody with you?"

Elmer went limp in the saddle as the strength went out of him along with the tension. "Nope," he croaked.

Miss Charlotte called, "Are you all right?"

"Aw, sure," he answered. But when he slid from the saddle, his knees went limber. He landed in a heap.

Lute said, "Come in the cabin. We're not going to have a light any more." He was standing in the doorway with his rifle ready, watching into the darkness.

Miss Charlotte said, "Varina is asleep in the lean-to. She doesn't know anything special happened."

Foolish is the lucky one, Elmer thought. All hell could bust loose, and she'd never know it.

He remarked, "I don't think he'll come back."

Lute laughed, one short laugh. "I don't think he will. Getting run off by a runt of a boy with an empty gun."

"It wasn't empty," Elmer explained. "I had one chamber loaded."

"Did you now?" Lute sounded half smothered. "One charge, so you was all ready for bear!" He moved aside as Elmer entered the cabin, but he stayed near the doorway watching into the night with the rifle over his arm.

Elmer took three deep breaths and asked, "How's Pa?"

Lute cleared his throat, and Miss Charlotte said softly in the darkness, "Elmer, come over here to me. Please?" She put her arm around his shoulders, and he tried to stop shivering. "Lute?" she prompted.

Lute told him then. "Your pa died just before Steve got him to town. Steve stayed to see he got a good funeral. Your pa wanted him to."

Elmer stepped away from the gentle pressure of Miss Charlotte's arm, and his voice was gruff in his own ears. "I been figuring," he said. "I can make out all right, but Varina—she needs looking after. Maybe we could make a deal."

"What kind of a deal, Elmer?" Miss Charlotte's voice was like rippling creek water.

"If you was to take her back East with you," he stumbled along, "I'd turn over our stock to your brother, and maybe it would bring enough to pay for raising her." He could not remind her that she owed him anything; he was suddenly a man, burdened with a man's gallantry. He was asking her for a favor. "If it ain't enough," he offered, "I kin earn the rest after I git bigger."

She said, "Oh, Elmer!" as if she might cry any minute. "I—I might not go back East," she said. Lute, standing there black against the night, jerked his head.

"I don't want her raised out here!" Elmer cried out frantically. "Ma always said this ain't no country for women!"

"It will be," Miss Charlotte promised. "It's going to be, before long. Men like you and Mr. Kimball will make it. This is going to be a good place to live."

He was not a man any more. He was eleven years old and had nothing more to do with problems that were too big for him. He put his hands up to his face and began to sob. He cried for a long time, and neither Lute nor Miss Charlotte said a word or made a move.

When he was through, Lute spoke as if nothing had happened. "Tomorrow," he said, "you can be a kid if you want to. If you haven't forgotten how. You got that coming to you. But tonight I need a partner."

Until dawn, Elmer stood in the doorway with his new gun in his hand— the Peacemaker that had been Buck Saddler's. Lute prowled around farther away with a rifle, listening and watching. Nobody came.

TWELVE YEARS LATER, VARINA MERRICK spent her double eagle to buy her wedding clothes. Elmer, stiff and solemn in a new suit, tall and sturdy, a good hand at anything he undertook, gave the bride away. He had almost forgotten how hard he tried to give Varina away once before.

᭥

The author of seventeen books, fifty-two short stories, and countless magazine articles, Dorothy Johnson had a writing career that spanned more than sixty years. Known for works such as The Hanging Tree, The Bloody Bozeman, *and* Buffalo Woman, *Johnson wrote well-researched stories and nonfiction about the West. Three stories, "The Hanging Tree," "The Man Who Shot Liberty Valance," and "A Man Called Horse," were made into feature films starring Gary Cooper, James Stewart, and John Wayne. Born on December 19, 1905, in McGregor, Iowa, Johnson grew up in Whitefish, Montana, an experience she recounts in* When You and I Were Young, Whitefish. *After graduating from the University of Montana in 1928, where she studied with H. G. Merriam, Johnson worked as a book and magazine editor in New York City from 1935 to 1950 before returning to teach in the University of Montana's School of Journalism from 1953 to 1967. Johnson, who said she wanted to be buried under a tombstone that said, simply, "*PAID," *died of Parkinson's disease on November 13, 1984, in Missoula.*

❦ *Elizabeth B. Custer*

From *Boots and Saddles, Or Life in Dakota with General Custer*
OUR LIFE'S LAST CHAPTER

O UR WOMEN'S HEARTS FELL WHEN the fiat went forth that there was to be a summer campaign, with probably actual fighting with Indians.

Sitting Bull refused to make a treaty with the Government, and would not come in to live on a reservation.Besides his constant attacks on the white settlers, driving back even the most adventurous, he was incessantly invading and stealing from the land assigned to the peaceable Crows. They appealed for help to the Government that had promised to shield them.

The preparations for the expedition were completed before my husband returned from the East, whither he had been ordered. The troops had been sent out of barracks into a camp that was established a short distance down the valley. As soon as the general returned we left home and went into camp.

The morning for the start came only too soon. My husband was to take Sister Margaret and me out for the first days march, so I rode beside him out of camp. The column that followed seemed unending. The grass was not then suitable for grazing, and as the route of travel was through a barren country, immense quantities of forage had to be transported. The wagons themselves seemed to stretch out interminably. There were pack-mules, the ponies already laden, and cavalry, artillery, and infantry followed, the cavalry being in advance of all. The number of men, citizens, employees, Indian scouts, and soldiers was about twelve hundred. There were nearly seventeen hundred animals in all.

As we rode at the head of the column, we were the first to enter the confines of the garrison. About the Indian quarters, which we were obliged to pass, stood the squaws, the old men, and the children singing, or rather moaning, a minor tune that has been uttered on the going out of Indian warriors since time immemorial. Some of the squaws crouched on the ground, too burdened with their trouble to hold up their heads; others restrained the restless children who, discerning their fathers, sought to follow them.

The Indian scouts themselves beat their drums and kept up their peculiar monotonous tune, which is weird and melancholy beyond description. Their war-song is misnamed when called music. It is more of a lament or a dirge than an inspiration to activity. This intoning they kept up for miles along the road. After we had passed the Indian quarters we came near Laundress Row, and there my heart entirely failed me. The wives and children of the soldiers lined the road. Mothers, with streaming eyes, held their little ones out at arms-length for one last look at the departing father. The toddlers among the children, unnoticed by their elders, had made a mimic column of their own. With their handkerchiefs tied to sticks in lieu of flags, and beating old tin pans for drums, they strode lustily back and forth in imitation of the advancing soldiers. They were fortunately too young to realize why the mothers wailed out their farewells.

Unfettered by conventional restrictions, and indifferent to the opinion of others, the grief of these women was audible, and was accompanied by desponding gestures, dictated by their bursting hearts and expressions of their abandoned grief.

It was a relief to escape from them and enter the garrison, and yet, when our band struck up "The Girl I Left Behind Me," the most despairing hour seemed to have come. All the sad-faced wives of the officers who had forced themselves to their doors to try and wave a courageous farewell, and smile bravely to keep the ones they loved from knowing the anguish of their breaking hearts, gave up the struggle at the sound of the music. The first notes made them disappear to fight out alone their trouble, and seek to place their hands in that of their Heavenly Father, who, at such supreme hours, was their never-failing solace.

From the hour of breaking camp, before the sun was up, a mist had enveloped everything. Soon the bright sun began to penetrate this veil and dispel the haze, and a scene of wonder and beauty appeared. The cavalry and infantry in the order named, the scouts, pack-mules, and artillery, and behind all the long line of white-covered wagons, made a column altogether some two miles in length. As the sun broke through the mist a mirage appeared, which took up about half of the line of cavalry, and thenceforth for a little distance it marched, equally plain to the sight on the earth and in the sky.

The future of the heroic band, whose days were even then numbered, seemed to be revealed, and already there seemed a premonition in the supernatural translation as their forms were reflected from the opaque mist of the early dawn.

The sun, mounting higher and higher as we advanced, took every little bit of burnished steel on the arms and equipments along the line of horsemen, and turned them into glittering flashes of radiating light. The yellow, indicative of cavalry, outlined the accouterments, the trappings of the saddle, and sometimes a narrow thread of that effective tint followed the outlines even up to the headstall of the bridle. At every bend of the road, as the column wound its way round and round the low hills, my husband glanced back to admire his men, and could not refrain from constantly calling my attention to their grand appearance.

The soldiers, inured to many years of hardship, were the perfection of physical manhood. Their brawny limbs and lithe, well-poised bodies gave proof of the training their outdoor life had given. Their resolute faces, brave and confident, inspired one with a feeling that they were going out aware of the momentous hours awaiting them, but inwardly assured of their capability to meet them.

The general could scarcely restrain his recurring joy at being again with his regiment, from which he had feared he might be separated by being detained on other duty. His buoyant spirits at the prospect of the activity and field-life that he so loved made him like a boy. He had made every plan to have me join him later on, when they should have reached the Yellowstone.

The steamers with supplies would be obliged to leave our post and follow the Missouri up to the mouth of the Yellowstone, and from thence on to the point on that river where the regiment was to make its first halt to renew the rations and forage. He was sanguine that but a few weeks would elapse before we would be reunited, and used this argument to animate me with courage to meet our separation.

As usual we rode a little in advance and selected camp, and watched the approach of the regiment with real pride. They were so accustomed to the march the line hardly diverged from the trail. There was a unity of movement about them that made the column at a distance seem like a broad dark ribbon stretched smoothly over the plains.

We made our camp the first night on a small river a few miles beyond the post. There the paymaster made his disbursements, in order that the debts of the soldiers might be liquidated with the sutler.

In the morning the farewell was said, and the paymaster took sister and me back to the post.

With my husband's departure my last happy days in garrison were ended, as a premonition of disaster that I had never known before weighed me down. I could not shake off the baleful influence of depressing thoughts. This presentiment and suspense, such as I had never known, made me selfish, and I shut into my heart the most uncontrollable anxiety, and could lighten no one else's burden. The occupations of other summers could not even give temporary interest.

We heard constantly at the Fort of the disaffection of the young Indians of the reservation, and of their joining the hostiles. We knew, for we had seen for ourselves, how admirably they were equipped. We even saw on a steamer touching at our landing its freight of Springfield rifles piled up on the decks *en route* for the Indians up the river. There was unquestionable proof that they came into the trading-posts far above us and bought them, while our own brave Seventh Cavalry troopers were sent out with only the short-range carbines that grew foul after the second firing.

While we waited in untold suspense for some hopeful news, the garrison was suddenly thrown into a state of excitement by important dispatches that were sent from Division Headquarters in the East. We women knew that eventful news had come, and could hardly restrain our curiosity, for it was of vital import to us. Indian scouts were fitted out at the Fort with the greatest dispatch, and given instructions to make the utmost speed they could in reaching the expedition on the Yellowstone. After their departure, when there was no longer any need for secrecy, we were told that the expedition which had started from the Department of the Platte, and encountered the hostile Indians on the head-waters of the Rosebud, had been compelled to retreat.

All those victorious Indians had gone to join Sitting Bull, and it was to warn our regiment that this news was sent to our post, which was the extreme telegraphic communication in the Northwest, and the orders given to transmit the information, that precautions might be taken against encountering so large a number of the enemy. The news of the failure of the campaign in the other department was a death-knell to our hopes. We felt that we had nothing to expect but that our troops would be overwhelmed with numbers, for it seemed to us an impossibility, as it really proved to be, that our Indian scouts should cross that vast extent of country in time to make the warning of use.

The first steamer that returned from the Yellowstone brought letters from my husband, with the permission, for which I had longed unutterably, to join him by the next boat. The Indians had fired into the steamer when it had passed under the high bluffs in the gorges of the river. I counted the hours until the second steamer was ready. They were obliged, after loading, to cover the pilot-house and other vulnerable portions of the upper deck with sheet-iron to repel attacks. Then sandbags were placed around the guards as protection, and other precautions taken for the safety of those on board. All these delays and preparations made me inexpressibly impatient, and it seemed as if the time would never come for the steamer to depart.

Meanwhile our own post was constantly surrounded bv hostiles, and the outer pickets were continually subjected to attacks. It was no unusual sound to hear the long-roll calling out the infantry before dawn to defend the garrison. We saw the faces of the officers blanch, brave as they were, when the savages grew so bold as to make a day-time sortie upon our outer guards.

A picture of one day of our life in those disconsolate times is fixed indelibly in my memory.

On Sunday afternoon, the 25th of June, our little group of saddened women, borne down with one common weight of anxiety, sought solace in gathering together in our house. We tried to find some slight surcease from trouble in the old hymns: some of them dated back to our childhood's days, when our mothers rocked us to sleep to their soothing strains. I remember the grief with which one fair young wife threw herself on the carpet and pillowed her head in the lap of a tender friend. Another sat dejected at the piano, and struck soft chords that melted into the notes of the voices. All were absorbed in the same thoughts, and their eyes were filled with far-away visions and longings. Indescribable yearning for the absent, and untold terror for their safety, engrossed each heart. The words of the hymn,

> E'en though a cross it be,
> Nearer, my God, to Thee,

came forth with almost a sob from every throat.

At that very hour the fears that our tortured minds had portrayed in imagination were realities, and the souls of those we thought upon were ascending to meet their Maker.

On the 5th of July—for it took that time for the news to come—the sun rose on a beautiful world, but with its earliest beams came the first knell of disaster. A steamer came down the river bearing the wounded from the battle of the Little Big Horn, of Sunday, June 25th. This battle wrecked the lives of twenty-six women at Fort Lincoln, and orphaned children of officers and soldiers joined their cry to that of their bereaved mothers.

From that time the life went out of the hearts of the "women who weep," and God asked them to walk on alone and in the shadow.

This poignant excerpt from Elizabeth B. Custer's Boots and Saddles, Or Life in Dakota with General Custer, *published in 1885, depicts the hollowing fear experienced by army wives as they see their men march into battle. Elizabeth Custer was the wife of Lieutenant. Colonel George Armstrong Custer, and she traveled with his Seventh Cavalry as they headed west to fight the Battle of the Little Bighorn on June 25, 1876. After his death, Elizabeth Custer wrote several books about George Armstrong Custer, including* Following the Guidon, *published in 1890, and* Tenting on the Plains, *published in 1895. She lived from 1842 to 1933.*

Gwendolen Haste

RANCH IN THE COULEE

He built the ranch house down a little draw,
So that he should have wood and water near.
The bluffs rose all around. She never saw
The arching sky, the mountains lifting clear;
But to the west the close hills fell away
And she could glimpse a few feet of the road.
The stage to Roundup went by every day,
Sometimes a rancher town-bound with his load,
An auto swirling dusty through the heat,
Or children trudging home on tired feet.

At first she watched it as she did her work,
A horseman pounding by gave her a thrill,
But then within her brain began to lurk
The fear that if she lingered from the sill
Someone might pass unseen. So she began
To keep the highroad always within sight,
And when she found it empty long she ran
And beat upon the pane and cried with fright.
The winter was the worst. When snow would fall
He found it hard to quiet her at all.

THE REASON

She told them when they came and found him there
That he had tried to kill her with the knife—
Although she knew that he would never dare
To threaten her—much less to take her life.
So they who had seen his rages let her go.
But brooding on it in the later years
She felt she might have stood each curse and blow,
His shouting anger or his brutal jeers,
But on that day her heart was tired and sore
With God's austere and high indifference.
She saw the withered fields beyond the door,
The rotting barns, the filth, the broken fence,
And all her faded days, robbed of delight,
Where everything but weariness had fled,
So when he came in lowering that night
She took the rabbit gun and shot him dead.

THE SOLITARY

Whenever she's in town she leaves the shops
And wanders off to beauty on a street
Shaded by pleasant trees, where bungalows
Are white and green, where clover lawns are neat,
Where zinnias and bright nasturtiums bloom
Each house is built close to another one
So women every afternoon can sit
Upon the porches when their work is done,
And talk to other women and crochet.
Autos rush by. A cheerful phonograph
Sends sudden music, while across the lawns
A group of noisy children play and laugh.

Then she goes back and climbs into the Ford
To ride long miles out where there is no sound
Except the wind, a rooster's crow, the hens,
The eternal crickets singing from the ground,
And past the further hillside a faint smoke—
All that she sees of any other folk.

Gwendolen Haste, who wrote between 1922 and 1946, depicted the harsh realities of Western life in her poetry, a break from the more romantic visions of previous Western writers. Born in Streator, Illinois, in 1889, Haste graduated from the University of Chicago in 1912 and won The Nation's poetry prize in 1922. She worked with her father to edit The Scientific Farmer in Lincoln, Nebraska, and in Billings, Montana. She eventually moved to New York City, where she worked on the staff of The Survey and worked with the Poetry Society of America from 1928 to 1935. Her selected poems were published by Boise State University's Ahsahta Press in 1976. Haste died in New York City in 1979.

B. M. Bower

From *Lonesome Land*
COLD SPRING RANCH

OR ALMOST THREE YEARS THE letters from Manley had been headed "Cold Spring Ranch." For quite as long Val had possessed a mental picture of the place a picture of a gurgly little brook with rocks and watercress and distracting little pools the size of a bathtub, and with a great, frowning boulder—a cliff, almost—at the head. The brook bubbled out and formed a basin in the shadow of the rock. Around it grew trees, unnamed in the picture, it is true, but trees, nevertheless. Below the spring stood a picturesque little cottage. A shack, Manley had written, was but a synonym for a small cottage, and Val had many small cottages in mind, from which she sketched one into her picture. The sun shone on it, and the western breezes napped white curtains in the windows, and there was a porch where she would swing her hammock and gaze out over the great, beautiful country, fascinating in its very immensity.

Somewhere beyond the cottage—"shack," she usually corrected herself—were the corrals; they were as yet rather impressionistic; high, round, mysterious enclosures forming an effective, if somewhat hazy, background to the picture. She left them to work out their attractive details upon closer acquaintance, for at most they were merely the background. The front yard, however, she dwelt upon, and made aglow with sturdy, bright-hued flowers. Manley had that spring planted sweet peas, and poppies, and pansies, and other things, he wrote her, and they had come up very nicely. Afterward, in a postscript, he answered her oft-repeated questions about the flower garden:

The flowers aren't doing as well as they might. They need your tender care. I don't have much time to pet them along. The onions are doing pretty well, but they need weeding badly.

In spite of that, the flowers bloomed luxuriantly in her mental picture, though she conscientiously remembered that they weren't doing as well as they might. They were weedy and unkempt, she supposed, but a little time and care would remedy that; and was she not coming to be the mistress of all this, and to make everything beautiful? Besides, the spring, and the brook which ran from it, and the trees which shaded it, were the chief attractions.

Perhaps she betrayed a lack of domesticity because she had not been able to "see" the interior of the cottage—"shack"—very clearly. Sunny rooms, white curtains, bright cushions and books, pictures and rugs mingled together rather confusingly in her mind when she dwelt upon the inside of her future home. It would be bright, and cozy, and "homey," she knew. She would love it because it would be hers and Manley's, and she could do with it what she would. She bothered about that no more than she did about the dresses she would be wearing next year.

Cold Spring Ranch! Think of the allurement of that name, just as it stands, without any disconcerting qualification whatever! Any girl with yellow-brown hair and yellow-brown eyes to match, and a dreamy temperament that beautifies everything her imagination touches, would be sure to build a veritable Eve's garden around those three small words.

With that picture still before her mental vision, clear as if she had all her life been familiar with it in reality, she rode beside Manley for three weary hours, across a wide, wide prairie which looked perfectly level when you viewed it as a whole, but which proved all hills and hollows when you drove over it. During those three hours they passed not one human habitation after the first five miles were behind them. There had been a ranch, back there against a reddish-yellow bluff. Val had gazed upon it, and then turned her head away, distressed because human beings could consent to live in such unattractive surroundings. It was bad in its way as Hope, she thought, but did not say, because Manley was talking about his cattle, and she did not want to interrupt him.

After that there had been no houses of any sort. There was a barbed-wire fence stretching away and away until the posts were mere pencil lines against the blue, where the fence dipped over the last hill before the sky bent down and kissed the earth.

The length of that fence was appalling in a vague, wordless way. Val unconsciously drew closer to her husband when she looked at it, and shivered in spite of the midsummer heat.

"You're getting tired." Manley put his arm around her and held her there.

"We're over half-way now. A little longer and we'll be home." Then he bethought him that she might want some preparation for that home-coming. "You mustn't expect much, little wife. It's a bachelor's house, so far. You'll have to do some fixing before it will suit you. You don't look forward to anything like Fern Hill, do you?"

Val laughed, and bent solicitously over the suitcase, which her feet had marred. "Of course I don't. Nothing out here is like Fern Hill. I know our ranch is different from anything I ever knew—but I know just how it will be, and how everything will look."

"Oh! Do you?" Manley looked at her a bit anxiously.

"For three years," Val reminded him, "you have been describing things to me. You told me what it was like when you first took the place. You described everything, from Cold Spring Coulee to the house you built, and the spring under the rock wall, and even the meadow lark's nest you found in the weeds. Of *course* I know."

"It's going to seem pretty rough, at first," he observed rather apologetically.

"Yes—but I shall not mind that. I want it to be rough. I 'm tired to death of the smug smoothness of my life so far. Oh, if you only knew how I have hated Fern Hill, these last three years, especially since I graduated. Just the same petty little lives lived in the same petty little way, day in and day out. Every Sunday the class in Sunday school, and the bells ringing and the same little walk of four blocks there and back. Every Tuesday and Friday the club meeting — the Merry Maids, and the Mascot, both just alike, where you did the same things. And the same round of calls with mamma, on the same people, twice a month the year round. And the little social festivities—ah, Manley, if you only knew how I long for something rough and real in my life!" It was very nearly what she said to the tired-faced teacher on the train.

"Well, if that's what you want, you've come to the right place," he told her dryly.

Later, when they drew close to a red coulee rim which he said was the far side of Cold Spring Coulee, she forgot how tired she was, and felt every nerve quiver with eagerness.

Later still, when in the glare of a July sun they drove around a low knoll, dipped into a wide, parched coulee, and then came upon a barren little habitation inclosed in a meager fence of the barbed wire she thought so detestable, she shut her eyes mentally to something she could not quite bring herself to face.

He lifted her out and tumbled the great trunks upon the ground before he drove on to the corrals. "Here's the key," he said, "if you want to go in. I won't be more than a minute or two." He did not look into her face when he spoke.

Val stood just inside the gate and tried to adjust all this to her mental picture. There was the front yard, for instance. A few straggling vines against the porch, and a sickly cluster or two of blossoms—those were the sweet peas, surely. The sun-baked bed of pale-green plants without so much as a bud of promise, she recognized, after a second glance, as the poppies. For the rest, there were weeds against the fence, sun-ripened grass trodden flat, yellow, gravelly patches where nothing grew—and a glaring, burning sun beating down upon it all.

The cottage—never afterward did she think of it by that name, but always as a shack—was built of boards placed perpendicularly, with battens nailed over the cracks to keep out the wind and the snow. At one side was a "lean-to" kitchen, and on the other side was the porch that was just a narrow platform with a roof over it. It was not wide enough for a rocking-chair, to say nothing of swinging a hammock. In the first hasty inspection this seemed to be about all. She was still hesitating before the door when Manley came back from putting up the horses.

"I'm afraid your flowers are a lost cause," he remarked cheerfully. "They were looking pretty good two or three weeks ago. This hot weather has dried them up. Next year we'll have water down here to the house. All these things take time."

"Oh, of course they do." Val managed to smile into his eyes. "Let's see how many dishes you left dirty; bachelors always leave their dishes unwashed on the table, don't they?"

"Sometimes—but I generally wash mine." He led the way into the house, which smelled hot and close, with the odor of food long since cooked and eaten, before he threw all the windows open. The front room was clean— after a man's idea of cleanliness. The floor was covered with an exceedingly dusty carpet, and a rug or two. Her latest photograph was nailed to the wall; and when Val saw it she broke into hysterical laughter.

"You've nailed your colors to the mast," she cried, and after that it was all a joke. The home-made couch, with the calico cushions and the cowhide spread, was a matter for mirth. She sat down upon it to try it, and was informed that chicken wire makes a fine spring. The rickety table, with tobacco, magazines, and books placed upon it in orderly piles, was something to smile over. The chairs, and especially the one cane rocker which went sidewise over the floor if you rocked in it long enough, were pronounced original.

In the kitchen the same masculine idea of cleanliness and order obtained. The stove was quite red, but it had been swept clean. The table was pushed against the only window there, and the back part was filled with glass preserve jars, cans, and a loaf of bread wrapped carefully in paper; but the oilcloth cover was clean—did it not show quite plainly the marks of the last washing? Two frying pans were turned bottom up on an obscure table in an obscure corner of the room, and a zinc water pail stood beside them.

There were other details which impressed themselves upon her shrinking brain, and though she still insisted upon smiling at everything, she stood in the middle of the room holding up her skirts quite unconsciously, as if she were standing at a muddy street crossing, wondering how in the world she was ever going to reach the other side.

"Isn't it all—deliciously—primitive?" she asked, in a weak little voice, when the smile would stay no longer. "I—love it, dear." That was a lie; more, she was not in the habit of fibbing for the sake of politeness or anything else, so that the words stood for a good deal.

Manley looked into the zinc water pail, took it up, and started for an outer door, rattling the tin dipper as he went. "Want to go up to the spring?" he queried, over his shoulder. "Water's the first thing—I'm horribly thirsty."

Val turned to follow him. "Oh, yes—the spring!" She stopped, however, as soon as she had spoken. "No, dear. There'll be plenty of other times. I'll stay here."

He gave her a glance bright with love and blind happiness in her presence there, and went off whistling and rattling the pail at his side.

Val did not even watch him go. She stood still in the kitchen and looked at the table, and at the stove, and at the upturned frying pans. She watched two great horseflies buzzing against a window-pane, and when she could endure that no longer, she went into the front room and stared vacantly around at the bare walls. When she saw her picture again, nailed fast beside the kitchen door, her face lost a little of its frozen blankness—enough so that her lips quivered until she bit them into steadiness.

She went then to the door and stood looking dully out into the parched yard, and at the wizened little pea vines clutching feebly at their white-twine trellis. Beyond stretched the bare hills with the wavering brown line running down the nearest one the line that she knew was the trail from town. She was guilty of just one rebellious sentence before she struggled back to optimism.

"I said I wanted it to be rough, but I didn't mean—why, this is just squalid!" She looked down the coulee and glimpsed the river flowing calmly past the mouth of it, a majestic blue belt fringed sparsely with green. It must be a mile away, but it relieved wonderfully the monotony of brown hills, and the vivid coloring brightened her eyes. She heard Manley enter the kitchen, set down the pail of water, and come on to where she stood.

"I'd forgotten you said we could see the river from here," she told him, smiling over her shoulder. "It's beautiful, isn't it? I don't suppose, though, there's a boat within millions of miles."

Oh, there's a boat down there. It leaks, though. I just use it for ducks, close to shore. Admiring our view? Great, don't you think?"

Val clasped her hands before her and let her gaze travel again over the sweep of rugged hills. "It's — wonderful. I thought I knew, but I see I didn't. I feel very small, Manley; does one ever grow up to it?"

He seemed dimly to catch the note of utter desolation. "You'll get used to all that," he assured her. "I thought I 'd reached the jumping-off place, at first. But now—you couldn't dog me outa the country.'"

He was slipping into the vernacular, and Val noticed it, and wondered dully if she would ever do likewise. She had not yet admitted to herself that Manley was different. She had told herself many times that it would take weeks to wipe out the strangeness born of three years' separation. He was the same, of course; everything else was new and—different. That was all. He seemed intensely practical, and he seemed to feel that his love-making had all been done by letter, and that nothing now remained save the business of living. So, when he told her to rest, and that he would get dinner and show her how a bachelor kept house, she let him go with no reply save that vague, impersonal smile which Kent had encountered at the depot.

While he rattled things about in the kitchen, she stood still in the doorway with her fingers doubled into tight little fists, and stared out over the great, treeless, unpeopled land which had swallowed her alive. She tried to think—and then, in another moment, she was trying not to think.

Glancing quickly over her shoulder, to make sure Manley was too busy to follow her, she went off the porch and stood uncertain in the parched enclosure which was the front yard.

"I may as well see it all, and be done," she whispered, and went stealthily around the corner of the house, holding up her skirts as she had done in the kitchen. There was a dim path beaten in the wiry grass—a path which started at the kitchen door and wound away up the coulee. She followed it. Undoubtedly it would lead her to the spring; beyond that she refused to let her thoughts travel.

In five minutes—for she went slowly—she stopped beside a stock-trampled pool of water and yellow mud. A few steps farther on, a barrel had been sunk in the ground at the base of a huge gray rock; a barrel which filled slowly and spilled the overflow into the mud. There was also a trough, and there was a barrier made of poles and barbed wire to keep the cattle from the barrel. One crawled between two wires, it would seem, to dip up water for the house. There were no trees—not real trees. There were some chokecherry bushes higher than her head and there were other bushes that did not look particularly enlivening.

With a smile of bitter amusement, she tucked her skirts tightly around her, crept through the fence, and filled a chipped granite cup which stood upon a rock ledge, and drank slowly. Then she laughed aloud.

"The water really *is* cold," she said. "Anywhere else it would be delicious. And that's a spring, I suppose."

Mercilessly she was stripping her mind of her illusions, and was clothing it in the harsher weave of reality. "All these hills are Manley's—our ranch." She took another sip and set down the cup. "And so Cold Spring Ranch means—all this."

Down the coulee she heard Manley call. She stood still, pushing back a fallen lock of fine, yellow hair. She turned toward the sound, and the sun in her eyes turned them yellow as the hair above them. She was beautiful, in an odd, white-and-gold way. If her eyes had been blue, or gray—or even brown—she would have been merely pretty; but as they were, that amber tint where one looked for something else struck one unexpectedly and made her whole face unforgettably lovely. However, the color of her eyes and her hair did not interest her then, or make life any easier. She was quite ordinarily miserable and homesick, as she went reluctantly back along the grassy trail. The odor of fried bacon came up to her, and she hated bacon. She hated everything.

"I've been to the spring," she called out, resolutely cheerful, as soon as she came in sight of Manley, waiting in the kitchen door; she ran toward him lightly. "However does the water keep so deliciously cool through this hot weather? I don't wonder you call this Cold Spring Ranch."

Manley straightened proudly. "I'm glad you like it; I was afraid you might not, just at first. But you're the right stuff—I might have known it. Not every woman could come out here and appreciate this country right at the start."

Val stopped at the steps, panting a little from her run, and smiled unflinchingly up into his face.

The author of sixty-eight novels set in the American West, B. M. or Bertha Muzzy Bower began publishing stories in 1900, but her first real success came with Chip of the Flying U, *published in 1906. After that, she regularly published books. Some of her more well-known works include:* Her Prairie Knight *(1907),* Jean of the Lazy A *(1915),* Cabin Fever *(1918),* Casey Ryan *(1921), and* Lonesome Land *(1911), which was republished in 1997 by the University of Nebraska Press with an introduction by Pam Houston. Bower was born in Minnesota on November 15, 1871, but moved with her family to Montana in 1888. After working as a teacher in the Great Falls area, she married her first husband, Clayton J. Bower, at the age of nineteen. After her death on July 23, 1940, Bower's children gave her papers to the University of Oklahoma Libraries' Western History Collection.*

Ruth McLaughlin

DESTINY

I HEARD ABOUT THE FIRE IN WINTER, and three months later I travel the narrow highway east across the state. No traffic, only miles and miles of prairie hills, roughening at river breaks, and in long valleys stubble fields of last year's wheat. Through town after tiny town I slow, the highway tamed to a street, at last entering Culbertson just before Montana's seamless shift to North Dakota.

I continue east in slow motion to the farm. This ten miles I've more than memorized; I feel my body tugged toward each landmark: the homestead shack, still sturdy, whose occupant, a Chicago transplant, hanged himself in the teens. In the next field a lone tree, huge now, that someone once had swerved around with a plow. Far from water the tree has somehow year after year survived. I feel the pull of worn fence posts, gray as bone, some misshapen. When I was small I imagined the ugly ones as fierce, staring at me. Now as I pass they seem subdued, merely old.

Beyond them I think I see the first gleam of spring in prairie grass. I picture our small white house on its hill, long windows overlooking our land east and west, and south half a mile to the highway. Today is sunny, just an edge of winter in chill air. The sky overhead is blank, an innocent blue; perhaps my 90-something friend in town heard wrong in January on her sheriff's scanner: "The Alexander house burning up in snow."

Then I round the last curve and see on our hill just a blackened chimney in open air. I'm shocked at how complete the fire has been.

I turn north up the gravel road whose weeds scour my car's underside. Beyond the ruins of the house, a coal shed, two garages and the upright granary remain. On other visits here I've looked for their decline. I've half-wished for the buildings to lean and collapse, model how to unfasten from this land. I've wanted to find a roof torn off by wind, linoleum curling up in corners of the house. Instead the sturdy buildings say the farm's gone on as always in my family's absence. In five years I've watched a single slow decay: down the gentle slope of hill past the long red barn, corral poles are loosening and shrugging down.

Our family had a 97-year fling here; now we are gone. Ten of us were left behind, six of them children, planted in two cemeteries.

I didn't think I'd feel so cheated staring at the rubble of our house. But as I grew, our farm was more than just a home. Our fenced pastures and oblong fields on slopes of hills seemed permanent, the end stage of this land: our family's destiny.

Grandpa Hawkins, my mother's father, the first of us in our corner of the state, told the story of his journey here as if it were ordained. My brother and I listened as we hoed his windbreak. Twice a year in summer, starting when we were small, Grandpa drove Dwight and me from our neighboring farm to labor. We chopped at weeds that the disk couldn't reach, fireweed and Russian thistle smothering seedlings of blue spruce. It took five years of hoeing before the new trees that didn't belong here—particular about wind and drought—outgrew the weeds that did. Grandpa refused to plant an ordinary windbreak, scrub Chinese elm and caragana, that didn't need a hoe.

Midmorning, Grandpa strode down the path to visit, overalls drooping on his small frame; he looked pleased with our chore. He recited how he had stepped onto a ship in Sweden at age sixteen, arriving six weeks later in New York. In Milwaukee and St. Paul he'd tried his hand at the fur dressing trade; finally in 1903 he boarded a train for North Dakota. He got off and on again in Williston—too civilized—and at last found land across the Montana line that resembled his childhood home, except that a dry coulee instead of a creek wound through it.

I listened to my grandfather's story of his long voyage ending here, an unvarying text. I heard it as a mantra: our family's destiny.

At the end of his story Grandpa laughed, throwing back his head, blue eyes and gold tooth flashing, as if he'd delivered a giant joke. The laughter puzzled me; though now, stepping out of my car and crossing our prairie yard to teeter on the edge of our once-house—laughter doesn't seem so strange.

Surely this farm was my father's destiny. After two failed homesteaders, he was the first to make a living on this place.

Our farm's dirt roads are his; and the two coulees dammed for stock water, fringed by cottonwood, ash, and Russian olive. He stamped out fields north and west of our caragana and Chinese elm windbreak, alternating wheat and summerfallow, and fenced the apron of prairie south to the highway and east and west to hills at the horizon.

For five years on visits here I've entered the empty house, this time an irregular field outlined by the foundation's concrete scar. Now the house seems even smaller without its walls: just a divot on the expanse of prairie.

I'd step into the kitchen with its silent cupboards, stroll through the mint green living room with gray linoleum, and enter my little bedroom from whose wardrobe dolls gaped. In the closet of another bedroom, ghosts of my mother still hung: cotton housedresses abandoned decades ago when she at last joined the fashion switch to slacks.

Now a till of shattered asbestos shingle overlays the burned house, like new soil. So far, nothing grows here in spring. Prairie grass has declined entrance; there's no caragana or Chinese elm, and of course, no blue spruce. But I think that somewhere fireweed and Russian thistle have begun to imagine the empty field of our house.

I identify something at my feet: glass from the kitchen light fixture, spun into a fantastic shape. I study the borders of the burn again, trying to build the field of trash into a house, with air walls. At the far corner is my brother's room through which a twisted metal bedstead heaves. In the living room beside the anchoring chimney is a skeletal couch. I peer beneath twists of drainpipe and stovepipe—except for shingle siding, only metal is in pieces bigger than my hand—and see the old Underwood, my mother's typewriter. It looks intact—carriage, space bar, keys—as if equally blackened hands could settle here to write a letter, though the desk beneath has vanished.

Now I see that just a few feet away there's no trash mess; the walls folded inward as they burned. I feel a tincture of childhood shame. The cramped house always seemed a reflection of our family, one that would shrink in on itself on trips to town, anticipating stares. I wish that the death of our home, our family, hadn't followed this predictable course.

I wish that the house had blown up, scattering pieces in the windbreak trees and on the prairie. Years from now, someone roaming this land might stumble on our durable remains. He would kick at the shield of oven door or finger the glinting saucer of a flue stop from the chimney, and picture us here.

But I can't believe the low-browed hills won't think of us forever. East and west, and south to the abrupt edge of highway, the hills seem the same: wind-dimpled, excited for spring. I'm half-surprised the prairie grass could manage a new season without our anchoring house.

Growing up I thought these hills favored us. South across the Missouri River, my father's father failed on land whose scanty soil discouraged grass and wheat.

Of course a glacier had favored us. The last late Wisconsin glacier creeping from the north had halted just before the Missouri River: a thousand-foot-high shelf of ice. Then—as if fashioning a template for future immigrants—it departed. Boulders fell through rotting ice, fouling our fields; as 10,000 years later, failing homesteaders left behind a litter of shacks and machinery. But the glacier in its long retreat released a gift of Canadian silt and clay and mineral-rich rock dust, gentling the debris into long hills to grow protein-rich prairie grass and wheat.

The glacier formed our hills, grass grew; three generations of our family spent a minute of history here, then vanished.

On my last visit I stopped at Grandpa Hawkins' farm three miles west, home to the blue spruce windbreak, sold to another farmer some thirty years ago. The log barn and chicken coop remain; pole fences are intact. But the new owner did not bother to keep chickens or milk a cow. He erected a cavernous steel machinery shed south of the house, dwarfing it, and making insignificant my grandfather's low sheds and barn.

The owner's widow greeted me at the door. She said mysterious things had begun to appear, as if heaved from the earth like the glacial rocks we picked and dumped at corners of the fields each spring. She'd discovered a turn-of-the-century Swedish dictionary in the attic, and a "W" branding iron that I'm certain was not my grandfather's, though no one else occupied his land.

There's no one left to ask.

Now our farm has a new owner. He lives miles away, our land only a patch on a quilt of farms he operates with giant machinery. I glimpse one beyond the granary, a hulking yellow grain drill three times the size of our John Deere model nearby. Also dwarfed beside it are my father's sickle mower and the sharp-tined dump rake. The owner's machine, seldom used here, is like scat to mark the land his own.

I can't believe that our grain drill and slender mower will join the ranks of the dead past. All around the prairie on the tops of hills, along flanks of hills and overgrown in coulees are rusted binders, plows and harrows—machinery left behind by fleeing homesteaders. In my childhood the tools were only a curiosity, something to fix the eye on from my corner of the car—past my father's large shoulders and my mother's round ones—on snail's pace trips to town. Surely the machinery's owners had not thought their destinies were here.

Our farm's new owner struck the match that burned our house. For five years he ignored my sneaking up here, ignored the museum we'd left behind. High in a cupboard was the green plastic doughnut maker my mother used just once, her doughnuts grease-laden and small. In my dim bedroom's wardrobe were bride and groom dolls in moldering dress, a wooden black baby with a sock shirt, and Dennis the Menace. On my last visit Dennis was jaunty still despite the absence of an arm below the elbow.

At the far end of the burned rubble I spy the dull gleam of metal ingots—knobs from my mother's 1940s waterfall veneer dresser? I zero in on the location of the snowy-channeled black-and-white TV: gone. But alongside the tipped shell of the refrigerator is a nest of broken and grayed ceramic. I think of the vaporized TV and try to imagine what could have survived the fire: electric insulators? My mother's cracked ovenware, old as her marriage?

The fire must have been immense. The skinny cottonwood behind the house, a volunteer with roots dug deep into the open drain field, is blistered and limbless on the fire side.

I suddenly wish that I had been here, starved as I am for a transforming event. That's how I pictured my parents' deaths and the end of our farm would be: suffused with meaning, an alchemy. Like fire.

Not ordinary. Not as my father predicted last year, saying suddenly over the phone from his little house in town: "I'm just afraid when you call someday I won't be here."

I look toward our windbreak. The slender trees are dying, a few tangled together as if clinging to each other in death. I'm surprised. I'd thought that the trees, small-leaved in anticipation of drying winter winds, summer drought and moisture-robbing weeds, would last forever.

Then I hear my grandfather's laughter again. It hadn't mattered that he planted an impractical blue spruce windbreak, one that switched to dying the moment he left the farm: his replacement hadn't time on his hands—or grandchildren—to hoe, haul water in a tank from town, and shovel dikes to direct spring snowmelt. Now the rows of evergreen are gap-toothed, at least every other tree dead. But a handful of them tower raggedly, visible miles away.

I look down our footpath over which pigweed has hopefully flung bright tentacles, beyond the little white gate to the prairie rising and falling to its seam of highway. The highway is the same, cars appearing from a long way off, passing slowly with the elegance of animals. On summer nights my parents sat outside on kitchen chairs counting cars east and west.

Beside me in the grass, or in the burned-out skull of our house, I hear a cricket's trill. We're all gone except for me, and my brother who fled the farm at seventeen, landing in California. He rarely visits.

I feel like a sole survivor, the ugly cottonwood, black-blistered. For years we ignored the tree, my father unwilling to nurture more than a front yard spruce. We waited for the tree to die. But it lived, and thrived on our gray bath water, and dishwater from the kitchen sink.

At my feet is the grave of the dirt-walled cellar, a small room entered separately from outside, home to potatoes over winter. Pitched into it is the kitchen coal stove, white enamel skirts blackened.

I take momentary satisfaction in the huge sound its crashing down must have made, stirring our farm to life again.

In summers Dwight and I were made faint by the odors of the stove's noonday meal—frankfurters cauterized in an oven dish, potatoes steaming. In winters we perched beside it when the road outside had vanished, a sweep of snow even rising up the barbed wire fence. We knew that the school bus would pass us by for at least a day. Back and forth our father stamped carrying coal, his overshoes leaving a puddly mess on the floor. Dwight and I scooped melting snow from the linoleum and tossed it onto the stove to hiss, seeing whose pile could stay alive the longest.

Now I wonder why the new owner burned the house. It's dangerous if he decides to run cattle; they could topple into the open cellar. Did he want to put to rest all our ghosts? Was he tired of finding the tracks of my twice a-year visits?

My old friend Edna said in town: "The fellow probably burned the place to keep bums out."

But I think we're all still here, wandering in and out of sheds and the grease-fouled truck garage, inhaling the granary's clean wheat scent. From the fenced pen in the pasture that held weaner pigs, bristle-haired, squealing at our approach, I think I hear their voices carried on the wind. My hands still feel the slickness of the long manger pole inside the barn, burnished smooth by the milk cow's throat as she plunged her head over it into hay.

I turn to leave the farm again; once more I've managed to sneak onto this land with the owner absent. Then I see something in the rubble.

It's a slender bottle I can't place. It looks old, perhaps a Hawkins souvenir saved by Mother. The bottle is sturdy, and survived better than I the conflagration of the house. "Duraglass" is embossed on one flat side.

I tip the soot-blackened bottle into my hand, and glittery particles tumble out. A patent medicine hoarded by my grandparents? Another brand of the hope that brought them here?

Grandpa Hawkins' hope even overrode the practicality of busting virgin sod to plant wheat. The prairie grass resisted breaking, fraying the strength of four harnessed horses. Grandpa chopped the ground with an axe to dig the steel plowshare in, then it turned sod over in curls unbroken for a quarter mile. He sometimes had to file a new edge on the plowshare each night.

Borne on by glittery hope, the homesteaders did not stop to ponder the grass's resistance, an adaptation to survive drought and shredding hailstorms that wheat, oats, flax and barley could not: long roots of native grass were bound to one another, intertwining.

In our county, settlers turned over 800,000 acres of virgin prairie— more than half the land. The work was done long before my fifties childhood, but one year when I was small, the owner of a high pasture north of ours broke the sod and planted wheat. My father called the man "Eddie Sodbuster," giving him a new last name. For years, Dad spoke admiringly of how Eddie had busted sod, recalling it even after the man gave up farming and sold out. I never learned Eddie's real name.

Now Eddie Sodbuster's field along with others is returning to native grass, paid for by a federal conservation program. Back-to-nature could take fifty years, though the program accelerates the process by requiring landowners to knock down weeds. Thistle grows first in bare ground, choked out by sturdier pigweed and fireweed, finally overtaken by short-lived grasses that prepare soil for the return of sod-forming western wheatgrass, needle and thread, green needlegrass and blue grama.

This century's settlers on empty land are not short, wiry Scandinavians, but short, wiry prairie grasses.

In retrospect my grandparents seem foolish, believing that tall wheat with short roots, not entwined, could buffet drought and hail and grasshoppers like native species. Some hope-in-a-bottle—as I hold in my hand—put them under a spell.

But I am not free of the spell. I know that I will take the little bottle home and place it in a window where I can glance at it often. I am also bound like grass here.

I'm not alone. My brother could not wait to get out, but he has kept current on farming. He knows about tractors replacing those of our era, with radios and air- conditioned cabs, and even with Global Positioning Services that—he recently told me—keep the tractor from swerving an inch off a straight furrow. He said that now all plows are obsolete; with "minimum tillage" the ground is barely scratched for sowing, and chemicals instead of machinery control weeds.

Grandma Hawkins, who of our family suffered the most here, still seemed bound to her land. Short and plump, her legs encased year round in cotton stockings, she snugged a man's billed cap over her iron gray bun, and roamed the farm between chores. As a child I liked to join her, skipping ahead then slowing my walk to her arthritic pace. In spring we searched for crocus in the pasture, heading north through the corral past the windmill with its weeping wooden tank in which she drowned kittens each year. I avoided the tank when alone, believing it was depthless. Meadowlarks, returned in spring, teetered near on fence posts. Grandma interpreted for me their liquid song: "Oh, you're a pretty-little-girl."

We looked for low-growing purple crocus, so beautiful and brief it seemed not to belong here; the plant was soon succeeded by homely sunflower, milkweed and wild onion. Its plump blossoms were the only ones Grandma picked, lasting a few days in a small dish. Friends have encouraged me to plant crocus in my back yard. But I've never believed a nursery plant would be the same as the solitary one that broke through the brown prairie after numbing winter, sometimes pushing up in snow.

Grandma would halt at a spot in the pasture where the windbreak dwindled; I knew to imitate her silence there. Crocus erupted, meadowlarks sang, hills all around heaved and fell in memory of another time, as we paused at three babies' graves.

Ruth McLaughlin grew up in northeastern Montana on land her grandparents homesteaded. She graduated from the University of Montana, and in 1978 received an M.F.A. from the University of Arizona. Her work has appeared in two dozen magazines and in four anthologies, including Best American Short Stories. *She was the recipient of a 1999 Montana Arts Council Individual Artist Fellowship. She currently teaches writing in Great Falls. "Destiny" is the opening chapter of her recently completed memoir* Bound Like Grass.

✿ Nannie T. Alderson and
Helena Huntington Smith

From *A Bride Goes West*

SOMETIMES I WONDER IF TOO much hasn't been said about the grim aspects of frontier life. Later on in my marriage I came down to hard, bare facts; to loneliness and poverty. But that first spring and summer I was anything but lonely in spite of the lack of women. I had much to learn and hard work to do. But I had no children to look after, I lived in surroundings of great beauty, I was happy in my marriage, and pioneering still seemed rather romantic.

We had plenty of visitors. Although the ranches were far apart—our near neighbors being five to ten miles distant—the men were always riding around looking for lost horses or moving stock, and as summer time approached, reps from miles away—even hundreds of miles—would come riding by on their way to join the roundup, and they would stop with us. A rep was a cowboy sent out by his outfit to represent them on some other part of the range, and gather up stray cattle bearing their brand. There were no fences, the cattle drifted for many miles, and these riders came to us from long distances—from the Belle Fourche in South Dakota, from Sun Dance on the edge of the Black Hills. Each would be traveling with a string of horses, his bed packed across the back of one. He would ride in, turn his horses in with ours, and stay for a meal or a night. If for the night, he would just throw his bed down out of doors. Later I heard that quite a joke was made on the roundup about the number of reps who found it necessary to pass by the Zook and Alderson ranch.

Once a week the mail came by horseback courier from Birney postoffice, twenty-five miles across the divide. Often it brought belated and unexpected wedding presents. The carrier was a young red-headed cowboy named Fred

Banker, who spent the weekend with us, making the return trip to Birney on Monday. As he was a pleasant young fellow with a good singing voice, he was quite an addition to our musical evenings, and he and Johnny, Brown, and my husband, soon learned all the songs I knew on the guitar.

One week he brought a motherless colt he had picked up on the road over. Apparently the Sioux Indians, who were visiting the Cheyennes, had left it by accident, or because it was too weak to travel. When Freddie rode over the hill the appearance of extra bulk in the saddle occasioned some wonder at first. As he rode up he said: "There was no wedding present for you this mail, so I brought you this colt."

About the same time one of the bachelor neighbors brought me a motherless calf, also carried across his saddle, so I sent to Helena, the state capital, to have a brand recorded and thereupon entered the stock business. Our firm's brand was the sugar bowl and spoon; my individual brand was the first three letters of my maiden name with a bar underneath, <u>TIF</u>. The orphan stock that wore my brand was pretty pathetic, especially the calf. He was known as a "poddy," for feeding skimmed milk gave him a big stomach, and there was a sad look in his eyes, due to undernourishment. We called him Jack after the neighbor who brought him, and we kept him till he was a big five-year-old steer. He was what they called a "rough steer"—but he brought enough to buy a much-needed carpet to cover the splintery boards of my room. Those were later and harder times.

In 1883 we were all very young. Mr. Alderson was twenty-eight, and he was the oldest. I was twenty-three at the end of the summer; Johnny Zook and Hal were my age, Brown was a year younger. Our friends were in their twenties or early thirties. If we were empire builders we didn't feel like it or act the part. We made a game of everything, even the garden.

In April Mr. Alderson and Johnny and Brown took the plough and started breaking ground for a garden plot on a level space near the house. I shall never forget how tough the sod was; it didn't want to be ploughed. For longer than human memory the grass had grown and died and its roots had interlaced to form one of the strongest sods ever seen. Our little saddle horses weren't raised for such work, and besides they were only on grass, as we had no grain to give them, so they tired easily. The men could do just a few furrows at a time, and it took several days to make our small garden. But we planted it eventually with peas and lettuce and potatoes, and we turned the sod back over them, which was all we could do. We had fresh vegetables that summer, but the potatoes were quite flat.

While they were ploughing I would finish my housework—or just leave it unfinished, I'm afraid— and would go down there and watch them. When the horses had to rest the boys would come over and sit by me. Mr. Alderson was wearing a gold ring which became too tight as he worked, and he took it off and put it on my finger. A few days later it was gone.

We were working on the garden again when I noticed it was missing. I rushed back to the house and searched. I looked where the wash water had been thrown out, but the ring was nowhere. Brown had followed me up to the house to see what the matter was, and he now said soothingly:

"I'll bet Walt or some of them have hid that ring on you."

I said: "Go back down there and tell them I'm crying my eyes out"—but even that didn't produce the ring.

Next day I discovered a bruise on my forehead, and the moment I saw it I knew where the ring was. A few days before this the boys had taken the wagon and gone up into the hills to load pine poles for a fence. Of course I'd had to take my crocheting along and ride with them, perched on the running gears, and I'd sat under the pine trees and crocheted while they cut the poles. The gnats were thick on those warm spring days and in batting at them, as I now recalled, I had hit myself a crack over the eye with the ring.

I said to Brown, "I know where the ring is. It's up where you all were cutting poles."

He said: "You'll never find it. A magpie has got it by now."

But we saddled and rode up there, and I could see it gleaming in the pine needles before I got off my horse.

No, we were not very serious then. We didn't mind the hard things because we didn't expect them to last. Montana in the early Eighties was booming just like the stock market in 1929, and the same feverish optimism possessed all of us. I believe the same thing was true of many other frontier communities. Our little dirt-roofed shack didn't matter because our other house was building. And even the new house was to be only a stepping stone to something better. We didn't expect to live on a ranch all our lives— oh, my no! We used to talk and plan about where we would live when we were rich—we thought of St. Paul. It all looked so easy; the cows would have calves; and two years from now their calves would have calves, and we could figure it all out with a pencil and paper, how in no time at all we'd be cattle kings.

Well, it wasn't so. But there was glamour to it while it lasted. Raising cattle never was like working on a farm. It was always uncertain and exciting—you had plenty of money or you were broke—and then, too, work on horseback, while dangerous and often very hard, wasn't drudgery. There was more freedom to it. Even we women felt that, though the freedom wasn't ours.

To me at first ranch life had endless novelty and fascination. There were horses to be broken and cattle to be branded, because new ones that we bought had to have our mark of ownership put on them before they were turned out on the range. Something was always going on in the corral, and I would leave the dishes standing in the kitchen and run down and watch, sometimes for hours. This having a Wild West show in one's own back yard was absorbing but it was terrifying; I never could get used to the sight, but would marvel how anyone could stay on such a wild, twisting, plunging mass of horseflesh. The boys took it all quite calmly, and would call to the rider to "Stay with him!" as though it were just a show. My husband always rode the ones that bucked the hardest. It was awful to see his head snap as if his neck would break, yet I never could stay away. However, Brown learned fast to be a good rider, and before long offered to take the worst ones, as he wasn't married.

Sometimes the boys would run races on their favorite horses, and I would hold the stakes. I often went riding when I ought to have been at work. I had a dark blue broadcloth riding habit, with a trailing skirt, and a tightly fitted coat made à la militaire, with three rows of brass buttons down the front. The buttons were a gift from a cousin who went to Annapolis, but was expelled along with two or three other Southern boys for hazing a negro midshipman. My riding habit was even more inappropriate to the surroundings than the rest of my clothes. But the men liked it, and there were no women around to criticize.

My mounts were a chapter in themselves. Gentle horses, as the term is understood in more civilized parts, were almost as rare in Montana as kangaroos. Therefore it was a routine operation, when I was going riding, for one of the boys to get on the horse first with my side saddle and skirt and "take the buck out of him," after which I would get on and ride off, trusting to Providence that he was through for the day. All cowboys, wherever they worked, had each his "string" of eight or ten horses, which actually belonged to the company but which were regarded as the sacred private property of the man who rode them. What was referred to as my "string" consisted of one elderly bay cow pony known as Old Pete. Old Pete was neither good-looking nor a lady's saddle horse, but he was considered gentle because he didn't buck except on starting out, and he would tolerate a side saddle. One day, however, Brown remarked with a thoughtful expression: "I'm afraid Old Pete's going to blow up with you some day when you're riding him. He did it with me."

If he did "blow up" I knew what would happen, but at the time it was Old Pete or nothing. When the roundup came, however, I acquired a new and safer mount.

Many young people have told me how they envied the freedom of the unfenced range as we knew it. But I fear that to the girls of today we should have seemed very quaint. Being married, I felt like a mother to the bachelors, even when they were older than I was, and none of them ever called me by my first name. As for Mr. Alderson, I never could bring myself to call him "Walt," the way the boys did. We didn't do that, in the South. Back home you would hear women say: "Why, I couldn't call my husband George"— or William or Henry. "You'd call a *servant* by his first name!" Of course I couldn't address my husband as I would a servant—not even in Montana where there were no servants! I believe we stuck all the more firmly to our principles of etiquette, because we were so far from civilization. We could still stand on ceremony, even though our floors were dirt.

I should add that in time Mr. Alderson took to calling me "Pardner," which became shortened to "Pardsy," and that after awhile I called him "Pardsy" too. So perhaps we were not so stiff after all.

The boys were always scrupulous about swearing where I could hear them. But when they were working in the corral, they would forget that the wind could carry the sound up to the house. I caught nearly all of them that way at one time or another. Once I even caught Mr. Alderson. It was one day in the summer while they were finishing the new house. I had taken my darning and gone over there to sit, as I often did—because it was cooler there, and one of our new chairs, still done up in burlap, made a comfortable seat. A half-finished partition hid me from Mr. Alderson and Hal, who were working on the tongued-and-grooved ceiling. This was a difficult piece of work, and when Hal, in his irresponsible way, dropped his end of a board and tore out the whole groove, Mr. Alderson swore at him just terribly. I hated so to hear him, I dropped my work and ran to the shack—greatly to the delight of that scamp Hal.

No one could have been more unprepared for ranch life than Nannie Alderson. Born in 1860 in Virginia on a slave-holding plantation, Alderson was raised as a member of the Southern aristocracy. After she and her husband Walt married in 1882, they moved to his ranch in Birney in southeastern Montana, where she was suddenly cast in the role of a frontier wife. After the fierce winter of 1886 and 1887, Nannie and Walt gave up the ranch and moved to Miles City when they realized "they were no longer born up by the belief that [their] trials were temporary." Nevertheless, her memoir A Bride Goes West *(reprinted by University of Nebraska Press, 1969) is a vivid and moving portrait of a young woman in very unfamiliar and unforgiving land. When she was eighty-two, Alderson collaborated with Helena Huntington Smith—a journalist who also produced* We Pointed Them North *with "Teddy Blue" Abbott—to produce her memoir. Alderson died in 1947.*

Bonnie Buckley Maldonado
In collaboration with Patrick F. Buckley III

BENEATH THE NORTHERN LIGHTS

I am home
beneath the Northern Lights,
my annual pilgrimage
to this ancestral place.

The path down the coulee
seems steeper this year.
I hear the yips of young coyotes
coming out to hunt,
their elders telling them to hush.

When we lived here,
I saw a great gray wolf
sitting by my bed.

Sunset's red fades into gold;
the Sweet Grass Hills vanish
as I drop down from the rim.

A screech owl swoops
in front of me, not speaking,
just checking out his territory.

If I cross this steep ravine
and a stream slick
with rotting cottonwoods,
I'll see where
Timber Coulee widens,
runs to Little Jerusalem,
part of the Buffalo Plains
once called home.

Foundation stones
outline the last
of Blarney Castle Ranch.
Elegant Victorian house
and out-buildings destroyed.
Great cottonwoods cut down;
took water from the pasture.

But it isn't ranch buildings
or trees that bring me here.
It is where I come
to breathe family,
to hear their stories.

I have taught the children
to see the Indians
luring great beasts
over the buffalo jump
not far from where I stand.

There are other stories, too,
so that they will know
how the West was won or stolen.

I am here at last,
and now it is near dark.

I will rest where the tall grass bends,
heavy with its burnished seed.
I can hear your voices,
Blackfeet voices,
Irish voices, children's voices,
the heartbeat of this place.

Later owl will come
to guide my footsteps
up the darkened trail.

BLARNEY CASTLE RANCH
1887–1937

Blarney Castle Ranch
was named for a castle
in County Cork,
for steep bluffs
rising from the deep coulee.

Victorian house of immigrant dreams,
twelve rooms and running water,
bathroom and electric lights,
a glass house for tomatoes.

Furnishings were shipped
from Marshall Fields,
during Pat and Annie's nine-month honeymoon,
along with their photograph
at Niagara Falls.

A living room big enough to hold
family, visitors, and a million Hail Marys.
A ladies' parlor with carved walnut
curlicues, and a rosewood piano for
Annie's entertainments.

Acres of garden,
hillside of potatoes
and Mr. DeLoy to tend them.

Formal portraits in gold frames

of five children: Johnnie, Mary,
Nellie, Patrick, and Francis.

School-room upstairs
for the first six grades
where Patrick studied
with his children,
giving the young teacher fits.

Relatives and neighbors come to dinner,
some spend the winter,
riding the grub line.

Stories and piano tunes swirl
around the stove in winter,
and on the summer verandah
voices carry stories to the stars.

Wild mustangs were bred with Belgians
for sale to the U.S. Cavalry,
for a terrible death in France;
for the post–Great War
Cavalry Remount Program.

Blarney Castle and its sheep camps
was home to thousands of sheep
and a string of herders and dogs,
cooks, and foremen.
The great sheep sheds
and a flock of other buildings
formed the heart of it.

Now sheep no longer gauge its days,
tipi rings and buffalo bones
are plowed under.

The ranch was foreclosed on
for a fifteen thousand dollar note
near the end of the Depression
by a ruthless banker,
stone shack torn down,
meant nothing to his son.

The house and most buildings
were demolished after 1949
when Blarney Castle became
a place for Hutterite children
to run and play.

ANNIE'S BONFIRE
Blarney Castle Ranch, 1937

An auction sale
is no place for private things.
Tonight they'll burn,
my last chore before
we leave tomorrow.

Dave built the fire for me
outside the kitchen gate,
where I step three times
a day to ring the dinner bell.

First my buff and buttoned
riding boots, hat boxes
tied in purple ribbons,
letters with Irish stamps,
sheet music for flute and piano,
my and father's duets.

Fifty years of newspaper stories,
half-sister Kate's scenarios,
Tim's high collars, and
Pat's Knight of Columbus cape.
My bridal trousseau
worn at Niagara Falls.
The dead baby's layette.
I couldn't use it for another.

I can't stop now.
There are too many keepsakes,
no longer with a home.

There is something else
that I didn't care for,
and I will be glad to leave behind:
the drinking.

Don't get me wrong.
Patrick worked harder
than any of us
to build his empire.

He accomplished miracles
with a third-grade education
and correspondence courses.
He loved his family,
and he also loved to drink.

The fire surged
in spears of purple,
flashed in poison green.

Everyone laughed
when I wouldn't speak
to him after one of his benders.

It might be a week or more
before he would amble in,
horse and buggy
finding their way home,
with him fast asleep.

He brought me
peace offerings:
the oak kitchen clock,
gray marble one, too,
until there was no room
for more offerings.

I tried to stay mad at him,
but had to laugh
when he slammed his salt shaker
on the oilcloth and said,
"My name is Pat Buckley
and I own this place."

This ranch is a paradise,
and the good times here
will be ours forever.

My idea was to invest in Bell Telephone,
instead of founding banks
that took away from the ranch.

If we had a fraction
of what was lost,
we could live out our lives here;
our children and grandchildren, too.
Without our home to keep us,
the only thing left is prayer.

Born in Choteau, Montana, Bonnie Buckley Maldonado grew up on a sheep ranch and oil field west of Sweetgrass. She earned undergraduate and graduate degrees from Western New Mexico University when she was a single mother and went on to complete a doctoral degree in counseling and psychology at New Mexico State University. After teaching for forty years, she is professor emeritus from Western New Mexico University. Her first book, From the Marias River to the North Pole, was published in 2006 by Sweetgrass Books, a division of Farcountry Press, and she has published in literary and educational journals. She has three grown children and lives in the mountains of New Mexico with her husband, two canines, and the ghost of a third.

May Vontver

THE KISKIS

"HADN'T YOU BETTER EAT in the house today? It is cold outside," the teacher suggested.

Pretending not to hear her the three Kiskis slipped silently through the door with their double-handled Bull Durham tin can. They stood in a knot on the south side of the school-house and ate from the one tin. From her desk Miss Smith observed that they now and then put one bare foot over the other to warm it. This was the second time they had disregarded her invitation to eat in the house with the others. The rest of the children had drawn their seats into a circle about the stove and begun to eat.

Teddy Kirk at last decided to enlighten the teacher: "They have only bread in their lunch-pail. That's why they won't eat with us."

Miss Smith made no reply. She suspected that the lunches of the group around the stove weren't very sumptuous either. She knew hers wasn't. The people with whom she boarded were homesteaders, too.

"What about these Kiskis? Who are they?" she asked Mr. Clark that evening at supper.

"The Kiskis?—Oh, they took up their claim here last fall. They are pretty hard up. They have only one horse. Kiski hauled out all the lumber for his shack and barn with it. Thirty miles it is to Hilger. I was hauling wheat then and I used to pass him on the road walking beside the load and pushing when it was uphill."

Miss Smith smiled crookedly. One horse in a country where four- or six-horse teams were the rule was somewhat ludicrous. It was pathetic, too.

"Now, now! You needn't look that way! Kiski broke ten acres with that horse of his last spring. Got the ground in shape and got it seeded, too. The horse pulled and the old man pushed and, by golly, they got it in." There was respect, even admiration, in his voice.

"They have eight children, though," Mrs. Clark broke in. "The two oldest girls are doing housework in Lewistown."

Eight children. That meant three at home younger than the ones at school.

"Have they any cows?"

"One, but she's dry now. It's pretty hard for them."

Miss Smith decided not to urge the Kiskis again to eat in the schoolhouse.

The Kiskis in school were painfully shy. Rudolph, the oldest, going on eleven, hid his timidity under a sullen demeanor. Once in a while, however, he could be beguiled to join in a game of "Pum-Pum-Pull-Away" or horse-shoe pitching. He was a good pitcher. Margaret, next in age, expressed her shyness in wistfulness. Johnny, barely six, refused to speak. Never would he answer a question in class. Never a word did he utter to the children on the playground. He might, now and then, have made remarks to his sister and brother in Bohemian, but, if so, he wasn't ever caught making them. Yet, he was by nature a happy child. When anything comical happened in school or something funny was said he would laugh out loud with an especially merry infectious laugh. It was plain that he observed and understood more than his usual behavior indicated. The teacher, mindful of her psychology texts, tried vainly again and again to utilize these occasions of self-forgetfulness by surprising him into speech.

At the beginning of the term in September every child had come to school barefoot. As the season advanced the other pupils, family by family, donned their footwear, but the Kiskis continued to arrive barefoot, although it was now late in October and getting cold.

"Why don't you wear your shoes?" "Aren't your feet cold?" "Haven't you got any shoes?"

With their bare goose-fleshed feet Rudolph, Margaret, and Johnny picked their way between the prickly pear cactus without answering. But it was plainly to be seen that more and more the continued questioning and the curious staring at their bare legs and feet embarrassed them.

Gradually the weather grew colder. The cracked gumbo froze to cement.

Still the Kiskis came barefoot to school.

Then the first snow fell. It was but a thin film. Disks of cactus and tufts of bunch grass stuck through. Yet it was heavy enough to show plainly the tracks of the Kiski children's naked feet.

One day when John and Margaret had planned to reach school just as the bell rang, to escape the inevitable and dreaded comments of the others, they miscalculated the time. All the children were on the porch watching as the Kiskis walked, heads down, toward the schoolhouse.

"I don't see how you can stand it!"

It was the irrepressible Teddy Kirk speaking. The others left their remarks unspoken, for this time Margaret answered and there was defiance in her indistinct mumble.

"We like to go to school barefooted. We get there quicker that way."

She did not tell them that they had not come barefoot all the way; that at the hill nearest the school house they had stopped and undone the gunnysacks wrapped about their feet and legs and hidden them under a rock. When they went home they would put them on again, for no one else went their way.

But little Johnny wasn't so good at keeping his mouth shut at home as he was at school. He didn't know any better than to tell that none of them had worn the gunnysacks all the day. Fortunately or unfortunately for the children, a little Old World discipline was exercised upon them. The next day they wore the gunnysacks all the way to school. They wore them all day, too.

Their schoolmates and their teacher after a while grew used to seeing the coarse string-bound sacks, but the Kiskis never became used to wearing them. No longer did Rudolph take part in the games. Margaret grew sullen and unapproachable like him. On pleasant days when the girls strolled by two's and three's with their arms about each other Margaret stood alone in a corner against the wall. Sometimes they invited her to come with them; but she never answered. All recess she would stand there just looking at the ground. At last the girls quit asking her. Margaret made believe that she did not notice either them or their neglect. No longer did Johnny's laughter ring out in unexpected places. All three were creeping farther and farther into their shells of silence. Finally Rudolph ran away. After two days his father located him in a barn, where he had been hiding in the hayloft. Unless he had milked the cows in that barn he had had nothing to eat during his absence. He was brought home and made to go back to school.

In November the threshers came to Kiski's place. Because the field there was so small, they made that threshing their last job before pulling out of the country. Mr. Kiski hauled the wheat to Hilger and bought shoes and stockings for the children who attended school.

Other school children, the smaller ones especially, always proudly displayed their new shoes the first day they wore them. Several times that fall the teacher had been asked to admire the pretty perforations on the toes, the shiny buttons, or the colored tassels on the strings. But the Kiskis were almost as painfully conscious of their new foot wear as they had been of the gunnysacks. They arrived with faces darkly flushed, sat down immediately, and pushed their feet far back under their seats. The teacher had hoped that to be shod like others would gradually restore their former morale. She was mistaken.

Kiski's cow had come fresh. The children had butter on their bread now. Miss Smith heard about it. She had occasion to pass by the children as they stood eating and she saw that it was really true about the butter. Yet the Kiskis would not eat with the others. They continued to go out at noon time. If the weather was severely cold or stormy they ate in the hall, quickly. Then they would come in, without looking at anyone, and go to their seats.

As the four-month term drew to a close Miss Smith's heart ached for the Kiskis. They had not learned a great deal from their books; she had been unable to supply them with the many bare necessities they lacked; and their own keen realization of being different had made their attendance a torture. They were so unapproachable, too, that she had found little opportunity to show them her love and sympathy. She had had but one chance that she knew of to do so, and she was grateful for that one occasion, though it had not affected the Kiskis' silence nor changed in the least their subsequent conduct.

It came about in this way. Miss Smith had been late to school. There had been a heavy snowfall in the night and she had not had previous experience in breaking trail. If she had not been new in the country she would have known that wading three miles through knee-deep snow takes considerable time. When at length she reached the school house the Kiskis were there standing about the cold stove. All were crying—even Rudolph! They had been too miserably cold and numb to attempt building a fire for themselves. As soon as Miss Smith had the fire crackling merrily she took Johnny in her lap, undid the new shoes and stockings, and began to chafe the cold little feet. And when his crying still persisted she began telling "The Tarbaby." She had noticed early in the term that he particularly relished this tale. And sure enough, at the very first "Bim" of Brother Rabbit's paw on the tarbaby's cheek Johnny laughed through his tears right out loud— something he had not done for a month. Miss Smith decided to tell stories all day. She felt justified in entertaining the Kiskis this way, for they were the only pupils who braved the roads that day. She had a great fund of fairy tales and folk tales and a gift for telling them; also she had that day an audience whom professional entertainers might well have envied her. Johnny leaned against her knee. She put one arm about Margaret, who stood on one side, and would have put the other about Rudolph on the opposite side had she dared. He was a boy and eleven. With shining eyes and open mouths they drank in "Cinderella," "Hansel and Gretel," "Snow White," "The Hag and the Bag," "Jack and the Beanstalk," "Colter's Race for His Life" and "Mowgli."

Only to replenish the fire and melt snow for drinking water did Miss Smith stop. Her audience was too timid and self-effacing to make any spoken requests, but after each happy ending their eyes clamored, "More, more!"

At noon the water on the top of the stove was boiling. Miss Smith put condensed milk and a little sugar in it and brought the hot drink to the Kiskis in the hall. For out there they had gone as soon as she announced that it was dinner time. They accepted with smiles and drank every drop, but without a word. Miss Smith, too, stayed in the hall to drink her tea with them. Then the storytelling went on again, until three o'clock in the afternoon, when the teacher bundled them up in some of her own wraps and sent them home.

Going back to her boarding-place, stepping carefully in the tracks she had made in the morning, Miss Smith reflected that should the county superintendent ever learn of her program for the day she would be in for a reprimand. In such a case, she thought, she would defend herself on the grounds that since formalized education had failed noticeably to benefit the Kiskis, it was not altogether unreasonable to try a little informality. Anyhow, she was fiercely glad that the Kiskis' school-term would include one happy day.

It was with sorrow and regret that Miss Smith made her way to the school-house on the last day of the session. With the other pupils she had accomplished something in the way of progress, but the Kiskis she would leave embittered, shyer, and more isolated than she had found them.

She had just reached the shack and barely had time to pile the kindling into the stove when she was aware of subdued noises in the in the hall. She thought absently that it was unusually early for the children to be arriving. When the door opened a crack to allow some one to peer in, she began to wonder what was going on. Then with a rush the three Kiskis were at the stove.

With her unmittened purple hands Margaret was thrusting something towards her. It was a small square candy-box of pristine whiteness. A wide pink silk ribbon ran obliquely across the top and was looped into a generous bow in the center.

"We brought you a present, Teacher," Margaret began breathlessly.

This time, however, Rudolph did not want his sister to be the chief spokesman. "There are fourteen pieces, Teacher. Two have something shiny around them. We looked."

And before Miss Smith had time to recover from this surprise a miracle came to pass. Johnny spoke, and he spoke in English!

"It is to eat, Teacher. It is candy."

Miss Smith said, "Thank you, children. It was very good of you to give me this."

She shook the stove-grate vigorously. The ashes flew into her eyes. She had to wipe them.

"Open it, Teacher. Open it now."

The teacher took the box to her desk. The Kiskis followed and stood about her watching. There really were fourteen pieces. Johnny pointed out the two with tinfoil. Each of the fourteen reposed daintily in a little cup of pleated paper. It was a wonderful box and Miss Smith was lavish with praises of it.

She held the opened box out to them. "Take one," she invited; and as they made no motion, "Please, do."

The three black heads shook vigorously. Johnny's hands flew behind him.

"They are for you, Teacher," they protested. "You eat."

But Miss Smith couldn't eat just then. More than anything else she wanted to see the Kiskis enjoy the contents of that box themselves. She felt small and unworthy to accept their astounding offering. But again, how could she refuse to accept it and kill cruelly their joy in giving? It was a gift not to be lightly disposed of. An inspiration came.

"Would you care if I shared it? There is enough so that every child in school can have a piece. Johnny could pass it around when they all get here. Would you like that?"

"Yes, yes, yes." Their black eyes shone.

Johnny carried the box to his seat and sat down with it. Rudolph and Margaret hovered about the teacher, happy, eager, excited. Rudolph explained how it all came about.

"Anna came home from Lewistown last night. Margaret and I wrote her a letter once and told her to buy us a present for you. We were afraid she'd forget, but she didn't."

Teddy Kirk was coming. Rudolph and Margaret saw him and ran out on the porch.

"We brought candy for teacher. You are going to get some, too. Johnny has it. Come and see!"

Teddy was too taken aback to say anything. They led him in easily. The pieces were counted again.

Other children came. Rudolph and Margaret met each new arrival before he got to the door. To each in turn Johnny exhibited the box and its contents. He did not mind being the center of attraction now. He made use of his new-found speech, too.

"I am going to pass it around," he told them. "When the bell rings I am going to pass it."

Rudolph and Margaret talked. They chattered. The other children kept still. They had to get used to these new Kiskis.

When the bell rang, a few minutes before time, everybody was in his seat. Johnny got up and passed the candy. Teacher saw to it that he got one of the shiny pieces.

Candy—candy of any kind—was a rare treat to everybody. These chocolates were very fresh. They had softy creamy centers. Some had cherries in them. The children had not known that sweets like these existed.

They took their time about the licking and nibbling. Delights such as these had to be given their just dues. There was no needless or premature swallowing. And to think that the Kiskis had provided it! The Kiskis were assuming importance.

The Kiskis ate candy, too. They beamed on everybody. They had had something to give and everybody thought their gift wonderful.

The sun shone. At recess the girls again walked about by two's and three's. Margaret walked with them. Teddy presented Rudolph with one of his horse-shoes, and Rudolph began to pitch it. Edward, the other first-grader, found a string in his overall pocket and promptly invited Johnny to be his horse. Johnny accepted.

He trotted; he paced; he neighed surprisingly like a horse. Then he kicked at the traces a while.

"You should say 'Cut it out,'" he instructed his driver.

That noon the Kiskis ate lunch in the school-house.

Born in Sweden, May Vontver came to the United States with her brother at the age of twelve. She finished her high school education in five years, then began teaching as well as homesteading in Fergus County, Montana. She studied with renowned English professor H. G. Merriam at the University of Montana– Missoula during summer school and published "The Kiskis" in Merriam's literary magazine The Frontier *in 1929. The story has been reprinted in journals around the world. She eventually served as county superintendent of schools in Petroleum County and received an undergraduate degree from the University of Minnesota at the age of fifty-six. During her time living in Billings, Montana, she was a member of the Montana Retired Teachers Association and the Theosophical Society and published stories focused on her life and family in Sweden, including "The Mistress of Langsten." In 1961, she published a novel* Utvandare till Nebraska (Emigrants to Nebraska) *with a Swedish publishing company. Vontver died on January 10, 1990.*

Tami Haaland

THE DOG

I hated seeing her
split like a shot deer, burst
from her skin because a truck shifted down
too late. I heard the shift
walking from the wheat to the house
thinking a month had passed
since the moon was big and we came home
facing it late one night.

We squatted to touch her head,
her hips, the rest sprawled, a steamy
sculpture, water falling from rock, her blood
still draining on harvest dust.

We dug near the wild plums
to ground so hard we had to beat
each piece with iron
and carried her in a green spread,
turned red, to a hole four feet deep.

The neighbors gathered under the yard light
to talk of broken wrenches,
headers run into rock,
how soon they would finish,
how much they would make,
while we covered her,

pushed the dirt down hard
in the dark.

In the morning
I scraped her liver into weeds
off the road, covered blood
to disappoint the flies.

FIRST TRIMESTER

For three quiet months it's not much more
than a mouse nest behind the pubic bone
so interior no one else can know.
A tiny cataclysm in the body
of the mother, it creates more earwax,
shiny hair, softer flesh, keener smell,
the need for fried eggs in the middle
of the night. It is a transformation
no more noticeable than aphids
colonizing the underside
of sunflower leaves or the soft larvae
of cabbage moths stretching themselves
along the broccoli's interior stems.

SCOUT MEETING AT MAYFLOWER CONGREGATIONAL

I step after them toward the open
door of the unlit chapel and stand
at the end of the aisle. Siblings
of scouts, these three and four-year-olds
tip toe into darkness, then halfway
to the altar they spook like horses
in a storm, tossing their heads and
galloping for the doorway's light.

One mother nudges her child away,
another grabs an arm. "Stay
away from there," she says. "A church
is no place to play." I watch the
remaining three, my young son
among them, dancing on toes
toward darkness, whispering into
the center where Jesus waits,
pretending not to notice their approach.

11:05

This is my tired poem when the ash
leaves turn and willows by the river
sift theirs to the ground; this is my
turning in poem, my singing poem
about the dog curled into old blankets
and cats rattling dishes in the sink.
This is for sleep, for you who have
begun to sink into the deep water
of dreams where I am swimming
to meet you in tall weeds and we
wait for the next big fish. This is my
swimming poem when we rise
to its belly, hold to its spiked fins and
follow it into the open waters of this lake.

Tami Haaland is the author of Breath in Every Room, *which won the 2001 Nicholas Roerich Poetry Prize from Story Line Press. Her work has appeared in various journals and anthologies, including* Rattapallax, 5 AM, High Desert Journal, *and* Ring of Fire: Writers of the Yellowstone Region. *She received her undergraduate and master's degrees from the University of Montana– Missoula and her M.F.A. from Bennington College. She teaches creative writing at Montana State University–Billings.*

◊ *Deirdre McNamer*

From *One Sweet Quarrel*

BLUEBUNCH WHEATGRASS, INDIAN RICEGRASS, tufted hair-grass, slender wheatgrass, blue grama.

Junegrass, squirrel tail, foxtail barley, prairie cordreed, sand dropseed, rough fescue, little bluestem.

The grass in 1910. It wasn't high everywhere. People like to say that, but it isn't true. It was deep in places, though, and it had a silvery sheen to it. The texture was different than it is today—very smooth and dense; not bunchy and harsh. You could walk it barefoot.

The buffalo of course had been gone for thirty years. Entirely. The last of the unshot were traveling the country, mangy and punch-drunk, in Wild West shows. But you could still see their wallows in the grass that spring, caves in the grass, big as rooms. And their big white bones too.

Somewhere in eastern Montana, passengers in a westward train huddled at the windows to watch two children ride a sled down a hill of that grass. The sky had no ceiling.

A solitary homestead shack, the sledding children, the hard clean sunlight, nothing else.

They rode the tawny grass slowly to the flatness, their small backs very straight. Then one of them waved a brown arm at the train, and it was as if the wave sent something to the people in heavy clothes who crowded around the windows, and the ones who stood smoking at the rail of the caboose, because they all laughed happily and at the same time.

This is how we are now, they thought. This is how we get to be.

〜〜〜

THEY CAME IN DROVES THAT year. Some of the train cars contained entire transported farms, minus only the land. Bundled and stacked fence posts, a flanky milk cow, a dismantled house. Stoves, dogs, washbasins, children. And soon, very soon, land to put it on—three hundred and twenty acres of it for the asking, the taking.

Other parts of the trains carried other kinds of homesteaders, including the ones in city suits and dresses and hats. Young men, young women, from Minnesota, Illinois, Wisconsin. Teachers, clerks, realtors, maiden ladies, who had all decided to be farmers now because the railroad had told them they could. The only illness in Montana comes from overeating, the railroad said in the brochures it sent to Europe. Bumper crops, year after year. Land for the asking.

Someone made a survey of the previous occupations of fifty-nine home-steaders in a northern Montana township. Twenty-three had been farmers. The rest included two physicians, three maiden ladies, two butchers, two deep-sea divers, and six musicians.

Which one is a deep-sea diver? The ruddy squinting one with the dirty shirt?

Six musicians?

⤺

MANY OF THESE WERE SECOND sons, unwed daughters, the ones with dimmer prospects, more to prove. More than a few had spent the Sundays of their childhoods in lace-doilied parlors with heavy dark furniture, growing up during those musty decades that flanked the year 1900 like large black-skirted aunts.

Now they had brilliant brochures in their vest pockets and valises. A smiling farmer glided his plow through loamy soil, turning up gold pieces the size of fists. The farmer's house on the edge of the field had a picket fence and bushes and a garden. Everything was unblown, well-watered.

Get it now before it's gone; your own free home! They came in waves. Olly olly oxen, all home free!

And the big aunts speaking too: Child, improve yourself.

JEROME CHANGED HIS NAME TO JERRY the day he stepped on the train. He rolled up his long white sleeves and made notations in a small leather diary with his new fountain pen, looking up from time to time to watch the grasslands flying past.

On that day in 1910, he wrote a sentence about the weather. *Fair and warm.* A sentence about the terrain. *Much land for the having and the grass appears to thrive.* He was, after all, from a generation that logged the days in dry one-sentence reports. It was as if they recorded some ideal emotionless self; a self not subject to despair or transport. Maybe they thought if you could write it neutrally, you could keep living it, keep stacking the days.

Sometimes, though, a small cry broke through and it all seemed to tumble. On September 11, 1952: *Vivian slipped away today, 4:15 P.M.* On Christmas 1952: *One long day since Sept. 11.* And then he would put down the pen and try to make his own body go as quiet as hers.

What must they have felt when they looked back on those dry little sentences piled up for a big fall? When they saw the entries on the days *before* unexpected disaster. *Bought two dozen chicks at Halvorson's. Strong wind from the east.* Did they read the words later and feel tricked?

A YOUNG MAN IN A DIRTY BLACK SUIT began to play "Red Wing" on a mouth harp. He had colorless patches on his skin, flat eyes and filthy hair. He was slumped in the corner of his train seat, one thin leg crossed over the other, his entire upper body a tent over his harmonica. Still learning the tune, he played it over and over, repeating phrases, stopping, starting again.

Jerry knew the melody, and it gave him a queasy feeling he tried to shrug off. The other passengers seemed to like the sound of it. One man whistled quietly along. A mother with a child in a blanket hummed it to her baby's head.

THE REVEREND FRANKLIN MALONE and his wife, Mattie, gave a tea for their son before he ventured West. The deacon's twin daughters—teenagers with orange hair in ringlets—sang "Red Wing." They sang without harmonizing, so they sounded like one person with a very loud voice. It was raining. His kindly Calvinist father presented Jerry with the fountain pen, telling him proudly what it had cost. Mrs. Ritter passed a plate of her famous lemon swirls. All the women commented on the lemon swirls. All the men and children chewed quietly. Jerry could have wept for the deadness of it.

Everyone at the tea was careful with him because of the problems he had developed last time he left Saint Paul—a bad, dark time that brought him home from a small college weeping, and then silent, and then refusing for a few weeks to leave his room because he had, in every way, come to a halt.

He doesn't know, as we see him on the train, precisely what went wrong, what shut him down. It had to do with tall doors opening wide on a cosmos that was not being made; it was finished. Fixed and airless for all time.

A membrane away from horror, that thought. What was the point of doing anything? What protection did a person have from the most terrible of fates or the most mundane?

Hints of what might lie behind those slowly opening doors had come upon him early. Maybe that is why he developed a habit of refusing, in the small choices of childhood, to do what seemed to be expected. He resisted. He bent his response.

But the world began to fill up with people who expected things of him—first family, but then teachers, coaches, friends, girls—and to refuse to cooperate became an increasingly vast and complicated undertaking.

By the time he went to college, the expectations of the entire world seemed laid at his feet, and all he could do, finally, was stop. He could not move an inch without cooperating. And he could not cooperate with a plan that wasn't his.

Sometime during the third week in his room at home, he had a simple thought: If I can feel myself to be at real risk, that may be evidence that free will exists. If I can feel myself chancing something, perhaps that means the outcome is not fixed. Perhaps that is a pale clue.

And so he decided to behave *as though* he were making real choices. He would measure the success of the effort by feelings of being in danger. It didn't feel authentic a first, this pretending. It felt like putting on a costume to see if he could fool himself in the mirror. But for much of his long life he would continue to do it. He would pretend he was a gambler, an adventurer, a person given to hazard. He would pretend that life was not accomplished, that it could still be made. It was the only way to feel hope.

And so, naturally, when a friend handed him pamphlets from the Great Northern Railroad—get it now!—Jerry Malone did not think long. He felt what he felt, and he got on that train.

AS A YOUNG MAN HE HAD REDDISH UNRULY HAIR, pale-blue eyes, a full mouth; an unconscious glower to his eyes and forehead, which perhaps made others more brusque with him than they might have been otherwise. The brusqueness stung him and deepened the glower he didn't know about, and so it circles.

He was still new to his life, though, and the wary expression wasn't constant. Sometimes he looked soft and hopeful, as he does now, resting his head against the chair seat while the train pounds west, the thin sound of a sentimental song from the previous century wafting from its open windows.

THE HARMONICA PLAYER RAISED HIS HEAD to look carefully at the tawny, unpeopled, unfenced place they were pushing through. A place that seemed to own itself.

By now, he had been playing "Red Wing" for hours; starting and stopping and starting again; ignoring requests for something new or for silence. Whenever the train stopped, everyone in the car looked at him hopefully. He didn't leave.

In a twangy Appalachian accent, he spoke his first words of the trip.

"*This*?" he barked, throwing an arm at the prairie. "Why, this ain't nothing to be *satisfied* with!"

They looked around them.

Somewhere the train had pulled away from towns, from roads, from rivers, hedges, and people. Somewhere it had reached a point—at night perhaps, when no one really saw—where it had catapulted onto some taller place. A place that was scoured and glowing and as ferociously innocent as a new-laid egg.

THEY PASSED THROUGH SHELBY almost four days after leaving Saint Paul. Clouds had moved in and given the sky a ceiling. It was late afternoon and drizzling.

Almost the end. Twenty-five miles to Cut Bank, and then the fence that began the Blackfeet Indian reservation. Then the Rockies. This was it. Jerry got off in Shelby, thinking he might get located there. Then he thought, I choose to go on. He felt the verifying trickle of fear as he stepped back on the train and went on to Cut Bank, to the very edge of the available plains.

Shelby had looked too provisional and unlit. The previous evening, a large fire had started in the outhouse behind a barbershop and spread to the warehouse and mercantile of one James A. Johnson. Johnson's store was destroyed, though the contents were saved. It would have been worse, far worse, without a snappy bucket brigade and the beginnings of a soaking rain. As it was, Johnson lost thousands.

Smoke mingled with drizzle in the flat afternoon light, giving little Shelby the look of a kicked-out campfire.

It did not look like a place that would be famous throughout the entire country in thirteen years. And James A. Johnson, resilient and flamboyant as he was, even then, did not seem like the kind of man who would be on the front page of the *New York Times*.

THESE ARE SOME OF THE NAMES they would give their twelve-by-sixteen-foot shacks and their quarter sections or half sections of land: Kubla Khan, Scenic Heights Farm, Peace Valley Ranch, Dulce Comun, Experimental Farm. The publisher of the *Cut Bank Pioneer Press* asked them to name their new homes and send the names to the paper for the record. Clonmel Ranch, Meadowbrook Heights, Boomers Retreat, they would write.

Only a few seemed to guess what might be coming: Grasshopper Ranch, Locust Hill, Bluff Arcade.

The shacks had tar-paper roofs, most of them, and you could buy the pieces precut at the lumberyard in Cut Bank—homestead prefabs for all those young people, men and women, married and single, who didn't know the first thing about building a building, farming a farm. Most of them had never set plow to earth at all, much less earth that had never been turned.

How was it possible for them to look around at where they were—treeless wind-strafed prairie—and call a shack Kubla Khan? Maybe they were wittier than we give them credit for.

THE WALLS OF THE SHACKS WERE PAPERED with newspapers. You could read your walls for recent news. The Unitarian Church Quartet, seventy-five miles to the south in Great Falls, had performed "In a Persian Garden" by Liza Lehmann. A man who claimed to be a dentist from Bozeman had been arrested for joyriding. Peruna was the medicine of the day for puny girls, Clemo for arthritis, Electric Bitters for female troubles, and Dr. King's New Life Pills for those times when a lazy liver and sluggish bowels made a man so despondent he wanted to die.

In San Francisco, Jack Johnson, the Negro with gold teeth and a scarlet racing car and white women, trained for his Independence Day prizefight with James Jeffries. Poor Jeffries had been coaxed out of retirement to pummel his three-hundred-pound body into something white that could silence the yappity cuckolding black man, but it wouldn't work. He would lie bruised and bleeding at the end, and his fans would race out all over the country to redress the insult by spilling blood.

In Colorado, a fifteen-year-old white brawler named William Harrison Dempsey was bathing his face and hands in a secret putrid brine, making them into leather for the days ahead. This wasn't in the newspapers.

WHEN JERRY STEPPED OFF THE HUFFING TRAIN at Cut Bank, the first person he spoke to was Vivian McQuarry, the woman he would live with for forty-one years.

She stood near a tall democrat wagon, the locator's wagon, in a white shirtwaist and long slim skirt. Her chocolate-colored hair was in a puffy chignon, and she had a flat straw hat perched atop it. The clouds had lifted and scattered. Vivian held her hat against a stiff little breeze. A slim-shouldered man wearing wire-rimmed spectacles bent with her over a map.

"Are you here to be located?" Jerry asked them. They looked up. The man nodded. The woman gave a happy ironic smile. "I'd give a lot to be located," she said. She had rosy skin, a wide smile, grave black eyebrows.

They laughed together at the strange new word, made introductions all around. Vivian McQuarry and her brother George, from Cleveland. Jerry Malone from the outskirts of Saint Paul.

The locator was a rabbity man with a big official plat book. He wore a suit and gumbo-crusted work boots. He collected their twenty dollars, made pencil notations, explained that tomorrow's trip would be north of town. Prime country.

A DECADE LATER, DURING THE BAD TIME BETWEEN THEM, Jerry and Vivian would wonder if they would have been so instantly alert to each other had they not been new people in a new place.

They would think that they had, perhaps, been predisposed to be exhilarated by each other because they were travelers then and were seeing everything with the seizing eyes of adventurers.

Jerry became, the moment Vivian saw him, as enchanted and familiar to her as her engraved dream of her long-dead father, which was actually just two impeccable images: one of him lifting her laughing aproned mother a few inches off the floor; the other of his strong young hand on a straight razor, drawing the edge along his stretched jawline.

Vivian struck Jerry—as she stood with one hand on her hat, the other on the wagon that would take her to her own land—as the very antithesis of the ordinary; a ravishingly odd woman who could keep him surprised the rest of his life.

It would occur to both of them later that the secret to the kind of love that beats the heart is to somehow keep yourself, in your mind, a traveler. That way, you don't make the mistake of wishing for an earlier version of a husband or wife, when what you really want is yourself when you were in motion.

IN CREAKING VOICES, HOMESTEADERS TELL their stories to earnest young people with tape recorders. Sometimes you will hear in the background, as they pause to pick their words, the restless whine of someone down a carpetless hall.

Will they tell you what the countryside looked like, or the train station, or how many people were at the train station, or what the weather was? No. That is for us to imagine. They will tell you instead about the smell of a neighbor woman's perfume at a country dance, about a Gros Ventre man in braids and a city hat at the Havre station, or the smell of burning cow chips on a fall day. They will remember the glowing newness of a neighbor's hand pump, the pretty pink gums of their young dog, a hamper filled with the bread they had baked in Minnesota. And a hot plate wrapped in woolen underwear for a father's rheumatism, the way a cook spit on a restaurant stove to test it, oil of cloves on a wound, strung cranberries on a Christmas bush, thousands of tiny red bugs in a pail of reservoir water, the taste of a rabbit pie.

They would write in their diaries: *Planted twenty acres of flax with help of Johnson boys.* Or, *Copper wash kettle arrived today.* But a woman might recall, most vividly of all, the way a neighbor kissed her before he went back

East to retrieve a young wife. A man might remember digging a well and going so deep that stars appeared in the tiny circle of sky above.

The sound of a wolf. The uncanny greenish color of oncoming hail. The smells: raw lumber, tar paper, cut flax, the exhaust of the store owner's automobile. The wet warmth of a chinook emerging from an arch of dark clouds.

FOR VIVIAN AND JERRY, IT WAS BARE GROUND that finally stood still, a wide vault of sky, some small new buildings with large spaces between them, the smell of raw lumber, and a cartoonishly high wagon with two long wobbly benches.

The locator pointed north toward the line that separated vast ground from vast sky.

"I'm here to locate you," he promised.

THE LOCATOR'S HORSE NUDGED JERRY hard in the back as they all huddled over a map and knocked him against Vivian and George. Jostled them all for a minute. The map crackled. Jerry smiled and gently pushed the horse's head back. "Beasts," he said gallantly. "Brain the size of a gopher's."

They ate at the Beanery, a long raw building near the station. Long-cooked stringy beef, mashed potatoes, beets from jars, bread, pie. Jerry and George bent their heads over the maps again. George's face was flushed with excitement.

They all took rooms at the new and boxy Metropolitan Hotel, where they put all their luggage and crates, and then in the morning the three of them met the locator at his high-seated wagon with its wheels that were almost as tall as they were and its two long seats, placed high for the long view.

The cart lurched and moved, and the horses quickly fell into a brisk walk that kept everything bobbing and moving. They headed north, leaving the scramble of Cut Bank's buildings behind. North and north in the bleached light for six miles. They kept to the grass along rutted wagon tracks. Occasionally they passed or caught sight of a shack out there on the grass. Occasionally they passed a field of blue flax. But mostly they saw prairie, prairie, tinged green, moving blankly in the breeze.

They stopped and the locator affixed some stakes to the ground and made a notation in his book. And they moved farther east and he affixed some more. One half section for Vivian. One half for George. One half for Jerry. They looked at each other and burst into full laughs.

Jerry had brought bread and cheese and dried beef, and they had dinner in the growing dark in the grass. The wind had stopped, a moon would be out, there were lanterns for the wagon, there seemed no huge hurry. They were located.

⤙⤙

THEY TRAVELED IN THE SILVER-LINED DARK toward the tiny winking gaslights of town. Not a dense line of them. Just there, there, there.

The homes of their childhood had been planted and close. Old brick and painted wood. Shade trees. Canaries in draped cages.

Here, the moon rode the sky, the stars shivered, Halley's leaped across the horizon. The wind rippled the grass; the clouds moved in small, liquid herds, breaking and re-forming. Small animals flickered. All of it was light and silver and moving.

⤙⤙

THEY TRAPPED RAINWATER AND BOUGHT MORE in Cut Bank for fifty cents a barrel. George hauled it out once a week in a wagon. It was straight from the Cut Bank River and the color of pale rust by midsummer. A Russian thistle grew by the back door of Vivian's shack. She thought it was handsome, so she drew a cupful of her precious water every day and watered it—the tall spiky purple-topped thistle that would make all the farmers so miserable in another few years.

Looking back, Vivian would see that she had been a fool about a simple weed. But at the time, the thistle was a discovery. Bending to trickle copper-colored water over it, she thought to herself, I shall make the prairie bloom!

George got a typesetting job at the Pioneer Press and spent weeknights in town at the Metropolitan. He brought Vivian a cat she named Manx. Manx had begun his life as a cat named Cotton. A year earlier, Cotton's nine-year-old mistress had cut off the cat's tail with her mother's butcher knife. Not all at once either. In inches. He left the house shortly after that and hung around the Beanery, where they fed him, and then he went to live with Vivian in her little ship on the grass.

SHE STRAINED HER FIFTY-CENT WATER, boiled it, boiled her clothes and rinsed them and blued them and wrung them and hung them to dry. The boards of her shack began to shrink, and she stuffed the cracks with catalogues and rags against the winter. She cut up the rabbits George brought her, cooked them, canned them. She made soap in the early mornings when it was still cool.

She helped Azalia Newcombe, three miles north, thrash her crop of navy beans. They stood on the roof of the chicken coop, two women in their twenties, and poured the beans into a tub on the ground below so the wind could comb the chaff away.

She named her homestead Flax View because Jerry Malone had planted a field of flax and she liked to watch it waving blue in the sun.

They didn't know anything then—had no idea what the soil and the weather and the fates had in store for them. They lived in their shacks on the edges of great patches of soft-blue flax, a shade of blue that would always be, for Vivian and for many others, the color of possibility.

ON THE LAST WEEKEND IN August, George and Vivian McQuarry, Jerry Malone, and scores of other homesteaders and townspeople drove their buckboards and wagons to Round Lake, north of Cut Bank, for a big picnic. The lake was the only substantial body of water for many miles in any direction. It was perfectly round without a bush or tree on its banks. It glimmered blankly, naked and prehistoric.

These were the kinds of people who looked at such blankness and saw something green, planted, producing. There was talk of building a pavilion for shade, and it wasn't hard to imagine that pavilion on a summer night not so many years thence, when the sky would be the color of lilacs and the band would be playing and the sound would carry through air made windless and soft for the occasion. They would have earned something like that: music on a soft summer night.

The air held the smoke of burning pine trees a hundred, two hundred miles west in the mountains, and of the grass fires in the eastern part of the state. The fires would burn themselves out, out of sight somewhere. No one was panicked. Today was a picnic. It had been a good summer, and the crowd was buoyant.

Look at them. How young they are! How rosy and cheerful. The men still have their city slouches. They wear the suits they wore on the train west. They don't know how to handle their horses or their farm equipment. Everything is still an experiment. Some of them politely scan the crowd for possible wives; for someone's sister who may have come out on the train. Everyone, man and woman, wears a hat.

Ten miles to the west, a fence runs along the Blackfeet reservation. The Indians have been put behind it somewhere.

A few children duck between the adults, ice cream smeared on their faces. A six-piece band sets itself up. Blankets are spread on the slick grass, the corners anchored with hampers and rocks. The women carry parasols. Their hands are still smooth.

Roderick Adams has brought a couple of cases of his homemade beer, and some of the men are drinking it. One of them climbs onto a buckboard and offers a toast to the first summer in God's country. Beers and hats and parasols lift skyward.

The band is a little rusty at first, but smoothes out. It's the first music most of the crowd has heard in months. They play all the familiar tunes.

When they start "Red Wing," a few people raise their heads quizzically, trying to think why it makes them pause. Then someone mentions the boy on the train and his infernal harmonica, and a small cry goes up. Stop! they plead with the band, laughing. We've heard enough "Red Wing" to last us the rest of our earthly lives. The sun is red.

Jerry Malone stands with two other men, smoking. Vivian watches him. He lifts his head to watch her too, and they wait a few moments to turn their heads away.

They look around at the crowd and all the space stretching beyond them, the wind-ruffled lake and the children wading at its edge. They keep their eyes away from the sun, which looks like a wound through the smoke, and concentrate on the people around them. On how happy everyone is.

Deirdre McNamer grew up in Conrad and Cut Bank in north-central Montana. She worked as a daily journalist for a decade, then turned to fiction and published her first novel, Rima in the Weeds *(Harper Collins, 1991). She has since published two novels,* One Sweet Quarrel *(Harper Collins, 1994) and* My Russian *(Harper Collins, 1999), and a fourth is forthcoming from Viking in August 2007. Her articles, essays, and stories have appeared in a variety of publications, including the* New Yorker, Ploughshares, Outside, DoubleTake, *and the* New York Times *magazine. She has been on the creative-writing faculty at the University of Montana–Missoula since 1995 and lives near the campus with her husband Bryan Di Salvatore.*

MOUNTAINS

Maile Meloy

From *Half in Love*
GARRISON JUNCTION

IT HAD BEEN SNOWING HARD for twenty-four hours and the snow stayed where it fell. A few cars crawled the streets, white lights emerging from whiteness, red taillights invisible until they were just ahead. The whole valley was socked in, the mountains invisible in the steady snow. Gina left the car running in the driveway with the heat on, and white flakes stung her eyes and melted on her cheeks. It would be worse up on the pass, where the snow came harder.

The phone was ringing inside the house, and the woman on the line asked for Chase. She said her name was Kathleen Sheehan and she was calling about a check; she said Chase would understand. Gina took down the Missoula number, put it in her pocket and went to the bathroom. Her bladder seemed to have shrunk to the size of a walnut. When she stood she felt shaky on her feet.

Chase came in, stomping his boots clean at the door. "How's your car running?" he asked. He had put off getting studded tires on his truck all fall, and no garage in town had time for him now. Gina had put hers on when the roads were still dry.

"I think we should wait out the storm," she said.

"Can't wait." He gathered a stack of manila folders and yellow pads for his deposition, his bare hands red from the cold. Gina wondered, watching him, if Kathleen Sheehan was a client—but then she wouldn't be asking about a check, she'd be explaining why she hadn't sent one.

Chase slid back the driver's seat of Gina's car as he climbed in, and lowered the seat back until he could see out the windshield. Gina buckled her seat belt over her queasy stomach. There were no cars on the valley road, and no cars coming from the mountains, only the snow blowing against the glass and the half-buried tracks ahead. A temporary orange sign posted where the road began to climb said: EMERGENCY VEHICLES ONLY.

"Chase," she said.

"This *is* an emergency," Chase said.

Gina supposed it was an emergency for her, too. She was going to visit her mother while Chase had his deposition, to try to explain. She hadn't slept since she told her mother she was pregnant, and the long nights were worse than the sick mornings, the dark patches flowering like bruises under her eyes. Her mother had said, "So you're going to be a whore like the rest of us." Her mother wasn't well, she knew that, but still she had sat up that night and thought about those women, her mother and grandmother, her lonely aunts, their absent men. Going to college and teaching school had seemed to put her in a separate category from them. No one was marrying when she met Chase—marrying mattered only to her mother, and life with him was good. No reason to change it, no need to.

Now it was ten years later, and the most militant of her college friends had tied various kinds of knots in courtrooms and churches and meadows. A wrongful-termination case in Missoula had brought on two bad years, when Chase was gone all the time, staying nights in a motel instead of driving home. Gina wasn't sure they had made it out of those years intact. She had seen the baby as a happy accident after Chase won his case, drunk on wine and praise, but Chase just saw it as an accident. And now there was Kathleen Sheehan on the phone.

The more immediate fear, as they drove up the winding road to the top of the pass, was that Chase would miss one of the invisible turns and they would go over the invisible edge and plummet to the valley below. The thick curtain of snow parted only a few feet in front of them, and Chase drove slowly, for him, into that curtain, following the disappearing tracks around each curve. The insides of the windows iced, and when she scraped the glass her own frozen breath showered her.

"This is crazy," Gina said.

"I could drive this road blind," Chase said.

There was still no visibility at the top of the pass, only the feeling of going down instead of up. Down was worse; the snow on the road had started to freeze into ice, and their wheels slid until the studded snow tires caught and held, slid and caught again. When the police roadblock stopped them in Garrison Junction in the valley below, Gina's hand was cramped from gripping the door handle, and they hadn't spoken for miles.

"How'd you get through?" the highway patrolman asked when Chase rolled down his frosted window. "That's emergency vehicles only."

"This *is* an emergency," Chase said. It was less convincing when he said it to the cop.

"Well, you can't go through," the officer said. There were white spots on his red cheeks, the beginnings of frostbite. "Road's closed both ways now. There's an accident ahead—a semi stretched out across the highway. No one's getting through today. You can wait in the cafe until the storm quits and we can get you back home."

They parked at the low-roofed white building with the sign for motel cabins, next to the single-pump gas station. Gina thought about the phone message, about mentioning it while they were still alone, but instead she got out into the storm.

The cafe was steamy inside with bodies, the linoleum slick with melted snow. Although the room was packed, it wasn't loud. Everyone seemed trapped and tired of it, no giddiness of adventure in the hum of their voices. Gina shook off her boots on the wet rubber mat and dodged the tables to the bathroom, where the roll of toilet paper had fallen into the melted snow on the floor.

When she came out again, a man stepped from the men's door opposite: tall with a dark mustache, in a heavy denim jacket with a dirty sheepskin collar. He looked her in the eye and hesitated, as if he wanted to say something, and then he moved on.

Chase had found two seats at a table by the window, next to an old man and an old woman with hard-worn faces, and Gina sat down.

"Jesus, I never seen anything like that," the old man was saying. He rubbed chapped hands over eyes gadrooned with wrinkles. His hair was bushy and white, and he had a truck-stop gimme cap on the table.

"We were going west right behind the semi," his wife said, voice low. "A car stopped on the road ahead because they couldn't see, and the semi piled right into them. Killed the man and the woman in the car. We ended up in the ditch to miss the wreck." The woman dropped her voice further. "The driver of the semi's here," she said. She cast her eyes to the center of the crowded room.

Gina knew who it would be, and waited until Chase had looked, then turned to see the tall man with the dirty sheepskin who had given her the hard look by the bathrooms. He sat alone at a small table, drinking coffee. He caught her eye and she nodded at him, feeling awkward, and looked away.

"Just killed two people," the old man said under his breath. "Poor sucker. I don't know how he stands it in here."

Gina thought of the couple in the car, so afraid of what was in front of them that they had forgotten what would be behind. She wondered if they'd been fighting about the road, if they'd argued about what to do, or if they'd agreed to stop. She thought of the view from the truck, the car materializing in the field of white.

"That must be what truckers fear, hitting someone," she said.

The old man widened his eyes. "You ever talk to those guys?" he asked. "We used to run a truck stop in Choteau. Those guys aren't scareda anything."

"Oh, Al, that's not true," his wife said.

"It is."

Chase gazed across the room. "You think they'll get that truck off the road today?"

"Not likely," the old man said. "Not in this storm."

Chase seemed to be thinking. His eyes, downturned at the corners, always seemed to be thinking—not plotting, just considering. She thought it was why juries liked him. Her mother had liked him, too, at first, and liking him might have carried the day with her, except she didn't trust any man at all. Gina's father had pushed her down the stairs when she was twenty, and everyone said the fall had left her a little off. Gina touched the piece of paper through her jeans, felt it crinkle. Finally Chase sighed, and pushed himself to his feet.

"I better go call the judge, then," he said. "Say I'm not coming."

Gina watched him go, past the table where the truck driver sat alone, to the line for the pay phone on the wall. She thought about calling her mother, but her mother wouldn't be expecting her yet. If she called now she would worry.

"You feeling okay, honey?" Al's wife asked her. "You look pale."

Al's wife had the dried-up look of long winters in smoky truck stops, and Gina thought she must look pretty rough to alarm her. But there was concern in the woman's voice, and Gina was grateful for it.

"I guess I don't feel so good," Gina said.

"What're you going on your guy's trip for if you don't feel good?"

Gina held her hands in her lap and knew by the word "guy" that their ringlessness had been noted. "I was going to visit my mother," she said.

Chase always said Gina was not her mother, but sometimes Gina had to be in the same room with her to make sure they were not the same person and she would not end up damaged, jobless and alone. Gina had started scanning the classifieds for waitressing jobs again—a compulsion, after ten years of teaching, but just to be sure.

"I'm Alice," the woman said. "We were going to see our daughter. Maybe our daughter can get together with your mother." She laughed. "I think your mother'd be disappointed if she got our daughter instead of you."

"I don't know about that," Gina said.

"You don't know our daughter."

"Now," the woman's husband said.

Chase came back to the table. "Can't get through," he said. "That line is all people trying the phone and finding out they can't get through. But they don't tell each other it doesn't work. Or if they do, everyone still wants to try it." He shook his head and sat down.

Gina stood. "I'm going for a hot chocolate," she said. "What can I get you?"

They all asked for coffee and Gina stepped over two children in snow-suits playing on the slushy floor. The waitress at the counter seemed too nice and too old to be a waitress, and Gina talked to her about the snow. When the coffees were ready, Gina felt the truck driver looking at her, and she carried the tray to the table, avoiding his eyes. She thought again of the couple in the car, braking in the road, unable to keep moving forward in the blinding snow. She wondered how soon they had noticed it coming, if they had seen the lights first or heard the shrieking brakes, and who noticed it first, and what they said.

"You're pregnant, aren't you?" Alice asked, nodding at the cup of chocolate. "You seem like a coffee drinker. And you've got the morning-sickness eyes."

"It's that bad, huh?" Gina said.

"Our Shelley's pregnant," Alice said, and she looked at Al as if daring him to say something. "She looks like she got punched in both eyes, too."

"Congratulations," Chase said.

"You, too," Al said. He clapped Chase on the shoulder. "I hope it's a fine kid you get."

Chase looked down at his hands. "I hope so, too."

Al and Alice would see his demeanor as modest and pleased, but Gina guessed Chase was thinking of the burden the baby would be to him, the drain on his time and sleep and money.

Al said, "I gotta move my knee a little." He shoved his chair back with a linoleum squeal, straightened with his hands on his thighs and lumbered away from the table.

"Don't mind him," Alice said.

"Nothing to mind," Chase said easily.

"Now," Alice said. "Why don't you marry this girl?"

Chase raised his eyebrows at Gina.

"I didn't—" Gina began, and she looked at the woman. "What do you mean?"

"No reason why not to," Alice said. "Or is there?"

Chase smiled at Alice, looked out the window and yawned a little self-conscious yawn. "Well, maybe I will," he said. "No reason why not to."

Gina pressed the paper message against her thigh again, a motion that had already become a habit, the feeling of wanting to touch it detached in her mind from what it might mean. Chase would have an explanation for Kathleen Sheehan, for the call. He always did. He would say Gina had to start trusting him someday. But his embarrassed yawn made her angry; the old woman had caught him off-guard, and that was hard to do. Gina heard herself speak.

"Someone called this morning, I forgot to tell you," she said. "A woman."

Chase looked at her, and she could feel him grow alert. "What woman?"

She took the piece of paper from her pocket and read out what she knew by heart. Chase kept the guarded look on his face for a second longer and then laughed. There was relief in his laugh, but Gina didn't know if he was relieved the woman was not who he'd thought, or relieved that once again he had a good answer.

"Katy Sheehan," he said. "Sure. She took some pictures for me, up in the Bitterroot, for a water-rights case. I sent her a check for them." He smiled as if he'd won.

Gina waited.

Alice said, "Why's she asking about the check, then?"

"I don't know," Chase said, serious now. "Come to think of it, I don't think I ever got those pictures."

The old man came back and sat down heavily, ignoring the silence at the table. "Phone's still out," he said.

The windows were fogged and the room was close and warm. Gina believed Chase about the check, but believing him didn't help. It just meant it was true she would have to start trusting him someday. "I'm going to walk around," she said. Her legs were less shaky now, and she stood, leaving the hot chocolate on the table. Alice had guessed right: she missed coffee.

One of the children in snowsuits had fallen asleep under his parents' table; the other played tic-tac-toe with her father in the gray borders of his newspaper. A teenaged girl slept against the wall beneath a print of a bugling elk, and her boyfriend slept with his head on the table, holding her hand. People without tables sat in mismatched chairs pulled from the motel cabins. The line for the phone was gone; everyone had accepted the downed lines and given up. The road back over the pass would open soon, and they could go home, and Gina would call then. She would not have seen her mother but she would have tried. And they would be safe at home, alive and whole.

Gina walked the perimeter of the room once, and when she looked up the driver was watching her. He swung the dregs in his coffee cup in small circles, then put down the cup and stood to go. The people around him looked up. At Gina's shoulder he brushed against her and paused, again as if to say something, then pushed open the fogged glass door and walked out into the snow. She felt the cold air on her throat. The bell tied to the hydraulic arm jingled as the door swung shut, and the room was close and warm again. The people who had watched the driver stand returned to their low conversations or their naps.

Gina went to the door and rubbed a clear spot in the pane. The driver had no truck, and there was nothing but the one-pump gas station out there. The blue denim jacket headed neither toward the gas station nor toward the police roadblock, but straight for the empty road. A cigarette burned in his hand. He would be invisible in the snow in a minute. She put up her hood and stepped outside, the air cold and bright in her lungs, the snow blowing against her face, and she could smell the smoke he left behind. On the other side of the highway were mountains, invisible now but leading, she knew, straight up into the white sky. She watched the dark jacket disappear into white, and then the legs that carried it, until the figure had vanished in the storm.

She shoved her hands in her pockets to keep them warm. She could find the frostbitten policeman and tell him the driver had wandered off. She could follow and see if she could find the man, though it was cold, and he was far away, and what would she say to him? She could tell Chase he was gone; Chase would have an idea about what to do. Or she could just let the driver go, and walk where he wanted. He might be accountable in some way, but no one could say the accident was his fault. Her face was wet and tingling with snow, and the smell of his smoke was gone. She wanted, with an unexpected force, for him to come back. But she imagined feeling what she'd seen in his eye, and what it might be like to walk away, and she went back inside, and let him go.

Maile Meloy was born and raised in Helena, Montana, and attended Helena High School. She is the author of the story collection Half in Love *(Scribner, 2002) and the novels* Liars and Saints *and* A Family Daughter *(Scribner, 2003 and 2006). Her short stories have been published in the* New Yorker *and* The Paris Review, *and she was a 2004 recipient of a Guggenheim Fellowship. She received an M.F.A. in creative writing from the University of California, Irvine, and she lives in California.*

❦ *Sandra Alcosser*

MARE FRIGORIS

Coming home late spring night, stars a foreign
Language above me, I thought I would know

The moons like family, their dark plains—sea of
Crises, sea of nectar, serpent sea.

How quickly a century passes,
Minerals crystallize at different speeds,

Limestone dissolves, rivers sneak through its absence.
This morning I learned painted turtles

Sleeping inches below the streambank
Freeze and do not die. Fifteen degrees

Mare Frigoris, sea of cold, second
Quadrant of the moon's face. I slide toward

The cabin, arms full of brown bags, one light
Syrups over drifts of snow. Night rubs

Icy skin against me and I warm
Small delicates—cilantro, primrose—

Close to my body. A hundred million
Impulses race three hundred miles an hour

Through seventeen square feet of skin and
Gravity that collapses stars, lifts earths

Watery dress from her body, touches me
With such tenderness I hardly breathe.

WHAT MAKES THE GRIZZLIES DANCE

June and finally snowpeas
sweeten the Mission Valley.
High behind numinous meadows
lady bugs swarm, like huge
lacquered fans from Hong Kong,
like serrated skirts
of blown poppies,
whole mountains turn red.
And in the blue penstemon
grizzly bears swirl
as they bat snags of color
against their ragged mouths.
Have you never wanted
to spin like that
on hairy, leathered feet,
amid swelling berries
as you tasted a language
of early summer—shaping
lazy operatic vowels,
cracking hard-shelled
consonants like speckled
insects between your teeth,
have you never wanted
to waltz the hills
like a beast?

A FISH TO FEED ALL HUNGER

On the porch like night peelings,
bags of red hackles.
The fisherman is dressing,
capes of moose mane around him.
In his vise, he wraps the waist
of a minnow with chenille.

We wade downstream. I am barefoot.
The fisherman stands, thigh deep,
seining insects. Perhaps today
in this blizzard of cottonwood
it is the caddis that rises,
after a year in mud, from larva
to phoenix in four seconds.

The fisherman ties an imitator
of hare's mask and mallard breast.
He washes his hands in anisette,
then casts back, a false cast,
watching the insects legs
break the water.

I line the creel with hay and mint
and lay in six pale trout. There is a pink
line that runs the length of a rainbow's
belly more delicate than an inner ear.
It makes the whole basket quiver.

The fisherman does not ask why I come.
I have neither rod nor permit.
But I see him watch me all afternoon as I bend
to brush down my rooster-colored hair.
He understands a fish to feed all hunger.
And the lure is the same.

MICHAEL'S WINE

Winter again and we want
the same nocturnal rocking,
watching cedar spit
and sketch its leafy flames,
our rooms steamy with garlic
and greasy harvest stew.
Outside frosted windows—
claw marks high on yellow pine,

Venus wobbling in the sky,
the whole valley a glare of ice.
We gather in the kitchen
to make jam from damsons
and blue Italian prunes,
last fruit of the orchard,
sweetest after frost, frothy bushels
steeping in flecked enamel pots.

Michael, our neighbor,
decants black cherry wine,
fruit he ground two years ago,
bound with sugar, then racked
and racked again. It's young and dry.
We toast ourselves, our safety,
time the brandied savory
of late November.

I killed a man this day last year,
says Michael, *while you were away.*
coming home from town alone,
you know the place in Lolo where the road
curves, where the herd of horses got loose
New Year's Eve, skidded around
white-eyed, cars sliding into them?
Didn't see the man until my windshield broke.

Could have been any one of us.
Twenty-nine years old, half-drunk,
half-frozen. Red and black hunting jacket.
Lucky I was sober. We stand there
plum-stained as Michael's face
fractures into tics and lines.
He strokes his wine red beard.
Michael with no family,

gentle framer's hands, tilts the bottle,
pours a round, as if to toast.
It was so cold, he says,
that when it was over,
he swirls the distilled cherries
under a green lamp, *there was less*
blood on the pavement than you see
this moment in my glass.

Sandra Alcosser, Montana's first poet laureate, has published in the New York Times, The New Yorker, The Paris Review and received numerous awards, including two National Endowment for the Arts Fellowships and the Merriam Award for Distinguished Contribution to Montana Literature. Her book Except by Nature (Greywolf Press, 1998) received four national awards, including the James Laughlin Award from the Academy of American Poets. Alcosser founded and directs the Master of Fine Arts Program in Creative Writing at San Diego State University and the International Writers Summer Program at National University of Ireland, Galway. She is poet-in-residence for Poets House New York and the Wildlife Conservation Society. She lives in Florence, Montana.

Annick Smith

VIRTUE

I LOVE TREES, THESE DAYS, more than I love men. The old woman in my bones opens her mouth and the brittle words come crabbing out. If a woman is old, what has she got to lose? Not skin, not teeth, not beauty. An old woman's children are gone, and she has outlived the men in her life; also her parents; also her sisters. When she sings, she sings off-key. She can dance on her old legs to tunes only she remembers. I'm talking about an old, old woman. I am not talking about myself.

I'm talking about an old woman with no teeth. Her nose droops toward her chin. She is tall and gnarled, rooted deep into the banks of her green river. She snares the white-bellied squirrels my dogs love to hunt. "Get 'em when they're fat," she says, "before the snow flies." I have seen a row of those squirrels hung on her clothesline by their tails, like socks.

I gather pinecones for Christmas money, I raid caches the squirrels collect all summer. You look for telltale petals of cones on a stump or scattered under a woodpecker snag, I kneel among roots of a great ponderosa. Nothing grows here because the tree has taken everything nourishing into itself. I toss aside the pine needles. My hands are sticky with sap.

The lumber mill in Bonner pays for cones by the bushel. It's seed. First, cut all the big trees down for two-by-fours and plywood, log houses in Japan. When the trees don't grow back on clear-cuts that face into the dry sun, or the steep hills that should never be logged, plant new ones. You must have patience if your crop is a forest in Montana. My ex puffs himself up like he's a boss. "It's our industrial forest."

I laugh. "What you've got there is nonsense." I want to talk straight for a change, but he wants lies after dark and forgiveness in the morning. My ex slams his fist on the table, his beer bottle skitters to the edge. He works at the mill pulling green chain. It's a job for young men, but he's not young anymore and won't admit it. His back aches every night. He gets falling-down drunk at the Milltown Bar and takes aspirin with codeine that was prescribed for my ankle, which was broke last winter, on the ice. "What you've got," I tell him, "is not a damned thing."

The night before I kicked my Jimmy out for good, he cried drunk crocodile tears. I was wasting my breath trying to change things. Nothing comes back like it's supposed to. Fifty years is an old logger. It's a woman who can't bear children. Fifty years means heartbroke.

THE AFTERNOON I MET VIRTUE I was headed for the big pines upstream from the mouth of Gold Creek. The trees are called yellow because their bark is the color of honey, an inch thick and layered like the pieces in a jigsaw puzzle. A yellow pine is nothing but a ponderosa come into venerable age, maybe five hundred years of growing. I imagine these woods in 1492. There were giant trees without number and no white man ever saw them. Damned few Indians, either, because this place was not on the way to anywhere and nobody lived here but the bear and the wolves, the elk, the deer and cougars.

The clear-cut hills are laced by logging roads and skid tracks, only stumps and slash, no topsoil left. The yellow gumbo runs off into gullies and silts the rivers. You could cry here. And then you'd see Virtue's tall green trees. Her mile-square patch of old growth is a park thinned by fire. The pines, larch, and Douglas fir reach up 130 feet with pagoda branches; you could lay a child head-to-toe on their stumps. Sun sifts down to the understory of young trees, grass, and berry brush. When you walk on the silent needles, squirrels scream. There is the drumming of a blue grouse, and the swish, swish of raven's wings. If a breeze comes from the west, you hear the trees talking. In a north wind the trees moan and crack. When cones are ripe, they fall like bullets.

The back of my Suburban was loaded with bushel baskets. My two shepherd dogs sat on the seat behind me, ears up, noses out each window. We turned off the gravel road and into the private forest where hand-lettered signs read NO TRESPASSING…NO SNOWMOBILES…NO HUNTING. On the biggest sign were the newly painted red-scrawled words, I MEAN IT!

Knapweed brushed my axles and I had to put the rig into four-wheel-drive because of the mud holes. At the edge of the deep woods, a trail branched off toward Gold Creek. I inched my rig down until the trail ended at a locked gate, for I am a nosey-Gus and always want to see what is forbidden.

The woods opened to a meadow fenced with hog wire six feet high. Someone didn't want any living thing to come in or go out. In the middle of the compound stood a hewn log house chinked with white cement; its shake roof was mossy and patched with tar paper. There was a garden of cabbages, onions, carrots, beans, and pumpkins—the sturdy vegetables that grow in Siberia, or Montana, where you can have frost on the Fourth of July. I called out, but no one answered.

When I opened the car door to get a closer look, my dogs bolted for the clothesline hung with squirrels and commenced to leap and snap. I was yelling at them, half-astraddle the locked gate, when a shot roared out. The dogs turned back, whimpering.

"What the hell do you want?" An old crone slammed out of the house, a twelve-gauge in her hands.

"I was just looking for pinecones." I scrambled off the gate and into her yard and pointed lamely at my bushel baskets. I gave Blackjack a swift sideways kick in the butt. "Get out of there. Sit!

"I'm Annie Dutch, from Bonner." I walked toward the old woman in a friendly kind of way.

"Virtue Fernando," she said, lowering her shotgun.

HERMITS ARE PEOPLE WHO DON'T LIKE PEOPLE. Or they're mystic nuts who believe God will come if they sit on some pole long enough. Or they're murderers hiding out from the law. If a hermit is an old woman, you could think she was a witch. We sit on Virtue's porch sipping elderberry wine. The fermented berries are bittersweet.

"If I fall, I get up," she says, "or I don't. Me, I never liked no constraints of the body or of the mind. I got my garden and my woods, my traps and my fishing."

Her woodpile is low, and I see no electric poles or telephone lines.

"The church folks up to Missoula," she laughs, spraying the purple wine from her purple toothless gums. "The Catholics. They're due soon as the first hard freeze. They'll haul me a couple cords of larch. And they'll tithe up a bunch of canned goods and sugar, flour and coffee. Beans. Tuna fish. Peanut butter. Whatever's cheap and leftover in the cupboards."

I ask if she is Catholic. "Maybe," Virtue grins, "maybe not." A woman needs a man, I think, or a child, another woman—even God in a pinch. I ask if she is lonely.

"The Fish and Game," she says, "he comes around on his snowmobile, fetches me a road-killed deer or some elk shot in the gut. Most folks think I'm crazy. I'm glad when they go home." She wraps her sweater tight around her chicken-wrinkled neck.

Virtue wants what no one can bring her. She hungers for cactus and lizards, the bats, the hummingbirds. "Some things," she says, "are worth the remembering."

MY HOUSE IS A CLAPBOARD boxy thing with a front porch looking out to the only paved street, which is also Highway 200, in the company town of Bonner. The town is old as the century, built by Anaconda when they owned the state of Montana—copper and forests, newspapers and politicians, and the working stiffs who took the boats from Ireland or Finland, Italy and Bohemia, or hopped the freights from the slums of New York and Chicago. My dad was a bohunk miner in Butte. He came out West to find freedom, but all he ever found was another goddamn slavemaster.

All the look-alike houses are strung along the windy canyon of the big Blackfoot River, where lumberjacks used to float logs to the mill. You can tell my house by its sky-blue color and the peonies and iris, painted daisies and columbine. I detest the plastic flamingos that Lila collects next door. What I do in the mornings is deliver mail from the false-front P.O. which sits kitty-corner across the highway from my house. I stop at every mailbox twelve miles east to Bear Creek Road, and know the names of every log-hauler, school teacher, and two-bit rancher on every dirt road. I get to see who's got the collection bureau on his butt and who's raking in checks, and sometimes

I read the postcards from lovers and relatives gone to Disneyland or France, which keeps me daydreaming until the mail is delivered.

"You've got to live your own life, Ma." That's what Heather tells me when she calls from Seattle. Heather is my baby girl who is studying to be a lawyer. She thinks anyone can pull themselves up by their bootstraps like she does, and be anything they want.

"What life would that be?" I ask.

The boys just want me to do what I've always done. Gary's married and selling real estate in Bozeman. I'd like a grandkid, but he's too busy courting movie stars and rich people who are moving in like killer bees. They wear Stetsons, breed cutting horses, tear up their hands fixing fence. I guess they want to prove they're tough as any cowboy. "When you've got millions, why do you have to prove anything?" I ask Gary.

"That's why they're rich, Mom, and that's why you and Dad are poor," he tells me. "You never had a profitable idea in your whole life."

Gary doesn't know I wanted to join the Peace Corps in the '60s, wanted to open my wings in the big world. So many months of winter, slinging burgers at Ruby's Cafe, trying to work my way into a university education,

I'd choke on the chill, smoky air from the mills and yearn for cities in the sun—Nairobi, Singapore—far away places where I did not know the language. I was nineteen and I wanted my life to matter.

Buddy's the only child of mine I understand. He was the athlete, wanted to play professional baseball and be what his dad only dreamed of. But Buddy wasn't pro material, and he's off to Alaska on a fishing boat. When hunting season comes, he'll be flying home like a Canada goose and there'll be venison in the freezer, and cases of beer, and a bunch of his friends dealing poker in the living room with the tape deck turned up so loud the neighbors will be calling the cops.

As for me, my days are predictable. All I want to do anymore is walk in the woods with my dogs and talk to red-tail hawks and hermits.

⌒

THE SNOW WAS SPITTING the next time I got back to Virtue. It was coming Thanksgiving, so I packed a frozen turkey breast, my homemade cranberry sauce, and canned yams into the Suburban along with some *Arizona Highways* magazines I'd picked up in a used bookstore called The Bird's Nest. I bought a bottle of brandy. Not that cheap stuff from Christian Brothers, but French cognac in a gilt box that cost me most of a week's load of groceries.

Smoke rose from Virtue's stovepipe and the meadow grass glowed silver. This was the first snow of fall, and my Suburban made it to the locked gate with no trouble. I stamped my felt-lined Sorels on Virtue's doorstep, shifted my load onto my left hip, and knocked hard as I could. I called Virtue's name, but there was no sound except my voice echoing back from the snowy hills, and the soft boom of my fist against the door.

In my mind I saw Virtue lying stiff and dead; but I knew there was a fire in the stove, and the door was unlocked. The front room was dusky. Her twelve-gauge rested in its rack by the door. A Coleman lantern hung from a low beam, burning a gas-blue flame, and the plank floor was sprinkled with ash and splinters around the homemade woodstove, one metal barrel joined by pipe to a second barrel. Beans simmered on a camp stove in the lean-to kitchen, and the air smelled of feet from the knitted socks hung up to dry above the sink. The back door led to a catchall pantry, where Virtue had stacked her jars of huckleberries and elderberry wine. The hind end of a deer hung on a hook, along with a couple of skinned rabbits.

Bam. A spring-loaded rat-trap snapped shut on my toe. The pantry was mined. Another trap held a pack rat large as a kitten. "Virtue!" I yelled, wondering where the hell she had gone off to.

A well-worn trail led to an outhouse that looked like an upended coffin. It was from there Virtue emerged in her patched together squirrel-skin coat "I give up on you," she says, shuffling toward me in unbuckled galoshes. "And here you catch me on the crapper."

Virtue shrugs as we unpack her Thanksgiving treats. "Don't know one day from the next, and it don't matter. When I was a girl, I made a calendar. Bunked in the attic with my little sisters, and we'd check off each day with a red *x*. We was waiting, you see, until the day we'd get away."

The way she talked, time would be like smoke. Start with fire, which goes up the chimney and dissolves into cold mountain air. I was astounded that a woman could stay hidden in the woods so long. "You've stuck here for over seventy years?"

"Hell, no," she said. Virtue had been born and raised in this log house, and she was determined to die here. But the middle, that's another story.

WE SETTLE DOWN AT THE ROUND OAK TABLE with our French cognac, two tin cups, Virtue's magnifying glass, and the stack of *Arizona Highways*. She loves saguaro cactus. The old ones, maybe 150 years, are tall as a tree and riddled with nesting holes for owls and songbirds. In May, the saguaros grow white waxy flowers on top of their heads, "like Easter hats," says Virtue. She calls them church ladies because they look so smug. "And I give them names: Gertrude for Mama; Flora, Grace, and Serena—those were my sisters."

Virtue makes a sound in her throat, somewhere between a growl and a laugh. "Mama, she thought if she named us after angels and flowers and such, that's what we'd grow up to be."

My mother had no such high hopes. All she could think of for me was plain Annie, and my brother is John. I ask Virtue if she has any children. No, Virtue is thankful for the girlhood fever, which burned the fertility out. Her sister Flora got pregnant with a logger who already had a wife, and then Flora ran off to Seattle and died of the influenza. Grace found religion from a missionary Mormon preacher with a black beard, who believed in polygamy. "Pop run 'em both out," Virtue says. "Called her a whore and him a dirty heathen. Serena died an old maid, and me, all I ever wanted was to be free as a man. What I loved about the desert was you could see each thing clear. There was no mess about it."

"Free as a man," I say, thinking about Jimmy consorting in the bars. Virtue sinks into her memories, and I do not know where memory leaves off and the tale-telling begins. She had gone to Arizona to work in the aircraft industry while Alfred (her second husband, we never got around to her first) was shooting at Japs in World War II. When the telegram came, which starts out 'We are sorry to inform you …,' Virtue headed for the hills. Running for cover, she says, is not a bad idea.

Virtue ran to Apache Junction, at the foot of the Superstition Mountains near Phoenix. There was a black-eyed woman in that town, with her gang of Mexicans and Indians. Virtue hired on as cook and packed food up to their camp at the base of Haystack Needle, where they were searching for the Lost Dutchman gold. No one has ever found that gold. "It don't exist," she says.

Virtue's Fernando was the Yaqui wrangler who ran the mules. He and she would eye each other in camp. One night Fernando came into the cook tent where she slept on a cot. The sky of the desert isn't black, like ours, says Virtue, it's purple-blue, and soft, and the quarter-moon hangs upside down, which reminds me of westerns I saw as a child. I imagine Gene Autry with his bandy legs, the tents glowing yellow, and sparks from the cooking-fire shooting up to the sky.

She remembers the mesquite burning. It must have been her on fire—a widow woman sending out her signals. She says she was asleep. I picture Fernando's brown hand. The hand strokes her thigh. It lights the berry bush of her sex. Maybe the Indian's fingers were gentle, not urgent like my Jim's used to be, before he lost interest and went chasing after the bar girls with their tight little buttocks.

"His belly was warm…." Virtue's voice slips into silence. She takes another slug of cognac. I do too. At this rate, we'll both be smashed before dark.

They went to the barrio of Guadalupe at Easter time. Fernando tied a deer head on his head, and wore deer hooves for rattles. He stripped half-naked, stuck his chest out like a rutting animal, and danced the deer dance at Holy Week. There were violins and a harp player, a flute and something Virtue calls a water drum beating the deer's heart. When Fernando tossed his antlered head and picked up his feet, she says, you'd be seeing a man turning himself into a sacred beast. They never got married in church, but Virtue took his name. "Jules Fernando," she says, "was the only person, man or woman, never let me down."

When Virtue's father died and left her his woods, she came back to

Montana because land, she says, lasts longer than love. Fernando thought the land owned you. He wanted to die in his desert. The Yaquis believe in a real world, which is the desert, says Virtue, and they believe in another world, which is the desert you would dream, covered with flowers and running water and the spirit deer they sing to.

Virtue scratches her head; I back away. Maybe she has lice. I wait for her to continue the story. I, myself, have yearned to live a life of magic and romance. Virtue laughs her growling laugh and sits back in her chair. "Of course they're full of shit as a Christmas goose."

She nods her head, and then she falls into sleep the way old people do, as if sleep is the same as waking.

I WANTED TO TALK TO VIRTUE about my Jim, how beautiful he was when I met him—the grace with which he moved in his baseball uniform, how he was all golden in the afternoon. The American Legion played at Dornblazer Field. We'd sit in the stands, me and the other girls, along with the millworker moms and the professors' tailored wives. The diamond was green, the dandelions were yellow as butter.

Now, because my days seem so dumb, I've become addicted to Virtue's life. I itch to hear her stories and listen to wind in the tall trees. Sometimes I wonder how a ponderosa views the world. I think I might like being a tree, talking with ravens and the bluebirds in my branches. Then in my daydream this logger comes down this trail, and it is Jim on his Harley, the one we rode when we'd go out to the woods and make love so long ago.

My friends say I should go out and meet people. What they mean is I should find a man. I'm not bad looking—a little thick in the waist, with fat bulging around my hips, but my legs are still good, and I color my hair chestnut. Some nights I wake up and I'm hot and wet between my legs, and I reach down under the covers. But it's embarrassing, alone in the dark. You can't make good love to yourself.

I think about Virtue and her Indian, Fernando. Should she have stayed with him in his desert? Should I go back to Jimmy? Virtue has lived alone in her woods for forty-three years. I wonder what she does all those nights with not even a dog or cat to stroke. Some days I think it will be a blessing to get old. Not like my mother, who just faded down to a soft-voiced ghost, watching television and baking cookies for her grandkids. When Daddy died, Mother sold everything, put herself in a nursing home, and went to bed. It was her turn to be waited on, she said, and when the care wasn't good enough, she wept. Mother died covered with bedsores.

No, I want to be old like Virtue in her forest. I want to study the birds and the seasons, to stand solid and uncaring as a yellow pine, making demands on no one, and no one making demands on me.

IT WAS A NEW YEAR. The morning was blue, the temperature somewhere around ten below, hoarfrost gilding every branch and weed, so bright I had to wear my sunglasses. In the fields around the plowed gravel road where I parked the Suburban, snow stood high enough to hit my knees. It would be five miles on cross-country skis. Lucky for me, someone had ridden the logging road up to Virtue's place in a snowmobile, making a smooth hard trail I could glide along. The dogs padded in my tracks.

We skirted the clear-cuts, their stumps topped with high snow hats. I scooped a mitten full of white flakes, and their dry cleanness made my mouth tingle. My path was crossed with the deft, heart-shaped tracks of deer, and the larger tracks of elk. Also rabbits, and the tiny mouse roads that go from one clump of weeds to the next. I was soaked in a fine deep sweat when we finally reached Virtue's clearing. The sun stood high as it gets in winter and a light breeze shook sequins of snow from the pines. Knowing the old woman's dislike for my dogs, I tied them to a tree near the house.

Large, waffled, spoon-shaped tracks led out from Virtue's back pantry. Snowshoes. I took off my skis and followed the path to Gold Creek, where the water runs too fast to freeze. The tracks led to a beaver dam and the ice- slick pond behind it.

The peace of the woods broke with the crack of a rifle. I dove into the snow. My bad ankle gave way, and I was pissed off as a wet cat. I decided to stay where I was and announce myself. "Hello, it's only

Annie. Hello…Do you hear me?"

My tethered dogs started barking from their tree, and then the old woman stepped slowly up over the creek bank in her snowshoes and ragged furs. She blinked in the glare and held a .22 rifle in her right hand. The gun was aimed at me.

"Annie!" I shouted my name. "Virtue, it's me, Annie Dutch!"

"Get the hell off my land."

"You get that gun pointed the other way," I shouted again, "and I will." She's lost her mind, I thought. Slowly, I raised myself out of the snow.

Virtue moved closer, her lower lip twitching, her blank blue eyes coming to focus on my face. I could see she finally recognized me.

"No wonder you got nobody," I scolded. "You crazy old nutcase. I'm going home, and I'm taking the presents I brought you with me."

Blood streaked Virtue's bare hands. And there was a smear of red on her cheek, where she had pushed hair out of her eyes.

"You all right?" I asked.

"Come help me," she said. "Long as you're here."

Virtue led me down her snowshoe path toward some chewed-off little cottonwoods near the pond. A staked chain anchored in the bank led to a steel trap that was clamped to a beaver's neck. The terrified animal was bloody, but still alive. He crouched ready to spring. His small round ears lay tight to his skull. His buck teeth were bared.

"Trap should've drowned him." Virtue poked the tip of her snowshoe at the beaver. "Spring's about worn out. Can't set 'em like I used to. Tried to bust his head, but he near-to bit my finger off."

Virtue's rifle flashed in the sun as she held it out to me. "I ain't gonna shoot him. Pelt's no good with holes in it. Here, you finish him off with the butt."

I have always hated killing things. I will catch a grasshopper that jumps into my kitchen, his amazing legs pushing against my palm, and toss him into the wind. The reason I'm not a good fisherman is you have to kill the fish to eat him.

"No," I said.

Virtue placed her free hand on her hip. "You got any pity, you'd be killing him clean, not slow and messy like me."

Of course, she was right. My toes were numb. With each step, I sank to my shins. The .22 was familiar in my hands.

When I was a girl in the smoke-black mining town of Butte, my dad would take me and my brother, John, to hunt pheasants in the Deer Lodge valley each October. It was my job to scramble through thorn apple brush and weeds, to scare the birds from their hiding places and retrieve them when they were shot, so soft and smelling of blood. I loved the creek bottom willows and yellow stubble fields. I loved the blue and iridescent green around a cock's neck. What was distinct from a distance—the lines and curves of land against sky, a bird flushed from cover—blended close-up into plucked breasts and steaming guts, feet thrown into the soup-pot, meat and not bird.

The beaver was three feet long, and fat, fur dense brown underneath, with a top layer of bristling long hairs tipped silver, like a grizzly bear's. The long paddle-shaped tail was black and scaly, and he held his forepaws up, like tiny clawed hands ready to strike. His rat's eyes glowed red in the sun, and his snout curled back to reveal the almost comical teeth.

I raised the rifle's worn mahogany butt like I would raise a splitting maul, then lowered it. Smashing a live thing's skull was beyond my capabilities. So I righted the weapon and aimed square between the beaver's eyes, the stock of the rifle wedged tight against my shoulder. And then, like my daddy had taught me, I gently squeezed the trigger.

MY GIFT OF SILK LONG JOHNS (powder blue to match Virtue's eyes) lay in their tissue paper on her round oak table, along with the silk sock-liners and gloves. She liked the touch of them, and lifted the pantaloons in blood-splattered hands.

"Must have cost you a fortune."

"Silk from China." I did not mention that I'd got them on sale from a sportsman's catalog overstocked from Christmas.

"I've got China tea," she says, "honey from my hive."

Virtue and I had dragged the heavy beaver back to the house. She had gutted him on the spot, and we left the intestines for coyotes. Then she skinned him. Later, she would stretch the pelt, Indian fashion, on a round willow frame. "It'll be yours," she said. "You earned it."

After we had drunk our tea in silence, I followed Virtue into the curtained-off alcove that was her bedroom. It was bare except for a sagging bed, a down comforter, and an old oak dresser with its cracked mirror. There were no pictures on the walls, only a moth-eaten deer's head with faded Mexican paper flowers strung around it like a crown. A crocheted afghan in a pattern of roses covered the locked cedar hope chest where Virtue hid her secrets.

She dug around in the chest until she came up with a legal-sized manila envelope. Pushing her new silk underwear aside, she spread official-looking papers across the table.

"I been thinking about heirs," she said. "Don't have any except for a pack of Grace's Mormon kids I never saw and wouldn't like if I did, and I am surely not leaving my land to the government. Champion's offered me near half a million," she said, "and every gyppo outfit in the county is after my trees."

Virtue regarded me with a calculating glint. "What do I need money for? I want you to have my property, but only if you take care of it like I do."

She asked would I thin the trees and pull the weeds, keep the garden up and the hunters out. "No gadgets, no electricity, no telephones, no indoor toilets. You got to live on it," she said, "to keep it."

I sat quiet a long while, trying to sort out how I felt. "For once in my life," I finally said, "I'd like to do what pleases me, and no one else." Virtue snorted.

I couldn't believe I was refusing 320 acres of virgin forest. My son Gary would be confirmed in his notion that his mother was a fool. I thought of Jimmy, he would die for this property. What sweet revenge, me rich and him having no claims at all.

"I'll think about it," I said.

"Fine," said Virtue, "just don't think about it too long." Skiing back to my car through blue afternoon shadows, the cold settled around me in a mist of frozen air. My dogs shivered in my tracks, and I concentrated on movement. Mini-icicles dripped from my nose and tears froze my lashes shut. My bum ankle ached. All I could think of was the beaver. I rubbed at my shoulder, where the rifle had kicked back. I felt the panic in the beaver's eyes. Virtue had baited him with his own musk.

FEBRUARY IS THE WORST MONTH. I pulled the covers over my head. I was a squirrel in her nest, or more accurately a mouse. Virtue had to be holed up too, the snow three feet deep, a cold-snap pulling the temperature down to thirty below three nights running. I wondered if she was alive, if her mind had snapped completely, but I had lost the desire to go to her. For a while there, I hated Virtue's guts. She had trapped me all right, and if I didn't do something quick, I'd be strangled.

The day I put my blue house up for sale, the realtor's sign where everyone could see it, the phone started ringing. People I hadn't talked to in months inquired: "Are you getting married again? How much are you asking?"

I wasn't asking much—only fifty thousand for three bedrooms—but there was rot in the basement, the plumbing was shot, and I was in a hurry. Which made Jimmy call from the Milltown Bar. "Just what the hell are you doing?"

"It isn't any concern of yours," I told him. In our divorce, I got the house and no alimony. He got the Dodge pickup. I agreed to share one last drink with him, not in my place where who knows what could happen, but in front of his pals, where he'd be constrained to behave himself.

In the Milltown Bar, the stuffed mountain goat's head in its Plexiglas bubble has lost its white sheen and turned yellowish. Jim is dressed in his black canvas pants held up by suspenders, loggers high-heeled black boots, a red-checkered shirt open to reveal the sparse gray hairs on his chest. He's started to grow a beer belly, but his shoulders are wide and strong as ever.

"You're looking good," he says, noticing my purple sweater.

Jim has his beer and his shot lined up in front of him; he's had several shots from the look in his eyes. "No whiskey," I say. "You can order me an Irish coffee."

"You going to find you a rich old bastard?"

I tell him I've consulted with our daughter, Heather, who is my legal adviser, and I have made a will. Half of the house money goes into a tax-free fund for my old age—about twenty thousand, and it'll grow. I'll keep five thousand to travel on until I decide what to do with the hind end of my life. The rest will be split among the kids, except for a couple thousand in trust for Jim. When his liver gives out from the drinking, I'll be footing the bill.

Jimmy pats my knee, too surprised to say anything. I lay my hand on top of his blunt scarred fingers, and that old tender feeling rises to my throat. I lick the whipped cream from my steaming Irish coffee. There's no way to explain my feelings to this man, who is still so beautiful.

I'm going to pack my Suburban with summer clothes and my dogs, and I'll head down the Rockies to Utah and Colorado, New Mexico, Arizona. Good work will come to my hands. I'll find some traveling companions—long-haired kids or old people in Airstreams, other divorcees. We'll go to bingo parlors and shop for turquoise earrings. Like a bird with radar in her head, I'll follow rivers when the snow flies, and go home to the cool forest in summer.

I'm going to see Virtue one last time. "Here's the deal," I will tell her. "I can take your land, or leave it, but you'll have to trust me." There will be no conditions—none.

I have been puzzling about a story Virtue told about the Yaqui people in the olden times. What I love about her story is the young girl who talked to a tree. It was a twin girl and a paloverde, or maybe a new-leafed mesquite with the wind whispering. This slip of a girl received the gift of talking to trees, but the price she had to pay was to sing the tree's prophecies.

The girl sang about white people coming and their terrible deeds, and some of the Indians were so afraid they hid in the underworld of flowers and never came out. That's what Virtue chose. The rest stayed on the hot sand and were baptized by priests. They prayed for a better life in heaven. I have learned never to believe in promises, but faith is another matter. There is a third road—and that's the road I'm taking.

I want to see what I have never seen—cactus bloom and cave paintings. I want to walk with strangers on red rocks under a moon that is upside down, and find a man who dances like a deer. There are deserts under deserts under deserts, and time, and this is my time to see each thing clear. I will study the lizards and the bats, and if I'm lucky, maybe I'll hear the water drum that beats like a heart.

Annick Smith is the author of In This We Are Native *(Lyons Press, 2004),* Homestead *(Milkweed Press, 1996), and* Big Bluestem *(Council Oak Books, 1996). She edited* Headwaters: Montana Writers on Water and Wilderness *(1996) and coedited, with William Kittredge,* The Last Best Place: A Montana Anthology *(Montana Historical Society Press, 1988). Her essay "Grandmother Land" is included in the anthology* Kiss Tomorrow Hello: Notes from the Midlife Underground *(Doubleday, 2006). Smith produced the film* Heartland *(1981) and coproduced* A River Runs Through It *(1992). Born in Paris and raised in Chicago, Smith has lived for more than thirty years on a homestead ranch in the Blackfoot River Valley.*

Geraldine Connolly

MOREL HUNTING

Fast the tent city of pickers, past the drainage ditch,
fallen cedars, you search for elusive morels at the far
edge of the North Fork. How sure you are that you must
have them—devils' thumbs, like foreign cities, or new love,

fleshy and sexual—accidents of fire and water risen
from the charred timbers like Lazarus. Along the rushing
spring run-off, ashen skeletons of lodge pole litter
the muddy loam. Only a vision with brandy and butter,

veined domes drowned in shallots atop grilled tenderloin,
keeps you hunting them, driven, clutching your empty
basket, wanting a fleet taste of the sublime unmanageable—
riotous as a preacher in a forest caught on fire.

LYDIA

There was life before us,

my sister and I discovered,
looking at photographs

we shouldn't have been looking at
of the English girl my father

was engaged to during the war.
Here she is right in front of our eyes,

the woman before my mother,
in a black lace cocktail dress,

a cigarette in a holder,
pensive, earthy—waiting

in front of the carved wooden radio,
for news from the front.

This is the war, after all,
and here she is again, somewhere

on an English beach, draped
across my father's shoulder

all of her silky skin radiant
above the soft folds of sundress.

They stand in front of a sign
that reads "Seaside Cottages,

two dollars." And here she is
again, painted onto the cockpit

of my father's plane with hardly
anything on at all, and here he is

in his flight jacket, looking,
in fact, happy. My sister and I each

lift our pencils like cigarettes,
taking long sultry drags to puff

out invisible rings. They rise
in the air like silver nooses

that will catch our father
and hold him to us.

DEEP IN THE BARN

Gold the straw
deep in the barn
bright in the still
and failing dusk,
still as the evening
beginning above,

silent as a crow
while darkness
comes on

and gold the wish
made on the straw,
the wish to return

hung in the air
like a piece of dust
that lingers

in drifting light
but will not fall.

⟿

Geraldine Connolly, who lives in Bigfork, is the author of two poetry collections, Food for the Winter *(Purdue University Press, 1990) and* Province of Fire *(Iris Press Publishing Group, 1998), as well as a chapbook,* The Red Room. *Her work has appeared in* Poetry, Chelsea, Gettysburg Review, *and* Shenandoah. *She has won two National Endowment of the Arts fellowships in creative writing and a poetry prize from the W. B. Yeats Society of New York. Her work appears in many anthologies, including* Poetry 180, *edited by Billy Collins,* Sweeping Beauty: Poems About Housework, *edited by Pamela Gemin, and* Crazy Woman Creek, *edited by Nancy Curtis and Linda Hasselstrom.*

🍃 *Debra Magpie Earling*

BAD WAYS

O
N THE FLATHEAD RESERVATION YOU can come to a spot in the road where the wind smells like sulfur, a dark smell, something you think you should be able to leave behind you, but it will be in your clothing and in your shoes. And there will be a darkness in the way you see things, a darkness you wish you could leave. The Indians say it is because of the old white-man ghost that haunts the Dixon side of the river, the old white-man ghost that rode through the land before Dixon was a town, because there were some Indians a long time ago and these Indians had listened to too many white men and they had found themselves hungry with only empty pockets of land, land that had a stinging edge, a bitter taste like the silt dark water on a beaver pond, a land they couldn't leave, or see beyond, or even move for a short time, a land where the dark fish began leaving the rivers as if they were being washed away by an angry, pulling current.

This was an end to the land, they told themselves, and not because their enemy the Blackfeet pressed in on them but because the land itself was being corralled. They had seen more than deer caught on the miles of thorn wire. They had seen small bundles tied tight with strands of horse hair and for the first time they didn't know who had placed the small bundles around them. It was a medicine that called them to bad dreams and woke them dry-mouthed and praying. And they knew that whoever had put the small bundles on the ripping wire was afraid of more than small hunger, whoever had left the bundles was afraid of a withering heat that could speak to them at night like a bad animal caught in their throats, afraid of old power dying on their tongues so that day by day their people would begin to stink with loss. And the power did leave. And these Indians so long ago had to bury their shit because they were locked in small pieces of land, because their skin began to itch and the soles of their feet burned, because the strands of their hair lined with small white eggs. And a deep hunger made them small and so hungry, at night they dreamed of small bits of food in the mouths of birds, so hungry the sides of their bellies bloated like deer and their ribs became hard. And when they slept, they slept on soil or cattails ground to pitiful dust by the stiff bones of their asses because in their hunger they tried eating their elk blanket robes by boiling them clean in water. But the elk hide was thick and the water in which they boiled the hides stayed flat and bitter. The water did not foam up with the sweet smell of bone marrow. Then the hides turned green and the elk died twice.

When the white man came, he came with a shining watch, gold lined the back of his teeth, and he liked to smile because of it. He told these hungry Indians, the whole time playing with the coins in his pockets, that he wanted to play a gambling game with them, an Indian gambling game, and in exchange he'd like to get himself an Indian woman. And the Indian men laughed because all of their women were so hard you could count their bones. They had lost their breasts, and their hair was coarse from lack of any oil.

"Just the same," the white man had told them, "I want one of your women."

And the Indian men, the few that would talk to him, were curious about this. They wanted to know what he wanted with their women. The white man looked them straight on.

"I don't care who she is," he said. "She can be ugly or beautiful. I want her to dance for me. I want her to dance like a small deer for me alone."

Then the white man winked at the Indian men and they were not sure what he meant by this gesture though they knew it meant more than what he was saying. Still they never thought to ask what it was exactly that the white man wanted. He wanted it all, they believed, to lie with an Indian woman in tall grass, to press into her, to sleep. They were only thinking of the bright gold at the cuff of his sleeve, the blinding white stones in his rings, his pockets deep with coins.

Some of these Indian men began to think about this.

"What game could we play with you?" they asked him.

The white man was quiet. He shrugged his shoulders as if he didn't have a game in mind, as if he didn't know how to win. The Indians named off stick games and foot races, story games and mazes. The white man put his hands on his hips and looked at the ground. And these Indians began to feel bad, thinking maybe this white man couldn't gamble with them. Then they mentioned hunting games and fishing.

"I will fish," the white man said. "I will fish these waters and I will fish by myself and I will bring in more fish than all five of you. And if we fish a draw," he said, "you will have my money. All my money."

And these few Indian men looked at each other not wanting to smile and show the white man they had already won this game.

"Okay," they said, "you go on and fish, but fish by yourself," they said, feeling their winnings. "And if you only catch one fish, one big fish, you win."

"Well," said the white man, "you are being more than fair, but I must ask for the company of an Indian woman while I sit by the riverbank fishing."

The Indian men looked at one another. This request did not seem so unreasonable. Their hesitation must have seemed like reluctance to the white man.

"Here," he said to them, "you can hold on to my horse until I return."

"We don't need your horse," they said, because they believed that they were winning.

So these Indian men, the ones that were talking to the white man, began listing all the women in the camp. They thought of Broken Feet and Long Man's daughter. They thought of Small Salmon, how she was graceful and quick and pregnant. They thought of a woman who liked to sleep with all the men in camp, and laughed to recall she smelled like river mud and onions. They thought of Humming Blood but knew she wasn't right in the head. Then they thought of White Crow. She wasn't pretty and no man had spoken for her. She was quiet and never talked. She wouldn't complain if they forced her favor. They began wondering why she had been overlooked for so long, why Long Man had not made her more available. The Indian men snuck up close to White Crow and were surprised when she smiled at them, pleased at all the attention they were giving her. She stood up proudly and walked down the river to meet the white man. The Indian men waved White Crow on and sat down to wait for their treasures.

They sat a long time. They looked towards the river and talked among themselves. They wanted to feel the heavy coins in their hands. One talked about the gold watch and how he would smash the face to stop the white man's time. They laughed at this, stopping time. They looked at the sun. Much time had passed. They did not tell this white man he had to be back by a certain time. They worried a little. Maybe they should try to catch a few fish. Maybe he was already having such a good time with White Crow he wasn't going to come back and settle his bet. Maybe he had already gotten what he wanted while they sat in camp waiting like fools. They remembered White Crow waving to them, White Crow walking to the river. They began talking about how pretty she was and how they had overlooked her for too long. They got it in their minds that they should go see what was going on with the white man and White Crow.

When they saw the river and the white man's horse, they hunkered down behind the river brush, watching for the two of them, White Crow and the white man. But they only saw the white man sitting close to the water, and beside him were larger fish than they had seen in a long time. They went down to the white man, admiring his fish. And he tossed the fish over to them. Fish flapped on the dry rocks in front of the Indians. Fish, their puffing gills powdered in dust, their green tails sweet and slick. Fat fish the length of a short man's legs. The white man smiled at these Indians. The Indians looked at each other and smiled at the fish. For so long the river had run dry of food. The Indians forgot all about White Crow, so busy they were with all they thought they were gaining. All of them hungry with the hope of fish.

"What are you doing to get these big fish?" they asked the white man. "We have tried everything but our peckers."

They laughed and the white man laughed, too. And they laughed harder as he lifted his hand and pointed down past the big rock where his silver line bit the water. What are you using? swam in their heads. What are you using. Using? They leaned forward where the water sunk deep to shadows. They looked past the mirror of their faces, down past the first tips of weeds, down again to where the water swirled once beyond a red rock pocked by the turning current, down to where White Crow danced dead in the water. Her eyes were dark and open, looking up from green darkness, looking up to see them all looking down on her, lost to water, White Crow, her long hair a tangle of weeds.

The white man pulled the rings from his fingers, the coins from his deep pockets, and tossed them onto the hard ground. Gleaming. The Indian men could hear the high, tinny sounds of silver dollars bouncing off rocks, a hundred small lights they could see from the corners of their eyes falling to darkness.

And when the Indian men pulled White Crow up from water, their hearts split with tears to see the open wound of her, the openness of her flesh fluttering to the open mouths of fish. White Crow slit from her woman hole to the hollow of her throat, her lungs now ghostly fish, her warm heart nibbled and cold.

Then these men, these Indians, they did back to the white man what the white man had done, not thinking of what it might do to them, not thinking what more it would take. These Indians, they beat the white man hard with river rocks until his breath stopped. They took all the things he wore on his body. They took his shiny black boots, even a picture in his pocket of a small-eyed white woman. They beat the teeth from his gums with a wedge rock and dropped his long-rooted teeth in their pockets. Then they did to the white man what he had done to White Crow. They put a knife up the hole of his ass. They slit him between his balls. They held their breath while they slit the pocket of his stomach and broke the pee sack. The Indians took the white man's white horse and painted it red with his blood. Then these Indians held the white man up above their heads and shoved the muzzle of the horse into the white man's hollow torso like a death mask, bound his body round the horse's head and neck with tight thongs. The blind animal's nostrils quivered with the scent of its owner's blood.

Then these Indians sent the horse back as far as he could make it to the white man's camp. But the horse stood still and when they slapped its haunches, the shied horse bolted, caught up in tall river bramble, the naked ass of the white man splayed over the horse's neck, the white man's arms and legs beating the sides of the struggling horse. And when the horse fell, it couldn't toss its head to get back up for the weight of the white man. And when the horse died and the white man and the horse began to bloat and stink by the river, the other Indians broke camp and tried to leave the smell and the bad feeling. But they couldn't get far enough away from the stink so locked on the land they were. Even though they wept for White Crow, the white man, and the pitiful horse, they couldn't escape what these Indian men had done nor what the white man had started. Not even after these Indian men had buried the white man and his horse, not even after the other white men came looking and could not find the white man or his horse or even catch the dry whiff of his white bones, the stench of the horse's blue gases, the bad smell, followed the tribe.

These Indians, they brought some bad things here a long time ago. They brought the ghost of a white man to us because they gave him a place to shit his bad desires. And we must remember that something has gone wrong with us, something has made us scared of ourselves and what we know. Something has made us step back from the water and hold our shaking sides. We have lost ourselves when we let the white man come too close, when we give ourselves away. And we need to go back to the water first, to listen, to embrace the ghosts that shiver our bellies. And sometimes when we are fishing in the smooth lakes in slow circles, when in the greenest currents the fat pike leap from the water with snapping teeth at dusk and the sky overhead is still and clear and the fish are blind, we are close to White Crow, her blood puffing clouds in the deep water, calling us. And there is a bad smell here sometimes coming up from the rivers and streams when we are deep in our dreams of big fish beneath our boats opening their mouths to our hooks. A bad smell we should not ignore, like the musk smell of a deer that has died without prayer. Because little by little, over all these many years, the power is still leaving us, and we have to hook it, snag it like a great struggling fish and pull it back.

WINTER DEEDS

D ON'T ASK ME WHY I agreed to do it or why I did it. I've been asking myself the same damn question now for at least three days. It was money. I was drunk. The way I see it, I did both of them a favor. Stoner and the man near Charlo. But it scared me. I got spooked again, real good this time. I felt something strange standing out there in that man's field. I kept touching the crotch of my pants like I'd pissed myself when I hadn't. At one point I remember looking up at the moon and it was so bright, but only on me, as if anyone looking out in the black fields could see me like one big asshole standing in a hard light. In the moonlight I could count the buttons on my coat. I could see the wart on my left hand and the twist-skin where the rope had almost burned my thumb off when I was fifteen. The halter buckle was shining silver, so bright I had to squint my eyes. I was drunk enough to say hell with it, to get back in my truck and drive the hell away from there, to drive past Pretty Chief's house and yell for him to come out.

I went there to this stranger's house like Stoner had asked me to with every intention of killing that quarter horse, of stringing it up on the man's porch like a used gunnysack. Chop a hindquarter for chops for the dog. I don't know what I had to be afraid of. I'd seen a hundred horses killed, maybe more. Too old to be living, lame, sway-backed, broken-down nags. And hell, here I spent an hour getting ready like I was stalking, like I didn't know the horse was kept in a steal-easy corral close to the house on good nights and in the third stall over from the Dutch barn doors on winter nights like we been having. You tell yourself things, things you don't want to hear when your heart goes sour and you're walking too fast toward trouble. But I was bad that night, standing at the corner of this stranger's house, smoking. He had a few horses, not much, but I knew I was hearing the horse I was going to be killing. Those horses know. I heard his box kick in the stall, straight out, not hard but nervous, testing, ready to run. He could smell my blood, the noose in my hand, the blade of my iron knife. I was getting a little cold waiting but I thought I should wait even though there was nothing going on in the house. The man was sleeping or else he could be waiting at a black window with a power scope, an elk rifle that could split a man. I took my chances like a cowboy. I stepped out from the house. I listened to my footprints, the puff of my breath. I looked behind me but the house was still. The son of a bitch didn't sleep like any rancher I knew. I smiled to myself. Hell, once this was over I could kick back for a whole hard season. I could hire me a ranch hand to boss around. I could screw Louise maybe in a fine hotel in Missoula. I'd smoke a good cigar while warming my ass in a tub full of hot soapy water. I'd squeeze me some big tits, have a real good time. With money like this I would hammer the thick heads of a hundred head of cattle.

The barn door was open a ways. I walked in like I owned the place. I made small noises deep in my throat and puffed out my breath in deep heaves, trying to give this horse my scent. I pulled out my lighter and lit the darkness for a short while. I could see the nostrils of the other horses first, then their huge, quiet eyes, open wide to me, their ears starched. I walked carefully past them. I reached in my pocket for small bits of sweet apple. They sniffed but would not taste. I saw the quarter horse, not in the third stall but in the very last stall over. He stood calm-eyed and quiet in his stall, alert and powerful. I lifted up my lighter and he backed off. I could see the deep muscles in the horse's shoulders, the withers defined by light, the rump was like a driving force, a mass of engine in horse flesh. I grabbed the jaw, a cutting horse, a good one. I was glad I didn't bring my special choke bit. The horse was trusting. I slipped the halter over its Roman head. I snapped the lighter and looked at this horse again. I had wanted a horse like this since my father first made me ride his hell mare. A mare, not a stallion, that threw me from her back three times and knocked me off against the corner of the corral, running a dead heat so hard that she spun off my kneecap.

This horse was obedient. Still, I was the son of a bitch that could kill him. I felt the edge of my knife through its leather holster. I walked him on out past the barn, out back to the fields. I could see him. I didn't talk to the horse like I do. I reached under its barreled throat and felt for a strong pulse of blood. The blood surged through the horse, a heat I could feel like power near the base. Some asshole told me once to slit the tongue of a big animal like a snake's tongue so the blood will choke the sound of killing, or just slit the tongue and rope the mouth, have a cup of coffee and come back in an hour. Done. I thought. I looked down the horse's mouth. A stupid idea from too many bar belts. I put my hand down on the great chest of the horse and decided to stab him hard, three times. Slug him. The blade deep. Drop him. I stepped back to take off my coat, and the back of the horse quivered. "Just do it," I said to myself. I reached into my pocket and took out the leather sheath. I put it between my legs to hold on to it and took off my coat. "Just do it, you son of a bitch." I could hear the pull of the knife through leather. I was ready. I gritted my teeth. I grabbed the halter and pulled the horse close to me. I could smell the sweet sweat of its mane. I had the reins in my fist and the horse's head up when I felt a breath on my back so hot I wondered if my skin was already freezing. I turned to look behind me and I saw nothing. Nothing at all.

I positioned the point of my blade to the horse's big chest. I pumped my arm and lifted it far back, behind me. I thrust down with all the power in the sleeve of my arm, with all the muscles in my back. I wheezed in the struggle of my own strength but something happened. My arm didn't move. My arm didn't move one inch and I looked behind me and there it was, still suspended in air, ready to go. "You are a drunk son of a bitch," I said to myself. But my arm wouldn't move. It hung there almost for the longest time. And I turned and had me a real good look in the dark. And for one crazy moment I could've sworn I saw something, something like a ghost, standing just beyond me, but I couldn't see much. What I really saw was bones, blue bones. I could count ribs like a fat coil that was busted down the center and had lifted up. I could see a man's ribs. I could see the thighbones. And I wasn't spooked just then. If anything, I was dry sober. I was standing cold in a dry wind in snow, dry sober, looking at a ghost that should have been a sight for drunkenness but I was sober. It was the ghost of a man. I knew that, the way you know for no reason at all, that someone is watching you from behind. I wasn't afraid. I loaded that horse up in the back of my rig and drove on out to Whiskey Flats. I let that horse go on five thousand acres of raw land, not knowing why, just knowing that was the thing to do at the time. I saw the spray of its tail, lifted high, beautiful, as he headed out. I didn't worry about the winter. I didn't worry about the drop of the thermometer on bad nights, the slick rocks, the bad drops. I let that horse go free. I turned it loose on a night so cold I saw the blue bones of a ghost. And I didn't care about Stoner just then. I could make up a story. I could just say the farmer came out when I was ready to drop his horse so I took the horse and ran. I could tell him I dropped the horse, one shot in the Whiskey Hills. But that son of a bitch, I know he'll be thinking, just like I'd think myself, that I took the horse for me but even if I did, he'd owe me. He'll owe me big for this one.

I got Roy Hearn to wake up in the middle of the night. I pounded at his window so the lazy son of a bitch would get up before daylight. He didn't even ask me what I was doing on his porch at two in the morning. He sold me one of his glue horses, pick any one, he said. And I went out back and felt guilty as hell to look at all these broken-down horses, scarred, some limping, waiting for the truck to take them into Bozeman. No longer horses, no longer good rides or a cowboy's freedom. Now they were meat.

I found one the same color as the farmer's horse, the same color. I put that horse down right there. Roy yelled out his window once at me. "Trying to sleep," he said. But the horse had already gone to rest. I skinned it right there with the other horses huddled against the farthest fence. Hell, they know what's going on. I held my nose. The whiskey was still in me somewhere, threatening to come back up my throat at the smell, the deep gut smell, the bad smell of death that should have come years ago. Animal death ached in my nose. I popped the knife into hard bone. Stung my fingers like a son of a bitch. I drained some blood into a water pouch I kept behind my seat. When I had gutted the horse, I pulled the hide away from the corral. I left the meat still steaming. I figured Roy would appreciate the extra meat for no money. I got in my truck and turned to look at the corral. Smoke rose up from the shivering horses' backs and I thought to myself they'd be steaming like the other horse, but only in a butcher's concrete room in a few days and maybe I'd done this one horse a favor. But I'm a son of a bitch. I don't need a dozen doe-eyed horses flinching back from me to tell me. I know I'm a son of a bitch.

By the time I got to the first curve in the road to Charlo, I had to pull over my truck and lose the whiskey. I could feel the chafe of whiskers on my collar. I saw the farmer's house again. I got out of the truck and lowered the tailgate. A powder of snow covered the horse hide. I put my gloves on and opened the hide out flat and a heavy heat rose from it. A bitter smoke. There was a feeling of morning rising in the air. The colors were flat. The mountains were edged now. The stars were thinning.

I looked at the man's house in the distance. He had slept through this long assault. He was still snoring. A sorry son of a bitch. I reached into the truck and picked up the water bag. I slung the horse hide on my back and my bad knee bowed. My boots crunched the field snow. I felt the cold in my battered ass, the click of my teeth. Everyone must be sleeping.

About halfway to the field, I realized what a sorry son of a bitch I really am. A crazy asshole that has chased a good man's horse to hell, lost a good night's sleep and at a minute to morning is still up, pranking like a schoolboy without a lick of brains. I had lost my heart for the job. I decided to hell with Harvey Stoner. I'm leaving the carcass on the corral. And I left. By the time I got back to my truck my knees were buckling with cold. The back of my head was tight and I looked up to see the farmer's light glowing in the distance. I rolled down my window as I was driving away, still in semi-darkness. I left my headlamps off. I stopped once, listening for an angry voice but I heard nothing but the popping of my tires over frozen road. And all the way home I could hear a crying so hard I would look into my rearview mirror to see if someone was in the truck bed behind me. But there was no one, not in the lonesome truck bed or the seat behind me. There was no one, only me.

OLD GHOSTS

A SMILING WOMAN PICKED HER UP about a half mile from the Vullets' house and when Louise told her that she was Indian the woman stopped talking. The woman's face was a shadow in the warm car. The woman steered her car onto the first wide spot in the road. She had reached across Louise's lap and had tugged at the door handle while the car was still moving. The woman's face was tight and for a moment Louise thought that she was smiling. The car pulled to a slow roll and stopped. The woman pushed the door out so hard the springed hinges creaked and the door came back fast at Louise. The woman drew her chin in tight to her chest and stared up at Louise. Louise got out of the car and before the woman had the door closed she was off again.

Louise watched the spin of the woman's tires on the slick roadside. The woman rode the pedal. Louise heard the high whine of the wheels grinding. The wheels spun so hard they almost burned. When the tires finally took hold, the car whiplashed down the highway for such a long way that Louise began hoping the car would right itself again.

Night was pressing hard over the hills, a charcoal face, Louise thought, the chest and front legs of a giant horse running, clouds turning. She stood at the road and looked over at the dull silver river. She could see the black water where the animals had chipped a hole in the ice. Day was sinking. Through the naked trees she heard the river's voice. Louise told herself it was only the ice, the fingernail-thin ice pulling on the shore. Louise squinted at the water skin rattling on the river, the place where the current ran hard. The still-water place where her sister had died last summer. She stood for a long time watching the spot of her sister's death hoping she could call her sister back. For a moment there was no sound. Snow snaked on the road. She watched with her eyes clear and seeing. She watched with a heart in her chest, her heart slowing. She could feel the day around her slipping. The closer you are to life, the closer you are to death, her grandmother had told her. She wondered if now was one of those times. When she heard the ice crack she felt the break along her spine, an opening. She listened to the shrill splitting river. A sound like a woman moaning crossed the water bank.

A mule deer leaped from the dense brush and clipped across the changing river. Louise heard its hollow clocking steps kicking ice and then its hooves broke to water. The ice creaked like an old door closing. She saw, not wanting to believe what it was she was seeing.

She saw the deer's dark eyes roll up white, a clear splash of water gurgling. And then the river was silent. She stood for a moment looking toward the dense call of water. This was the place where her sister must have looked up once maybe or again and again without seeing or seeing only this panic of water rising up her neck. Louise's hands trembled. She ran toward the river, not taking her eyes off the hole where the deer had broken through. Brambles scratched her face. She slipped and fell and saw the chuffing mouth of the hole, a small hiss of water smoking and the animal gone. She got back up, chased the river run from the bank, watching the still river place, her own heart strangled by the thought of water, trying to see beneath green swirls of ice, hoping she hadn't seen the deer fall through, still hoping she could save it somehow. But she knew the water ran fast here and never froze. She had never known there to be a fishing hole here in winter. Water only glazed.

The deer was gone.

The wind chattered in the red bramble.

She stopped running and felt her breath tight in her chest. How many times that summer day, Louise wondered, had her sister lifted her face up from the water only to smell this place here, the burn of nettle, the smell of sky meeting water? The last memory for Amelia must have been the sweet smells the river inhales in slow pockets that somehow turn into the length of a long summer and become the only thing we remember. A blind and blinding memory.

She pointed her steps homeward and felt the wind gather speed. It pushed at her back. She felt her nerves stinging cold. The tips of her ears itched. She began to wonder if she had ever seen the deer. She watched her feet. The snow was so cold-dry she could hear the squeak of her footsteps and a sudden quiet. The quiet that meets the day at evening. Her breath steamed in front of her. She tried to think of home. She tried to think of a warm place. She saw only the big poster bed in Stoner's house. The small pillows. The framed pictures on the walls. She could almost feel the heat rushing up the vents, heat rushing to the pulse in her throat, hot, the first glare of summer again and again, so hot she would drop her clothes and stand naked to open-mouthed Harvey Stoner just to feel the breath of the furnace. She could stand barefoot and naked on the hot brass plate, press her hand to the window, and melt ice in a winter that dipped to twenty below, and never feel the sting of cold. She would stand on the vent until the scorch of hot brass nipped the tough soles of her feet.

He would lie on the bed sometimes. He would lie on the bed and unzip his pants to touch himself, to watch her. She would hold her breasts for him. He would cry sometimes. She would drape herself in a white sheet and pretend to be his daughter. She would braid her hair. And Harvey Stoner would kiss her. She could smell cigarette smoke in the deep pores of his skin and she would pull back from him. He would kiss her hair until her hair would unwind from its braid. And he would smile and sleep. And she would sneak downstairs to visit his wife's pantry.

In the dark, in a room bigger than her grandmother's house, she would feel the full stacked shelves. She would touch the store-bought cans of peaches, plums, pears, the shelves without beans or sacks of dry meat. She could feel no mouse turds or spider webs. The room smelled like boxes of apples, Macintosh or Transparent. And while Harvey Stoner slept she would drink the juice from a cool can of apricots. She would eat his sweet peaches in the good-smelling room. And then she would walk home, leaving Harvey to find a row of empty cans lining his wife's clean kitchen counter.

Louise had never really seen Mrs. Stoner before today. In the distance she had always looked like a woman who had a lot of money. In her passing car she always looked satisfied and happy. She looked almost young. But today Louise had seen her face up close. She had seen the face of a woman who had slept with Harvey Stoner for fourteen years. Fourteen years of new cars and big rings. And she saw in the woman's face a mean sadness. Years of wondering, years of younger women, girls, really. And Louise hated Harvey Stoner. Once she had slept with another man just to get the scent of Harvey Stoner off her skin. The nights he pulled her into his car to suck her breasts were the nights she wouldn't go home. She would stay outside her grandmother's house. Now Harvey Stoner could touch her and it didn't matter anymore. She felt only small tugs on her skin, a heat on her belly, and then he was gone. And the less it bothered her, the less it mattered to her, and the more he wanted her. And the more he wanted her, the less it mattered to her. Until he became small to her. She wasn't sure what she wanted from him now. All Louise could feel was her hunger. A want that stayed with her like a small bird that chirped in her dreams, woke her hungry.

SHE WAS COLD AND TIRED. She would sit down by the roadside just for a minute, she told herself. She hugged herself and squeezed her hands beneath her arms. She blinked her eyes to the cold, to the dark coming. She sat still to the silver river and the silver-pink sky. She sat still. She sat as if her breathing had left her. The hills were turning dark against the pale sky. The flutter of birds had quieted to night. She could see the shadowy branches of the cottonwoods down by the river. She remembered the hushed noises of a hundred settled birds, then the rush of robin's wings leaving. She thought of her sister Amelia. Her sad, sweet smile. All the sweet, wild roses were gone. The huckleberries, sarvis berries, Indian celery, were long sleeping beneath the knee-deep snow. The fat deer had chased the new growth far up the timberline. And the mule deer she had seen was now cradled in the swirling river far down the river, swallowed, rocking to dark silt. The land was deep in the crushing sleep of winter. Louise blew breath into the cup of her white palms. She stuffed her hands back into her pockets and felt the tight curl of her fingers, the burn of blood. She would sit down on the roadside for just a moment, she told herself again. When she closed her eyes she could see the pale sun.

It was Jules. Jules in his blister-blue truck, his headlights smoking. He had lifted her from the roadside and carried her to his truck. He had made her mad. She had slapped him for waking her when the good dreams had just started to come. The windshield was frosted with his breath. The moonlight was white. She could smell the sweat of horses, the scratch of heavy wool at her face. Jules had thrown his horse blanket on her. She couldn't open her eyes even when she knew Jules was pounding the dashboard to wake her. The heater hummed. And she turned toward sleep. He slapped at her face until the roots of her hair were fire. "Christ," he whispered. "Christ." There was white moonlight. The curve of the river flashing. The sleepy shift of the truck rounding curves. And Jules whispering. Whispering to the sound of the slick hum of wheels. "I'm taking you to my home, Louise. You'll be fine. I'm taking care of you," he said. "I need to go to Missoula tomorrow early. But I'll be back. I'll be back," he said. She thought he had kissed her hair. And she remembered that he had carried her into a dark house that smelled like camphor and tobacco. He had taken off her clothes, jerked her arms out of her sleeves. She opened her eyes to see his sleek chest, to see him naked and pulling back the blankets on his bed. She remembered the heavy pull of sleep again, the blankets, the thick heat of Jules's hands cupping her buttocks, the way her teeth chattered even in sleep.

"Jesus," he said. "You could have died out there."

She heard him in the morning as he was leaving but he did not say goodbye. She lifted the curtain and saw the dark light of dawn. She pulled the covers back up and closed her eyes. She thought she was alone.

THE WOMAN WAS IN THE KITCHEN and Louise watched her lift her hand above her eyes as if she were squinting into the bright sunlight or as if she were waiting, watching for someone. Louise knew that she was in the house of Jules Bart. She remembered the rooms. She could see his work pants on the floor of the kitchen, a pair of long underwear over a chair. The woman walked carefully to the cookstove and opened the door without gloves. The fire was so hot, Louise could feel it from where she stood but when she walked closer the kitchen was cool. She could place her hand in the stove even though she could still hear the crack of the hot wood fire. The kettle hissed on the stove without steam.

The woman was dressed in a long skirt. Her hair was brown, light brown, and over her ears was a fresh spray of bluest lupine. The woman looked out the window and wiped her hands on her apron. Someone was coming. Louise looked outside. The snow was falling and she wondered if she might be dreaming.

Louise walked barefoot into the living room. She could hear birds outside, hundreds of birds, and yet she knew it was winter. She listened closely. From the far field she could hear the mourning dove and meadowlark. She opened up the door to hear better. She opened up the door to see summer, and an ice-tingling wind shot through the house and slammed all the doors shut.

Louise turned to the woman. "Hello," Louise said to the strange woman, "hello." The woman did not answer her. It was as if the woman did not see Louise at all and when Louise stepped into the kitchen she felt cold. Her teeth chattered and her shoulders ached from shaking.

Louise turned to see the woman throw a shawl over her shoulders. She was clear as water now. The hair of a ghost, the pale eyes of a ghost turning to Louise. Louise could see death now turning to pass through the door of Jules Bart's house. Louise could feel the cold lifting from the woman like heat lifts from the road in hottest summer. Nothing. And beyond her leaving, in the dream of the smallest second, the pale, green grass of a spring morning. Buttercups and buds.

Louise found her pants and her shirt in the bedroom. She found a pair of dirty socks that weren't hers and decided to put them on anyway. She grabbed her boots and dressed as she moved to the door. She knew she had to get home, that her grandmother would be worried about her. She slid her stocking feet on the floor of the dining room. She bent over to tie her boots and heard someone. She heard someone talking. It sounded like a young man with a cracking voice. She was hoping it was Jules.

Louise does not want to see them but she sees them. She puts her chin to her chest and prays that she is dreaming. When Louise looks up she sees the woman again. This time the woman is unmoving. This time Louise knows the woman is dead. She is laid out on the dining room table. She is shoeless. Her toenails are long and yellow. Louise holds still.

A young man, a boy, really, enters the room with a steaming bowl of water. He looks like Jules but he is only fourteen years old at most. He sets the bowl down and Louise gets a sudden whiff of spearmint. He has scented the water. The smell makes Louise lonesome for summer and she remembers the warm smell of sweet grass above the river.

The woman is still on the table. Louise looks at the woman's dress, the long folds that drape to the floor. It is a heavy dress. The woman's hair is in a tight knot at the top of her head. Her face has been wind-beaten smooth. The young man takes the pins from her hair one by one and her hair untwists from her head and touches the floor. Her hair is brown and silver and the boy brushes her hair carefully. She can hear the whistle of his breath through clenched teeth. He brushes her hair for a long time, smoothing each brush stroke with his hand. Louise feels a tightness in her chest. Even though it is winter she can hear the quaking aspens outside shivering silver. Louise hears the warm wind. She wonders if she steps outside if she can hold this time.

He washes his hands for a long time and then he carefully unbuttons the woman's dress. There are many buttons but he takes his time. His hands shine at her throat. There is a quiet in the room made quieter by his breathing. He unbuttons every button, unsnaps every snap, and when he is finished he struggles to remove the dress from her. He props her left elbow, trying to yank the sleeve. He doesn't cry. He seems angry now and he tears the dress up the left sleeve and bares her arm. He tears the dress again, exposing both of her thick arms. He dips a washcloth in the steaming water. He hisses. The water is hot. Louise can smell spearmint. He lifts the woman's wrist and swipes her arm twice. The boy takes a long breath. The woman is heavy on the table in her long skirt and bodice. She has more clothes on than the living. Louise knows the boy will undress her.

He starts with the bodice. He unlaces it. Louise hears the slap of the laces unthreaded. Her body opens slowly as if she has been bound tight all of her life. The woman's breasts blossom. They are large and white. The boy doesn't look at them. His hands are long and slender. He tries to undo her slip. He walks to the end of the table and tugs at the hem of the slip, trying to pull it off her. Her body moves down the table a bit. He jerks again and when he looks up to see her breasts jiggling he stops his effort. His neck is red and his face looks hot. He stands for a moment. He looks at the woman's face and then he digs in his pocket. He pulls out a small closed knife. He opens the blade with his teeth and slits her skirt open. By the time he gets to her full hips he realizes she is naked. He realizes he has passed the cuff of his hand through the hair between her legs. Louise closes her eyes for a moment, knowing she is seeing something that she should not be seeing. He pulls a breath so tight into his chest and stumbles back so fast Louise knows he has touched the woman in a private way. He backs up for a moment. He looks at the floor. He looks at the door.

Louise thinks that he is finished. She feels that he will leave this task. But he goes back to the woman. He strains the hot cloth in his fist without wincing. He washes her face. He places the cloth to her breast like he's not touching her at first. And then he is washing her hard. He is washing her like a table. And he cries. He puts his head down on her chest and he cries hard. Louise realizes he is alone. There is no one for him. He cries so hard the table shakes. He sucks at the woman a little, then he sucks her breast hard. Louise bites her lip, surprised at how she feels, how his sadness grips her chest. He cries open-mouthed at the ceiling. He puts his head back down on the woman's chest. His mother, Louise thinks, feeling stupid for not knowing that from the beginning. His dead mother. He stops crying for a while. He looks up straight at Louise and she sees the young face of Jules Bart. She wants to hide from him but she knows he cannot see her. Jules Bart looks up like he realizes he is not alone. He has been seen.

And then the man comes in. He has seen Jules. He has seen Jules at his mother's breast crying. He is pulling the gloves from his hands. Jules Bart kneels down and covers his head and all Louise hears is the sound of the man's dull fists on the backs of Jules's hands, his arms, his hollow chest.

Debra Magpie Earling is a member of the Confederated Salish and Kootenai Tribes of the Flathead Reservation in Montana. She is the author of the novel Perma Red *(Blue Hen Press, 2002).*

Mary Ronan

From *Girl from the Gulches: The Story of Mary Ronan*
as told to Margaret Ronan, edited by Ellen Baumler

THE JOCKO VALLEY

A CCORDING TO DUNCAN MCDONALD, THE last factor at
Fort Connah:

> The Flathead Agency is situated on a small tributary
> of the Jocko River. One mile to the rear a chain of lofty
> mountains rise abruptly from the valley—forming no
> foothills—and towering grandly above the scene. The
> mountains are covered with a dense forest of fir, pine
> and tamarack. Nearby are several clear mountain lakes,
> abounding in speckled trout, and from one of those lakes
> a waterfall or cataract over one thousand feet high plunges
> into the valley, forming one of the tributaries of the Jocko
> River. The valley is about five miles in breadth and twelve
> miles in length with excellent farming land, cultivated
> by Flathead Indians and half-breeds. Following down
> the Jocko to its confluence with the Pend d'Oreille River
> the valley closes, and the Jocko rushes through a narrow
> gorge. At the junction of the Jocko and Pend d'Oreille
> River, the valley again opens into a rich and fertile plain,
> where a large number of Indian farms are located.
>
> St. Ignatius Mission, where the Indian boarding and
> manual labor school is established, is some seventeen
> miles from the Agency. This Mission is one of the largest
> institutions of the kind in the U.S. and is presided over
> by a number of Jesuit priests, lay brothers and Sisters of

Providence. A large convent, church, school house and dwelling are surrounded by a picturesque Indian village of some seventy snug log houses, where principally Pend d'Oreille Indians dwell and cultivate the rich soil in the surrounding valley. The Mission Valley is a broad, extensive and well-watered plain with ranges of mountains on both sides. From the Mission to the Flathead Lake—a distance of thirty miles—and around its borders there are farming lands enough for thousands of settlers. The Indian name for the lake is *Skalt-koom-see*, which means Wide or Big Sheet of Water.

Peter Ronan reported to the United States Commissioner of Indian Affairs in August 1877:

Flathead Lake is embossed in one of the loveliest and most fertile countries, surrounded by towering cliffs and mountain ranges. It is some twenty-eight miles in length, and has an average width of ten miles. In the center of the lake is a chain of beautiful islands, and upon its clear, broad bosom wild waterfowl of every description, even sea gulls, disport themselves. Around the foot of the lake is another Indian settlement where snug houses, well-fenced fields, grazing herds and waving grain, give evidence of the rapid advance of those Indians in the ways of civilization and thrift. Here the Pend d'Oreille River takes its rise, rushing and leaping through narrow gorges, and widening out into a broad stream, winding through lovely valleys for hundreds of miles, when it falls into the Pend d'Oreille Lake, a sheet of water larger than the Flathead Lake.

I have quoted at length because these descriptions reveal a situation for the Indians quite different from the present one. I bear witness to the fact that at that time many of them did have snug log houses, well-fenced farms, waving fields of grain, and grazing herds of horses and cattle; and there was evidence of husbandry and thrift and of the advance of the Indians in ways of civilization.

The confederated tribes of the Flathead, the Salish, Pend d'Oreilles, and Kootenais at once bestowed upon my husband the title *Scale-ee-hue-eel-i-me-kum,* White Chief. That he was indeed and more; he became their advisor, mediator, patriarch, and champion. So concerned was he in their affairs, in counseling them, in seeking to solve their problems, to get justice for them and redress for their many and grievous wrongs, and so successful was he in the administration of his office as an agent of the government that he spent the remaining sixteen years of his life among the Indians on reappointments through Republican and Democratic administrations.

Once, in council with the confederated tribes, General John Gibbon, who looked upon the solution of the Indian question as dependent upon the transfer of the red man to the guardianship of the army, suddenly put the question to Flathead Chief Arlee: "Do you like your agent?" Arlee replied, "As agent of the government we respect him; as a friend and advisor and neighbor we love him; and I trust I may never live to see the appointment of his successor." With a few notable exceptions, that, for instance, of Major John Owen, always the understanding friend of the Indians, the history of the affairs of the Flathead Reservation under the various agents had been one of everlasting trouble, or misappropriation of Indian and government property and of constant court proceedings. Mr. Ronan, in writing to his people in Malden of his appointment as agent of the Flathead, concluded that this was the condition to a notorious extent. He wrote, "No doubt your reading of 'Indian Rings' and thieving agents gives you the idea that it is hard for human nature to withstand the temptation of becoming a public robber, but make your mind easy on that score. I came into the office with clean hands, and with clean hands I shall go out."

True enough, just as my husband thought, I was delighted with the beauty of the place. There I spent twenty years, the most interesting and difficult of my life. Something stirring, exciting, dangerous, was always pending, threatening, happening. The old agency was isolated from civilization, but the situation was so lovely, and fishermen and huntsmen found the streams and country all about such a paradise for their sports, that after the first summer, as long as I lived on the reservation, I was never again alone in my home with my own family. As there was no hotel nearer than Missoula, a half day's journey by wagon or on horseback, and my husband was lavish in his hospitality, all comers were our house guests for as long as they chose to stay. Keeping my household organized, attending the needs of growing children, the insistent demands of a baby—during the most of those years there was a child under three years of age—counseling with my husband when, in our mutual concerns, we felt that two heads were better than one, all this combined to keep me in the midst of enthusiastic activity and burning with a sense of quickened and multiplied consciousness.

My difficulty came upon me in having to play the gracious hostess almost continually to members of Indian commissions, transcontinental surveys and railroad commissions, senatorial commissions on appropriation for the reservation, special agents of the government, generals of the army and other officers; a papal delegate, archbishop, bishops, and priests; an English and an Irish earl, a French count; sportsmen from abroad, the East and the West; scientists, millionaires, journalists in search of a story, celebrities, friends, relatives; and Indians—chiefs, tribesmen, and squaws with their papooses. There was no retinue of trained servants in the background to prepare and serve food and to dispense other necessities and comforts for this multitudinous and very human pageant of guests. My "help" usually consisted of a Chinese cook, an Indian laundress, and a young girl to act as nursemaid for the children and to help me with the sewing, for I made nearly all my clothes and the children's. I am glad to remember that in those busy years I never felt overworked or abused or longed for my little children to grow up. There was always something especially appealing about the worn little shoes, scattered about in the evening, which made me resolve that the next day I would try to be more patient and sweeter.

If I had the ability, the heart, and the endurance to capture and to relate the complete story of these years, to tell of the people and of the events that came and passed in perpetual flight into or beyond memory, my story would fill volumes. Since all that is actual is in a moment gone, reducing experiences to groups of impressions, I can only hope to trace faintly the main line of my story and to capture some of what is so fugitive by the aid of my old scrapbook with its accounts, in letters and newspaper clippings, of events as they were long ago recorded.

Mr. Ronan carried out the plan sketched in his letter of May 31, 1877, came to Helena in "the nice spring wagon," and conveyed Mrs. Lambert, the children, and me the hundred and fifty miles to the Flathead Reservation in a very comfortable manner, according to our ideas at that time. Mrs. Lambert with her little daughter Grace, who was just Mary's age, and I with my baby Gerald, not yet three months old, sat on the back seat. Mary, not yet two years old, and Vincent, just past three, sat beside their father on the journey. We spent the first night at Deer Lodge. At the hotel in the evening M. J. Connell, who was at that time a clerk in the store owned by E. L. Bonner, called upon us. During the second day we stopped a little while at New Chicago (hopefully named!)—then a settlement of some ten or a dozen houses—now I am told, no such metropolis! At the store of Archie A. McPhail, I met his wife, Annie McCabe, with whom as a little girl I played in Bannack, fourteen years before. We drove on and spent the night at a stage station—at Bearmouth, I think. At noon each day we would stop for a meal and a rest at a stage station.

Mrs. Lambert and I were young, happy, and forward-looking. We did not find the care of the children irksome at all. The weather was pleasant and sunny, so sunny that my wrist, exposed between my sleeve and glove as I held my baby, was all blistered. The country was beautiful beyond power of description. The spicy fragrance of June blossoms, especially of wild roses which hedged the road and of syringas, which almost over-powered it, delighted us into forgetfulness of burned wrists, arms aching from holding the baby, during hours and hours of jolting over rocky roads that followed river bottoms or clung along mountain slopes, of toiling up long, long grades or scraping down with brakes set, of pitching down steep banks into deep fords. Between Deer Lodge and Missoula, a distance of eighty miles, the Missoula River had to be forded about twenty times.

On the evening of the third day of our journey we arrived in Missoula and went to the hotel on West Front Street kept by Mr. and Mrs. William Kennedy. The old friends were expecting us and greeted us warmly. Fifty-five years ago Missoula was a little village, and most of the log houses were clustered around the vicinity of Higgins Avenue bridge, where the Missoula Mills, the property of F. L. Worden, stood; the village extended a block or so east and west on Front Street, and north on Higgins Avenue.

Early in the morning we started on the last twenty-eight miles of our journey to the agency. At the mouth of the Coriacan Defile (now called O'Keefe Canyon), we stopped at the log ranch house of Baron O'Keefe, for through all the years, since the Alder Gulch days, I had kept up my friendship with Mrs. O'Keefe, née Hannah Lester, by letters, and since my marriage, Mrs. O'Keefe and her two little girls had visited in Helena. In spite of urgent invitations we did not stay long enough to get down from the wagon, for we were anxious to reach our new home.

Mollie O'Keefe, a girl of about twelve years of age, came down the roadway from the cabin and stood beside her mother at the gate of a zigzag rail fence, on which a bluebird perched and sang. Mollie was radiantly beautiful. Her wavy blond hair was caught back from her face and hung in ringlets about her shoulders. Her eyes were blue as the bird's plumage, her cheeks delicately pink, her skin clear as porcelain and smooth as satin. She was tall for her years, slender, willowy, and lithe. My words may sound extravagant; they are only futile in their attempt to picture Mollie O'Keefe as I saw her that morning, looking like the princess of the old fairy tales, who dwelt in the castle rather than the pioneer child who lived in the tiny log cabin in the shadow of the high hills that flanked the narrow canyon. She stood, a lovely picture; still I see her so.

The weariest, most wildly beautiful stretch of our way lay through the narrow Coriacan Defile. Besides following the windings of the canyon, the road twisted and turned around great boulders; the roadbed was as rocky as a river bottom, in fact it lay along what must have been an ancient riverbed. We traveled next for four or five miles through the dense, majestic Evaro woods, slaughtered years ago; down Evaro Hill to the ford of Finley Creek, then a roaring torrent for none of the water had been diverted for irrigation. Just beyond the ford we emerged from a grand grove of yellow pines, and I saw for the first time the fruitful valley of the Jocko. It was lovely and lush in June growth, the grass and flowers spread knee-deep across the prairie; here was a great blue patch of lupine; there, a rippling splotch of pink clarkia. A band of wild horses, grazing in this luxuriance, raised their heads, startled, whinnied, and broke into a gallop. Pitched against backgrounds of occasional clumps of trees, smoke-stained tepees could be glimpsed. Best of all, in the distance, at the end of a road that looped in long curves almost across the valley from west to east, was visible a little settlement, the agency, our home, a cluster of houses showing white in the late afternoon sunshine.

Directly to the east and to the south of the agency buildings, not two miles away, rose, so abruptly that they seemed to lean forward, great wooded pyramids of mountains, their dark blue intensified by deep shadows. To the northeast, in a gap in the mountains, was a magnificent view of one of the jagged snow-capped peaks of the Mission Range and a glimpse of a waterfall on its craggy side, barely distinguishable from the snow. To the north were rolling brown hills; back of us, to the west, were higher wooded hills and mountains. So beautiful the valley was, it seemed to me that day I had entered a place like unto the garden of paradise.

At the agency stockade gate Harry Lambert waited to welcome us. We went into the house described in my husband's letter and found a delicious dinner prepared and ready to be served to us by the cook. Mr. Ronan had hired a clean efficient white woman to cook for us, the sister of Ovando Hoyt, the agency miller. We were tired, but not too tired to be gay during our house-warming dinner. Then Harry took his wife and little daughter to their cottage just across the way.

When Mr. Ronan had had sufficient time to make improvements, the agency settlement, built in a hollow square, covered in all about an acre of ground. It consisted of our residence in the center of the south side of the square; on the west were the agent's office, a storehouse for government supplies for the Indians, a cottage for the government clerk, a granary, and a long narrow building with living quarters for the Indian interpreter and the agency employees (miller, sawyer, carpenter, stableman, etc.). On the north there was a barn, a carpenter shop, and a blacksmith shop; to the east a grist and sawmill. In the southeast comer was a house that included the residence, office, and drugstore of the agency doctor. In the yard back of the agent's residence were various small buildings: an icehouse, milk house, smokehouse, chicken house, washhouse, etc. All the residences were weather boarded and enclosed with low picket fences; the yards were planted with flower gardens and shade trees. All the buildings and fences in the settlement were painted white or whitewashed, except the sawmill, which was red; the roof, too, of the big barn was red. A picket fence six feet high enclosed the whole agency square; in the center of each side— north, east, south, and west—was a gate wide enough for a wagon to drive through. At night these gates were closed to keep out wandering stock. A fence-enclosed vegetable garden, a pasture with a zigzag fence, cattle sheds, while the houses for the sawyer and blacksmith were outside the stockade to the north and west.

In time Mr. Ronan set out an orchard on the ground between our house and the doctor's. In it were several varieties of apple trees (among them the McIntosh Red), wild plum trees, currant, gooseberry, raspberry and blackberry bushes, and strawberry plants. In the midst of the orchard he had built a little cottage for the gardener. Back of the cottage was a big root cellar, and still farther back was a pond for water storage in the summer time and from which to cut ice in the winter. He devised a system of water works: a cold stream was run through the milk house; cold water was piped into the kitchen sink. A bathroom, with a big tin tub, was improvised in a small room off the kitchen. Hot water had to be carried in pails from the large tank attached to the kitchen stove and emptied into the tub; cold water was carried in pails from the sink. But the water drained out through a rubber tube into a narrow irrigating ditch—a truly great convenience!

After a number of years the government allowed a sufficient appropriation so that additions were built on to several of the residences. On account of the numerous official guests that it was necessary to entertain, the two-story addition to the agent's house was somewhat pretentious for the times, consisting of a large "parlor" and several bedrooms. The house came to have, during most of the years that we lived in it, eleven rooms, besides a fair-sized storeroom, pantry, bathroom, and three hallways. The largest of these the children named "the hall of death" because in it were many mounted trophies of the chase: a black bear, a mountain goat, elk, moose, deer, and caribou heads. Practically all the lumber used in these buildings was turned out in the agency mill and most of the building was done by the agency employees, with the carpenter as head contractor.

Straight across the prairie to the north, scarcely two miles away, out of Big Knife Canyon, came tumbling and roaring the cold, sparkling waters of the Jocko. Often in the late afternoon Mr. Ronan would walk, ride horseback, or drive to the Jocko and return in perhaps an hour with twenty or thirty trout hanging from the crotch of a willow branch, in plenty of time to have them cooked for supper. All about just outside the agency stockade were quantities of prairie chickens and pheasants. We would drive out a little way with the children in the spring wagon and Mr. Ronan would shoot the birds from the wagon. The children loved to be lifted down to run to get the birds. Even that first summer sturdy little Vincent did this sort of retrieving. In season for each we went on gay expeditions to gather huckleberries, chokecherries, wild plums, Oregon grapes, and elderberries. These I preserved or made into jelly or jam in great quantities and put them away in gallon earthen jars.

We needed to use every resource. We were provided with shelter, heat, light, some staple supplies such as flour and sugar, and we were privileged to utilize for our own household products from the government demonstration farm, garden, and orchard. My husband's salary was $125 a month, payable in quarterly installments. Oftener than not, however, until the railroad came through, the payments were delayed a month or two or three. The currency to pay the salaries of all the government employees on the Flathead Indian Reservation and allotments to the Indians was expressed to Missoula, where my husband had to go to receive it and then drive back with a pouch containing thousands of dollars over that lonely, twenty-five-mile stretch of hill country, mountain, forest, and canyon to the agency. The trips to Missoula for the money were always made secretly. Sometimes Mr. Ronan took with him a trusted guard, but oftenest he made the trip alone, always armed. He was never accosted by robbers, but I was never a moment at ease until his perilous errand was done.

We kept hearing stories of the trouble which had been rife since May among the non-treaty Nez Perces, led by Chief Joseph, and the white settlers in the Wallowa Valley in Idaho, backed by the United States soldiers under the command of General O. O. Howard. Except for an uneasy feeling when I listened to these rumors, the first weeks at the agency passed like a happy dream. When I sat by the "parlor" window or on the long, narrow porch across the west side of the house, rocking my baby or sewing, I could see my husband going about the agency square with hired men or colorfully blanketed Indians. When he was not off on trips of inspection, he could be home for every meal.

In those happy-go-lucky, idyllic days before a household budget was heard of, we would have regarded it as a breach of hospitality to have submitted to the Department of the Interior an expense account for the ubiquitous inspectors, special agents, and other officials on government business who stayed at our house and sat with us at table for days, weeks, and sometimes months at a time. As a matter of fact, it never occurred to either of us to do so. I suppose we were simple, unsophisticated, and unbusinesslike. We were products of our times, and every stranger was welcomed like an invited guest. Our latchstring always hung out.

Mary Ronan came to the Flathead Indian Reservation as the wife of Indian agent Peter Ronan. This selection from Girl from the Gulches: The Story of Mary Ronan *(Montana Historical Society, 2003) was edited by historian Ellen Baumler, who used material from a thesis originally published by Ronan's daughter Margaret. Ronan's work depicts an early-day Montana: from the streets of Virginia City, where "rough-clad men with long hair and flowing beards swarmed everywhere," to the Flathead Indian Reservation, where "the situation was lovely, and the fishermen and huntsmen found the streams and country all about such a paradise for their sports that after the first summer as long as I lived on the Reservation, I was never again alone in my home with my own family." Born in Louisville, Kentucky, in 1832, Mary Ronan came with her family to Virginia City in 1863, the same year the Vigilantes became known. Born in 1852, Ronan lived on the Flathead Reservation until she died at the age of eighty-eight in 1940.*

Janet Zupan

PLUNGE

Your bed is warm, a beach for me
sanderling with salted wings settling near berm

The ocean gives a thousand mile fetch
waves curl in the confusion

I'm free of the tides and polar
winds that cage the clouds

The sky is wide with the pulse and spiral
of spring. Sparrows outside our window

cling social on the whipping branches
Afternoon is a flute, notes rising

up the sill into memories of water and runoff
fool's watercress in an overhang of sun

Love's unreason draws us away
like clouds making escapes

on daring winds, like a downstream
moving us beyond thought to the draw

of our lateral lines, feeding
like bream, traveling toward

salt marsh and sea aster.

REFUGEE

In bristlespine, the woman alone
is denied another mercy.

Branches scrawn the wind,
flaming sleep to a catsclaw.

Dream is beyond reckoning.

Flay trees dot the sunsmoke,
No parchsongs, no lord candles.

Night is not a velvet entrance

but a region of thorns where rest
is a state found only

in arms of prayer trees
along the edge

of a funeral range.

PRODIGAL DAUGHTER

I'm the wind in full moan
no matter how he flips the windwindow.
Wrappers hiss on his dash. I've cracked

a weedy face in the road he travels
tapped valves loose in the truck
he never paid off. Speeding down

Pearblossom Highway, he sees
one after another piñon or yucca
contorted from years of gust

and devils. Forty miles
through their squatting shadows
is the only town, full of fruitstands

boarded by night. The Ford cuts
a fast shadow across
their wooden faces and he thinks

of my skin, smooth as cherries.
By the end of today's map, he'll fall
a hundred miles short

his destination. He rests
in a Palmdale curve. The star-
pocked night is round as an eye

fair as the coyote giving
a father's cry from the canyon
dreams are a lull until

sandstorms come between him
and the horizon. When he wakes
I'm there, hungry

around creosote and sage,
with the shifting shoulders
of a dune, moaning low.

Janet Zupan earned her M.F.A. in poetry from the University of Montana–Missoula in 1996. Her poems have appeared in various journals, including Apple Valley Review, Talking River Review, *and* Cumberland Poetry Review. *Her essay "Vertigo" was part of the collection* I Thought My Father was God, *edited by Paul Auster (Henry Holt and Company, 2001). She presently divides her time between writing and her job as an instructor at the University of Montana–Missoula. Janet resides in Missoula with her husband Kim.*

Melissa Kwasny

READING NOVALIS IN MONTANA

The dirt road is frozen. I hear the geese first in my lungs.
    Faint hieroglyphic against the gray sky.

Then, the brutal intervention of sound.
    All that we experience is a message, he wrote.

I would like to know what it means
    when first one bird swims the channel

across the classic V, the line flutters, and the formation dissolves.
    In the end, the modernists must have meant,

it is the human world we are weary of,
    our arms heavy with love, its ancient failings.

But that was near the first war, not in 1800,
    when a young German poet could pick at the truth

and collect the fragments in an encyclopedia of knowledge.
    There is a V, then an L, each letter

forming so slowly that the next appears before it is complete.
    The true philosophical act is the slaying of one's self,

Novalis wrote and died, like Keats, before he was thirty.
    They have left me behind like one of their lost,

scratching at the gravel in the fields. Where are they
    once the sky has enveloped them?

I stand in the narrow cut of a frozen road leading into mountains,
    the morning newspaper gripped under my arm.

But to give up on things precludes everything.
    I am not-I, Novalis wrote. *I am you.*

If, as the gnostics say, the world was a mistake
    created by an evil demiurge, and I am trapped

in my body, abandoned by a god whom I long for as one of my own,
    why not follow the tundra geese into their storm?

Why stay while my great sails flap the ice
    as if my voice were needed to call them back

in the spring, as if I were the lost dwelling place for title flocks?

LEPIDOPTERA

more brilliancy, starriness, quain, margaretting!
–Gerard Manley Hopkins

The Wood Nymph steadies itself on a grass blade
with one of its six legs. It landed clumsily.
It has been mating in air. Common Sulphur
on the sunflower. Cabbage White on the yarrow.
Black trim of the Pine White caught in a web.
Perhaps the argument begins here, when I am late,
when things are browning. A week ago,
all was gauze-green, billowing in the breezes.
One could hardly choose between velvet and cob.
There was coolness for thirst, the equivalent
of our gin and tonics. The bulbous spree of mullein,
yellow-tipped, made the pasture a candelabra.
And as the butterflies steered through this forest
of soft things and the eccentric, of towers, tridents,
the sun-warmed mint, the musk of thistle,
they would land and close their wings as if in prayer.
One reads the world the best one can,
bloom of bull thistle changing from fuchsia to purple,
the purple not a color but an event.
Even the berries are translucent.
This is how it must be for them, the vegetable world
standing between them and the sun, glimmer
through fir trees in the morning: priests, intermediaries,
interlocutors. Why does the female Wood Nymph
have no eye spots and the male have two?

Why do Wood Nymphs visit flowers more than others?
Would you trade your eighty years
for their two weeks of bliss, blue gentian, a chance
to mate in air? It takes years for some species—
egg to caterpillar, to pupa, gates of the chrysalis
to open wide—yet two years of the non-ecstatic
are life, too. And aren't there times
when they have felt, as we in turn have felt,
that gorged with such goodness they could die now.

COMMON BLUE

for Grace

Their eggs are laid on lupine. Tiny jade
hairstreaks I could easily mistake for dew.
Too precious. Too incidental,
these trills that flounce in my potato patch,
drawn from dryland origins to the domestic
stain of water from my hose.
What an old woman would study, I think
as you hand me the guidebook, distracted
by the replica of a parasol
growing out of a bleached cow pie.
The Siamese kitten with his butterfly eyes
comes running, his mouth full
of swallowtail, his breath smelling of borax
and sugar I have poured
over the ant hills in the garden.
He is young and intent on eating poison.
We bushwhack through paradise,
what is there to say except to lament
the daily evidence of its passing,
how the Common Blues scatter from my shade.
And you, so fragile, so sick, so thin,
your diet restricted, keep pointing out
the bearded face of larkspur.
When the angels fell, a 15th century bishop says,
there were 133,306,668 of them.
It takes us all afternoon to cross the field.

The body, it is so sad what happens to it.
If you fell, you would dry up instantly.
But these are not Angelwings
who disguise themselves as leaf or shred of bark,
who are named after the stops
in meaning our language must make room for:
the Comma whose wings look battered,
or the violet underside of the Question Mark.
To keep the mind from clenching, you say,
is the main thing. Even the most
beautiful days always seem to have death in them.
As Valentinus says: our fall into love and sleep.
You especially like the dark Alpines
with their furred bodies and lack of marking.
And the Sulphurs, yellowed scraps that fall
from a myth of origin that doesn't include us.
When we find them, we will wonder
who is still alive. We speak of our souls with such
surface ease. But who will take such care for us?
You bend and bend to the scrappy blue sea,
your back turned to the moon fluttering above you.
I have been thinking so much of strength
this week, yours and mine, I mean,
the field of attention that can be strengthened.

Melissa Kwasny is the author of two books of poetry, Thistle *(Lost Horse Press, 2006, winner of the Idaho Prize) and* The Archival Birds *(Bear Star Press, 2000), and two novels,* Trees Call for What They Need *and* Modern Daughters and the Outlaw West *(Spinsters Ink Books, 1993 and 1990). She edited* Toward the Open Field: Poets on the Art of Poetry 1800–1950 *I. Her poems have appeared in a number of journals, including* Ploughshares, Poetry Northwest, Seneca Review, Cutbank, Willow Springs, Bellingham Review, *and* Threepenny Review. *She lives outside Jefferson City, Montana.*

TOWNS

Joanna Klink

PORCH IN SNOW

There you are, snow filling the air,
in the midst of silence. The porch still with ice
and the distances shifting in us,
snow falling in slips to the streets.
Winter, there is no prayer but this,
to hold fast in the time of few choices.
An animal moves through the backyards, its eyes
precise and lit, the premise of everything I believe,
a whiteness that measures the sadness
of the creature unsure where it will sleep.
And every conviction you held of what it means
gone, the evening long gone. And it may be
a shining in your eyes as other sleepers enter homes.
Restless with ice, an animal crosses the wide field
in you, a darkness that asks
everything for measure, spacious world,
the animal moves against all winter,
a grace of feeling we had not imagined.
This also comes into the winter garden
while a car starts, snowlight falling across the alley
in radiant extension of everything I cannot
see. As if the night were utterly changed,
as if you would turn to enter the rooms again,
lit against cold, and there were no further sorrow
possible for you, in any form.

WINTER FIELD

What better witness than this evening snow,
its steady blind quiet, its eventual
completeness, a talc smoothing every surface

through the lumen tricks of ice.
No one who comes here hastens to leave,
though the mineral winter makes a dull

math of cold inside the bones, a numbness
thinning into each fingertip and eye.
Faint injury traveling toward earth in

shifting silence, a softness in the weather
passing through us, dark moods of snows—
a sense of peace so deep we extend out

into the blackness of our lives, dread and failure,
and feel no hint of terror, only the premonition
of drift-design, the stars behind the snow

burning in ancient immanence over the field.
What lights a world gone blank with despair?
You were here once; you will be here again.

ANTELOPE

In the head of a child, the ice holds.
The snow sifts for hours toward the earthline,

a graylight ground with stars. I would have come
without thought to this place, where the present

extends forever into ice, and the seasons, bright-in-
dark, fall on the crystal threshold, a hard frost

driven deep into the lake stretching over the surface
clouds. Sense, memory, the herd arriving in dusk,

ears pricked, without need or recognition, keeping
their openness alive. What were our hopes

when we first heard that it broke—a sound of dust
in the white expanse, their bodies ghosted

where our minds would have them stall.
And nothing came to interrupt injury,

the fir trees motionless under hours of snow,
a silence clean of every concept. They came

because they believed they would be held,
as in each moment there is no hint of future pain.

First visible animal of the dusk, sleek shape
full of omissions, you are allowed to pass.

All day the snow fell. Around the lake, the air
filled with moths, light as pencil outlines.

Note to "Antelope": *Eighty-five antelope fell through thin ice and
drowned on January 9, 2004, while moving south across Fort Peck Lake
in Valley County, Montana. Antelope have been making the crossing for
hundreds of years.*

⤳

Joanna Klink is the author of two books of poems, They Are Sleeping
(University of Georgia Press, 2000) and Circadian *(Penguin, forthcoming in
2007). She teaches in the graduate creative writing program at the University
of Montana–Missoula.*

Madeline DeFrees

CLIMBING THE SKY BRIDGE STAIR
ON MY WAY TO SUZZALO LIBRARY

           I pause on the landing to admire
the *Dancer with the Flat Hat* by Sculptor
Philip Levine. The cast bronze figure enacts his
favorite theme—the ambiguity of
balance—including his own. Work with cement and
metal is brutal. Witness two artificial
knees, a back subjected to the knife and uncounted
injuries to the hands. I tip my head
back to look up at

           the six-and-one-half-foot
figure, feel positional vertigo
return, and grip the railing to keep from
falling at the Dancer's feet. Given the weight of
the artist's materials, the incredible
feeling of lightness
means a triumph of art over matter. How better
to salvage one's grief
as body slowly turns

           stone, already tied to
a drowning spirit, than by putting a flat
hat on one's sorrow, making
the soul and its body dance in ambiguous balance?

THE POETRY OF SPIDERS

Who knows if they sing in their webs? McPherson asks.
Unlike Little Miss Muffet, who bolted
in fright, she links spiders to music in spite of
Frost's design. *A dimpled spider, fat and white,*
sounds cute enough until we spot the *moth...dead wings*
carried like a paper kite. In Gallagher's poem,
beginning to say No *is to wear a tarantula in your*

buttonhole/yet smile invitingly. Most spiders don't
devour their mates, we tell ourselves,
and screw our courage to the sticking point, less
confident when we confront the Black Widow
whose red hourglass calls up Lowell's *spiders...*
Swimming from tree to tree that mildewed day...Where
gnarled November makes them *fly.*

                    If we could learn to
harvest spider silk, we'd breed mini-machines for
silk production and bleed Whitman's
noiseless patient spider. But that's been tried and
failed. A better way to go: join Wrigley's
walk along the forest path and read the signs: *tatters*
of...webs, wind-swung,/making his dark shirt and jeans

an odd diaphanous tweed. Spiders hide in layers of myth
as complicated as their webs: Arachne's suicide,
Meleager's murder. In his story we learn
that amber comes from birds' tears. Should McPherson be
onto something, who knows if a spider,
trapped in fossil resin, may sing from that ornamental
prison to create a bird-and-spider duet?

IN THE HELLGATE WIND

January ice drifts downriver
thirty years below the dizzy bridge. Careening traffic
past my narrow walk
tells me warm news of disaster. Sun lies
low, can't thaw my lips. I know
a handsbreadth farther down could freeze me solid
or dissolve me beyond reassembling.
Experts jostle my elbow.
They call my name.
My sleeves wear out from too much heart.

When I went back to pick up my life
the habit fit strangely. My hair escaped.
The Frigidaire worked hard while I slept my night
before the cold trip home.
Roots of that passage go deeper than a razor
can reach. Dead lights
in the station end access by rail.
I could stand still to fail the danger,
freeze a slash at a time, altitude for anesthetic.
Could follow my feet in the Hellgate wind
wherever the dance invites them.

The pure leap I cannot take stiffens downstream,
a millrace churned to murder.
The siren cries
at my wrist, flicks my throat, routine
as the river I cross over.

Your strategies were natural and sure.
Light from a used sun flooded the street
where I stood, half woman, half nun, exposed.

THE SHELL

My sealed house winters in its triple shell —
storm-windowed, weather-
stripped, and double-locked. I knock
icicles from the low eaves and watch the cold
come back cold
air condensing under doors. Sculptured carpet
snow below the cocomat. Once
I wanted that
blood too thick and hot
for comfort, all breath closer
than my own. Ice
forms again on the lintel, hardens
against the screen.

                    In your light
sleep I pull back the drapes,
let the cold
light down, leave the flue open. Animal signs
of a long siege. Later
the barometer falls. Wind
hollows a track through the chimney. Casings
crack as they swell. The house
settles into the frozen ground.

Madeline DeFrees's eighth poetry collection, Spectral Waves, *was released by Copper Canyon Press in June 2006.* Blue Dusk: New and Selected Poems, 1951–2001 *(Copper Canyon Press, 2001) won the Lenore Marshall Poetry Prize from The Academy of American Poets/The Nation as well as a Washington State Book Award. She lives in Seattle and teaches in the low-residency M.F.A. program in writing at Pacific University in Forest Grove, Oregon. DeFrees taught at the University of Montana–Missoula from 1967 to 1979 and at the University of Massachusetts–Amherst from 1979 to 1985.*

❦ *Patricia Henley*

THE SECRET OF CARTWHEELS

T HE WINESAP TREES ALONG THE ROAD were skeletal in the early evening light. I stared out the school bus window and cupped like a baby chick the news I looked forward to telling Mother: I'd decided on my confirmation name.

"What's nine times seven?" Jan Mary said.

"Sixty-three," I said. *Joan.* That was Mother's confirmation name, and I wanted it to be mine as well. She'd told me it was a name of strength, a name to carry you into battle.

"I tore my cords," Christopher said. He stood in the aisle, bracing himself with one hand on the chrome pole beside the driver, who wore a baseball cap and a big plaid mackinaw.

The bus driver sang, "Don't sit under the apple tree with anyone else but me." I knew we were nearing our stop, the end of the route, whenever the driver sang this song. We were the last ones on the bus. Although the heater was chuffing hard, frost in the shape of flames curled along the edges of the windows.

"Sweet dreams," the driver said, as we plodded down the slippery steps of the school bus.

Aunt Opal's pale green Cadillac was parked at an odd angle near the woodshed. I knew something was wrong—she never drove out from Wenatchee to visit in the winter. I remembered what our mother had told me the night before. Before bedtime we all lined up to kiss her good night, and when my turn came, she'd said, "There are signs in life. Signs that tell you what you have to do." Her voice had frightened me. I didn't want to hear what she had to say.

Jan Mary said, "Who's that?" Her knit gloves were soggy, her knees chapped above slipping down socks.

"Aunt Opal," Christopher said. His voice was dead and I knew he knew and understood.

Our breath came in blue blossoms in the cold, cutting air, and a light went on in the living room. I didn't want to go in, but I kept trudging through the snow.

Inside, everything was in its place, but our mother was gone, which made the house seem cold and empty. Four-year-old Suzanne stood on the heat register, her grubby chenille blanket a cape around her shoulders. Her hair had been recently brushed, and she wore plastic barrettes, a duck on one side, a bow on the other. When I remember those years at home, this is one of the things I focus on, how nothing ever matched, not sheets, not barrettes, not cups and saucers, not socks. And sometimes I think the sad and petty effort to have matching things has been one of the chief concerns of my adult life. Aunt Opal perched uneasily on a ladder-back chair with the baby, Laura Jean, on her lap. Laura Jean, eyes roving, held her own bottle of milk, and when she saw me, her look latched on to me and she stopped sucking and squirmed and kicked. Her plastic bottle clunked onto the floor. Aunt Opal's white wool pantsuit stretched tightly across her fat thighs. Her teased hair stood hard and swirled. Ill-at-ease, she shifted her weight gingerly as though she might get dirty. I thought I saw pity in her eyes, and I looked away. Christopher and Jan Mary hung back by the kitchen door, Christopher banging his metal lunch box softly against his leg.

"Where's our mother?" I said, scooping Laura Jean away from Aunt Opal.

"Now I hate to have to be the bearer of bad tidings," she began. "I know this will be hard on you children. I don't know what your mother was thinking of." She got up and stalked over to Suzanne, her spike heels dragging on the linoleum.

"Just tell me where she is." The baby stiffened in my arms. This was the first time I'd ever issued a command to a grownup, and I felt both powerful and worried. Without our mother there, I was suddenly older.

Aunt Opal took a few seconds to adjust one of Suzanne's barrettes. "At the VA hospital," she said. "She's sick. Surely you must have known? She needs a rest. She's gone away and left you."

Christopher and Jan Mary went meek as old dogs into the living room and turned on the television. I snugged the baby into her high chair, wrapped a receiving blanket around her bare legs, and began peeling potatoes for supper. Suzanne sat in her miniature rocker, holding a Dr. Seuss book upside down and mouthing the words she knew by heart. I remember thinking if we could just have an ordinary supper, do our homework, fold the laundry, say our prayers, then it would be all right with mother away. We might feel as though she'd just gone through the orchard to visit a neighbor, and that she might return at any moment.

"You'll have places to go, of course," Aunt Opal said, lighting the gas under the stale morning coffee. The sulphurous smell of the match lingered.

"Places?"

"Christopher can stay with Grandma and Grandpa. Janice will take the baby."

"We'll stay here together," I said.

"Roxanne," she said, pouring coffee into a flowered teacup. "You can't stay here alone with all these children."

I remember feeling small and powerless then, and I saw that I still needed to be taken care of—in fact, wanted to be taken care of—but I did not think I would be. I had no trust in anyone, and when you are a child feeling this way, every day becomes a swim through white water with no life jacket. Many years went by before I allowed myself to wonder where my father was during this time.

"How long will we be gone?" I said.

"It's hard to say," Aunt Opal said, sighing. "It's really hard to say."

I was thirteen, Christopher twelve, and Jan Mary eight. We went to St. Martin's and rode the public school bus home, aware of our oddity—Christopher's salt-and-pepper cords instead of jeans, the scratchy scapulars against our chests, the memorization of saints' names and days and deeds. The week before our mother went away, I had stayed home from school twice, missing play auditions and report card day. She had written excuses on foolscap: *Please excuse Roxanne from school yesterday. I needed her at home.*

Our father worked in another state. The house was isolated, out in the country; our nearest neighbor lived a mile away. During the summer I loved where we lived—the ocean of apple blooms, the muted voices of the Spanish-speaking orchard workers, the wild berries, like deep black fleece along the railroad tracks. Winters were another story. We heated with wood, and the fine wood ash smudged our schoolbooks, our clothes and linens, our wrists and necks. The well was running dry, and we children shared our bathwater. By my turn the water was tepid and gray. Our mother fed the fire, waking sometimes twice in the night to keep it going, and her hands and fingers were cracked, swollen. I wanted to cry whenever I looked at them. The loneliness was like a bad smell in the house.

In the evening while the others, the younger ones, watched "I Love Lucy," she sipped Jack Daniel's from a jelly glass and told me her secrets, plucking me from childhood's shore. Very late, when the others had gone to bed, she'd curse our father in a whisper. One night, when she had filled that jelly glass for the third time, and wanted company, she told me about her true love, a woman she'd known in the WACS during the war when they worked together in the motor pool in Dayton, Ohio. You can learn too much too soon about your mother's past. The weight of her concerns made me turn from her and wish that something would save us from the life we shared with her. I couldn't make the wish while watching her split and bleeding hands light a cigarette. But later, lying confused and rigid in the double bed I shared with cuddling Jan Mary and Suzanne, I wished that our mother would go away.

ALL OF THE MOVING TOOK place at night. Aunt Opal drove Suzanne, Jan Mary, and me up the Entiat River to Entiat Home, a place local people called the orphans' home, but in truth the children there were not orphans but children whose parents could not care for them. The frozen river glittered in the moonlight. The fir trees rode in dark procession along the far bank. I sat in the front seat, a privilege of the oldest. The car was vast and luxurious and foreign. Most of the way, no one spoke.

Finally, from the cavernous backseat, Suzanne said, "Where's the baby?"

Don't ask, I thought, don't ask. I tried to send this silent message to Suzanne, but she didn't get it. Blood beat in my head.

"Laura Jean might need us," she said.

"Laura will be fine. Fine, fine," Aunt Opal said. "She's with your cousin Janice, who has another baby for her to play with."

Her jolly voice made me feel as though someone was hugging me too hard, painfully. When we'd left Christopher at Grandma and Grandpa Swanson's I'd felt sick to my stomach, not because I would be separated from him—no—but because I wanted to stay there too. I wanted to cling to Grandma Swanson and say, Take me, keep me. But I was the oldest. I didn't cling and cry.

I would miss Christopher. We had fallen into the habit of sitting in the unfinished knotty-pine pantry, after our baths and the dishes were done, listening to the high-school basketball games on the staticky radio. We knew the players' names and numbers. Together we had anticipated the mystery of going to high school.

Aunt Opal turned slowly into the uphill drive, which was lined with billows of snow. The dark was my comfort—I didn't want to see everything at once. We parked in front of a red brick house with two wrought iron lamps beside the neatly shoveled steps. Silence leaped at us when Aunt Opal shut off the engine. The place seemed a last outpost before the black and convoluted mountains, the Cascades, which, I imagined, went slanted and ragged to the sea. Then quickly, nimbly, a man and woman came coatless down the steps and opened the car doors, greeting us as though we were their own children returning home. The woman was thin and wore pearls and a skirt and sweater. The man had hair as black as an eggplant. Their voices were cheerful, but they kept their hands to themselves, as though they knew we would not want to be touched by strangers.

One moment we were in the dark, the car, the winter mountain air; the next, all three of us were ushered into the blinding white room, which was like a hospital room, with white metal cupboards, white metal cots, and everything amazingly clean and shiny under the fluorescent lights, cleaner even than Grandma Swanson's house.

We sat on the edge of one cot without speaking to one another. Snow dripped in dirty puddles from our saddle oxfords. The floor was black and white like a checkerboard. In the hallway, out of sight, Aunt Opal spoke with the man and woman—"Well behaved," I heard her say—and then she departed with all the speed and indifference of a UPS driver. Through a tall window in the room I watched her headlights sweep across the cinnamon bark of a ponderosa pine. From someplace faraway in the house came Christmas carols, wreathed in pure recorded voices. My body played tricks on me; my head hurt; my stomach knotted in an acid snarl.

Suzanne growled in a baby way she had when she was tired or angry. I pulled her onto my lap and she sucked her thumb. Consoling her was my only source of reassurance.

Jan Mary stamped the dirty puddles with the toe of her shoe. "How will we get to school?" she said.

"We'll go to a different school."

"I don't want to."

"We don't always get to do what we want," I said, shocked at the way I parroted our mother.

The woman in the pearls came into the bright room and leaned over us, one arm around Jan Mary's back.

"I'm Mrs. Thompson," she said. Her words were stout with kindness, which seemed a warning to me, as though she could hurt me, and she smelled good, like flowery cologne. She's someone's perfect mother, I thought.

"You'll need baths before bedtime, girls," she said. She strode to the oak door across the room and opened it, then switched on the bathroom light. "You have your own pajamas?"

"Yes," I said, nodding in the direction of the cardboard *Cream of Wheat* carton, which held my clothes. Each of us had packed a carton with our best things.

"You can help your sisters bathe, Roxanne," she said. "Then I'll check your heads for lice."

"Our mother wouldn't allow that," I said.

"What did you say?"

"Our mother wouldn't allow us to have lice," I said. My voice seemed inordinately loud.

"It's just our policy," she said. "Now get moving. It's late."

We bedded down the first night in that same room, on the single cots made up with coarse cotton sheets and cream-colored wool blankets with a navy stripe around the edge. The light from the hallway bridged the high transom of the closed door, and I didn't sleep for a long time. Our presence there rebuked our mother, and I felt that humiliation as keenly as though I were she. I kept thinking, We'll be better when we go home—we'll work harder, knock down the cobwebs more often, check Jan Mary's homework, throw out the mismatched socks. Keeping domestic order was, inexplicably, bound up with being good, blessed. The fantasies that lulled me to sleep were of cupboards packed with thick folded towels, full cookie jars, an orderly abundance like perpetual fire against the night.

The next morning I lay there, warm but wet, with the covers up to my neck. Suzanne and Jan Mary were still asleep. A cat meowed urgently in the hallway. The windows were long and divided into panes of wavery old glass. Outside it was snowing; the dry, fine net of winter. There was an old cottonwood tree in the yard that had been struck by lightning some time ago. The split in the main trunk had been girdled with an iron band; it had healed, and now the scar tissue bloomed over the edge of the metal ring. I wondered what time it was and what would happen next. The procedure of moving, being dropped off like a litter of kittens, had been bad enough, and now I had to admit I'd wet the bed. I dreaded telling someone, but wanted to get it over with.

I thought of Mary in *The Secret Garden* and the way her spite protected her. I remembered the places I'd read the book: on the school steps at recess in second grade, under the cooling arms of a juniper tree when I was eleven. My own spite and anger could not protect me. They were repulsive thoughts I couldn't bear to admit to myself, because then I'd have to admit them to the priest. I'd told him once that I'd wished our mother would go away. I'd wished it for my birthday, which seemed to magnify the sin. He did not understand the power of wishes, and for penance he gave me a mere five Hail Marys. And now our mother *was* gone and I tried to imagine her inside the VA Hospital, but I could only picture the rusted iron bars, the flaking pink stucco walls. It was down by the Columbia River. The summer I was ten, a male patient people called *a crazy* had deliberately walked into the river and drowned.

The door opened, Mrs. Thompson peeked in, and Jan Mary and Suzanne sat up in their cots, their choppy hair all askew, eyes puffy with sleep.

"Time to get up, ladies," Mrs. Thompson said. She wore a robe of some soft peach fabric.

"Snow," Suzanne announced.

I threw back the covers, and the cool air sliced through my wet pajamas and chilled me. I forced myself to slither across the floor.

"Mrs. Thompson," I said officiously, as though I spoke of someone else, "I've wet the bed."

"Oh?"

"What shall I do?"

She stepped into the room and closed the door. "Does this happen often?" She walked to my cot, with me close behind.

"Roxie wet the bed, Roxie wet the bed," Jan Mary sang.

I flung her a murderous glare, which silenced her at once.

"Sometimes," I said vaguely. By this time I had no feelings in the matter. I'd killed them, the way you track down a mud dauber and squash him.

Mrs. Thompson quickly jerked the sheets from the bed and carried them into the bathroom, holding them at arm's length from her peachy robe.

"Please," I said. "Let me."

She dumped the sheets in the tub. "Run cold water on them. Add your pajamas. Rinse them good. Ask your sister to help you wring them out and then hang them over this shower curtain. When they dry, we'll put them in the dirty laundry." I felt I'd depleted whatever good will there'd been between us.

The entire six months at Entiat I followed this routine. I managed to keep from wetting the bed four times in that six months, by what miracle I could not tell. I tried prayers and wishes, not drinking after six in the evening. Nothing worked. I lived in the Little Girls' House, though my age was borderline—they could have assigned me to the Big Girls' House. And every day all the little girls knew what I'd done when they saw my slick and gelid sheets hanging like Halloween ghosts in the bathroom.

Mrs. Hayes, the dorm mother of the Little Girls' House, had two immense tomcats, Springer and Beau, whose claws had been removed. They lived like kings, always indoors. Everyone called the dorm mother Gabby Hayes behind her back. She was in her fifties and smelled of gardenias and cigarette smoke. Her lipstick was thick and cakey, the color of clay flower pots. She prided herself on her hair—it was coppery and resembled scrubbing pads we used in the kitchen. If someone broke the rules, she would announce to the group at large, "That's not allowed here." The chill in her voice always arrested the deviant.

Life in the Little Girls' House was orderly, neat, regulated. Before school in the morning we did our chores, young ones polishing the wooden stairs, older ones carting the laundry in duffle bags to the laundry building. Some were assigned kitchen duty, others bathrooms. Everyone, down to the four-year-olds, had work to do. I was impressed with the efficiency and equanimity with which work was accomplished. I wrote letters to our mother, in my experimental loopy left-hand slant, suggesting job charts on the refrigerator, new systems we could invent to relieve her of her crushing burden.

There were twenty-three of us. Jan Mary and Suzanne naturally gravitated toward others their age. They slept away from the oldest girls, in a drafty long hall near Mrs. Hayes's apartment. Our family ties were frayed, and I was genuinely surprised when I met Jan Mary's musing blue eyes in recognition across the dinner table. She seemed to be saying, How in the world did we arrive here?

The first day at the new school I was issued a faded blue cotton bloomer for PE. At St. Martin's, PE had meant softball on the playground. At the new school the locker room was my personal hell: the body smells, the safety-pinned bras, the stained slips, the hickeys, the pubic hair growing wild down our thighs. Sister Michael had always told us not to look at ourselves when we bathed, to be ashamed and vigilant. In the locker room we girls were elbow to elbow in the narrow aisle beside the dented pink lockers.

"What is your *prob*lem?"

"The F word. That's all he knows these days."

"My mother won't let me."

"Bud's getting a car for his birthday."

Their conversations shimmered around me like a beaded curtain. We couldn't help but see one another—our new breasts, our worn underwear—but the talk kept us on another plane, a place above the locker room, where we could pretend we weren't totally vulnerable, absolutely displayed.

Georgia Cowley, a squat freckled woman, ruled that class with a cruel hand. When I entered the gym for the first time, she waved sharply in my direction and I went over to her.

"Name?"

"Roxanne Miller."

"We're tumbling, Roxanne Miller," she said, writing something on her clipboard. "You ever tumbled?"

"No, ma'am." I looked at the girls casually turning cartwheels, blue blurs, on the hardwood floor. My hope of fading into the wrestling mats for the hour fluttered like a candle in a storm.

"Come out here with me," she said.

I followed her to the sweaty red mat in front of the stage.

"We start with forward rolls. Squat down."

I squatted, glancing desperately around to see if there was someone I could imitate. All motion had wound down, and the girls were gathered in gossip knots, chattering and watching me with slitted eyes. I remember staring at Miss Cowley's gym shoes; there were dried tomato seeds on the toes.

"Tuck your head. Now one foot forward, hands on the mat."

She gave me a little shove to propel me forward. I fell sideways, my pale thigh plopping fishlike on the floor. The girls giggled and hot tears swelled in my head. The seconds on the floor expanded, seemed to go on forever.

"Get up," she said. "Sit over there on the bleachers for a while and watch. You'll get the hang of it." Then she blew her chrome whistle, and the girls lined up to do their forward rolls.

On the bleachers, a Negro girl from Entiat, Nadine, slid next to me, sighing hard. "Got the curse," she said. "I'm sitting out."

"You can sit out?"

"Sure 'nough." She scratched her skinny calf. "You know the secret of cartwheels, Roxanne?"

"No," I said, interested, thinking there might be some secret I could learn from her, some intellectual knowledge that I could translate into body knowledge.

"Catch yourself before you kill yourself," she whispered, as she retied her sneaker. "Catch yo-*self*." And then she leaped up and turned a few, flinging herself into them with her own peculiar flick of her pink palms above her nappy head.

"Jefferson," Cowley barked. "Sit down and keep quiet."

For the rest of gym period, Nadine and I wrote messages on each other's backs, using our index fingers like pencils through the scratchy blue bloomer blouses.

AT CHRISTMAS WE WERE FARMED OUT. I do not know how these decisions were made. Certainly I don't remember being asked where I would like to go for Christmas. Suzanne went with Mr. and Mrs. Thompson. Jan Mary was taken by Aunt Opal. I went to stay with the family of Darla Reamer, who had been our neighbor for five years. Darla was two years older than I was. When I'd been in fifth grade and Darla in seventh, we rode the school bus together and wrote love notes to one another using a special language we'd developed, a lispish baby talk in writing. Later that year she chose another girl as her best friend and left me miserable. Going to spend Christmas with her and her family, enduring their charity, was like an arduous school assignment I had to survive to attain the next grade. Her mother gave me a Shetland sweater and a jar of Pacquins hand cream. Her father took me out in the wind-crusted snowy field to see his apiary. We went to church, and those brief moments kneeling in the oak pew and at the altar, with its starlike poinsettias, were the only familiarity and peace I experienced. Darla spent many hours on the telephone with Julia, the one who'd taken my place. I was relieved when Mr. Reamer drove me back to Entiat on Christmas night. Many girls were still away and Mrs. Hayes let me stay up late. I drank hot chocolate alone in the dining room and wrote our mother a letter of false cheer and fantasy about the future.

IN THE OLDER GIRLS' SLEEPING QUARTERS, after lights out, under cover of dark, some girls took turns revealing fears, shames, wishes expressed as truth. When this talk began, their voices shifted from the usual shrill razzmatazz repartee about hairstyles, boys at school, and who'd been caught smoking. They spoke in church whispers.

"My mother tore my lip once. I have five stitches."

"My father's coming to get me on my birthday."

I didn't participate in this round-robin, but instead lay on my stomach, my pillow buckled under my chest, and watched the occasional gossamer thread of headlights on the river road. It seemed there was so much freedom and purpose—a will at work—in night travel. Their talk was sad and low, and I, in my isolation, dreamed of going away, of having the power, the inestimable power, to say *I'm leaving.* Boys could somehow run away and make it, survive. But everyone knew that a girl's life was over if she ran away from home, or whatever had become home, whatever sheltered her from ruin.

Some nights, if we heard the rush of Mrs. Hayes's shower, we would sing in our thin voices a maudlin song that was popular at the time—"Teen Angel." One night the community of singing gave me courage, and after the song faded, I said, "I saw my mother hit my father with a belt."

As one they sucked in their breath. Then Nadine said, "No *wonder* your mama in the hospital, girl."

And the others laughed, a false, tentative snicker. I hated Nadine at that moment and felt heartbroken in my hate. I'd always tried to be nice to her, because our mother had said they were just like everyone else inside.

On Valentine's Day, we received a crumpled package wrapped in a brown grocery sack and tied with butcher twine. Inside was a cellophane bag of hard candy hearts stamped BE MINE and I LOVE YOU. Our mother had enclosed three penny valentines and on mine she wrote, "I'm home now with Laura Jean and Christopher. See you soon." She was home! I'd given up on mail from her, but I'd kept writing. I tried to imagine her there with Christopher and the baby, without me to help her, and the thought made me feel invisible, unnecessary in the world. Don't think about it, I said to myself, and I began then the habit of blocking my thoughts with that simple chant. *Don't think about it.*

IN APRIL WE WERE ALLOWED to go home for a weekend.

"Your neighbor's here," Mrs. Hayes whispered in my ear, early that Saturday morning. "Help your sisters dress. I'll give him a tour while he's waiting."

I had a great deal to be excited about: seeing Christopher, going to our old church, being with our mother. Our mother. Her life without me was a puzzle, with crucial pieces missing. I had high hopes about going home. Our mother was well; everyone—Mrs. Hayes, Mr. Reamer—said so.

We met him by his pickup truck. His khakis were spattered with pastel paint; he said he'd been painting his bee boxes. We fell into silence on the drive home. The thought surfaced, like the devil's tempting forefinger, that though we were only an hour's drive from our mother, we hadn't seen her since that morning in December when we went to school not knowing life would be irrevocably changed by the time we returned home. Did she know that morning that she wouldn't see us for four months?

Spring was alive down in the valley. The daffodil leaves were up along the driveway, though the flowers were still just pale shadows of memory, curled tightly and green. Mr. Reamer parked his pickup truck and sat hunched, arms folded across the steering wheel, waiting for us to get out.

We were all shy, bashful, and I hung back, urging Jan Mary and Suzanne forward with little pushes on their shoulder blades.

Jan Mary flinched and said meanly, "Don't push."

"Don't spoil it now," I said.

And we three walked forward in a solemn row down the gravel drive toward the house. We wore our next-best dresses. Mine was a taffeta plaid with a smocked bodice and a sash, and I'd worn my cream-colored knee highs, saving my one pair of nylons for Sunday morning. I hadn't wanted to go home in nylons—they were a new addition to my sock drawer and I was afraid our mother would say I was growing up too fast. The house looked the same, sagging at the roof comers, the gray paint blistering along the bottom of the door. It was a sunny day. Darla Reamer's cocker spaniel came yapping out the drive, flipping and bouncing the way cockers do. As we drew near the house, I saw that Darla was sitting with our mother in that small patch of grass in front of the house. Someone had put a wooden cable spool there for a table, and Darla and Mother sat near each other in lawn chairs. Darla was painting Mother's fingernails.

"Here come my girls," Mother said, waving her free hand.

Music was on inside the house and we could hear it through the open window: *you made me love you.* I didn't know what to do with Darla there. I'd imagined our mother embracing us, welcoming us, with significance. My heart shrank in disappointment, a rancid feeling, everything going sour at once. Suzanne, being only four, went right up to our mother and slipped her little arms around her neck and kissed her cheek. Jan Mary said, "Will you do mine, too, Darla?"

Laura Jean started crying from somewhere in the house. Mother, startled, rose partway from her chair and then sank back, waving her wet fingernails and looking helplessly at Darla. There was a raw, clean smell about the yard, like corn silk when you go outside to shuck corn in the summer dusk. Darla looked older, in a straight linen skirt with a kick pleat in the back. She had on slim flats and tan-tinted nylons. Her hair was in a French roll.

"I'll get her," Darla said, and she went in the house, letting the screen door slam. Suzanne was close on her heels.

Mother pulled me near, her arm around my waist. "How's my big girl?" she asked. She'd had her black hair frizzed in a permanent wave and her nails were painted fire-engine red. With one hand she shook a Lucky from the pack on the table. A glass of whiskey and melting ice was on the ground beside her chair. Her knuckles looked pink, but the cuts and splits were healed.

"Fine," I said.

"Darla's been helping me," she said.

I held my breath to keep from crying.

I felt exhausted, not the clean exhaustion of after-dark softball but a kind of weariness; I was worn out with the knowledge that life would be different, but not in the way I had imagined or hoped. I didn't want to forgive her for being the way she was, but you have to forgive your mother. She searched my eyes and tried to make some long-ago connection, sweet scrutiny, perhaps the way she'd looked at me when I was a new baby, her first baby. I looked away. Jan Mary gnawed delicately at her cuticles. Christopher came around the corner of the house swinging his Mickey Mantle bat, his leather mitt looped on his belt. The new spring leaves were so bright they hurt my eyes.

Patricia Henley's first novel, Hummingbird House *(MacAdam/Cage Publishing, 2000), was a finalist for the 1999 National Book Award and the New Yorker Fiction Prize (2000). Her second novel,* In the River Sweet *(Pantheon, 2002), was named a best fall book by the* St. Louis Dispatch, *the* Chicago Tribune, *and the* Seattle Post-Intelligencer. *She has also published three collections of stories (*Friday Night at Silver Star, The Secret of Cartwheels, *and* Worship of the Common Heart*). Friday Night at Silver Star won the 1985 Montana Arts Council First Book Award. Patricia teaches in the M.F.A program at Purdue University.*

✻ Mary MacLane

From *The Story of Mary MacLane by Herself*
FEBRUARY 3, [1901]

T HE TOWN OF BUTTE presents a wonderful field to a student of
humanity and human nature.
There are not a great many people—seventy thousand perhaps—
but those seventy thousand are in their way unparalleled. For mixture, for
miscellany—variedness, Bohemianism—where is Butte's rival?

The population is not only of all nationalities and stations, but the
nationalities and stations mix and mingle promiscuously with each other,
and are partly concealed and partly revealed in the mazes of a veneer that
belongs neither to nation nor to station, but to Butte.

The nationalities are many, it is true, but Irish and Cornish predominate.
My acquaintance extends widely among the inhabitants of Butte. Sometimes
when I feel in the mood for it I spend an afternoon in visiting about among
divers curious people.

At some Fourth of July demonstration, or on a Miners' Union day, the
heterogeneous herd turns out—and I turn out, with the herd and of it,
and meditate and look on. There are Irishmen—Kelleys, Caseys, Calahans,
staggering under the weight of much whiskey, shouting out their green-
isle maxims; there is the festive Cornishman, ogling and leering, greeting
his fellow countrymen with alcoholic heartiness, and gazing after every
feminine creature with lustful eyes; there are Irish women swearing
genially at each other in shrill pleasantry, and five or six loudly-vociferous
children for each; there are round-faced Cornish women likewise, each
with her train of children; there are suave, sleek sporting men just out of
the bath-tub; insignificant lawyers, dentists, messengerboys; "plungers"
without number; greasy Italians from Meaderville; greasier French people

from the Boulevarde Addition; ancient miners—each of whom was the first to stake a claim in Butte; starved-looking Chinamen here and there; a contingent of Finns and Swedes and Germans; musty, stuffy old Jew pawn-brokers who have crawled out of their holes for a brief recreation; dirt-encrusted Indians, and squaws in dirty, gay blankets, from their flea-haunted camp below the town; "box-rustlers"—who are as common in Butte as bar-maids in Ireland; swell, flashy-looking Africans; respectable women with white aprons tied around their waists and sailor-hats on their heads, who have left the children at home and stepped out to see what was going on; innumerable stray youngsters from the dark haunts of Dublin Gulch; heavy restaurant-keepers with toothpicks in their mouths; a vast army of dry-goods clerks—the "paper-collared" gentry; miners of every description; representatives from Dog Town, Chicken Flats, Busterville, Butchertown, and Seldom Seen—suburbs of Butte; pale, thin individuals who sing and dance in beer-halls; smart society people in high traps and tallyhos, impossible women—so-called (though in Butte no one is more possible), in vast hats and extremely plaid stockings; persons who take things seriously and play the races for a living; "beer-jerkers"; "biscuit-shooters"; soft-voiced Mexicans and Arabians;—the dregs, the élite, the humbly respectable, the off-scouring—all thrown together, and shaken up, and mixed well.

One may notice many odd bits of irony as one walks among these. One may notice that the Irishmen are singularly carefree and strong and comfortable—and so jolly! while the Irish women are frumpish and careworn and born earthward with children. The Cornishman who has consumed the greatest amount of whiskey is the most agreeable, and less and less inclined to leer and ogle. The Cornish woman whose profanity is the shrillest and most genial and voluble, is she whose life seems the most weighted and down-trodden. The young women whose bodies are encased in the tightest and stiffest corsets are in the most wildly hilarious spirits of all. The filthy little Irish youngsters from Dublin Gulch are much brighter and more clever in every way than the ordinary American children who are less filthy. A delicate aroma of cocktails and whiskey-and-soda hangs over even the four-in-hands and automobiles of the upper crust. Gamblers, newsboys, and Chinamen are the most chivalrously courteous among them. And the modest-looking "plunger" who has drunk the greatest number of high-balls is the most gravely, quietly polite of all. The rolling, rollicking, musical profanity of the "ould sod"—Bantry Bay, Donegal, Tyrone, Tipperary—falls much less limpidly from the cigaretted lips of the ten-year-old lad than from those of his mother, who taught it to him. One may notice that the husband and wife who smile the sweetest at each other in the sight of the multitudes are they whose countenances bear various scars and scratches commemorating late evening orgies at home; that the peculiar solid, block-shaped appearance of some of the miners' wives is due quite as much to the quantity of beer they drink as to their annual maternity—that the one grand ruling passion of some men's lives is curiosity;—that the entire herd is warped, distorted, barren, having lived its life in smoke-cured Butte.

A single street in Butte contains people in nearly every walk of life— living side by side resignedly, if not in peace.

In a row of five or six houses there will be living miners and their families, the children of which prevent life from stagnating in the street while their mothers talk to each other—with the inevitable profanity—over the back-fences. On the corner above there will be a mysterious widow with one child, who has suddenly alighted upon the neighborhood, stealthily in the night, and is to be seen at rare intervals emerging from her door—the target for dozens of pairs of eager eyes and half as many eager tongues. And when the mysterious widow, with her one child, disappears some night as suddenly and as stealthily as she appeared, an outburst of highly-colored rumors is tossed with astonishing glibness over the various back-fences—all relating to the mysterious widow's shady antecedents and past history, to those of her child, and to the cause of her sudden departure,—no two of which rumors agree in any particular. Across on the opposite corner there will be a company of strange people who also descended suddenly, and upon whom the eyes of the entire block are turned with absorbing interest. They consist of half-a-dozen men and women seemingly bound together only by ties of conviviality. The house is kept closely-blinded and quiet all day, only to burst forth in a blaze of revel in the evening, which revel lasts all night. This goes on until some momentous night, at the request of certain proper ones, a police officer glides quietly into the midst of a scene of unusual gaiety—and the festive company melts into oblivion, never to return. They also are then discussed with rapturous relish and in tones properly lowered, over the back-fences. Farther down the street there will live an interesting being of feminine persuasion who has had five divorces and is in course of obtaining another. These divorces, the causes therefor, the justice thereof, and the future prospects of the multi-grass widow, are gone over, in all their bearings, by the indefatigable tongues. Every incident in the history of the street is put through a course of sprouts by these same tireless members. The Jewish family that lives in the poorest house in the neighborhood, and that is said to count its money by the hundred thousands; the aristocratic family with the Irish-point curtains in the windows—that lives on the county; the family whose husband and father gains for it a comfortable livelihood—forging checks; the miner's family whose wife and mother wastes its substance in diamonds and sealskin coats and other riotous living; the family in extremely straitened circumstances into which new babies arrive in great and distressing numbers; the strange lady with an apoplectic complexion and a wonderfully foul and violent flow of invective—all are discussed over and over and over again. No one is omitted.

And so this is Butte, the promiscuous—the Bohemian. And all these are the Devil's playthings. They amuse him, doubtless

Butte is a place of sand and barrenness.

The souls of these people are dumb.

Unorthodox, fiery, feminist, and openly bisexual, Mary MacLane was a controversial writer whose shocking books were bestsellers. Born in 1881 in Winnipeg, Manitoba, MacLane moved to Butte when she was ten years old. She published her first book, The Story of Mary MacLane *(reissued by Riverbend Books, 2002), which sold 100,000 copies in 1902. MacLane used the money to move from Butte to Greenwich Village, where she continued to write. She wrote two other books,* My Friend, Annabel Lee *(1903) and* I, Mary MacLane: A Diary of Human Days *(1917), and an autobiographical silent film entitled* Men Who Have Made Love to Me. *MacLane died in Chicago in 1929, and her work remained out of print until 1993, when* The Story of Mary MacLane *was republished in an anthology entitled* Tender Darkness.

✤ *Frances Kuffel*

FIRST LOVE

J ULIE IRONBITER WAS THE NEIGHBORHOOD waif. What evangelical offshoot her parents belonged to, I don't know, but between it and their business they had no expectations of Julie or her older brother, Cal. Cal was fourteen and had his own friends, but Julie was a loner, preferring the fields and alleys of our Montana lumber town to the loneliness of home. She lived a few doors down from us, in a big Victorian sunk in overgrown cottonwoods, its first floor given over to chiropractic offices. Julie was like a house cat gone wild, peering in windows but never joining the circles of light.

Until my brother lured her with the promise of television.

It was spring—mid-May. Tommy had been playing baseball down by the river and noticed Julie wandering along the railroad tracks. He swept her up as he and his friends headed home.

"Heck, Lizzie," he said later. "It was getting dark and it's scary down there. It was no big deal."

So maybe it was just a confluence of circumstances—the sky fading to the mildness of Necco Wafers, the big boy who casually assumed she'd come along with him and approached her frankly, happily, one time only, kid, no problem.

Or maybe she'd been watching *him*.

At any rate, by the time he shepherded her up the back steps he could tell us she was a good speller, had never been swimming, liked chocolate ice cream and believed that the world was going to end, in thirty-three days at 2:37 in the afternoon.

Her parents were at a church meeting and wouldn't be home until late so my mother pressed her to stay for supper. And Tommy had told her about *Star Trek*, which she spoke of wistfully as we washed up.

"Flying around in the sky like that," she mused. "It would be wonderful. It will be like that soon, for the faithful."

I was silent and perplexed. On the one hand, *we* were faithful. We went to confession and Mass every week, attended St. Regis Grade School and gamely ate pancakes with the Knights of Columbus once a month. On the other hand, I had plans for the summer.

"What if you're not?" I asked finally.

She cast her eyes to the light over the bathroom mirror. "The sky will be blotted out and there will be earthquakes. You will live in mountain caves and die of pestilence."

I didn't like this business of "you."

"How do you know who will get to fly around and who will die?"

"We will be wearing white robes." She looked at herself in the mirror as though exchanging some kind of vow and recited, "'There are the men who have passed through the great ordeal; they have washed their robes and made them white in the blood of the Lamb.'" She unscrewed the cap of my mother's face cream and sniffed. "This smells good. We don't have stuff like this at home."

That was the key. People with cold cream and TVs would be falling into smoking fissures, while the people like Julie—messy and friendless—would be lifted up on cloud mattresses to heaven.

WE BECAME THE MOST RELUCTANT OF FRIENDS.

I knew very well I was Tommy's proxy. When Julie learned he brought ice cream home that first night with his own money, she was hopelessly smitten. And she was enchanted with *Star Trek*. Sitting stiffly on the couch next to my mother, Julie Ironbiter began to see the next thirty-three days of her earthly existence as a bittersweet proposition.

While I didn't much like this strange girl, I was grateful for the company. Our neighborhood divided itself by what schools we attended, and no one my age from St. Regis lived nearby. Of course, my friends turned her into the butt of their jokes when they eventually met her, making up a jump-rope song they sang loudly whenever she was slinking around:

I – ron
bi – ter
swing it
tigh – ter
Easy, easy,
over.

And I screamed it loudest of all.

But on the days that I did not see my friends, I allowed Julie to seek me out; we squinted a hostile appraisal of each other before quarreling over what to do.

Television solved the problem, since my mother had taken it upon herself to feed Julie whenever she was with me and her parents were at one of their church meetings, which was pretty much always. TV provided all the fodder we needed for games: space explorers, flying nuns, spies, gun-slingers, and Indians.

Especially Indians. Julie had a lot of practice at padding silently through the fields along the river and considered herself quite a talented Cherokee. She was an insistent teacher. Like the Injuns in *Daniel Boone*, we counted coup whenever we found out something particularly gratifying, and it was as Dan'l and Mingo that we hid in weeds, crawled under barbed wire fences and perched in maple trees to check out what Tommy was up to.

Thus we learned that Tommy was going steady with Mary Helen Wendt and that he had kissed her among the storage boxes in the church basement, and that because of that kiss she had chosen Thomasina as her Confirmation name. We were hunkered in a dry ditch when we overheard this bit of brag-ging and Julie turned to me with eyes gray with solemnity and betrayal.

"In *church*," she breathed indignantly as the boys continued walking on in their rock-kicking way to someplace else.

It looked bad. You didn't have to be Catholic to see how bad it was.

"He must love her," I ventured. "And it was only the basement."

"Sins of the flesh-sh-sh," she hissed.

"He can confess it," I said, but she only looked at me. "We got our coup,"

I said, desperate to turn the subject. "Let's go spy somewhere else."

"Okay, who next?"

I thought a moment. "How about your brother for a change?"

"We have to cross Paxon Street," she said. "Are you allowed?"

Paxon was the main thoroughfare of town, the demarcation line of my freedom, but since I'd become Dan'l Boone in the wild frontier fields along the Bitterroot River, I thought I could risk it.

Julie had told me very little about her brother, Calan, an eighth grader at McKinley School. He was tall for his age, with a faint brown mustache, scraggly dishwater hair and narrow eyes. His face reminded me of a bowie knife, its features converging at his nose. They both had that back-country look you saw at the grocery stores on Saturday or at fair time when ranchers flooded the town. Later I learned that their father had failed at dry-bottom ranching out near Cohagen, and moved the family to Billings while he went off to Minnesota to study chiropractic medicine. They were hard-looking people, their gaze piercing as they sought out the failures in everyone they met.

"Calan'll be over at the Coombs's place," Julie told me as headed south on Paxon. "I've been there a couple of times for church. Billy is 16."

"Who's Billy?"

"Billy *Coombs*," she said impatiently. "He can drive. Cal goes over there after school. They go shoot gophers or ride around. They might not be there."

This startled me. These boys wouldn't go running to my mother if we annoyed them. They'd settle it themselves.

A blue Ford Julie said was Billy's was out front when we got there, and music blasted from the house peeling white paint. A large orange cat threaded its way between garbage cans and regarded us suspiciously. I drew closer to Julie and whispered, "Wanna go home?"

She stepped away from me in disgust. "You wanted to come. We might as well count coup."

Julie made her way along the house, pausing under what I took to be the dining room window and motioning for me to catch up. There was no shrubbery to hide in, just bare cement foundations meeting an unhealthy lawn.

"There's no way they can hear us," Julie said in a nearly conversational voice.

"I thought you weren't allowed to listen to music like that."

She ignored me. "You'll have to stand on me to hear anything," she said and dropped to all fours. "Climb up."

I looked stupidly down at her.

"C'mon, dummy. But take your shoes off."

I slid my sneakers off and stepped gingerly onto her back. "Does it hurt?"

"No, but hold onto the windowsill. That'll help."

I peered inside and found, to my relief, that no one was in the room. There was a lamp hanging from the middle of the ceiling but nothing else. I jumped off Julie and squatted down next to her. "It's empty," I said.

"It's the meeting room, dope. The Coombs's house is our church. What did you *hear*?"

"Nothing. I didn't listen. I thought I was supposed to see something… will they get mad if they catch us?"

"Mingo wouldn't be afraid." Julie rolled onto her knees again. "Get up there and listen."

I climbed up once more, not so gently this time.

"So?"

"They're talking about girls, and what to do Friday night," I said.

Julie watched the cat lick its paw under a lilac bush as she thought. "We'll have to go up on the porch," she decided. "We haven't learned anything yet."

I caught her arm. "Wait a sec," I gabbed frantically. "We caught 'em listening to music they're not supposed to have on, right? That's coup."

She pulled her arm away. "It's not enough. We need more." She started to crabwalk along the side of the porch when a screen door creaked open and voice announced it was time to make a cigarette run. Julie froze.

"What the hell are *you* doin' here, Julie?" the cigarette voice said. "Hey, Iron-butt. Your sister's here." The screen door banged again.

I began backtracking toward the alley, figuring even Dan'l would sometimes abandon a partner, if only so he could break her out later.

I hadn't counted on Mingo's big mouth. I'd just turned the corner onto Willow Street, affecting as jaunty a walk as I could, when the blue Ford pulled up.

"That her, Julie?" a boy's voice asked, and the passenger door swung open. I looked up the street wondering if I could make a break for it, but Julie's voice floated out from the dark interior. "Get in, Lizzie. Billy's givin' us a ride home."

"You girls are really stupid, wandering so far away," the driver, whom I took to be Billy Coombs, said. Julie and I were crammed in the back seat with Cal and another boy who stared at us in unblinking silence.

"Yeah," Cal agreed. "What if a stranger picked you up? Ever think about that? Nobody'd even notice you two."

"We were just playing," Julie said.

"Playing," Cal snorted. "Spying's more like it."

"We were playing scouts," I said brightly. "Like on *Daniel Boone*." The other boy turned his gaze on me. There was no recognition in his flat green eyes. "Like on TV." Julie dug her arm in my side.

"TV, huh?"

"Weren't you guys going for cigarettes?" Julie asked. "Aren't you having some *fun* before the Seventeenth?"

Billy and Cal exchanged looks. I relaxed slightly. We were on familiar ground again: sibling blackmail, and we had more to lob than they did.

"Take the brats home," Cal said to Billy. "Then we'll go to the DQ for ice cream."

Julie thrust her lower lip out, but I nudged her and rolled my eyes. In a time that required supreme faith, I knew ice cream was not a promise to believe in.

TOMMY WAS SITTING AT THE top of the stairs when I came out of the bathroom. I wiped my mouth with the back of my hand, the sour taste of vomit mingling with toothpaste.

"Not feeling so good, Liz? Car ride make you sick?"

So he'd seen us getting out of Billy Coombs's car at the corner. I'd hoped he'd been too busy with his friends to notice.

"It was Julie's brother's friend. It was okay."

Tommy gave a low whistle. "Calan Ironbiter runs around with people who have cars. I guess you want to, too, huh?"

"No," I said wearily. My face felt hot and I badly wanted to climb into bed and go to sleep. "It was horrible. They're horrible boys and hate them. I hate Julie Ironbiter, too."

Tom laughed. "Well, she'll be gone soon."

"You mean the Seventeenth?"

"That or they'll be too embarrassed to show their faces."

"Do you think it'll…you know…*happen*?"

"Naw," he said. "They're just a bunch of Holy Rollers."

"But Julie says a rocket scientist got it out of the Bible. Someone from NASA."

"Oh for Pete's sake, Lizzie. Don't you think the Pope would be in on something like this if it were true? You don't see the Monsignor getting ready to blast off in a couple of weeks, do you? It's like Dad says, their rocket scientist is probably some plumber from Coeur d'Alene."

"I guess," I said doubtfully. Tommy, Dad, the Monsignor and the Pope were too much for me to argue with, but I began to think about putting aside some cans of soup and blankets in the garage out back. Just in case.

TOMMY TOOK IT UPON HIMSELF to patch things up between Julie and me, inviting us separately to come down to the river diamonds the next day. We could fetch balls, he said, and keep the bats in order. Julie spent the first game slavishly picking up equipment while I yawned in boredom.

By 4:30, though, even Julie had had enough.

"Wanna go?" she asked. "We could pick a bunch of flowers. For your mother."

Julie hadn't thought of such a thing before but I knew my mother would be pleased and we spent the next hour sneaking into back yards and along alley fences. My mother was impressed, even though it meant washing ants out of peonies in the middle of getting dinner ready. She shooed us off to wash up for supper.

But instead of heading into the bathroom, Julie stopped and put her finger to her lips. "Let's play in Tom's room."

"It's boring in there."

"No it isn't," she answered, pushing me down the hall. "We can look for clues."

Tommy's room was buried in a drift of school shirts, papers and Boy Scout stuff. I shut the door behind us and crossed my arms. "Clues for what?"

"We won't know until we find them."

As far as I could tell, all we would find out about my brother was that he was doing a geography report on India and had hoarded his Easter candy. But Julie was going through his drawers, carefully lifting things out. She found his class pictures, going all the way back to first grade. Julie pored over them.

"Show me Mary Helen," she demanded and thrust his second grade picture at me.

"Mary Helen didn't live here then. She moved from Butte in fifth grade. Her dad's with Montana Power."

Julie snatched the photo back and flipped ahead three years.

Four rows of fifth graders smiled up at me. Mary Helen Wendt was in the second row. She had light-colored ringlets and dimples. I pointed her out to Julie. She studied the black-and-white picture a minute and then shuffled it back into place.

"I'll be prettier than that," she said, and her voice was hard with determination. "Let's go watch TV. Your mom's making pot roast. It smells good."

ON THE FIRST OF JUNE, the rain set in. We found ourselves indoors after a vernal May, the water table rising through the grass from a hard runoff. Tommy got out Monopoly and began a buying frenzy. He included Julie and me in his obsession, telling her that this was no more gambling than running a business. "It's commerce, you see," he said, sorting out stacks of play money. "Good practice."

I felt my life being usurped. Tom cheered Julie on, giving her advice about when to stay in jail and how to hoard money; I lay on the living room floor hating them both. When Tommy asked a couple of his friends over and my luck didn't change, I put on my galoshes and left. "What's wrong with her?" I heard Mike DiGrazi ask and Julie piped back, "Oh, she just doesn't *get* how to play."

I thought seriously about never going back. I wondered if I could walk all the way to St. Ignatius where the state orphanage was.

I'd meandered half way up the block when a gate clapped loudly behind me. I turned to find Calan Ironbiter standing in front of it, his hands stuffed deep in his ski-jacket pockets, looking as if he couldn't remember what he'd come out for.

"O'Brien, right?" he asked when he noticed me. I nodded cautiously. "Isn't Julie with you? I thought you guys were regular Siamese twins these days."

"She's at my house." My voice sounded hoarse. "She's playing Monopoly with my brother."

He shrugged his shoulders and looked vacantly up the street for the next item of business. There was only a rain-river hurrying in the gutter downhill. "You're not playing with them? Where ya goin'?"

It was my turn to shrug. "No place."

"Me either," he said. "This day is for the dogs, ain't it? For the cats and dogs," he amended and grinned. I smiled too, wanting to stay on his good side without getting too chummy. "My folks are up at St. Lawrence Canyon." He yawned and stretched. His jacket pulled up his T-shirt and I could see a row of black hairs running up from his belly button, like feather stitching. "I'm sick of homework. Why bother? Two weeks to go. Might as well have some fun, right?"

I nodded weakly.

"So you wanna do something? Play with Julie's big brother since she's got yours?"

I racked my brain for excuses. "I...gotta go."

"You said you weren't going anywhere. What's there to do on a day like this? Look at your feet. I mean, you're caked with mud. You wanna come in and see our house? I bet Julie's never had you over, has she?"

I shook my head. I didn't want to go in their house, but Calan was also right: there wasn't anyplace to go. Even the public schoolyard was chained shut.

"Come on," he coaxed. "We'll make sandwiches and I'll show you my dad's offices. It's kinda cool."

I knew this was a bad idea, but what they don't tell kids is what a trance someone older, with an actual idea in his head, can produce. There I was, at loose ends, mad at everyone, too scared to think—of course I went in. Of course I accepted a bulky sandwich of peanut butter and mayonnaise which I was too nervous to decline. We left the dank yellow kitchen and walked down a grim hall to the front office, where orange plastic chairs lines walls covered in an indistinguishable brown paper.

"This is the waiting room," he informed me. "Stay here and I'll be right back."

I sat tentatively in one of the molded chairs. I thought about throwing the sandwich away, but I knew he'd notice, or his parents would, and I didn't want to leave a trace that I'd been there.

After a few minutes, he called out in a high-pitched voice, "The doctor will see you now." I got up and went over to the open door, peering in. Cal was standing in a white coat next to a steel table. At the end of it hung a plastic human skeleton. Cal patted the thin mattress and told me to hop up.

The skeleton clicked as I did so.

"I'm going to manipulate your spine. That means, handle it, like my dad does. You have to take your jacket off.

With the sandwich leaking mayonnaise all over my hand, I didn't know how to proceed. He reached over and pulled the zipper down, took the sandwich and, gallantly, helped me out of my coat. "Now lie on your stomach," he said. The skeleton rattled again as I rolled over.

His hands were strong, and surprisingly warm, on the back of my neck.

THAT WAS TWELVE DAYS BEFORE the end of the world.

I watched myself turn into Julie in those days, furtively looking in on life, humbly grateful when my mother served me dinner.

At 2:30 on Monday afternoon, June Seventeenth, I hunched over my multiplication tables worksheet with one eye alternating between the clock and the windows. The minute hand trudged to 2:37, then 2:38. The only sounds were the chuffing of traffic and Sister Joseph's rosary clacking against desks as she stooped over our work.

By three o'clock, nothing had happened.

At 3:15 we were dismissed into an afternoon scrubbed clean as a plate. I soon caught up with Tommy and his gang. They were jostling each other off the sidewalk into the muddy gutters as Mary Helen Wendt and Stacia Hennessy clutched their books to their chests and kept a safe distance. When Tom saw me coming, he raised his arm and shouted, "Hey, Lizard! We're still alive!" His friends laughed and parted ranks for me to join them.

My brother almost never walked me home. It had happened twice: on the first day of first grade, and on the afternoon I wet my pants during confession. But he was in a mood as expansive as the sky, and he put his arm around my shoulders and rubbed my hair fiercely with his knuckles. "What d'ya think, Lizard? Those old Ironbiters must feel stupid as boiled owls about now."

"Kal Kan Ironbiter and his weird sister Droolie," Mike DiGrazi said. "I hope they have some bed sheets left to sleep in."

I was silent as they railed on, drifting off toward their own houses. Tommy and I walked the last block home alone.

"So say something, Liz. You hate them so much I thought you'd be gloating."

I grimaced. "Who cares about them? They're stupid. They thought they could get away with anything and still go to heaven." I stopped and looked up at Tom. "Maybe they will."

"Get away with what? Just 'cause you're jealous of Julie doesn't make her bad."

"No, but her brother is," I said vehemently, and then backtracked: "And I'm not either jealous. She has a big crush on you, and you don't know what he did, so just shut up."

"Hey." Tom caught my arm and pulled me to a stop. "What did he do? Did he call you names? Did he scare you?"

"No," I said, biting the corner of my mouth to keep from crying. "He… he didn't do anything. Leave me alone."

"What did he do, Liz?"

"*Nothing*," I gulped. "Nothing. Go away."

"He did, too. Tell me."

"No."

"So he *did* do something. Tell me what, Liz, or I'll *make* you."

I didn't answer.

He looked down at me for a long moment. "Did he do something bad to you?"

Bad. In one word we could sum up every sin we'd been taught to avoid. Bad was stealing. Bad was killing. Bad was sex.

I turned my eyes to the sidewalk and said nothing. I didn't have to.

Tommy slammed his books to the cement and swore. "I'll get him," he said.

AND THEN THERE WAS DREAD.

Actually, there were many dreads, like mites loosed on a still afternoon. Would Tommy tell our parents? His friends? Would Calan, older and bigger, kill him? Would he kill me? Somehow the idea that I might have died in the apocalypse wasn't as bad as dying at the hands of the boy who had plunged me into wishing I could die to begin with. I kept a tense vigil for signs that my secret had gotten out. If it did, I told myself, I'd run away. I'd left the survival gear out in the garage. At least it was summer. Maybe I could live in the woods.

But it was like that long afternoon in math class waiting for the end: the days ticked by and nothing happened. The Ironbiter house remained locked and curtained tight, no sign of their car, no garbage left out for collection.

It was the next Monday, the first real day of summer vacation, that my mother called upstairs for me. Julie was at the back door, wanting me to come out and play. My mother must have grown tired of the queer girl's assumption into the family because she didn't try to convince me to come down. Her voice drifted up through my open window; it sounded kind but firm as she told Julie that I was busy inside. I shivered when I heard the back gate clatter shut. Something irreversible was in motion and everyone was in on it, all because of me.

As for Julie, she seemed, Tommy told us, to have taken the failure of the

Second Coming in stride, believing it would come another time, with a readjustment of the NASA scientist's calculations.

Tommy might as well have been playing at TV hero himself, the way he chatted Julie up for information and canvassed his friends' siblings who went to the public high school for gossip about Billy Coombs. From Julie, he learned that Cal was mostly living at Billy Coombs's house now and, she added, that Billy was going to enlist in the Navy as soon as he was old enough. He wanted to go fight in the war. Then, just after the Fourth of July, Billy went off to work the first hay harvest on a big ranch past Arlee. Even Calan Ironbiter had to go home sometimes.

But he'd come home with the expectation of leaving again. Old Man Ironbiter decided it was time to pull up stakes and leave Montana once and for all. Tommy smirked when he told us this. "Julie says they're moving to the South. Boise. She says it's warmer there." He snickered and moved a forkful of green beans through his mashed potatoes. "I told her to take plenty of suntan oil and to be sure to wear a helmet. Those coconuts can really hurt when the fall off the trees."

A U-Haul appeared in their backyard. I watched Calan carrying boxes of stuff out of their house and heaping piles of junk for the trash man to collect.

Tommy was watching too. He'd found his chance.

He and his friends had taken to hanging out in our backyard. They'd gotten out their old bows and arrows and set up a target. "We want to go bow hunting this fall," Mike told my father. "Do you want to come, too?"

While one of them practiced, the others sat on the back fence, trading baseball cards and keeping tabs on what was going on two yards down.

In the still heat of the afternoons, with the windows open and the trees and birds quiet, I would hear everything going on in the yard. I overheard Julie say that their landlord was giving up the lease without any problems. I heard Tommy promise he'd come visit her in a couple of years. I heard the boys' laughter when she left and Tommy kicked the fence so hard the slats reverberated up the side of the yard. "So what? I'm breakin' her heart," he said with an ugly laugh. "Calan broke more than that." Their voices died to their previous steady hush. The kind of steady of plots.

I knew what they were doing and I did nothing to stop it. They all knew what had happened, thanks to Tom, and treated me kindly while looking closely to see if I was marked, as for a sunburn or hair cut. I stayed in my room. My mother didn't know what was going on, satisfied that the boys had a new passion and assuming that I was going through some phase that would soon be over. I badly wanted to believe her, but first I wanted Calan Ironbiter to pay. As I listened to the thwack of arrows hitting the cork target, I imagined the muffled target of flesh, its damage less certain.

IT WAS SUNDAY. The next day I would start Camp Fire Day Camp for two weeks. On the same day, August 1, the Ironbiters were moving to tropical Boise. Calan and Julie were allowed to leave church at noon while the adults stayed on. We got home from Mass at 11:30 and Tommy tore through the kitchen in his rush to change clothes and get outside. I sat at the kitchen table sharing a pull-apart with my father and sipping milk as Tom banged around upstairs. He reappeared as suddenly as he'd fled, standing in the doorway with his baseball bat in his hand.

"C'mon, Liz. You gotta get out of this house for a change. Go put on some shorts and come with me." I chewed the last bit of sticky crust slowly. "Hurry, will ya, Eliz-butt? Daylight's wastin'."

We met up with his friends at the DiGrazi house and circled through the alley into the Ironbiters' backyard of overgrown grass and tumbling, shaggy hedges.

"You keep Lizzie with you," he told Mike, and turned to Ben Szinski. "When they come, jump out and grab Julie. Keep her quiet and keep her out of my way." He scanned the hedges and big elms. "Keep both girls quiet. And remember, this is *my* fight. You're here because we want him to know he can't get away."

Mike DiGrazi took me by the hand and led me off to hide behind a sprawling snowball bush. The others took up similar positions, in the hedges or perched low in the trees. Ben crouched behind the garbage cans, ready to spring out and get Julie.

Calan was preaching at Julie as they came up the alley. "Now remember, we gotta go back to the Coombses at five for supper." He shut the gate behind them. "No disappearing today. You have to help out for once." Julie was about to start arguing when Ben jumped out and clapped one hand around her mouth and the other around her chest. Calan didn't even notice she'd dropped out of step with him as he walked up the sidewalk. "I'm sick of this stupid town," he continued. "I wanna get out of here as fast as possible."

The door of their screened-in porch creaked open and Tommy stood up and thumped his baseball bat against the top step. "The town's sick of you, too, Ironbiter, but we got business to settle before you leave." Tommy's friends, six of them, all with baseball bats, stepped or dropped out of their hiding places. Mike pulled me forward to the center of the yard. My mouth was dry and I could feel my eyes smarting. This was as close as I'd been to Calan Ironbiter since that afternoon seven weeks ago. Calan was looking around at the ambush party until his gaze settled on me.

"So the big baby told on me. Couldn't keep her mouth shut. I shoulda knowed." He shook his head and spit at my feet. Tommy walked up to him and shoved him back a step or two. "Your sister's a whore, O'Brien. She deserved it." Mike had put his arm around my shoulder and pulled me close to his side. "Aren'tcha, kid? Aren'tcha a whore. Aren'tch gonna do it with *him*?" Calan nodded at Mike. "And then all the rest of your brother's little friends."

Tommy looked over at me. "Got anything you want to say, Lizzie?" I shrank closer to Mike's side. "Go on," Tommy said, gently.

"He's bad," I muttered and turned my face to the crook of Mike's arm.

"Hear that, Ironbiter? You're bad. Bad people get punished." I heard a body fall to the ground. It was hot and hadn't rained since early July and the sound was barely softened by the Ironbiters' yellowing grass. I looked up to see Calan sprawled at Tommy's feet. Tom moved in quickly and kicked Calan in the knee. I noticed he hadn't changed to his sneakers after church, and his wing tips left a gray streak on Calan's black Sunday trousers. He pulled his leg up, grunting in pain, and Tommy darted around and kicked his in the side of his stomach. "Harf," Calan exhaled and rolled over and began to pick himself up.

"Okay," he said. "You wanna fight over the little baby, let's fight." He swung at Tommy, catching him in the jaw. Tommy dropped his bat and lunged at Cal, who stepped aside so that Tommy dove into empty air and fell to the ground. Then they were in a heap, Calan's black legs entwined with Tommy's blue jeans, punches landing with the hollowness of unanswered questions. Calan was bigger than Tommy, and you could tell he'd done a fair lot of fighting before. Tommy was getting the worst of it, his nose bleeding and a rip in his pants. I wondered what the point was. They'd brought bats, why not even up the fight? Tommy was going to lose, and I could imagine Cal and Billy talking about us. "First I fucked the kid sister, then I beat the shit out of her moron brother."

It wasn't what I wanted at all.

I jabbed Mike in the side with my elbow and broke free, racing for the bat Tommy had dropped before the scuffle began. Dancing wildly around them, as much to avoid the grasping arms of Mike as to try to keep up with the grappling, I circled the boys, nudging them apart with the bat until I had a clear target.

I held it like a golf club and putted straight at Calan's right ear, hard enough that it must have crushed the lobe. Blood began to trickle down his jaw, the first of Calan's blood drawn in the fight. I brought the bat down on the flat of his stomach. He lay there, dazed, stretched out open, beginning to cramp from the last blow. Tommy pulled himself to his knees and looked up at me. I held the bat uncertainly, not knowing how badly I'd hurt him, or what to do next. "Good girl, Liz," Tom panted. "Finish him off."

I rested the bat on the ground. "How?" This was all new to me, this rage, this power. Tommy stood up and limped over. "We can't do to him what he did to you, but you can hurt him there. Kick him, Liz. Kick him in the crotch. Kick him as hard as you can, and if he doesn't cry, do it again until he does. He dropped to hold Calan's arm to the ground. Mike came over to hold the other one and Frankie Blankenship grabbed his feet.

And I kicked.

"TELL ON US, JULIE, and your brother will go to jail. Got that?" Tommy asked as we filed out of the yard. She nodded, her thin blond hair scratching against her collar. She looked from Tommy to Calan, her face quivering between loyalty to, and fear of, both boys. "Good. You tell him that, too."

Tom shut the gate and hobbled over to us. His upper lip was caked with blood drying black and there was an ominous dark stain spreading around the rip in his jeans. "We're going to the river, Liz. I gotta clean up. You go home. Tell Mom and Dad you got bored. I'm gonna spend the night at Mike's. I'll call later and get permission. You stay inside. They're leaving tomorrow. No one will ever know what happened."

"I don't want to go home," I said. "I want to go down to the river with you." I was too worked up to go home to my books and dolls and my crisp new Camp Fire outfit, and I suddenly realized I felt, for the first time all summer, like being outside, like running and yelling and making too much noise and getting in someone's way. I want to hang out and gloat with Tommy and his friends, *my* friends.

"No," he said. "I gotta clean up and then I'm going to Mike's. We gotta lay low today. You're better off at home. Go home, Liz-butt. You did good, but now you have to go home."

It was only one in the afternoon, the last day of freedom before camp, a freedom I hadn't even had yet, and hours to wait before the wind would kick up and volley through the trees, tousling like boys fighting in the grass as thunder groaned in the far mountains.

Frances Kuffel is a native of Missoula. She worked as a literary agent in New York City for fifteen years and now walks dogs. Passing for Thin: Losing Half My Weight and Finding My Self *was published by Broadway Books in 2004, and her second book,* Just This Once: An Anatomy of Relapse and Recovery, *will be published by Basic Books in 2008. She is a weekly columnist for the* San Diego Reader, *and her fiction, poetry, and essays have been published by* Self, Psychology Today, Tri-Quarterly, Prairie Schooner, The Massachusetts Review, Glimmer Train *and* The Georgia Review.

Frieda Fligelman

NARROW STREETS I

Our only view
In looking out on nature
Is seeing neighbors
Going through the necessary
Stupid things of life—
Eating and dressing
Shaving and playing cards.

Oh gosh! I'd give my bath-tub
For ten miles of straight-lined prairie!

SOLITUDE
(Silence is Thought)

Dear Friend, do not misunderstand the silence.

Silence is thought
Too intimate and sudden
To trust to letters.

Silence is thought
Requiring welcome gestures:
 Reading, I reach to press your hand,
 Walking, I glance with questioning smile,
 Lying at rest, I seek repose against your breast—

And what are words
When one has need of kisses.

HALL BEDROOM SCHOLAR

Longing for plentiful shelf-space,
The mind roams in wishful expectation
Among well-ordered drawers and
                    card-catalogues,
Like a pioneer who gazing on
                    broad prairies
Sees the clean-laid furrows of
                    plotted fields
As ripening grain.

IF I WERE THE QUEEN OF SHEBA

I can imagine
Being the Lady Sultan
Of Arabia
With something like a harem
Full of lovers—

But they would not be slaves
No more than doctors
Are slaves to suffering patients
Or professors to eager students
Or actors and performers
to our need of re-creation.

And I would send
for Ahmed or Abdullah
And then for Ali, Shem and Japeth,
Yakut, Iram, Bouberkr, Es-Saheli,

And then exhausting memory for names
Call for the one who's gentle as a hound,
And then the one who's timid as a doe
That hardly dares to come
And lick the hand for salt;

Then I would call for him
Who loves to strut,
Thrusting his head about
Above his beautiful shoulders
Like the huge-antlered deer,

Who seems to wave a proud and graceful flag
As he runs lithely forth
To seek his food;

And then perhaps,
The beautiful youth
With resolute noble eyes—
I would not touch him
Save to stroke his hands,
Enquire of the progress of his plans
For an attack to conquer
Some rude problem
Of the universal pain.

And all would come
With firmly glistening limbs,
Clean from cool baths
Or working in the breeze.

They would be glad to come,
As glad to go;
Returning to their fascinating art or craft
Where some fair damsel
Is their bright companion.

For they would not be slaves
Locked for my pleasure,
Waiting in anxiety
The imperious call of master.

They would come gladly
As a beautiful pause
In their beautiful work—

Our caresses
Would be the joining limbs
of comrades creating beauty;
Our curving arms
Against the pillows
And each other
Would make designs
To rival autumn trees.

And as the leaves dropped
From our longing
And a short winter covered us
With gentle snow,
Slowly we'd melt away
Into delicious drowse of passing winter

And after half-an-hour
Spring would come again.

The birds, and singing youth
At charming tasks
Outside the windows
Would wake and call us
Not to waste in an unconsciousness
The little space of life
Which must be used to hold
So many joys.

Born January 2, 1890, and raised in Helena, Frieda Fligelman attended the University of Minnesota and the University of Wisconsin, and then moved to New York for graduate study in sociology, economics, and anthropology. After passing her comprehensive exams at Columbia University, she worked as a sociologist and went abroad to attend the National School of Living Oriental Languages in Paris. Fligelman was known for demonstrating a theory that a non-western language was as complex as modern European languages. But when she presented her published papers to fulfill the dissertation requirements, the department chair at Columbia refused her work. Frieda's achievements were not adequately recognized until 1944, when the World Congress of Sociology dedicated a volume entitled Language in Sociology to this Montana scholar. In 1948, Frieda returned to Helena to care for her ailing stepmother and lived in the then-new Hustad Apartments. Fligelman lived in Helena until her death on January 16, 1978.

Kate Gadbow

BUFFALO JUMP

MR. CONROY CAME TO ST. THERESA'S in late October of my sixth grade year. He "stepped in" because Sister Mary Damien, the new nun that year, "cratered." That's how my father put it, though I wasn't sure exactly what he meant.

I had begun to think St.Theresa's Parish got more than its share of odd clergy: Dominican nuns with foreign accents and frightening tempers, tongue-tied priests who couldn't sing. I'd been to church once in Seattle, and to Catholic school with cousins in Denver, and the nuns and priests in those places were different—more professional or something. I could imagine Pope John XXIII saying to one of his cardinals or bishops, "send that one to northern Montana. She can't do much harm there."

This impression had come to me gradually, though, since nobody openly criticized the clergy. I sensed it when I saw my parents exchange a look after one of Father Wilder's wandering sermons. After one of us kids came home with some strange recommendation: Sister Mary Paul says if you get a rock in your shoe you should leave it there and offer it up; Sister Monica says it's a venial sin to wear sleeveless blouses. "Sister means well," my parents would say, even as they removed the pebbles from our shoes or bought us cool summer clothes.

Some of the kids at school said this or that nun was "mean," but that's as far as it went. The nuns lived in a different realm and had secret, holy power.

Only Donny DeVay didn't seem to realize that.He was a thin, nervous boy with auburn hair curling onto his forehead.I'd loved him since I was ten. In fifth grade we'd had Sister Xavier, a fierce German with a jutting chin and hard gray eyes. Donny set himself against her early on, and by spring he was being ordered to her "office," a closet next to the classroom, nearly every day. We would hear five or six sharp smacks of the paddle but never a noise from Donny. Then both of them would come back, Sister panting and holding Donny by the collar or ear, Donny red-faced and tight-lipped but never, ever crying.

It wasn't that Donny did anything really bad. Mostly he just answered a question from his seat rather than standing, or used a slightly insolent tone of voice. I think it was his cool distance that drove Sister Xavier to fury, and her inability to change him in any way. By the end of the year she couldn't even take time for the office. She shook him, hit him across the face or ear with the flat of her hand. Once, only once, she smacked him with the rosary that hung from her waist. Afterward, she stared open-mouthed at the welts that bloomed on Donny's cheek, then rushed out of the room and was gone for what seemed a long time.

In some ways I could understand Sister Xavier's frustration with Donny, since I was equally unsuccessful at getting his attention. But I think that was what fascinated me too—his distance. He seemed to have some secret knowledge, some core of self-respect that couldn't be touched, not even by the paddle.

I didn't really try to get to know him better. Instead, I contented myself with daydreams, mostly situation in which nameless, faceless enemies— usually people but sometimes grizzly bears—were about to hurt me, when Donny would appear and stare them down with the same hard gaze he leveled at Sister Xavier.

SISTER MARY DAMIEN WAS A DIFFERENT KIND of nun. For one thing she was beautiful, movie star beautiful. And she grew up in Florida, not some unheard-of region of a European country. She carried herself like a model and wore her habit as if it were a prom dress, not camouflage. She was funny too. When somebody didn't understand what she taught, or when the class got loud and out of hand, she'd go to the wall and softly bang her forehead against it like Charlie Brown in the comics. I thought that was charming. I began doing it at home when my brothers or sister drove me crazy, or when my parents told me I couldn't do something. "Quit that, Patty!" my mother would say. "You'll hurt yourself."

Sister Mary Damien charmed Donny DeVay out of any thought of rebellion. The first time he tried something, she stopped him with a touch on his arm and some teasing banter that seemed almost like flirting. Donny opened up to her as he had to nobody else. He began to pay attention in school, even to tell jokes, although Sister was often the only one who got them. I liked the new nun most of the time, but began to feel a tight knot in my chest when she twinkled at Donny, or when one of his puns was the cause of the head-banging.

Before my jealousy could become really painful, though, Sister Mary Damien was gone. And without warning. There she had been on Friday—smiling, telling jokes. And on Monday we had a substitute and the school board was looking for a teacher, because Sister Mary Damien had cratered.

I brooded over what had caused this cratering. Maybe it had been the early blizzard on Sunday that swirled around the oil tanks at the edge of town and sent dry twigs and hard snow rattling down the streets. The prospect of a winter of that might have been too much for the nun's Florida-warmed blood. Or maybe, over the weekend, she had met a handsome stranger who convinced her that her vocation wasn't real—although the only place I thought she'd likely meet a stranger in Fenton was at a bar downtown or the Husky House on Highway 2. It was hard to imagine Sister in either place.

My parents weren't helpful with the details, so I was left with a mystery and the image of an old pickup on our friend Susan's ranch, its windows broken and grass growing through the wheel wells. It cratered when I was seven.

MR. CONROY'S CHILDREN HAD ALWAYS gone to St. Theresa's. There were lots of them: Mike in my class, an older boy in high school, several more sprinkled through the lower grades. But I didn't remember ever seeing him until the first day he was my teacher. My parents said he'd spent the last four winters in Dillon going to the teachers' college. He'd finished school but not his student teaching, so he didn't have a certificate. "Close enough for me," my father said. He was on the parish board that voted for the replacement and was happy that his children would finally get "a little male influence" at school. There'd been some opposition at the meeting—on the basis of the certificate and "other things" my father said.But his side won.

Mr. Conroy was Blackfeet Indian. That in itself wasn't so odd , since Fenton was right next to the reservation. I always had two or three Blackfeet kids in my class. But I realized I'd never known an adult Indian before. I also hadn't known a man who taught grade school. Most of my friends' fathers worked in the oil business like mine did, or ranched or worked in stores. They·were gone all day and even on the weekends didn't have much to do with kids. I thought, before I met Mr. Conroy, that he must be a sort of motherly man, or grandmotherly like Father Wilder.

He wasn't motherly. He was lean and tall, taller even than my father. He always wore a white shirt and started the school day by rolling up the sleeves with large, long-fingered hands. His black hair, combed straight back, gleamed with Vitalis. What I liked best about him were his eyes, kind and sad and crinkly at the edges, and his voice that was deep and husky, a heavy smoker's voice, I'd realize later.

With Mr. Conroy's arrival, Donny DeVay began to slip from his position in my fantasies. Mr. Conroy was relaxed and reasonable. He didn't need to be resisted. On the second day, Donny decided to challenge him anyway by getting up and walking to the back of the room during a writing assignment. Donny paged through the dictionary for a while, then just stood there, looking out the window. Mr. Conroy waited, longer than Sister Xavier ever would have, then very quietly said, "Better get back to work, Donny."

Donny glanced at him, then moved back to the dictionary.

"You already did that," Mr. Conroy said, still smiling.

"I'm doing it some more," Donny mumbled, and all of us froze, waiting for the explosion, the office, the paddle.

Mr. Conroy shrugged and went back to his own writing. Five minutes later, when Donny had flipped all the pages of the dictionary several times and didn't seem to know quite what to do next, Mr. Conroy stood up and walked to the back of the room. We all turned to watch and Donny tensed, gripping the dictionary stand and waiting for the inevitable.

Mr. Conroy didn't hit him. He didn't even stop smiling as he slung Donny or his shoulder like a sack of grain and walked to the front of the room where he held Donny's ankles and hung him upside down, head several inches from the floor.

The class roared with laughter at Donny's ridiculous arm-waving, at the silly smile Mr. Conroy put on, like a rodeo clown doing a trick. They kept laughing as Mr. Conroy stood Donny on his feet and walked him to his desk then tousled his hair. I laughed too until I looked at Donny's face and saw, for the first time in his long career of school torture, tears in his eyes.

I felt confused the rest of the day. I was upset with Mr. Conroy for humiliating Donny to the point of tears. But I was mad at Donny too—for the way he slammed open his desk and took out a book, for the prissy set to his mouth as he stared at the book and wouldn't look at anyone.

The worst moment came at the end of the day as we lined up to leave. I stood behind Donny, and Mr. Conroy stood in the doorway handing out homework and saying goodbye to each person. When Donny's turn came, Mr. Conroy put a hand on his shoulder and said, "Hey. No hard feelings, okay?"

Donny shook the hand off and muttered, "Get your Indian hands off me," and then bolted for the stairs before Mr. Conroy had time to react.

The way Donny had turned the word "Indian" gave me a sick feeling in the pit of my stomach that worsened when I glanced at Mr. Conroy. I had expected him to be furious, ready to chase after Donny. He wasn't though. Instead, he looked sort of ashamed, as if *he* had said or done something he had to cover up. He flushed and looked down, then raised his eyebrows and forced a smile as he handed me my papers.

Donny and Mr. Conroy avoided each other after that. Unlike the nuns who demanded a standing response even for a "Yes, Sister" or "No, Sister," Mr. Conroy let his students stay seated. So Donny didn't have to refuse on that count. If Donny's voice was insolent, Mr. Conroy chose not to notice. Mr. Conroy taught, and Donny stayed as guarded and distant as ever.

I was the one who changed. When I looked at Donny, I no longer admired the proud set of his shoulders or the way his fiery hair fell on his forehead. Instead I saw the narrowed eyes, the sour twist to his mouth. I began to suspect he had no secrets. Or if he did, they were small, ugly ones.

Donny himself was gone from my daydreams, but the soft caves of feeling remained. And they began, gradually, to be inhabited by Mr. Conroy. At first I daydreamed classroom encounters after school or at recess; then I began to imagine meeting him away from school. Sometimes it would be down by the river where my brother Andy dared me to walk Devil's Underpass, a narrow sandstone ledge halfway up the river's rimrocks. If you fell off, you'd more likely be scraped on rocks than killed. But when you were on the ledge, with the overhanging wall above pushing you out and a slippery film of loose sand under your feet, it seemed you might die.

I had never made it all the way across the Underpass. In one fantasy I would be alone, determined to go the distance. When I finally did—scraped, sweaty, triumphant—I'd turn to see Mr. Conroy standing on the riverbank, gazing at me with wonder and love. In the other Devil's Underpass scenario, I would get hurt or stuck halfway across. Before I even had to shout for help, Mr. Conroy would be there, wordlessly guiding—or carrying—me to safety. In these daydreams, or the other ones that involved the rented pasture by the oil tanks where I biked to ride my horse, there was never any kissing and hardly any talking. It was mostly an exchange of long, loving gazes—hazes that filled both our hearts.

In real life, Mr. Conroy did look at me kindly. But he looked at everyone that way, except his son Mike. His treatment of Mike was the only thing about Mr. Conroy that bothered me. Mike was a placid, moon-faced boy who had never been an outstanding student. He kept up his mediocre ways after his father took over. While Mr. Conroy had endless patience with the rest of the class, he couldn't abide Mike's fumbling guesses.

"Think, boy," he'd say. "Try to think, will you?" And his voice would rise and sharpen in a way it never did with the rest of us. Mike would hang his head—doubly embarrassed that the teacher who thought him stupid was also his father.

I wondered if Mr. Conroy treated his high-school son that way. I hadn't known the older boy well at St. Theresa's, but the past spring I'd seen him throw the javelin at a track meet I went to with my friend Lisa and her mother. Unlike Mike, Howie Conroy was long and lean like his father. When his turn came to compete, he walked on the field with a big elegant stride, the javelin balanced on his fingers. As he ran, then stretched back for the launch, Lisa's mother breathed to a friend beside her, "My God. Isn't he beautiful? A beautiful brave with a spear."

In spite of my sympathy for Mike, I made excuses to myself for Mr. Conroy's shortness with him. Maybe Mr. Conroy hadn't wanted to have all those children. Maybe his wife had tricked him into it. Maybe he just wanted to be free.

BY MID-DECEMBER, I BEGAN TO FEEL SINGLED OUT by Mr. Conroy. I'd worked like the devil on all my assignments, and he started to write what seemed like special comments on my papers, and to compliment my thinking in class. And then there was the time when I'd had a rotten cold for a week and the skin beneath my nose was raw and red from blowing, my voice like gravel. As I left the classroom on Friday, Mr. Conroy handed me my homework, then gently touched my cheek with his knuckles. "Take care of yourself," he said.

It was all he said, but his tone of voice was enough to make me blush as I ran down the stairs, and to make Lisa, who'd been in line behind me, raise her eyebrows and purse her lips when we got to the sidewalk. "Take care of yourself, dahling," Lisa taunted as we kidded sideways down the snow-packed street. "Take care of yourself, Babycakes. For me."

FOR CHRISTMAS, I ASKED FOR A PAIR OF MOCCASINS from the Museum of the Plains Indians in Browning. My mother was pleased; she thought I was beginning to take an interest in local history.

My mother was a history nut. She belonged to the Montana Historical Society and bought books about Indians and Lewis and Clark. She was writing a play for the 1964 Territorial Centennial, and some of the paintings and drawings she did had historical themes. She and her friend Ellen had set for themselves the goal of visiting every spot in the area where Lewis and his party had camped.

The past July, both our families spent what had seemed to me an unbelievably long afternoon at Camp Disappointment, a bare, hot hill on the reservation where Lewis figured out he wasn't going to reach the Saskatchewan River. In September, the two women took all of us kids, eight total with Ellen's four, to a spot on the Marias River where local boy scouts and historians said Lewis's men had killed some Indians.

Ellen passed out sandwiches while my mother read from Lewis's journal, stopping every now and then to pull back strands of dark hair the wind whipped into her face. She had to stop even more often when she got to the part about one of the Fields brothers stabbing an Indian, because my youngest brother Matt kept interrupting her.

"Where did he stab the Indian?" Matt asked.

My mother stopped reading to tuck the book under her arm and her hands in her jeans pockets. She walked to a nearby cottonwood tree and counted paces away from it, then turned and said, "I'd say about here, Matt."

Matt shook his head. "No, *where.* Where on his body?"

Andy snickered. "In the bee-hind," he whispered to the rest of us. Andy was thirteen then, and most of his jokes had to do with behinds and other body parts.

MY MOCCASINS SMELLED LIKE BEEF JERKY. I wore them all Christmas vacation even though they weren't very comfortable; the soles weren't padded and they had no arch support. I wanted to wear them to school when it started again, but my mother said no at first. "They're more like slippers—for wearing around the house," she said. "They're not real shoes."

I argued until she gave in and said I could take the moccasins to school if I wore snowboots on the way. It was important to me that Mr. Conroy see me in them.

Mr. Conroy did comment on my moccasins, but only briefly. He said they were "real nice," the same thing he said about the jackknife Doug Peabody got for Christmas.

Over the vacation, I had begun reading my mother's Indian history books and I wanted Mr. Conroy to know I understood him in a way the other white kids in class did not. I began to slip things about Indians into reports. If the assignment was to write about an animal, say, I'd look up the Blackfeet name for that animal and get it in somehow.

Usually Mr. Conroy ignored my Indian references. But one time, when he'd told us to write a story and I'd written out a Blackfeet legend on the creation of the world, he returned the paper then squatted beside my desk so he could look into my eyes. His gaze held such soft affection, and such a strange mixture of sadness and amusement, that I had to look down at his arm stretched across my desk rather than into his face. "Makes sense, doesn't it?" he said.

Given this slight encouragement, I became obsessive about Indians in the same way I had about saints the year before. I read biographies and studied family names and histories. I found stories of Indian warriors who, like Saint Joan, fought and died under orders from voices in their heads. And there were other connections. I read and reread descriptions of the Sun Dance, of leather thongs skewered under chest muscles, in the same way I'd invariably opened *Lives of the Saints* to Rose of Lima flogging herself in a locked room in Peru.

⟿

SUSAN, OUR FAMILY FRIEND WHO RANCHED south of town, usually stopped by for coffee on her weekly grocery runs. She was there one January afternoon when I shuffled through the kitchen in my beaded moccasins.

"Say, those are nice," Susan said. "I used to have a pair just like them when I was a kid."

My mother reached out an arm and pulled me close. "I think it's been good for Patty to have Howard Conroy for a teacher. She's becoming a real Indian historian." She rubbed my arm, gave me a squeeze. "And you should see Howard with the kids, Susan. That wonderful Indian gentleness."

Susan told me I'd have to come to the ranch some time and we'd go up the Two Medicine River and look for arrowheads at the piskun there.

Andy had been digging in the refrigerator. "What's a piss-can?" he asked, with a sly look at our mother.

"A buffalo jump," Susan replied. "You know, where the Indians ran the buffalo off a cliff so they could get meat for the whole tribe at once. They named the Two Medicine for a double piskun. Jack knew where it was. I'll bet we could find it."

I found a book by a man named McClintock who interviewed a chief called Brings-Down-the-Sun about piskuns in the area. He talked about the "Women's Piskun" from a time when men and women lived in separate bands, and "Ghost Piskun Creek."

"On the shoreline is a miniature cliff about 3 feet high," the chief said. "If you visit the place early in the morning you will see many mice. We believe these mice are the ghosts of buffalo, which take the forms of mice whenever people look at them."

The idea of a buffalo jump fascinated me, especially when I thought about it from the buffalo's point of view. I'd just discovered the concept of irony, and the buffalo's situation seemed heavy with it. Here you are, one of a thousand huge, powerful buffalo being chased by one or two puny men on horses. You think you're outrunning the enemy. You feel safe because you're surrounded by friends and family. Then—suddenly—you're vaulting through space. As you land, the ones you love become deadly weapons, crushing your bones. It made me shiver.

My hair was short and curly, but I decided to grow it out so I could wear braids. I bought some little beads at the Ben Franklin and made a necklace I thought looked vaguely Indian. I studied the beadwork on my moccasins thinking I might try sewing some on my school coat, but it looked too complicated and I gave up that idea.

In spite of all my reading, I was having trouble finding a connection between the Indians in the books and Mr. Conroy. Part of the problem was that most of the books I could find ended in the late 1800s. They didn't talk about Indians today. The last paragraph of *Blackfoot Lodge Tales* did say: "The Blackfoot of today is a working man. He has a little property which he is trying to care for and wishes to add to. With a little help, with instruction, and with encouragement to persevere, he will become in the next few years self-supporting, and a good citizen." I didn't think that said much. That could have been written about anybody.

Another part of the problem was that, while Mr. Conroy talked about lots of things, he didn't talk much about himself. From Mike I learned they lived outside town on a reservation allotment where they ran a few horses. Also, Mr. Conroy mentioned in passing that he had gone to Starr School.

I thought Star School was a wonderful Indian name for a school—like cloud school or sun school. Later, my mother told me Starr School was a boarding school on the reservation named by Jesuits who started it. Still later, during the AIM days, a college professor would call it an abomination—native children taken from their parents and force-fed Catholicism, their language and customs beaten out of them. Still, I never quite erased that first image that came to mind: a lone Indian sitting on a hill studying the stars.

IN FEBRUARY, MY MOTHER INVITED MR. CONROY and his wife Roseanne to dinner. I was uncomfortable with that whole idea. We'd had Father Wilder over for dinner before, but never one of my teachers since nuns didn't socialize. I didn't want to sit across the table from Mr. Conroy's wife who, until then, had stayed in the back of my mind as simply a shadowy negative force.

When the Conroys came, I sat in a corner of the living room and studied Mrs. Conroy, trying not to be obvious about it. She was a small, dark-haired woman with pale, smooth skin—pretty in a soft, helpless sort of way. She didn't look strong enough to have given birth to all those children, much less take care of them and their horses. My mother had said Mrs. Conroy wasn't Indian, and that it had been "a problem for both of them" at times.

I didn't like the way Mrs. Conroy kept glancing at me and smiling. One time she even winked, as if she thought I was a baby who would appreciate that sort of thing. I also didn't like the brown striped tie Mr. Conroy had on, or his blue cardigan sweater. He didn't dress that way at school. In my living room, with my parents doing most of the talking, he almost seemed like a different person. He was nervous, careful. He crossed and uncrossed his legs in a girlish sort of way. He sat close to his wife and touched her wrist from time to time. I didn't like that either. I wanted him to be funny the way he was in school. To tell jokes and stories that would put admiring smiles on my parents' faces.

Finally, I got so nervous that I slid out of my chair and went into the kitchen where my little sister Bridgit was doing homework. My father came in a few minutes later to mix drinks.

"What's Mr. Conroy having?" I asked.

"A highball. Bourbon and water, I believe." He looked at me over his glasses, amused. "And Mrs. Conroy's having wine, your mother's having scotch, and I think I'll drink a bit of this Old Granddad, if it's okay by you. And what for you Miss Patty? Ginger ale?"

I shook my head. I was shocked, though I wasn't really sure why. It hadn't occurred to me that Mr. Conroy might drink. The only picture I had in my mind of Indians and drinking was the doorway of the Napi Bar in Browning that my family passed when we drove to Glacier Park. Even at ten in the morning, the door stood open, and men stumbled out to sit on a bench by the street and sip wine from bottles in paper bags, squinting in the morning sunshine. Sometimes there were fights in front of the Napi, and my parents would murmur and shake their heads as we drove by.

I didn't think Mr. Conroy would suddenly turn into one of those men draped over the Napi's bench, but I didn't want him to be like my parents and their friends at parties either—everybody red-faced, laughing too much at nothing, talking too loudly. I wished he'd asked for water.

As it turned out, Mr. Conroy didn't change at all. Everybody had one drink and then we had dinner. The Conroys made polite comments about the food and left early.

My mother saw them to the door. When she came back to the living room, she said, "Well. That was nice." She smiled at me, but had a little frown between her eyes as if something had disappointed her, but she couldn't quite put her finger on it.

The next day in school, my Mr. Conroy was back again. He wore his usual white shirt and dark pants that were covered with chalk dust by afternoon. Lisa and I stayed after to clean the blackboards. As we left, Mr. Conroy stopped us at the door with the stick he used to close the transom.

"Halt," he said, barricading the doorway, grinning at us. "Where does the Lone Ranger take his garbage?"

Lisa and I giggled and shrugged. Mr. Conroy raised his eyebrows and waited, tapping the stick against the door frame.

"Where?" I asked.

"To the dump, to the dump, to the dump, dump, dump," Mr. Conroy sang. He raised the stick and let us pass.

ONE SPRING WEEKEND, SOMETHING HAPPENED, and I heard about it in the usual way I heard about goings-on in Fenton: from kids at school repeating what they'd overheard from their parents, each version slightly different. Apparently Howie Conroy and two Indian kids from Browning had taken some beer from a truck in back of Buttrey's supermarket, only three blocks from our house. One version had it they'd held up the stockboy with knives, threatening to scalp him. Other kids said that was wrong—that the beer had just been sitting there on the back of the truck and somebody had seen them take it. Lisa said she heard the Browning kids had both served time at Pine Hills reform school. All versions agreed that Howie had been kicked off the track team.

I felt sorry for Mr. Conroy. He must have known from the way everyone watched him and whispered at recess that we were talking about it. He didn't say anything about Howie, but seemed tired and distracted. Mike Conroy got in a fight at first recess on Tuesday and had to spend the noon hour in Sister Xavier's office.

My parents always seemed slower than others on the taking up of rumors—or maybe just better at not talking in front of us kids. In any case, it took until Thursday for the subject to come up in our house, and then only because my parents were going to a parish meeting after dinner.

"Kid stuff. It's just kid stuff," my mother said. She was chopping carrots for a salad. "The only reason everyone's so hot and bothered about it is that these particular kids came off the reservation to do their mischief. They don't know their place." She said the last part very sarcastically, waving the knife in the air.

My father leaned against the counter holding a drink. He'd brought up the subject and now looked as if he regretted it, as he watched my mother resume her furious chopping. I was in the dining room setting the table, eyeing my parents, listening hard.

"It's no reason for them to call Howard Conroy on the carpet," my mother went on. My father started to say something, but my mother interrupted him, pointing the knife. "Why didn't they call Bob Hanley to a parish meeting when his dear drunk little Teddy drove through the wall of the Tastee Freeze?" Bob Hanley was the family lawyer. One of the stained-glass windows in the church had a small gold sign on it that expressed appreciation to the Hanley family.

"I don't think that's the reason for the meeting," my father said. "We have to decide if we're going to rehire Conroy or get another nun—and find out if he even wants to teach again. This thing may not even come up."

"It'll come up," my mother said. She reached for a head of iceberg lettuce and smashed it on the cutting board to extract the core. I liked the heightened sense of drama when my mother went into one of these righteous furies. Unless, of course, one was directed at something I had or had not done. Then it was awful.

When my parents came home from the meeting, I was still awake. I tiptoed to my usual spying place at the top of the darkened stairway. From what I could gather, the meeting hadn't gone well. My mother's lips were clamped in a furious line, while my father wore an odd, willing look—like there was something he wanted to believe but couldn't quite get straight in his mind.

"I can't understand that Charles DeVay—describing that upside-down business with Donny like it was some kind of Medieval torture." My mother had thrown off her jacket and was pacing in circles around the room, flinging out her arms.

"You have to admit, it's pretty unusual punishment." My father's tone was joking. He was trying to lighten things up, and I sympathized with him, especially when it didn't work.

"As if the DeVays really care what goes on at St. Theresa's next year. Julia told me two weeks ago they're sending little Donny the genius to a boarding school on the coast. Very exclusive—you know Julia."

I decided the DeVays probably didn't know the nuns had been beating on their little Donny the genius for years. It hadn't occurred to me to tell my own parents.

As if reading my mind, my mother went on, "And the nuns! That's the worst. I can't believe that Sister Xavier—'Vell, you know dees people have trouble wit trinking.' Right in front of Howard she said that, Lyle. As if her were some kind of animal that couldn't hear her, some kind of specimen. You'd think at least the nuns—people of God…" She was near tears and had to stop.

I was shocked by the viciousness—and accuracy—of her imitation of Sister Xavier. I'd never ever heard my parents speak badly of anyone connected with the church, although my father had told a Pope joke or two at rodeos, outside my mother's hearing. But then he was the one who had grown up in the church, had lived with it all his life. My mother had converted herself to Catholicism at eighteen—passionately, wholeheartedly. There didn't seem to be room for Pope jokes in her vision.

My father stopped my mother's pacing by putting his hands on her shoulders. "They're people, Faye," he said. "Just people."

ALL MY CHILDHOOD, I'D READ in books—usually books set in England—about soft, greening springtimes filled with twittering birds and blossoming life. But in Fenton, spring was late and dirty. The wind blew constantly; snow melted into icy, brown patches, and ugly things came up. That spring especially, I felt restless, unreasonably sad.

As the school year drew to a close, I found I wasn't daydreaming about Mr. Conroy as much. I wasn't sure if it was because he had changed, or I had. He was still patient and told an occasional joke, but he seemed tired, distant. He'd even stopped seeming to care if Mike learned to think.

The last week of school, my mother gave me something new to think about. She had decided to transfer all of us to the public school the next year—"pull them out" was the term she used when explaining it over the phone to her sister-in-law. My father was happy to go along since he'd never been convinced of the superiority of Catholic education. We'd still go to Mass; there was no question about that. The decision seemed to make my mother feel much better about "the Conroy thing," to solve it for her in some way. She stopped talking about it.

MR. CONROY WAS GONE FROM Fenton the next year. I didn't know where. Now, when I think back on it, that's what amazes and disturbs me: that I didn't know and didn't bother to find out. Through Lisa, I knew his kids were still at St. Theresa's. Howie was still in high school. Maybe Mr. Conroy had gone to teach somewhere else, or had gone back to Dillon for more schooling. Maybe he was staying home on the reservation, riding his horse or studying the stars.

At the time, Mr. Conroy and St. Theresa's seemed frozen to me— suspended in time—while I felt myself moving forward. To a new school, to real boyfriends, to a wider world beyond romantic obsessions like a crush on a teacher. Already some part of me knew you couldn't run too far with a thing like that, or you'd find yourself falling, unexpectedly, through air.

Kate Gadbow's novel Pushed to Shore *was selected by Rosellen Brown as winner of the 2001 Mary McCarthy Prize in short fiction and was published by Sarabande Books in 2003. Her stories and essays have appeared in various journals including* Epoch, Northwest Review, CutBank, Talking River Review, *the* Montanan. *She coedited* The Quill Reader, *published in 2000 by Harcourt Brace. Gadbow directs the Creative Writing Program and teaches undergraduate fiction classes at the University of Montana in Missoula, where she lives with her husband, journalist Daryl Gadbow. Their grown children, Grady and Alison, are fifth-generation Montanans.*

🍂 *Ellen Baumler*

DOROTHY'S ROOMS:
HELENA'S LAST, AND SOME SAY BEST, PLACE

A PRIL 17, 1973, IS A DATE ETCHED in the annals of Helena history. That was the day local police and sheriff's officers, armed with a court order, ended the long life of Dorothy's Rooms at 19½ South Last Chance Gulch. Voicing the sentiment of many Helenans, one outraged citizen proclaimed the motive of the afternoon raid due to the "the asinine morality of a pipsqueak." Inside, officials found 240-pound diabetic Dorothy Baker, nee Dorothy Putnam, sick with the flu. The only other individuals on the premises at the time were Dorothy's maid and a woman found hiding in a closet. The occupants were removed and the doors boarded up. Officers noted, among other things, a small statue in the kitchen that bore a prophetic statement: "It's a beautiful day… Now watch some bastard louse it up."

The final raid on Dorothy's Rooms came in a roundabout way because of Dorothy Baker's civic conscience. Downtown Helena was crumbling around her with buildings vacant and unsightly. Hoping that others might follow suit, Dorothy decided to fix up her property. In the fall of 1972, the City of Helena awarded her a $500 federal Urban Renewal grant to refurbish her building "for retail purposes." The ground floor had been nearly ready for commercial tenancy when the raid took place, but the granting of federal dollars attracted too much attention to her business. Affidavits from a Kalispell police officer and a Missoula sheriff's deputy, both friends of the court who had clandestinely visited Dorothy's Rooms, were the basis of the complaint. They maintained that they been admitted to Dorothy's place and assigned girls. One said that he paid a dollar for a drink (Dorothy did not have a liquor license) and $20 to watch the girl "take off her clothes and roll around on the bed." The questions went no further. That was enough for the county attorney, who alleged that Dorothy Baker's rooming house was being used "for the purpose of lewdness, assignation and prostitution." The district judge duly issued a temporary writ of injunction, ordering law enforcement to remove the occupants and secure the premises. This peremptory action came because the same county attorney had previously obtained a restraining order against Dorothy's Rooms in December of 1970, prohibiting her from operating a house of prostitution. Dorothy had ignored the order. The county attorney maintained, therefore, that ejecting the occupants and boarding up the building was necessary. The judge agreed.

Although "Big Dorothy" Baker ran a quiet and orderly house, said to have been "clean as a kernel of corn," it was not the first time police raided her business. In 1963, another crusading county attorney who eventually went on to the Supreme Court had unsuccessfully attempted to close her down. And a midnight raid on Dorothy's Rooms in 1969 landed Patricia Anne Garrison in jail for illegally selling liquor. Miss Garrison told the *Indepedent Record,* "It was the first time I ever did it." Despite these legal problems, Dorothy quietly continued in the business she had run at that location in Helena for nearly twenty years.

Dorothy, however, was not the first to operate the well-known house at 19½ South Last Chance Gulch. By 1927, her predecessors Pearl Maxwell and Ida Levy ran several upstairs establishments in neighboring business blocks. Pearl had been in Helena since at least 1918 when her "furnished rooms" were located on the western edge of Helena's downtown. She may also have been around the previous year when the older red light district along Wood and Joliet streets was ordered closed, along with red light districts across Montana, as part of the war effort during World War I.

Prohibition and reforms changed the way red light business was conducted in Helena and elsewhere, but they did not put an end to it. Dorothy's Rooms are proof enough of that. Back room speakeasies replaced saloons; brothels shut down and re-emerged in other locations as "furnished rooms," a convenient front for these activities. Montanans familiar with "furnished rooms" of the '30s like to point out that such places never mentioned exactly what was "furnished." By 1930, the old Wood Street district buildings were vacant and dilapidated, and even Helena's once elegant high-class "Castle" at 103 Joliet (demolished, along with the other early red light properties, during urban renewal) had a chicken hatchery next door. In the late 1920s, Helena's dispersed red light activities recovered and resurfaced, notably in the second floors of 17, 19, and 23 South Last Chance Gulch (then known as South Main Street). Ida Levy, Pearl Maxwell and a few others were permanent proprietors during the '30s and '40s.

Ida Levy came to Helena from New York City in 1913, was in residence at the International Hotel in 1918, and seems to have opened her South Main business in 1927. Those who knew her remember Ida as a handsome woman who wore jewelry that was so gaudy it didn't look real. But the diamonds and gems she wore were not only real, they were the *best*. Ida was fond of buying expensive neckties and gifts for her regular customers, spending substantial amounts on men's items at Fligelman's department store. Employees took careful note of Ida's purchases, and waited to see who would wear them after the holidays. After Prohibition ended in the 1930s, Ida's Silver Dollar Bar on the ground floor at 19 South Main, where the Windbag Saloon and Grill is today, was a favorite hangout for the CCC boys. Nor did Ida's place upstairs lack customers. In fact, marks of partitions in the flooring reveal that some of Ida's place was divided into a long row of tiny cubicles called cribs, the least prestigious of all carnal accommodations, banned by federal law in 1943. The Silver Dollar operated until 1957, but by this time Ida had long since retired and moved to Miami. She died there in 1963 at the age of 84.

Dorothy Baker took over Ida's place and eventually owned all three commercial properties at 17, 19, and 21 South Main Street. Customers visiting Dorothy's Rooms entered via a back gate and followed a series of steps down to the back door. Dorothy's accommodations included seven bedrooms and five sitting rooms, connected by long hallways. Each plushy bedroom sported a different color velvet bedspread and thick carpeting. A bar Dorothy operated on the sly was a favorite after-hours hangout for Helena's bartenders. The hospitable madam made the drinks in her kitchen. Locals knew the way to Dorothy's door, but out-of-towners looking for her sometimes got confused. One neighboring businessman, constantly pestered by Dorothy's prospective customers, finally had to post a sign on his door: "No Girls Here."

Dorothy's door was without a doubt the best-known door in town and perhaps in the state, through which among other things, paperboys received 5-dollar tips and school children selling fund-raisers—if they dared knock—could count on a sale. Parents used to wonder if the nuns at St. Helena School knew from whence many donations came. Each year at Christmas, Dorothy bought a hundred dollars' worth of used children's books to donate to the local children's homes. She wrote countless checks to charities and anonymously paid for more than one young person's entire college education. She would lend money without question and tip off the police to drug pushers. Besides that, she had a clientele that would make more than a few legislators blush. It is little wonder that the town reacted as it did when police closed her down.

Letters in support of Dorothy poured into the Helena *Independent Record* in the weeks following the 1973 raid. An indignant out-of-towner lamented, "You lost your best tourist attraction and a true asset to your town when you put the heat on the law to close Dorothy Baker's." Not all who voiced their support were men, either. One lady wrote to pass along her own father's observation that "a town without a whore house [is] a stupid place in which to live," sarcastically noting that another "boarded up place should blend well with the rest of downtown." Many reiterated Dorothy's generosity to the community, and one commended her as "a better citizen than a lot of newcomers with their mouths open and their hands out, bringing overrated ideas of progress [to] turn our community into a place just like the one they are running away from." Even law enforcement had to admit that Big Dorothy Baker ran one of the state's most prestigious houses, and she did it "as all good mamas should, with a heart."

Perhaps Dorothy could have mustered enough support to beat the rap; surely she read the heartfelt sentiments of her supporters. But on May 14, before she could have her day in court, Dorothy Putnam, a.k.a. Dorothy Josephine Baker, died in a Great Falls hospital of a sudden and acute illness. She left her brother and sister an estate valued at $60,000 including properties in the throes of urban renewal at 17, 19 and 21 South Last Chance Gulch. Wrecking crews blocked the well-beaten path to Dorothy's door. Her heirs filed suit against the City of Helena the following year, contending that urban renewal actions had financially devastated a ground floor tenant and forced him to move.

Urban renewal won out and Dorothy's heirs sold the building. By 1976 it had become Big Dorothy's Saloon, a legal bar once again. Since the late 1970s, the Windbag at 17 and the Ghost Art Gallery at 19 South Last Chance Gulch have been anchors along the block. Upstairs are offices and a few reminders of the building's former occupant. Visitors can still see Dorothy's bathroom, a 1960s showplace, done up in black plastic tiles floor to ceiling with hospital green fixtures. Her enormous square green tub, probably a necessity rather than a luxury given her ample proportions, features corner seating. Overhead lighting filters through a remarkable green plastic starburst in the center of a black ceiling.

A few of Dorothy's personal possessions and clothing items remain around town. Even the Montana Historical Society has its mementos: two "boudoir dolls" donated by a generous citizen and some clothing reputedly worn by Dorothy's employees. And, of course, those who have been around a while have stories about this mountainous Montana madam who was reality and legend in one. Her passing was widely noted, and a female legislator, also named Dorothy, even proposed designating Dorothy's Rooms an historical landmark.

Dorothy likely enjoyed her notoriety, and may have consciously modeled herself after another legendary Helenan. Josephine "Chicago Joe" Hensley was the first of Helena's colorful early madams in business from the late 1860s through the 1890s. She, like Dorothy, had an uncanny business sense, owned a great deal of real estate, quietly paid for the education of nieces and nephews, lent money to many a fledgling entrepreneur, gave generously to charities, and in later years was also a very, very large woman. Dorothy used two different middle names, Ione and Josephine. Was it a coincidence, or did Dorothy Baker choose the latter name and model her own career after Chicago Joe's? Clearly Helena's first and last madams had more in common than a name and girth: good business sense, generosity, and heart.

On a final note, a few years ago a traveler from New York City passing through Helena inquired at the Montana Historical Society library if it would be possible to find information about her great aunt. The lady explained that as a young girl she had idolized this favorite relative who had a very successful bar business in Helena. She wanted to know if it was still there and possible to visit. The proper and courteous lady went on to say that this aunt would visit her family in New York during the summer. She always took her nieces and nephews on wonderful shopping trips, buying them anything and everything their hearts desired. The librarian answered that they could trace the aunt in the city directories. "And what," he asked, "was her name?" The librarian was at a loss when he learned that Ida Levy was the great aunt. "Ida Levy!" he blurted out. "Why she was no bar owner. She was the best-known madam in Helena!" The lady was incredulous. Her family never had an inkling that Ida's lucrative business extended beyond the bar. As it turned out, the niece was thrilled to uncover her Aunt Ida's long-kept secret. She and her daughters enjoyed a meaningful dinner at the Windbag, the former Silver Dollar Bar, where Aunt Ida hadn't really made her money after all.

Ellen Baumler is the Montana Historical Society's interpretive historian. A popular member of the Montana Committee for the Humanities Speaker's Bureau, Ellen is a frequent contributor to Montana: The Magazine of Western History. *Her work has also appeared in a variety of publications. An award-winning author, Baumler is editor of* Girl from the Gulches: The Story of Mary Ronan *(Montana Historical Society Press, 2003), a finalist in the prestigious 2004 Willa Literary Awards. Ellen's most recent book,* Beyond Spirit Tailings: Montana's Mysteries, Ghosts, and Haunted Places, *is now recorded on CD with a musical score by composer/pianist Philip Aaberg.*

⚘ Cyra McFadden

From *Rain or Shine: A Family Memoir*

A FEW BLOCKS FROM MY SAN FRANCISCO apartment, a shop sells high fashion cowboy boots. Custom-ordered from Texas, in lizard, they cost $1,500. The same shop sells stovepipe jeans to tuck into the boots, sterling and turquoise belt buckles and Ralph Lauren's idea of Western wear.

The shop thrives, though there are no cowboys here, and so do similar shops in Beverly Hills, where on quaintly named Rodeo Drive, one sees pencil-hipped, forever blond TV producers in cow boy regalia, coke spoons dangling from the gold chains around their necks.

The West has been reinterpreted by Clint Eastwood, and nothing is more chic on the hills of San Francisco than a pickup truck. But I worry. Does anyone tell the rhinestone cowboys they'll never get the look right until they have broken every major bone in their bodies? That if they wear needle-toed cowboy boots for long, they'll soon have feet as misshapen as a ballerina's, com-ridden append ages that look like tubers and hurt like hell when the boots come off? That real cowboys don't wear tinted aviator glasses; they either disappear behind ink-black lenses or squint into the sun through eyes red as pickup-truck taillights?

Does anyone warn the owner of a creamy new Stetson that throwing a cowboy hat on the bed is bad luck? The next bronc will throw you on the same shoulder you broke competing in the bareback event in Cheyenne. Your wife will get tired of watching soap operas on TV, in the motel, while you're being stuck together with steel pins again, and leave you, taking the kids, the truck and Bob your Aussie dog. Your creditors will close in; many broken-down bronc riders have few other finely honed skills except spitting for distance.

Or so it was once. Now some cowboys on the circuit are MIT graduates or alumni of two years in Nepal with the Peace Corps. A few are black, finally staking out their claim on what has until re cently been an all-white segment of mythic America. San Francisco has a gay rodeo, though it's not sanctioned by the Professional Rodeo Cowboys Association, and though one brings up the subject in, say, the Cowboys Bar in Great Falls and then backs slowly, slowly out the door.

When Cy started out on the circuit, riders were mostly farm boys like himself, aspiring cowboys who harassed the horses on the family spread until they got their big break at Frontier Days in Fargo, or Waco, or Mandan. Some of them were fifteen but lied and said they were eighteen, some were veterans of thirty-five so full of steel by then you could pick them up with a magnet. Young or old, after a few lifetimes passed in seconds on the backs of horses named Powder River or Tailspin Terror, they walked like arthritic old men. Then as now, a few died. "Don't worry about it if the ambulance pulls out of the fairgrounds and the siren is going," Cy told me. "You start your worrying when they don't bother with the siren."

Though rodeo claims a good safety record, compared with other sports and considering the number of participants in it, injuries tend to be impressive. Horses roll on the riders they've bucked off, crushing ribs. To drive their point home, they trample them. Careering around the ring, when a rider is down, a bronc kicks with the force of a heavy-gauge shotgun.

Brahma bulls not only gore their fallen riders but have a knack for finding the soft flesh of the groin.

You can get hurt before you even get out of the chute, trying to get a saddle on a bronc that crushes your leg against the chute wall as easily as bending a straw.

Compared with cowboys, pro football players, in their helmets and padding, are at no more physical risk than chess players. So routine are injuries no one mentions the trivial, the cracked ribs and broken collarbones, and the riders don't cater to them: when my brother Terry was thrown and got his teeth rammed through his lower lip years ago, Tommy mopped up the worst of the blood, packed Terry's lip with ice and pushed his face back into something resembling a human face. Terry got on his next horse and rode.

Children are taught to be stoic before they're taught to feed themselves. Get your finger slammed in a car door at the fairgrounds and an embarrassed parent will swoop down on you. "For heaven's sake, will you stop that bawlin'! You can't get yourself in a lather over every whipstitch."

None of which matters, eternally taped ribs or wives clean out of patience, if you love the road. Cy loved it because he was fiercely independent; he'd sooner starve, he said, than work for somebody else. Pat loved it because it led away from Paragould, Arkansas, and poverty. I loved it because it was the life I knew. By my third birthday, I had logged 150,000 miles, occasion for an AP wirephoto captioned: "She Sees America."

It is inaccurate to say we saw America. What we saw was the western half of the country, the straight highways that shimmer in the heat across Nevada and Utah, the small-town fairgrounds where the rodeo was usually part of a country fair or paired up with a carnival. We saw hundreds of cafes called the Stockman's, the Wagon Wheel or the Gold Nugget, all of them serving mashed potatoes with an ice-cream scoop and offering you your choice of dessert, orange sherbet or orange sherbet. We saw hundreds of bars that still set the standard, for me, of a decent place to buy a bourbon-and-branch (in Montana, called a whiskey ditch).

A bar should be cool and dark, a cave hollowed out of the heat, and it should have a rail, ideally brass, where you can hook your boot heel, the better to settle in and ponder life. The bartender should greet you with "How're you folks today?" and then leave you alone; or if he knows you from other Frontier Days, "Cy, you old son-of-a-gun, how you been keepin'?"

No fake stained glass, no Perrier, and if the bar serves food, no friendly-puppy waiters crying, "Hi! My name is Roger. I'm your serving person tonight."

A decent bar will produce a napkin for a lady, one with cheerfully crass cartoons on it, possibly the only napkin in the place. The cartoons will feature steatopygic women wearing no underpants and surprised by a high wind. Caption: "Just Bummin' Around."

There should be the summer smell of beer sprinkled with salt the pleasant reek of sour mash bourbon, a rack with Planters peanuts in bags you have to rip open with your teeth, another rack with nail clippers and one with key chains: "Souvenir of Puyallup, Washington." A waitress is optional, but if there is one, her name should be Velma.

Walk out of such a bar on a hot day, into the glare of the street, open the doors of your car, with its melting tires, and you'll get an idea of what it's like to burn in hell.

These are some of the big-time rodeos Cy announced year after year: the Rodeo de Santa Fe, Santa Fe, New Mexico; the Snake River Stampede, Nampa, Idaho; the Pike's Peak or Bust Rodeo, Colorado Springs, Colorado; the Southwestern Exposition and Rodeo, Fort Worth, Texas; the Canadian Western Stock Show and Rodeo, Edmonton, Alberta. The small-time ones all took place, in my memory, in the same smoldering town with a ratty arena and a bar called The Last Roundup.

From the Black Hills Roundup in Belle Fourche, South Dakota, most years, we went to Cavalier, North Dakota, just across the border from Manitoba, and the farm where my father grew up. His father, Eli Taillon, and his mother, the first white child to be born in Pembina County and the former Philomine Dumas, still lived there. Born in 1870, she lived to be eighty-seven and left twenty-one great-grandchildren. Until my generation, it was a good Catholic family.

A tiny woman, Grandma Taillon still made her own lye soap in a boiling kettle in the yard; refused to "hook up to the electricity," so that the farmhouse, at night, swam in the shadows cast by kerosene lamps; killed chickens with fearsome skill. Preparing for Sunday dinner, she grabbed a hen by the neck and swung it in circles until its neck and its will to live gave out. Shrieks and the beating of wings and the figure of my grandmother, upright and still except for her implacably whirring arm. I tried to behave myself at her house.

Of Cy's nine brothers and sisters, all but two had left the farm and its backbreaking days. Uncle Henry worked it, and Aunt Ida, ageless in her great bulk, presided over the kitchen. A sea beast thrown up on land, Ida wore dresses the size of tents, made of printed sacking, and bedroom slippers with the tops of the toes cut out. Though she made shy overtures to me, I thought of her as made of the same dough as the bread she baked every day, soft, white and repulsive, and hurt her feelings by whining for store bread instead. Child of the truck stops, I hated farm food, especially those all too fresh chickens, and longed for french fries cooked in rancid grease.

We never stayed in Cavalier more than a few days. Pat was bored before the car came to a stop in front of the house, feeling correctly that she was out of place there. A woman who never could master the swivel-handled potato peeler, she had nothing to contribute in the way of usefulness, and no one called on her to rattle out a barrage of tap steps or do splits up a wall. Nor did any one else on the farm own a fitted cosmetics case or wear white lounging pajamas. Grandma Taillon and Ida knew nothing about either lip brushes or lounging.

"Go talk to Ida, damn it," Cy said when Pat complained. She and I exchanged horrified looks.

Thirty years later I became curious about Ida, but she was dead and it was too late to ask her why she never left home, never married, spent her own eighty-seven years at the pump handle and over the wood stove. I am left with her obituary and what it reveals about her lifetime of duty and hard work: charter member of the Tongue River Homemakers Club; 4-H leader; member of the Tongue River Sewing Circle, the American Legion Auxiliary, the Pembina County Pioneer Daughters, St. Bridget's Catholic Church and its Altar Society.

A patchwork quilt she made for us tells the same plain tale. With twenty varieties of fancy stitch, none repeated in the whole, the quilt is the work of a woman who loved her needle. But it's meant for utility, not beauty. The odd-shaped pieces of fabric are homely, cut from the sleeve of a worn cotton work shirt, a pair of whipcord pants or a flannel shirt. How Ida must have longed to cut just one sleeve off one of my mother's silk blouses or one cuff off her bell-bottomed satin pants, to feel the slippery stuff under her needle.

Pat and I were both outsiders on the farm because the language spoken there was mostly Canadian French. Cy spoke it. We neither spoke nor understood it. Much of the time, during those visits, Cy was hidden away, helping my grandmother take care of his father.

Grandfather Taillon was nearly deaf. All communication with him took place by shouting in French, and since he rarely came out of his downstairs room, from which there issued forth bellows and thumps, I thought he was mad. In several visits to Elm Croft, the farm's name, I saw him only a few times, a gaunt old man with Cy's strong cheekbones, yellowed gray hair and hawk's eyes. Though he spoke to me kindly, if unintelligibly, Cy quickly took him back to his room, seeming embarrassed by him and shooing him down the dark hall with what sounded like threats and invective. I think he must have wanted me to think of my grandfather as a gentleman landowner instead of a wild-looking old man, an apparition in long underwear.

Always, Cy's pattern was to treat things as grander than they were, as if the reality would compromise him. When he made me a gift of his ordinary violin many years later—or rather lent it to me, because he soon took it back—he insisted that it was a Stradivarius.

Nonetheless, he loved Elm Croft and the Red River valley in which it was situated, the flat, loamy fields surrounded by woods, the swimming hole with its heart-stopping rope swing and the farm animals, especially the horses.

Mechanization came late to the farm, and its horses were working animals that pulled threshers and bundle wagons for the haying. When Cy was growing up they also pulled the buggy, the light cutter, the sleigh and the Taillon brothers, who skied the frozen ditches in the winter, towed along at bone-rattling speed behind Old Ned, Cy's favorite. Ned, he wrote in an article called "Once a Farm Boy," was a roan weighing 1,250 pounds, "of uncertain lineage, with some Percheron blood."

In the same piece, he writes about the life of the place, the grueling hard work, the rosary his mother recited every night in French, with the family and the neighbors kneeling around her, and the joys of informal evening musicales. The family had its own orchestra of self-taught musicians, with all the children playing instruments—"fiddles, guitars, piano, xylophone, auto-harp, trumpet and drums"—except for Ida. She never learned to play, Cy notes, because she was too burdened with cooking and housekeeping chores.

With the other Taillon boys, he fished in the neighboring streams, hunted in the woods for bush rabbits, partridges and coyotes and ice-skated on the frozen Tongue River in the winters, when the temperatures dropped as low as sixty below zero. He played his fiddle and acted as a caller for square dances in farmhouses "where the musicians would usually stand in a doorway between two rooms filled with sweating and stomping revelers."

Elm Croft couldn't hold him. How can you keep a boy like Cy down on the farm after he's seen Fargo? But it formed him, so that the farm boy remained even when a reporter was describing him as "blasé and full of adjectives as a circus advance man." Resplendent in a satin Western shirt, boots and cowboy hat, on one of those visits he once took me out to the barn, where a colt had just been born. He had me smell its breath. "Sweet as new hay," he said. "Sweet as a baby's."

Yet he seemed happy to have left the place when we were back on the road again, with the world framed by the windshield. Shaking the dust of Cavalier off his feet, Cy merely traded it for different dust, but for him the dust on the rodeo arena was like greasepaint for actors. It had seeped through his skin; he missed it painfully when we were away long. In the winters, when there were no rodeos, he drank with more determination, got into more trouble—the infinite varieties of it having to do with money and women—and was dangerous to be near, volatile and looking for a fight. His restlessness was that of a bucking horse in the chute. My mother's mood wasn't markedly better.

A former chanteuse, as well as the tap-dancing sensation of St. Louis, Pat had a throaty contralto voice. She had no range at all but could have turned "Onward, Christian Soldiers" into a torch song. I remember her singing "Don't Fence Me In" along with the radio. "Let me ride thru the wide-open country that I love…Don't fence me in."

It could have been their theme song. I made the back seat of the car into a nest and filled it full of clothes, books, blankets and my collections: matchbooks, bar napkins, rodeo programs and swizzle sticks. They left laundry in towns all over the circuit because they were too impatient to wait for it to be ready; threw the windows and the door open when we slept in motor court cabins, to let in fresh air and cowboys looking for a place to bunk; seemed to think walls and a ceiling would cave in and smother them; rarely made it all the way through a movie. "Come on, now." My mother dragged me up the aisle, still riveted to Yvonne De Carlo, and out of the theater. "I can't stand to stay cooped up in this place."

Somebody usually picked up the laundry anyway, settled our bar bill and paid off the irate owner of the Drop Inn when we left his motor court at dawn, ahead of schedule and the bill. Film crews have retinues who follow them on location, sweeping up rubble and settling damage claims. Cy and Pat attracted a retinue of their own, loners drawn to them as a glamorous couple and admirers who saw themselves reflected in their high shine.

It was a thankless job, in their case. They didn't really care about bills and laundry or about orderly lives. But for the most patient of the loners, it eventually paid off.

Meanwhile we rolled along in the Packard, hell-bent for Dallas, Fort Worth, Baton Rouge, and Alabama City. We had our classy car, and gas money. We could sing three-part harmony to "San Antonio Rose." We had the Brahma bull by the tail.

A resident in the San Francisco area, Cyra McFadden was born in Great Falls in 1939 and raised on the rodeo circuit as the daughter of Cy Taillon, one of the most famous American rodeo announcers in the West. She describes this childhood on the road, traveling from rodeo to rodeo, fleabag motel to roadside café in Rain or Shine: A Family Memoir *(Knopf, 1986), and reprinted in 1998. On top of writing a biweekly column for the* San Francisco Examiner *for six years, McFadden published the 1977* The Serial: A Year in the Life of Marin County, *which satirized the trendy lifestyles of Marin County's well-shod residents and was made into a 1980 movie called* The Serial, *starring Tuesday Weld and Martin Mull.*

Sheryl Noethe

GOD'S RIFFLING TOUCH

It was springtime when I began to get well.
I stood on a bridge in the park and looked down at the water,
felt the sun in my bones.
Thousands of Bohemian Waxwings were stripping a stand of trees
in the most remarkable precision of chaos.
A stand of trees stood behind me.
The birds launched themselves at it, wings brushing my face,
their wind blowing back my hair,
they rushed and thrummed around and through me
as if I was just vertical wilderness.
My scarf flew away with them.
I turned and looked at several people gathering to watch.
"My friend," one said, "You have received a blessing."
The birds denuded the stand of its berries and
in a marvelous commotion of instinctual flight patterns gyred off into the sky
leaving me to wonder what next I must do with my life.

RURAL POETRY WORKSHOP

1.

I could hear them screaming from the auditorium.
It made me uneasy, suggesting a tension that pushed
at the surface, pouching into a weakening wall,
a dike ready to give.
The drummer told me he'd had bad sleep thinking about this day,
worrying that he wouldn't be interesting enough, that he might bore
the kids, that he might get a bad name, never be
asked back, that sort of thing. I said, look, you're an artist,
if there's a wild card anywhere it's the kids,
they're worked up and it's hot and they've eaten lots of
sugar, the parents will leave to go chat in the
hall, and the teachers decide it's not their job...
I could see I was making things worse so
I shut up and then the hundred and forty showed
looking at us with great lack of trust,
already suspecting we would try our best
to dupe them.
I took half the group to a classroom for the poetry workshop where they revealed
not a pencil or sheet of paper among them, not a care in the world.
    They settled into their chairs and looked at me expectantly,
    waiting to see how I'd handle it. I walked among them
    collecting one line per student so as to assemble a chant
    poem describing themselves as parts of nature, as color,
    movement and sound.
    The first boys refused, just shook
their heads and settled in farther beneath their
farm caps but I grinned hard, sweating,

and moved in closer, insisting they give me
one small metaphor each. They had no
idea my desperation was so much
greater than their desire not to speak.
I figured it could go two ways; either
I could engage them by the force of my will
and sheer rocklike wall of my faith
or it could all break down, we would reveal
that there was no connecting
luminous umbilicus between us,

2.

that language holds no contract, that one generation only waits
for the last one to die, and that entropy rules a formless sea.
We reassembled after an hour to perform our poets' chorus set to the drummer's
rhythms, bells and chimes.
I divided them into groups and assembled them on stage.
I walked child to child willing them to remember their lines.
One boy described himself as a deer drunk on beer and another
was a blistering badger crawling through the tunnel gap.
We finished our performance in less time than I'd hoped.
The teachers lined up their students to climb back onto the busses
and get home to chores
thankfully free of poets begging them for lines.
The drummer and I collapsed on the stage floor and I said,
the chaos wanted to touch us. I could
see it bulging behind the air, it reached
for us, I could smell it
and that's why you couldn't sleep
you had a premonition that it
knew your name and in the group
of children it would come
and lay its hand upon

you. But
we out ran it.
I helped him load his drums into the car. He said I made a good roadie.
It was mid afternoon and we were free. The road stretched ahead
like a curling ribbon. We sped back to our lives.
Chaos followed like a faithful dog.

THE SRI LANKEN'S GOLDEN BOOK OF DEATH

1.

I held a book. A Sri Lanken man handed it to me.
The spine was two strong twigs. The cover gold thin as tissue.
Markings indecipherable; could be Sankskrit,
Arabic, Aramaic, something more archaic

As I run my fingers along the text on the pages each name
Comes into my head and the person appears
I hear their voices, see their family around them,
Feel their terror rip from their chests like blood-soaked silk

I saw dark eyes with years of indescribable endurance of suffering
I could not lift my fingers from the pages; name without number
Extending my body beyond culture and language
Into the flesh.

Her golden paper-thin sari folding along her black hair.
I am the suicide bomber and his adoring younger brother
I could not lift my hands I wept as terribly as I've every wept
Until it woke my husband and he pulled me from the dreams of blood.

2.

This morning I call Judith and tell her the dream. I'm still shaky.
She whispers into the reciever. *All of America*
She says, *is having the same nightmare.*

Sheryl Noethe was born and raised in the Midwest. After she published The Descent of Heaven Over the Lake *(New Rivers Press, 1984), she moved to New York, where she worked as a poet in residence for five years and landed a job working at school for the deaf. During a residency in Salmon, Idaho, she met the man of her dreams in Luke's Bar and they married and began raising their family of dogs and one white one-eyed feral cat, Mike Tyson. She has published work in several journals, including* Cutbank, The Berkeley Review, *and the* Christian Science Monitor *and was awarded a National Endowment for the Arts fellowship. Her textbook* Poetry Everywhere, *based on her thirteen-year residency in Salmon, was published in 1994. She published a second book of poetry,* The Ghost Opening *(Grace Court Press, 2001). She founded and directs the Missoula Writing Collaborative.*

Mary Clearman Blew

PARANOIA

O N THE WINDSWEPT NORTHERN FACE of Montana, the town of Havre shelters under the bare bluffs of the Milk River. The town is a dot on the railroad map that connects a series of smaller dots across the Highline, a high brow of shortgrass prairie along the Canadian border. It is one of the most sparsely populated areas in the continental United States, with fewer than 100,000 people living along that 250-mile line. Self-contained and isolated by distance and weather, the people of Havre pride themselves on their ability to endure the baked dry heat of summer and the scant snow and minus thirty- or forty-degree temperatures of winter, just as they pride themselves on their town's outlaw past of wolvers and whiskey runners and railroad construction workers.

But Havre's outlaw days are long past. Coming into town, after driving the hundred or so miles up from Great Falls on Highway 87, the outsider is likely to feel the jolt of a mirage taking on shape and form: after so many miles of nothing but sky and sagebrush, here is this town of dusty cottonwoods and willows and irrigated lawns. "People live here?" a member of a Chicago dance troupe, come to Havre to perform at the local state college, once asked, incredulously.

Yes! We live here! And don't think for one minute that we'd rather live in your crime-ridden, congested, stinking Chicago! This is a friendly town where our kids can grow up safely and our neighbors will always offer a helping hand. We take care of our own here! We're doing just fine!

On the bluff above the town, facing into the wind, is the campus of Northern Montana College, established by local legislators in the 1930s in hopes of providing jobs to the community during those terrible years of drought and depression, and also of offering further schooling to the children of the tiny prairie towns and ranches of the Highline who otherwise lived hundreds of miles from a college or university. People in Havre are proud of Northern, which stands as another example of their pluck and self-reliance. Also, Northern is a campus where decent, conservative parents believe their children will be safe and sheltered from city temptations or from the radical ideas to which they might be exposed at, say, the University of Montana in Missoula.

A dark side of any isolated, self-contained community is how deeply it may fear outsiders. A particularly ugly incident during the summer of 1970 had fueled the fears of people all over Montana, when the headless, armless, legless body of a young man was pulled out of the Yellowstone River, near Livingston. Eventually the body was identified and the killers traced to a pair of hitchhikers who, by that time, had returned to California. Apparently they had murdered the young man for his car, but also for a grizzlier reason: when apprehended, one of the hitchhikers told police, "I've got a problem, I'm a cannibal," as he pulled a handful of human bones from his pocket and added, "These aren't chicken bones."

Californians! Hippies! Manson-style murderers! Flames and dark dancing figures, chants and blasphemies and slogans written on walls in blood!

The rumors that festered in and around Havre that fall might have been amusing if they had not led to such serious consequences. According to one popular story, hordes of hippies were camping in a public park a few miles to the east, getting ready to invade the town. As evidence, a woman wrote to the editor of the Havre *Daily News* that she had counted 130 hippies getting on school buses in the tiny community of Big Sandy, a few miles south of Havre. (Maybe what she had seen were the Indian fire crews from the Rocky Boy Reservation, going out to fight fires, suggested a wag.) However, fears were beginning to focus on two young men, one of them a black man, who had come from Philadelphia, of all outlandish places, to visit a local girl. The young men were shaggy-haired, they wore the disreputable clothing that young people even in Montana in 1970 were wearing, and they were disturbingly *other*. When the young black man was seen downtown in broad daylight with his arm around a white girl, community simmering came to a boil, and rumors went from preposterous to disturbingly plausible.

Was it possible, for instance, that a group of Havre businessmen—names were named, faces pointed out—actually had climbed a butte overlooking the town and burned a cross? *Oh! Yes! I was there! I watched them,* insisted a college student. *A friend of mine filmed it with a home movie camera, got all their faces.*

What certainly was true was that things had gone too far. The young men from Philadelphia had received death threats. But at that point, a respected Havre attorney called publicly for a return to reason. The two young Philadelphia men, he announced, were welcome to move into his home with him and his family and stay as long as it took for them to feel safe.

The attorney's willingness to speak out was, apparently, enough. If rumors of hippies or fear of out-of-towners hadn't dissipated entirely, at least they were no longer overt, and there was no more talk of cross-burning.

THE FACULTY AT NORTHERN MONTANA COLLEGE—the arts and letters faculty, at least—tended to keep themselves apart from the townspeople and to affect an amused disdain for their rumors. In truth, they were not a part of the town, although some of them had taught at Northern for twenty years or more. Then too, they had their own rumors to worry about.

Times were changing in academe in the nineteen-seventies, even at remote little state colleges like Northern. Everyone had read of the student protest movements on campuses in faraway places like Berkeley and Boston, or watched the jerky black and white footage of sit-down strikes and marches on the evening news, and while no one really believed that boys and girls from Highline towns and ranches were likely to start wearing beads and feathers or join radical societies or take over the president's office, the reports stimulated a disturbing thrill, like an electrical charge over a great distance. When, at a fall faculty meeting, a young professor of history whose office was located in the squat tower above Cowan Hall announced that he was requisitioning a length of rope to run out a window and let himself down in the event that students tried to hold him hostage, the laughter was nervous.

Among the faculty, there was a feeling that not only were their students changing in ways they could not have predicted, but so were the circumstances of their own lives. Northern Montana College had been staffed, during the nineteen-fifties and sixties, by recruiting seasoned teachers from high schools around the state. To be appointed at the college level was considered a reward for their years of service. No one thought of requiring them to hold doctoral degrees; a master's degree was all the education anyone would ever want or need. Unless you aspired to an administrative position, why waste years on the tedium and expense of writing a dissertation? There was such a thing as being *too* educated. The belief was widely held that, along with high academic achievement, came a lack of practicality and common sense. What wasn't wanted on an unpretentious campus like Northern was a pack of educated fools.

But now the professors at Northern were being told of new accreditation standards which required terminal academic degrees in appropriate fields, and these same seasoned professors were being presented with young colleagues who could write *Ph.D.* after their names but who had never taught in high school, who knew little and thought they knew so much.

To add to their unease, they were seeing women being hired, and not just as nursing faculty or as faculty in the two-year secretarial program. In spite of certain deeply-held beliefs that women were unfit for teaching college-level English courses, a second woman had just been hired in the English department to join the giggly ex-high school teacher who oversaw the teaching certification program. The new woman looked young enough to be a student, herself, but icily unapproachable, as though she feared that someone else's smile or greeting might shatter her surface like crazed porcelain. Something wrong there, but she had a Ph.D., so what else was to be said?

THE LONG-TIME CHAIRMAN of the English department had had to beat the bushes of Montana to staff his sections. Like their colleagues in other academic departments, most of the seven professors then teaching English had been lured out of one high school or another, although young Mr. Thackeray told how the chairman had driven out to wheat field where he was driving a combine and persuaded him to accept a teaching position instead of returning to law school in the fall. But by the early nineteen-seventies, however, it was becoming obvious that no longer was there a shortage of qualified candidates willing to live and teach at such a remote and windblown campus but, at least in the fields of arts and letters, there was a surfeit of would-be professors looking desperately for a job, any job.

But the former chairman had resigned after losing one of the fierce internecine wars that occasionally raged through the college, and the dean had appointed as his replacement a fiery little pot-bellied man who held a Ph.D. degree from Harvard and who was so deeply resentful of authority that he started battling with the dean the day he arrived on campus. True to his egalitarian principles, the new chairman had reorganized the English department as a co-op, shaken up the curriculum, and refused to evaluate the faculty. Now he was trying to hire a new young professor, and the dean for some reason was dragging his feet.

It was 1973 by now, times had changed, and hiring was now done through advertising and screening by a committee. The professors in the English department had supposed they would be looking for someone with a master's degree and high school teaching experience, but no, said the dean. They had to find somebody with a Ph.D., and so they settled down to read the tidal wave of applications that flooded into their offices. From these applications they selected a man from California whom we will call Paul Blevins.

"I SHOULD BE THE ONE to greet him," insisted the chairman, when the on-campus interview was finally arranged. The dean, for some reason, had taken a dislike to the California man from what he read in his paperwork, which enraged the chairman to the point of wanting to make the hire, sight unseen. But no, said the dean, there had to be a campus interview. All right, reported the chairman through gritted teeth to the gathered faculty. We'll play his little game. So the invitation was made to Paul Blevins, and the flight into the one-strip local airport arranged. The chairman would meet him and see him to his hotel room. Once he had had a chance to rest, there would be a dinner party to give everyone else a chance to get acquainted with him.

That Paul Blevins came from California was both impressive and frightening. That he also had a Ph.D. made everybody wonder why a man so well qualified really wanted to join them. Would he be *happy* here, they asked each other doubtfully. Would he *fit in*. But they had picked him out, and the dean finally had given them a go-ahead, and now they were anxious to get a look at him.

THE YOUNG WOMAN WITH THE FACE like porcelain about to shatter was assigned to pick up Paul Blevins at his hotel and drive him to the dinner party. Her husband reluctantly parked at the curb on First Street and waited while she ran in to fetch Paul Blevins; he hated all college faculty get-togethers, but he had no choice. He had to go along and keep an eye on his wife. While they both were in graduate school, he had been able to think of ways to keep her from going out and socializing, but since they had moved to Havre and she had had a real job, she was becoming more and more independent, and now his anger was blossoming, and also his suspicions. He knew she was naïve. Too naïve even to know when a pass was being made at her. Her behavior was drawing attention to her, and by extension to him.

The young woman, knowing herself on a knife-edge of civility which must last her and her husband through the evening, hurried through the lobby with its comfortable drone of black-and-white television and shabby chairs full of the shabbier old men who lodged in the old hotel. She had stayed in this same hotel three years ago, for her own interview, and it seemed to her that nothing had changed: same old men, same blurred television footage of faraway warfare. There would be worn chenille spreads on the beds upstairs, and tiny octagonal tiles on the floors of the bathrooms, where the sounds of conversations and flushing water from other rooms would be carried through the pipes, and where, at one or two or three in the morning, the faraway crash of freight cars coupling in the rail yards to the north would remind the sleepless guest that life continued elsewhere. She had lain awake the night of her interview, knowing that she was going to accept this job if it was offered to her, knowing that living in this town was going to change her, never guessing how much.

Now she climbed two flights of stairs and rapped on the door that was Paul Blevins's. For long moments no one answered, and she was just beginning to wonder whether she had made some mistake, wrong room number perhaps, when the door opened, and there stood a tall and robust man with a head of springy dark hair and a face so white that her first thought was that he must be in great pain.

"Dr. Blevins?" she faltered, feeling somehow that she had intruded.

He passed a hand over his face, as though hearing his name had intensified the pain.

"Yes," he said, "oh, yes." When he turned to reach for his coat, she saw that he was carrying a bottle of beer.

I WAS THAT YOUNG WOMAN, as much as anyone is the person she was thirty years ago. What can I say for myself? That I was so innocent of the ways of the world that I didn't recognize a drunk when I saw one?

That, although I had an uneasy feeling that something was seriously the matter with Paul Blevins, I lacked the self-confidence to say so?

Guilty on both counts. And yet, when I look back on that whole sorry episode, what strikes me is not just my lack of judgment, but the lack of judgment shown by nearly everyone who eventually was drawn into the Paul Blevins affair. It is as though, in the convergence of a certain set of circumstances—the iceberg, the ship—instincts more primitive than reason and judgment rise screaming to the surface as though they never had been submerged. Perhaps we can count ourselves fortunate if there is one, like the attorney who put out the flames of the great Havre hippie scare, who not only keeps his or her head but reminds the rest of us to keep ours.

TO UNDERSTAND THE PAUL BLEVINS AFFAIR, consider the size and isolation of the town and campus. The population of Havre in the nineteen-seventies was around eight thousand. The college, with about a hundred faculty and administrators and fewer than fifteen hundred students, lay nearly three hundred miles to the north of the University of Montana, over narrow black-topped highways that often were treacherous with winter ice and blizzards. To live at such distance from the rest of the world, at a time when cable television and public radio had not yet reached the Highline, when the internet was undreamed of, was to begin to believe that Havre and its campus was the only world that was.

For the older faculty, the college was an extension of the high schools in which they had taught most of their lives, and they felt lucky to be there. On the other hand, the younger, university-trained faculty, chafing at their circumstances, saw the college as a concept to be realized. The college-as-concept explained the radical curriculum revision the new English department chairman, with his Harvard Ph.D., had undertaken, and also some of his other innovations, such as rounding up a band of unemployed recent B.A. graduates, appointing them graduate assistants, and assigning them sections of freshman composition. He was apoplectic with rage when the dean, hearing of this program through his spies, fired all the graduate assistants and reassigned the composition sections to the professors. "You don't have a graduate program, so you can't have graduate assistants, and besides, there's no money to pay them," the dean pointed out. "Yes, but we *should* have!" raged the chairman.

The college-as-concept added its fuel to the battles among the Northern faculty and its administrators. Perhaps as a side-effect of a no-exit world, grudges were never forgotten and slights never forgiven. Faculty offices buzzed with plots, rumors, and counterplots, all at the deepest level of seriousness, and yet—again, perhaps because all the plots were on-going, all the rumors constantly metastasizing into new rumors—none of it was life-threatening. There were no cease-fires, but also there were no consequences.

That would change.

THE FALL SEMESTER OF 1974 began, as it always did, in the wheat dust and sunlight of late September. Cottonwood trees shaded the many-paned windows of Cowan Hall, with its echoing stairs and its warren of faculty offices at the south end of the second floor, and the students came sunburned and healthy from working harvest. These early days of the semester were as benign as though winter would never blast those lush leaves or rattle sleet against the windows, although in fact the first snowfall could silence the campus and town within a few weeks. The chairman of the English department called the first meeting of the fall, and everyone gathered in the dappled light of one of the big classrooms.

There at the meeting was handsome young Mr. Thackerary, who taught philosophy, and there was suave, toupeed Mr. Lisenby, who taught public speaking, and plump, chuckling Mr. Keller, puffing on his cigar, who taught British literature and could recite the plots of every Victorian novel ever written to anyone he could corner at a faculty party. There was Miss Erickson, who was working at getting rid of her giggle, and there was nervous, red-haired Mr. Neisius, who was supposed to have finished his doctorate the previous summer but hadn't. There I was, self-absorbed and frozen, and there was Dr. Paul Blevins. He was one of us, now. None of us saw any significance in the dean's hiring him on a one-year contract.

Later, as the semester wore on and the cottonwoods outside Cowan Hall turned briefly golden and then thrashed their way into sleet-whipped, subzero winter, we could all learn more about Paul Blevins and, for example, the magniloquence of his memo-writing. He could turn a request for a sentence or two requesting summer teaching into three or four pages of irony and hyperbole, he could object to some detail of campus governance with reams of satire embellished with the darkest imagery. But at that first department meeting, everyone was hopeful and curious, and many were the glances stolen at him as he sat in our semi-circle, handsome and expansive in his suit and tie. His headache seemed to be gone, his deep laugh rolled out at unexpected moments, and he gleamed with an inner amusement that told us he know a thing or two we didn't. All the while our little chairman beamed upon him, proud as a new papa.

While the men in the department seemed to see the chairman as a Quixote, flailing at the academic windmills of intellectual poverty on the one hand and parsimony on the other, I disliked him with an intensity that grew over the years I knew him. For him, women did not exist in academe. It was his duty, as he saw it, to fight for his colleagues and protect them from the dean, but of course his colleagues were men. Miss Erickson and I were—what. Adjuncts, perhaps. Useful takers of notes and instructors of freshman composition. My objections to my class assignments, or to my being overlooked for sought-after summer classes, were likely to be met with an absent frown, or—if pressed in department meeting—a startled titter. *Changing her mind is a woman's privilege*, he was fond of saying. Or, rolling his eyes, he would ask rhetorically, *What do women want?*

Writing about the man after all these years, I find myself wondering if I have invented him. Surely no such caricature could have existed. He's a figment of my imagination, an eater of my sins, a marionette that I've jerked through the decades in his shiny green suit and soiled necktie. I'm embarrassed to be writing about him, *whining* about him—and yet I close my eyes and there he is, nervously licking his lips with a shred of tobacco stuck to his tongue, although his only role at the present moment is as adjunct to the explosion of Paul Blevins that winter.

I might have paid more attention to the talk that almost immediately began to swirl around Paul Blevins if it had not been for the misery of my marriage. My husband and I had married in our teens, as undergraduates, and by now our ideas of ourselves had diverged. Because I had accepted the position at Northern, he had given up a job he liked, to come and teach at Havre High School. He hated Havre, and he hated the gossip, and he hated the transformation of his wife into *that young woman in the English department.* He felt exposed, felt himself the butt of unpleasant speculation.

"There are other jobs," he kept telling me.

"No, there aren't. Don't you remember how long it took me to find this one?"

I had finished graduate school along with a thousand other young Ph.D.s who were competing for too few positions in the liberal arts, and the job at Northern had seemed to me the last job in the world. I was certain that, if I gave in to my husband and resigned, I would never get another.

He would listen to my explanation, but in a few days he would come back to it. "There are other jobs."

Gossip always swirled on campus, and often it was vicious. What was said about me was that I required my students to hump me in my office, on my desk. What was said about Paul Blevins was that his wife was very young, which was true. That he had had an affair with her while she was in high school and he was her teacher, which had caused him to be divorced by his first wife and fired from his job, which might or might not have been true. That he and the very young wife and their baby son had moved into one of the cottages provided by the college for first-year faculty and covered all the windows with bookshelves and books so they could live in the dark like moles, which could have been true, but what did it signify?

There never was a source for these stories, which were told in the passive voice. *They were seen. He was seen.* If one believed the gossip, we all fornicated and frolicked in some shadowy state that existed simultaneously with our dull daylight drudgery, as though we were a department of doppelgangers. No wonder my husband snarled and tried to see through shadows.

One evening that fall, Paul Blevins showed up in the basement of Cowan Hall, where I was directing the college play. I glanced up and saw him grinning and beckoning from the double doors that opened into the theater. Wondering what on earth, I left my playbook and went out into the corridor to see what he wanted. Whatever it was, he was full of it; he was dancing on his toes, barely able to contain what he was about to import.

"They know all about you," he said, and he laughed, a long exultant skein of laughter that unwound itself down the echoing dark corridor and faded into the land of the doppelgangers.

"What?"

"Dr. Crowley and the postmaster. They know all about you."

I stared at him. Dr. Crowley was the president of the college. The postmaster lived up the street from my house. His youngest son was my son's age.

"It's a conspiracy. They're keeping track of the letters you've written to apply for other jobs. They're opening your letters to see what you're saying. I used to work in a post office," he explained, "so I know how they arrange these things."

What struck me, even in the moment, was how absolutely convincing he was. Whether it was the force of his personality, his energy, his massive body as he bent to confide the details of the plot he had uncovered, I was ready to believe him. Utterly. But I didn't believe him, because I had written no letters of application. There were no letters to open, no letters to conspire over.

I don't remember what else he said. I suppose I went back to play practice. I suppose Paul Blevins took himself off, laughing to himself and dancing up the stairs to the double plate glass doors which reflected him in a black sheen before he broke the illusion and disappeared in the direction of the parking lot. And if, thinking over his behavior, I had an uneasy feeling that something ought to be done, I didn't act on it. After all, what could I have done? Carried the tale to the department chairman? After all, it wasn't that much wilder a tale than some of the suspicions that buzzed up and down the corridors. Or so I told myself.

I did write in my journal that night, *Paul Blevins is crazy.*

I WAS WRITING FICTION AGAIN, after a hiatus of five or six years. Trying to write fiction. My husband was certain he was the secret subject of all my stories. He would stand over me and my typewriter, cocking his head as casually as though it were the most natural thing in the world for him to be reading the words as I wrote them.

"I see this time you've killed me off," he remarked, sadly, when one character turned out to be a widow.

"I'm not writing about you. Go away."

"Oh, yes you are. Why do you want to hang on to this job? There are other jobs."

"Go away, I'm trying to write." But he was on the attack now. Driven to distraction by rumors and shaken by the shift in our marriage, he tried to force us back to what we had been before my job—*the job!*—and he used the sharpest weapon he could find. "I want to get this situation settled, once and for all! You're thinking about having an affair, aren't you."

"No, I'm not! Why do you think that?"

"You're not the type that could handle an affair. You'd have a breakdown."

And so on.

Years later I learned that my seven-year-old daughter had lain awake, listening to our raised voices and sobbing softly to herself, small sufferer from the misery of marriage. "It always ended with you crying," she said. It was true; I always ended up in tears and my husband half-triumphant, half-abashed. He was terrified of losing me, he knew he was losing me, but he didn't know why, and all he could think to do was to insist and storm and accuse until he had reduced me to a sodden bundle of tears, which was not what he wanted at all.

What did I want? I knew my husband was right; the job wasn't even a good job, the college library was inadequate for scholarly research, and the teaching load was four classes a semester, most of them basic writing classes. I knew I was hurting him and hurting our children by my stubbornness. Why did I hang on to the job, why did I insist on writing fiction when my writing caused him so much distress? It was my fault, I knew it was my fault, and surely it wasn't worth it. And yet, just as I had plodded through graduate school through protests and recriminations, I kept writing and I plodded back to Cowan Hall every day, locked and frozen inside myself and trying not to give more offense than I was already giving.

Rumors aside, Cowan Hall was a safe place where secretaries typed in the administrative offices downstairs and the heat registers puffed away. Snow might swirl against those high single-paned windows, the wind might rattle against the glass, and conspiracy theories might abound, but Cowan Hall had withstood worse, and it stood four-square and solid under its squat tower, and I had my mailbox in the alcove next to the campus switchboard, and I had my small office with my name on the door, and the classrooms next door were filled with boys and girls in mackinaws and cowboy boots and blue jeans who knew as little as I once had, but were willing to learn. The saving grace of Northern was the solid teaching that went on there.

If I give up the job, I'll be at his mercy, I said to myself, without quite allowing myself to know what I meant.

WITH THE WINTER CAME FRESH SWIRLS of rumors about our embattled little chairman.He had been the subject of speculation ever since his arrival: how had a man with a Ph.D. from Harvard come to end his career on the Montana prairie? Who did he think he was? Did he have no sense of self-preservation? His quarrels were legendary; he had insulted Dr. Crowley, he had disobeyed the dean, he had picked fights with everyone from the manager of the book store to the cooks in the college food service in his whole-hearted belief that, through his own persistence and force of argument, he could transform the practical programs at Northern into a traditional liberal arts curriculum. Now came word that he was going to be removed as chairman of the English department. He couldn't be fired, because he had been hired with tenure. But, beginning with the next academic year, he would be just another professor with the rest of us, and someone else would be chairman.

Few events in academe, perhaps in the world, are so catastrophic that the survivors don't begin to speculate on what personal opportunity might open for themselves, and so it must have been with Paul Blevins. On the one hand (so rumor had it), the chairman had gone directly from the dean's office to Paul Blevins's office and woke his fears by saying, "They got me, and you're my protégé, so they'll be gunning for you next." On the other hand, the shoes that carried the old chairman from the dean's office to Paul Blevins's office could hardly have picked up another scuff before heads were together, calculating. *Let's see. Since they can't fire him, they won't have an open position. They can't hired from outside. The dean will have to look inside, which means one of us will be the new chairman. But which of us?*

Has to be someone with a Ph.D. Remember those accreditation standards? The chairman of a department has to have the appropriate terminal degree.

Paul Blevins?

THIS, I BELIEVE, IS THE direction Paul Blevins's thoughts spun. *Could he be so fortunate? But wait! There's Dr. Clearman. She's got a Ph.D. But they wouldn't, would they? Appoint a woman?—or would they?*

And so he showed up on my doorstep, late one evening. I went to see who could be knocking at such an hour and saw him grinning through the window and holding up his six-pack of beer. My husband took one look at him, gathered up his papers, glared at me, and moved down to the basement to finish grading.

Paul Blevins seated himself at my kitchen table and opened a beer. He had a story to tell, and he was looking forward to telling it, but first he downed his beer. Laughing, pausing to take deep draughts from a fresh beer, gleaming and giggling, he began an involved account of how he had learned that the local homosexuals were plotting to take control of Northern Montana College.

"I called Roger," he said, naming a young unmarried professor of art. "He said, *Hello?* I didn't say a word. I just waited on the line. After awhile he said, *Bill?*"

Paul Blevins exploded into laughter. "Can you believe it? He said, *Bill?*"

I was trying, in my literal-minded way, to understand what was incriminating about saying *Bill.*

"They almost caught me," Paul Blevins was explaining, his breath whistling at his narrow escape. "They had a party and invited me, but I knew enough not to go. Otherwise they would have caught me, too."

I felt as though I was listening to an eerie reprise of his postmaster plot, except that this one was less coherent. But in spite of his laughter and his fractured details, a narrative of sorts emerged. I think it emerged. Every story has not only a teller, but a listener, and every story contains not only what was told, but what was heard. It may be that I was too gullible a listener, it may be that I gave to his details a more distinct frame than Paul Blevins ever intended. He was to insist, in the aftermath, that he had been misunderstood. Misunderstood, or perhaps deliberately framed. But as he told his story, I was dazed by the names he listed, all of whom I knew, some of whom apparently were active members of the homosexual ring, some of whom were being blackmailed by the members of the ring, as Paul Blevins himself would have been blackmailed if he had attended the fateful party. Our former chairman was an active member of the ring, of course. *Of course.*

"I'll need your support," he ended. "They'll have their way on campus unless we stand up to them! We'll be an alliance of a true man and a true woman!"

Eventually, his beer drunk up, he took himself off, and eventually my husband came angrily back upstairs, and we quarreled, of course. Why did he have to go downstairs and leave me alone with a drunk? Well, why did I have to involve myself with drunks? Why, when most of the time he hovered over me, did he go off and leave me alone when I could have used his support? Well, why, when I brought these situations on myself, should he have to get me out of them?

So I never did tell him about the homosexual ring. But it worried me, and the next morning, when I ran into Miss Erickson as I hurried into Cowan Hall on some last-minute errand (I was traveling that day with a group of student actors in a children's play to a near-by town), I blurted out the whole tarradiddle. Miss Erickson's reaction was to laugh, which reassured me. It was a funny story, really. No need to worry further.

And yet, that afternoon, when the principal of the elementary school where my students were performing pulled me aside and said I was wanted on the telephone in his office I was stricken with dread.

It was the dean.

"I don't want to get into the details over the phone," he said, "but I understand one of our faculty has made certain allegations regarding others on our faculty. Is this true?"

I have never been a good liar. "Yes," I whispered.

"Are you willing to confirm what you were told?"

"Yes."

Why? Why didn't I do the decent thing and lie?

"I'll want to talk with you first thing in the morning," he said, and hung up.

My reaction was dread, spawned by a deep sense of guilt. This was *my fault.* At the very least, it was going to be construed as my fault, for listening, for *telling.* I crept home, crept around the house that night, crept to campus the next morning for my eight o'clock meeting with the dean.

As I opened the glass door into the suite of administrative offices, I glanced over my shoulder and saw the librarian unlocking the door at the other end of Cowan Hall. He gave me a curious glance. I knew what that meant. *She was seen on her way to the dean's office.*

I had made one phone call the night before. "Did you tell anyone?" I asked Miss Erickson.

"No," she said, puzzled. "Well—" and she named the dean of students. "I happened to run into him right after I talked to you, and I thought the story was so funny that I told him about it. He laughed and laughed."

In fact, the story had struck the dean of students as so funny that he had laughingly asked the academic dean what he planned to do about the homosexual plot. The academic dean had not been amused. Therefore his phone call to me, therefore, therefore.

"He was hired on a one-year contract," said the dean, after he had extracted my account from me, "and it won't be renewed. He won't be given a reason. The only person who needs to know is your chairman—he's still the chairman, until the end of the year—and he must be told why one of his faculty members will not have his contract renewed."

"He'll go right to Paul!"

The dean leaned back in his chair and regarded me. I seem to remember sunlight falling through the window behind him, making hollows of his eyes and patterning the shoulders of the off-the-rack suit all administrators wore in those days. He had been a football coach at a Montana high school before becoming a college administrator, and he was still very lean, with a graying crew cut and a face like a skull under a tight tanned mask of skin. He would go on to become Montana's commissioner of higher education before he was done. Before he was done. Before he and his wife and adopted son drowned in a sailboat accident. But all that lay in the unforeseeable future, and for now I shook under his gaze and dreaded my own future.

"He'll be warned not to," said the dean. As though that would be that.

THAT WAS MY MORNING. I dragged myself through the rest of my day, dragged myself home. I cooked dinner, I suppose. My husband had gone back to the high school to do some work of his own when the telephone rang. I knew, knew as certainly as though I had been writing the script, who was calling.

"Hello," I whispered.

There was a whistling silence on the line, as though over miles and miles. Finally, "Oh, yes!" sighed Paul Blevins.

I could think of nothing to say.

"I've been hurt," he sighed. "I've been badly hurt, and I'm going to see that others are hurt just as badly before I leave this town."

He waited, but it was as if I had no voice. I was shaking, I could say nothing, and finally, gently, he hung up the phone.

"What? What?" demanded my children. They were wild-eyed, sensing my fear.

"There's a bad man," I managed, and then the phone rang again.

It was Dr. Crowley. "Mary, did you get a strange phone call this evening?" he wanted to know.

"Yes," I sobbed, wondering how on earth he knew.

"We think he's dangerous," said Dr. Crowley. "Mary, is there anywhere you could go for a few days, or a few weeks? Out of town?"

"My parents' ranch," I said. "But my classes!"

"That would be excellent. Don't worry about your classes. Go to the ranch and stay there. Other than that, I don't know what to tell you, except to lock your doors and close your curtains and stay away from the windows."

He hung up. I stared at the phone. If only I knew more. After a minute I dialed his home phone number.

His wife answered. Her voice was pleasant and noncommittal, although campus lore in the aftermath would have it that her husband had called her, given her the same advice he had given me—lock the doors, close the curtains, stay away from the windows— without context, and then he had hung up on her.

"He's not here," she said. "He went up to his office on campus."

The college switchboard would have closed at five. He could call out, but no one could call in. I couldn't think what else to do. I wanted to pack, but both children were sobbing, so I gathered them up and rocked them until, finally, my husband came home.

"This is all your fault!" he screamed. "My busiest time! And now I've got to drive all night, to get you to the ranch!"

"I'll drive myself!"

By this time it was nearly midnight. Our headlights lit the empty street as, with the four of us crammed into the cab of the truck with what clothes

I had snatched together, we pulled out of our driveway. A few years later, a student who had been working as a police dispatcher told me that my house had been under surveillance all that night, but I saw no sign of police presence at the time. The town was silent, only a few dim security lights burning in stores. It was a week night and even the bars were quiet. All the noise in the world was contained in the cab of the truck with us, as my husband's fear and outrage and bewilderment twisted into diatribe. He had never asked for this flight into the night. He did not deserve the trouble I had caused him. He was up to here with it, he had had all he could take, and it was all my fault. For the three-hour drive through the darkest part of the night, over snowbound highways, my husband's voice ratcheted through my head. He may not have screamed for the entire three hours. It seemed, still seems to me, that he did. Then, at four in the morning, with the children settled into a state closer to stupor than sleep, we had driven through Lewistown, up the winding county road through pine forest, and were pulling up to the pole gate by the snow-covered barn. There was a light burning in the ranch house, a hundred yards on the other side of the gate.

LEWISTOWN, WHERE I WENT TO HIGH SCHOOL, lies in the shelter of several low mountain ranges. The wind is not as fierce as it is on the Highline, and the snow in winter lies deeper. There had been several feet of snow at the ranch that winter, and its white light fell through the windows of the old house. For three weeks my children and I lived in stasis, while Dr. Crowley and the dean negotiated with the state board of education to buy out the remainder of Paul Blevins's contract on condition that he leave town. Otherwise, as Dr. Crowley pointed out to me over the long distance telephone, he would hole up in his cottage and drink and brood, and who knew what he might do.

Rumors on campus had boiled over. My husband, who had turned around in the barnyard at four A.M. and driven back to Havre to teach the next morning, reported over the long distance telephone that he had had a series of calls from the chairman, begging to know where I had gone. The chairman had conceived the notion that if only Paul Blevins apologized to me, everything would be all right and Paul would have his job back. The chairman was sure everything could be smoothed over. He was telling everyone that I had gone to be with my sick father. No one had to know what I had done. My husband finally slammed down the phone, locked the house, and went to stay with a friend to get away from its incessant ringing.

"He was worried sick about his family. That was why he was so angry," my mother tried to soothe me.

For those three weeks my children played upstairs while I read and embroidered and worried about what would happen when we went back to Havre. One day my father took me to town, picked out a pistol for me, and made me practice firing it until he was sure I could shoot straight.

"Mom, are you going to wear that gun on your hip when you go back to class?" asked my son.

On another day my father hitched one of his teams of horses to a hay sled and took the children and me for a drive across snowbound meadows where sunlight danced on frost crystals and pine trees cast their blue shadows and occasionally dropped their snowcaps into a world that was otherwise peaceful. My children were bundled to their noses, and they got to hold the lines of the horses, and around the haystacks in the high pasture they saw deer that raised their heads at our silent passing and went on eating hay. I thought how it had been my choice to leave this place, a choice nobody understood, and now I would be going back to Havre, to try to piece together what was left of the semester. Dr. Crowley had called to say that it was safe, that Paul Blevins was gone.

ALL THIS TOOK PLACE DURING THE WINTER of 1974. That spring my husband told me that he was resigning his job at Havre High School and moving back to the Midwest. He no longer wanted to be married to me. The dean is dead—drowned with his family, as I have said—and Dr. Crowley is dead, and so is Mr. Lisenby. I suspect our fiery ex-chairman is dead, although I lost track of him after he retired. Miss Erickson is retired and living alone, in bad health. I visit her once or twice every year, and when, on my most recent visit, I told her I was writing about Paul Blevins,

I was surprised to learn that she did not remember him.

The only person I knew in 1974 who still teaches at Northern is young Mr. Thackeray, no longer young. I ran into him at a writers' conference last summer, and I asked him if he remembered Paul Blevins. He laughed and said he was probably the last person in Havre to see Paul; he'd helped him pack his books and odds and ends out of his faculty cottage and into a U-Haul for his move to—wherever he went. He was never heard from again.

I had returned, that winter, to a campus that was surprisingly calm. When I remarked on that calm to Miss Erickson, she had explained that when the rumors and speculation had reached the point where it seemed as though the English department was about to combust from its own excitement, Mr. Lisenby—suave, toupeed Mr. Lisenby—had gone around to everyone's office and said, in effect, *Pull yourselves together! Get over it! Enough!*

I went down to his office to thank him, but he only smiled.

Mr. Lisenby's wife had received a phone call from Paul Blevins on the night of threats. "Who are you?" Marian Lisenby was said to have said. "You sound like you're drunk. I'm hanging up."

Paul had had a busy night on the phone. Some of his calls were friendly, some were maudlin, and others, to members of his so-called homosexual ring, so threatening that some of the men were frightened nearly to hysteria. For years I wondered what would have happened if, during his call to me, I had had the poise to have said, as Marian Lisenby did, "Oh, Paul! You're drunk! Come off it!"

As I had with his postmaster conspiracy story, I must have let Paul think I believed his homosexual conspiracy story. I hadn't argued or tried to reason with him, hadn't dismissed him, but had listened and waited for him to go away. Now I wonder if he saw in me a naïve young woman who would believe anything he told her. I wonder if he thought his homosexual conspiracy story would frighten me into supporting him in his bid for the chairmanship.

If that is what he hoped, he was mistaken. The dean, mistrustful of Paul from the beginning, was only too glad of an excuse to be rid of him, and rid of him he was.

The other thing that happened that spring, besides the end of my marriage, was that the dean called me down to his office and offered me the chairmanship of the English department, thus confirming—what?—whose paranoia? My sense of complicity, certainly, that I have carried to this day.

Mary Clearman Blew grew up in Montana on a small cattle ranch that was the site of her great-grandfather's 1882 homestead. She attended the University of Montana, Missoula, and the University of Missouri-Columbia, where she received a Ph.D. in Renaissance literature. She has written or edited eleven books, including All But the Waltz: Essays on a Montana Family *(Viking, 1991), which won a Pacific Northwest Booksellers Award, and, most recently,* Writing Her Own Life: Imogene Welch, Rural Schoolteacher. *A novel,* Jackalope Milk, *is forthcoming. She has won numerous awards, including the Western Literature Association's Lifetime Achievement Award. At the present time she teaches creative writing at the University of Idaho.*

❦ *Melanie Rae Thon*

HEAVENLY CREATURES:
FOR WANDERING CHILDREN
AND THEIR DELINQUENT MOTHER

I. FATHERS

DIDI KINKAID AND HER THREE children by three fathers lived in a narrow pink and green trailer at the end of a rutted road in Paradise Hollow. One wintry November night, fifteen days after my father died, eleven days after he was buried, Didi's only son climbed the hill to our house, leaped from our bare maple to a windowsill on the second floor, shattered the glass above my mother's bed, and burst, bleeding, onto her pillows.

The house was dark, all his—Mother and I had gone to town that night to eat dinner by the hot-bellied stove in my brother's kitchen.

Evan Kinkaid helped himself to twenty-two pounds of frozen venison, a bottle of scotch, six jars of sweet peaches. The boy carried away my down comforter, a green sleeping bag, our little black and white television. He found Mother's cashmere scarf, rolled tight and tucked safe in a shoebox full of cedar chips, never worn because it was too precious. Now it was gone, wrapping Evan's throat, a lovely gift, something soft and dear for him to wear home and offer Didi. The starved boy crushed chocolate cookies in a bowl of milk and sugar. He stopped to eat, then slipped his hands in Daddy's gloves: deerskin dyed black, lined with the silky fur of a white rabbit.

In exchange, he left his blood, his dirt, his smell of bonfire smoke everywhere.

On the playground the next day, I saw the little wolf in sheep's clothing: Evan Kinkaid dressed in red wool and green flannel, my father's vest and shirt—both ridiculously loose, two sizes too big for a skinny child from the Hollow.

Why should the hungry repent? Evan Kinkaid wanted me to betray him. I stared, defiant as he was. *Mine,* I thought, *one holy secret.* Mother didn't deserve to know the truth, she who had sent me to school that day, against my will, against what I believed to be my father's deepest wishes. He would have wanted me home, with her, waiting till dawn to fold the clothes Evan tossed and trampled in their bedroom. Daddy would have wanted me to crawl under their bed, to find every stray sock, to lay my little hands on each one of his tattered undershirts as if cloth, like skin, might still be healed. Neither he nor I wanted to lie in the dark, listening to Mother scour and scurry.

By the mercy of morning light, Daddy hoped I would discover his last words, a note to himself still crumpled in the pocket of his wrinkled trousers: *Don't forget! Honey Walnut.* A loaf of sweet bread for me or a color of stain for a birdhouse?

The dead speak in riddles and leave us to imagine.

Face to face with the righteous thief, I made a vow to keep my silence. I was ten years old that winter day, arrogant enough to feel pity for this failure of a boy, Evan Kinkaid, stooped and pale, a fourteen-year-old sixth grader who had flunked three times, Evan Kinkaid who would never go to high school.

Less than a year later, Didi Kinkaid's pink trailer burned so hot even the refrigerator melted. By then, Didi lived in the Women's Correctional Facility in Billings, and Evan at the Pine Hills School for Boys in Miles City. Meribeth, seventeen, the oldest Kinkaid, a good girl, a girl who might grow up to be useful, lived in Glasgow with foster parents and eight false siblings. Fierce little Holly, just eleven—the dangerous child who once stole my lunch and slammed me to the wall of the girls' bathroom when I accused her—had become the only daughter of a hopeful Pentecostal minister and his barren wife in Polebridge.

So nobody was home the night the Kinkaids' trailer sparked, nobody real, though on any given night there might have been six or ten or twenty-nine tossed-out, worthless, wild kids crashing at Didi's, wishing she would return, their darling delinquent mother, dreaming she would appear in time to cook them breakfast, hoping to hear the roar and grind of her battered baby-blue Apache.

What a truck! Dusty, rusty, too dented to repair—you could squeeze thirty stray kids in the back and whoop all the way to Kalispell—you could pad the bed with leaves or rags or borrowed blankets, sleep out under the stars, warm and safe even in December.

Oh, Didi—slim in the hips, tiny at the waist—she might have been one of them, the best one, if you didn't spin her around too fast, if you didn't look too closely. The lost children built shelters of sticks and tarps in the woods behind her trailer. She let them drink beer in her yard. She gave them marshmallows and hot dogs to roast over the bonfire where she burned her garbage.

No wonder they loved her.

Any day now, Didi might honk her horn and rev the engine hard to wake them. *Sweet Mother of God!* Didi, home at last with four loaves of soft white bread and a five-pound tub of creamy peanut butter.

In half-sleep, the throwaway children kept their faith, but when they woke, they remembered: Mother in chains, Didi in prison. Of her seventeen known accomplices, three were willing to testify against her. *Three of them!* Sheree, Vince, Travis. *Traitors, snitches.* Three who still believed in real homes: mothers, fathers, feather pillows, fleece blankets.

Every night, these three lay alone between clean sheets, trying to be good, trying to be quiet, taking shallow breaths, hoping their clean and perfect mothers might slip into their rooms, kneel by their beds, and with tender mouths kiss them, kiss them, kiss them.

But only Didi came, in dreams, to mock and then forgive them.

Didi Kinkaid was made for trouble, slender but round, lovely to touch, lovely to hold, and mostly she liked it. To Didi Kinkaid, any roadside motel seemed luxurious.

What she liked best was the bath after, when the man, whoever he might be that night, was drowned in sleep on the bed and she was alone, almost floating, warm in the warm water, one with the water—not like the trailer where there was only a cramped closet with a spitting shower, three kids and twelve minutes of scalding water to share between them.

Any night of the week Didi might be lucky or unlucky enough to glimpse the father of one of her children—one good ole boy pumping quarters in the jukebox to conjure Elvis, one sweet, sorry sight for sore eyes slumped on a bar stool—and a feeling long lost might rise up: pity, fear, hope, desire.

There was Billy Hayes, Meribeth's father, and she'd loved him best, and she might have married him. But Billy was too young for Didi even when she was young—just sixteen when she was twenty—a skinny golden boy with a fuzz of beard and long flowing hair. Billy got sad when he drank and started looking like Jesus. She didn't have a chance with Billy Hayes, a boy still in high school, a child living with his parents. Didi knew from the start a woman from the Hollow could never keep him.

Now, the taxidermist Billy Hayes was old enough, and the years between them made no difference; his hair was thin and short; he had four kids and a wife named Mary. Mary Patrillo's patient parents had taught Billy Hayes to stuff the bodies of the dead and make the mouths of bobcats and badgers look ferocious, but the place he'd opened in Didi Kinkaid stayed empty forever.

When she told him she was pregnant, he never seemed to imagine any choice for them but having the baby—*I'll help you,* he said. And so it was: Meribeth came to be; and though Didi thought she'd loved Billy as much as she could love anybody, the child was her first true love, her first true blessing.

Billy helped her steal a crib and a high chair, booties and bibs, disposable diapers. *Shopping,* he called it. One night, their last night, he came to the trailer with a blue rubber duck and seven white rubber ducklings, toys to float in the tub Didi didn't have, so they put Meribeth in the kitchen sink with her eight ducks, and Billy, Sweet Billy Boy, hummed lullabies while he washed her.

Evan's dad was a different story, a mean sonuvabitch if ever there was one—Rick McQueen, Mister Critter Control, who was kind enough in the beginning, who rescued her at two-thirty one morning when she came home to discover pack rats had invaded the trailer. It didn't occur to her that a man willing to drown rats and feed cyanide to coyotes might harbor similar attitudes toward his own child. Evan swore to this day that he remembered his first beating. *Before I was born, when I was inside you.*

He banged his head and bruised his eye. Even now, when he's tired or mad or hungry, that place around the socket still hurts him. He traces the bone. *You have hard hips*, he says, and this much is true, so what about the rest of it?

Didi remembers how Evan kicked and punched, twisting inside her womb for days after the pummeling. She thought he'd choke, furious and desperate enough to strangle himself with his own umbilical cord. Maybe Evan truly remembers the beating, and maybe he's only heard Didi's story. Truth or tale—what does it matter in the end if a boy believes he felt his father's fists hammering?

You saved me, Didi says, and this is fact. The baby fought the man. If she'd had any inclination to forget, if she'd been tempted by Rick McQueen's tears, scared by his threats, or lulled by his promises, the baby unknown and unnamed reminded her night and day: *You let him stay, I'll kill him.*

Holly's father could have been any one of three people—it was a long winter, too cold, so it was hard to keep track of who was when, what might be possible. There was Didi's cousin, Harlan Dekker, and a fat man by the river whose name she's blissfully forgotten, and a third man too thin, like a freak, like the Emaciated Marvel in a cage at the carnival. *Half my life behind bars,* he said, *a guard, not a prisoner.* Now he lived on the toad, *free,* he said, in his rust-riddled Mustang.

The man who could suck his belly back to his spine didn't have the cash for even one night at a motel, so Didi, in her kindness, in her mercy, brought him back to the trailer, and they made love right there with three-year-old Evan and five-year-old Meribeth wide awake, no doubt, and listening. He had a pretty name, *Aidan Cordeaux.* The last part meant fuse, and the first was the fire, so maybe the flickering man did spark inside her.

Strange as it was, she often hoped the starved prison guard was Holly's father, that the night she'd conceived her youngest child, Evan and Meribeth had been there with her. *Little angels!* She felt them hovering all night, close and conscious, her darlings lying together in the narrow bunk above the bed where she and the Living Skeleton made love, where she touched the man's sharp ribs and knotted vertebrae, where she prayed, *yes, prayed,* for God to give him flesh, to restore him.

She heard her two children breathing slowly afterward, asleep at last, and the man was asleep too, up in smoke, and so she was alone, yes, but safe unto herself, blessed by her children, and the sound of their quiet breath was so sweet and familiar that she felt them as breath in her own body, as wings of sparrows softly fluttering. *God,* she thought, *his messengers.*

She was drunk enough to pretend, drunk enough to imagine. Later, the cries of feral cats in the woods sounded half-human, and she had to laugh at herself. What a hoot to think God might send angels to Didi Kinkaid in her trailer. *Just my own damn kids, but Christ, it was comforting.*

Her cousin Harlan was probably Holly's dad. It made the most sense: Holly and Harlan with that bright blond hair, those weird white eyelashes. Harlan's wife lived in Winnipeg all that winter, following her senile mother out in the snow, lifting her crippled father onto the toilet. Harlan and Didi met four times at the Kozy Kabins: twice to make love, once to watch television, once to be sorry.

More than anything, Didi wanted to believe Holly's father wasn't the fat man in his truck who passed out on top of her. She'd escaped inch by inch, hoping his cold sweat wouldn't freeze them together. She walked back to the Deerlick Saloon, to her own car, a yellow Dodge Dart that year, lemon yellow, a tin heap destined for the Junkyard. She thought she should tell somebody he was out there alone at the edge of the river. She pictured him rolling off the seat to the floor, pants pulled down to his ankles, ripe body wedged underneath the dashboard. He could die tonight, numb despite all that flesh, and Didi Kinkaid would be his killer.

But the bar had been closed for hours, and her fingers were so stiff she could barely turn the key in the lock of her car door, arms so sore she could barely grip the wheel. Didi didn't feel sorry for anybody but herself by then, so she didn't stop at the all-night gas station, and she didn't call the police when she got home—she didn't even tell Rita LaCroix, her neighbor, the babysitter—she just dropped into bed, shivering, and the truth was she was so damn cold she forgot the man, his flesh and sweat, his terrible whinny of high laughter.

In the morning, she smelled his skin on her skin and she used every drop of hot water in the shower, all twelve minutes, and she drank bright green mouthwash straight from the bottle and she listened to the news on the radio. There was no report of a dead man gone blue as ice by the river.

She figured he'd been spared and so had she, but when she thought of it now, she hoped to God she hadn't been cruel or stupid enough to abandon the one who was Holly's true father.

When Didi Kinkaid's child splintered the window above my mother's bed and entered our lives, her story became my story—her only son burst in my heart, her bad boy broke me open. My father was dead. Eleven months later, the second night of November, the night Didi's pink and green trailer burned and melted, I knew my mother was dying.

Didi had been in prison since August. When I imagined her children—the desperate ones she'd borne and the wild ones she'd rescued, when I imagined all the sooty-faced, tossed-up runaways left to wander—I understood there are three hundred ways for a family to be shattered.

Soon, so soon, I too would be an orphan.

II. FIRE

THE FIRE WAS REVENGE, INTIMATE AND TRIBAL. We came to witness, we people of the hills and hollows, lured up Didi's road by smoke and sirens. Through the flames, I saw the glowing faces of Didi's closest neighbors: Nellie Rydell and Doris Kelso, Lorna Coake and Ruby Whipple. I thought that one of them must have sparked this blaze—with her own two hands and the holy heat of her desire.

Who poured the stream of gasoline, who struck the match, who lit the torch of wood and paper? *Tell me now. I keep all secrets.* Was it one of you alone, or did all four conspire together?

For the small crime of arson, no respectable woman ever stood trial. The trailer was a temptation and an eyesore, a refuge for feral cats, a sanctuary for wayward children. Now Didi's home could be hauled away, a heap of melted rubble. *An accident,* Ruby said. *A blessing,* Lorna whispered.

Who can know for sure? Maybe the small boy called Rooster lit a pile of sticks to warm the fingers of his twelve-year-old girlfriend Simone so that it wouldn't hurt where she touched him. Maybe cross-eyed Georgia squirted loops of lighter fluid into the blaze just to see what would happen, and all the children danced in the dark, hot at last, giddy as the fire spread, too joyful now to try to smother it.

But I will always believe those four women in their righteous rage burned Didi out forever.

Didi Kinkaid trespassed against us: She harbored fugitives; she tempted boys; she tempted husbands. She slept with strangers and her own cousin— and despite all this generous love, Didi Kinkaid still failed to marry the father of even one of her children.

Compared with these transgressions, the crimes named by County Prosecutor Marvin Beloit—the violations for which Didi Kinkaid was shackled, chained, and dumped in prison—seemed almost trivial: receiving and selling stolen goods, felony offenses, theft of property far exceeding $1,000. To be precise: forty-one bicycles snatched by children and fenced by Didi over a thirteen-month period.

Forty-one, including the three treasures in her last load: a black and yellow 1947 Schwinn Hornet Deluxe with its original headlight, worth an astonishing $3,700; the 1959 Radiant Red Phantom, a three-speed wonder with lavish chrome, almost a motorcycle—and radiant, yes—worth $59.95 new, and now, lovingly restored by Merle Tremble's huge but delicate hands, worth $3,250; finally, the lovely 1951 Starlet painted in its original Summer Cloud White with Holiday Rose trim and pink streamers, worth only $1,900, but polished inch by inch for the daughter Merle never had. To him, priceless.

In court, Merle Tremble confessed: The jeweled reflector for the Phantom cost him $107. *A perfect prism of light, worth every penny.* He found a seat for the Hornet, smooth leather with a patina like an antique baseball glove, worn shiny by one particular boy's bones and muscles. *No man can buy such joy with money.*

For six years, Merle Tremble had haunted thrift stores and junkyards, digging through steaming heaps of trash to recover donor bikes with any precious piece that might be salvageable. Under oath, Merle Tremble swore to God he loved his bikes like children.

No wonder Didi laughed out loud, a snort that filled the courtroom. A man who believes he loves twisted chrome as much as he might love a human child deserves to lose everything he has, deserves fire and flood and swarms of locusts. But Didi's lack of remorse, her justifiable scorn, didn't help her.

For crimes named and trespasses unspoken, Didi Kinkaid received ten years, the maximum sentence.

Ten years. More than any man gets for beating his wife or stabbing his brother. More years than a man with drunken rage as his excuse might serve for barroom brawl and murder.

Didi's transgressions wounded our spirits. She fed the children no mother could tame. She loved them for a night or for an hour, just as she loved the men who shared all her beds in all those motel rooms, and this terrifying, transient love, this passion without faith that tomorrow will be the same or ever come, this endless offering of the body and the soul and the self was dangerous, dangerous, dangerous.

If she was good, then we were guilty. Exile wasn't enough. We had to burn her.

When Didi heard about the fire, she knew. *Busybody do-gooders,* she said, *always coming to my door with their greasy casseroles and stale muffins, acting all high and holy when all they really wanted was to get a peek inside, see if I had some tattooed cowboy sprawled on my bed, find out how many kids were crashing at my place and if my own three were running naked. Kindhearted ladies benevolent as that did the same damn thing to my mother. Ran her out of Riverton in the end. Killed her with their mercy.*

The bikes were just an excuse. *It could have been anything,* she said, *but in the end, I made it easy.*

III. BICYCLE BANDITS

DIDI NEVER ASKED THE STRAY children for anything. Rooster and Simone brought the first bike to her doorstep, a silver mountain bike with gloriously fat tires, tires nubbed and tough enough to ride through snow and slush and mud and rivers, a bike sturdy enough to carry two riders down ditches and up the rocky road to Didi's trailer. A small gift, for all the times she'd fed them. Rooster said, *I've got a number and a name, a guy willing to travel for a truckload.*

Stealing bikes was a good job, one the children could keep, without bosses or customers, time clocks or hair nets. They loved mountain bikes best—so many gears to grind, so many colors: black as a black hole black, metallic blue, fool's gold, one green so bright it looked radioactive. Rooster had to ride that bike alone: His Kootenai girlfriend was afraid to touch it.

There was a dump in the ravine behind Didi's trailer. *The Child Dump*, she called it, because sometimes it seemed the children just kept crawling out of it. They glued themselves together from broken sleds and headless dolls and bits of fur and scraps of plastic. Their bones were splintered wood. Their hearts were chicken hearts. Their little hands were rubber.

She expected them to stop one day—she thought there might be nine or ten or even forty—but they just kept rising out of the pit. In court, the day three testified against her, County Prosecutor Marvin Beloit said he had reason to believe more than three hundred homeless children roamed the woods surrounding Kalispell.

They slept in abandoned cars and culverts. Busted the locks of sheds. Shattered the windows of cabins. Desperate in a blizzard last winter, two cousins with sharp knives stabbed Leo Henry's cow in the throat, split her gut with a hatchet and pulled her entrails out so that they could sleep curled up safe in the cave of her body.

Three hundred homeless children.

Sleep was good, was God, their only comfort.

Nobody in court wanted to believe Marvin Beloit. *Not in our little town.* Didi pitied him—her brother, her prosecutor—a man alone, besieged by visions. She knew the truth, but couldn't help him.

Ferris, Cafe, Luke, Scoria—Hansel, Heidi, Micah, LaFlora—Dawn, Daisy, Duncan, Mirinda. These children offered themselves to Didi in humility and gratitude. Joyfully and by design, they became thieves. They'd found their purpose.

Sometimes when a child stole a bike, he stole a whole family, and they lived in his mind, a vision of the life he couldn't have: They pestered, they poked him. Nuke was sorry after he took the candy-striped tandem with a baby seat and a rack to carry tent and camp stove. That night he dreamed he was the smiling infant who had no words, who knew only the bliss of pure sensation. Wind in his face carried the scent of his mother: sweet milk and clean cotton, white powder patted soft on his own bare bottom. Daddy peddled hard in front, and the sun seemed so close and hot the baby believed he could touch it.

But Nuke woke on the hard dirt to the spit of his real name, *Peter Petrosky,* his mother's curse: *Not in my house, you little fucker.* Then he was an only child caught smoking weed laced with crack in his mother's house, in his father's shower. Doctor Petrosky was a genius, an artist with a scalpel who could scoop a pacemaker from a dead man and set it humming inside the chest of a black Labrador. Peter didn't wait to receive his clever father's pity or redemption. Sick with sound and light, the boy lay under his bed for an hour then climbed out the window. Now he was Nuke the nuke, a walking holocaust, sending up mushroom clouds with every footstep.

Wendy, Wanda, Bix, Griffin.

Tianna found a smoked chrome BMX with a gusseted frame and scrambler tires. She could fly on this bike, airborne off every mogul. Indestructible. *Tianna!* Thirteen years old and four fingers gone to frostbite last winter. *No more piano lessons,* she said, *no flute, no cello.* Tianna imagined sitting at the polished mahogany piano in her parents' cedar house, high on a hill, overlooking the valley. Oh! How strange and lovely the music would sound, true at last, with so many of the notes missing.

She might lie down, *just for a moment,* and fall asleep on her mother's creamy white leather sofa. Sleeping outside was torture. Tianna sucked and bit her stumps. The fingers she'd lost itched in the heat and stung in the cold. *They're still there,* she said, *but I can't see them.*

Naomi, Rose, Garth, Devon.

Angel Donner bashed into his own basement and stole his own bike, a black and orange Diablo Dynamo that any kid could see was just a pitiful imitation of a Stingray, worth less than fifty dollars new and now worth nothing. He remembered it under the Christmas tree, his father's grin, his mother's joy, his pit of disappointment.

Laurel, Grace, Logon, Nikos.

There was the one who called herself Trace because she'd vanished without one. *Idaho, Craters of the Moon, family vacation.* Cleo Kruse climbed out the bathroom window while Daddy and his new wife and Cleo's two baby stepsisters lay sweetly sleeping. *Knew I was gone before it was light, but didn't start looking till sunset. I read about me in the paper. Daddy thought it was just my way—doing all I could to cause him trouble.*

Trace was the little thief who jimmied the lock of the garage where

Merle Tremble had laced each spoke of his Hornet Deluxe, his Starlet, his Phantom. Cleo disappeared at eight, and now the girl gone without a trace was barely eleven. *Too big for your britches*, Daddy always said, but anybody could see she was puny. She wore loose T-shirts and baggy jeans, chopped her hair short, turned her baseball cap backwards. *I'm a boy*, she said, *halfway. That's the real problem.* She could never mind her p's and q's, never cross her legs in church, never sit still like a lady. Cleo Kruse was a six-year-old bully, suspended from first grade—two months for pinning and pounding a third-grade boy who called her *Little It*, who pulled her from the monkey bars, flipped up her skirt and said, *If you're a real girl, show me.*

Boy or girl, what did it matter now? Out here in the woods, down in The Child Dump, everybody was half-human. If you stole groceries to eat in Depot Park, you could convince yourself you might go home someday, scrub yourself clean, eat at your mother's table. But if one day in August you got so hungry you ate crackling bugs rolled in leaves, you had to believe you'd turned part lizard and grown the nub of a tail. Cleo had eaten bugs in leaves so many times she decided she liked them.

Jodie, Van, Kane, Kristian—Faith, Finn, Trevor, Nova. They broke Didi's heart with their gifts and their hunger.

Sufi wanted to twirl like a dervish, spin herself into a blur, turn so fast the back became the front, the air the breath, the girl nothing. She wanted to stop eating forever, to grow crisp and thin, to see through herself like paper.

She didn't believe in theft. If nothing belonged to anybody, how could anything be stolen? Objects passed, one hand to another, and this was good, what God wanted, so she was glad to ride the Starlet out of Merle Tremble's garage, grateful to be God's vessel, perfectly at peace as she watched Cleo buzz ahead on the Hornet, and Nuke disappear on the Phantom.

Caspar, Skeeter, Dillon, Crystal—Renee, Rhonda, Bird, JoJo—Margot, Madeleine, Quinn, Ezekiel. Swaddled in her narrow prison bed, Didi counts the lost children as she tries to fall asleep—so many came to her door, and now she wants to remember. *Cody, Kira, Joyce, Jewell.* If ninety-nine were found and one missing, she wouldn't sleep: She'd search the woods all night, calling. Nate carved his own name into his own white belly, a jagged purple wound that kept opening. *If my head's smashed flat, my mother will still know me.* Ray taught the others to make beds of boughs. Cedar is soft enough, and young fir with blistered bark smells of balsam, but spruce will stab your hands and back: a bed of spruce is a bed of nails.

Didi tries to rock herself to sleep, but the rocking brings the children close, and she sees their lives, so quick and sharp, one dark cradle to another.

Dustin, Sam, Chloë, Lulu—Betsy, Bliss, Malcolm, Neville. Oh, Didi, you sing their names. Mercy, Po, Hope, Isaac. Let them all join hands. Here is your ring of thieves. Let them dance like fire around us.

IV. THE LOVER

WHEN DIDI KINKAID WAS GOOD, she was very very good. She fed the poor. She sheltered the homeless. She lived as Jesus asks us to live: turned only by love, purely selfless.

But when Didi Kinkaid was bad, she abandoned her own three children, deserted Evan and Holly and Meribeth for nine days one January while she lived with Daniel Lute in his log cabin, perched high on a snow-blown ridge above Lake Koocanusa. Later, she swore she didn't understand how far it was, how deep the snow, how difficult it might be to find a road in the grip of winter.

She slept fourteen, sixteen, twenty hours. She woke not knowing if it was morning or evening, November or April. Daniel Lute's cabin whistled in the wind at the edge of outer darkness.

He fed her glistening orange eggs, the fruit of the salmon, its smoked pink flesh, his Russian vodka. Ten words could fill a day, a hundred might describe a lifetime.

They made love under a bearskin, *a Kodiak from Kodiak,* and the bed rocked like a boat, like a cradle, and the cradle was a box, sealed tight, sinking to the bottom of the lake far below them.

Daniel was a bear himself, tall but oddly hunched, black hair and black beard tipped silver, a man trapped in his own skin, condemned to live in constant hunger until a virgin loved him. Didi couldn't break that spell, and for this she was truly sorry.

On the seventh day, Daniel dressed in winter camouflage and left her alone while he stalked the white fox and the white weasel.

In utter silence, all the skinned Kodiaks walked the earth, bare and pink, like giant humans. Didi woke drenched in sweat, the skin of Daniel's bear stuck to her.

His fire flickered out. She'd never been so cold. She thought she'd die here, the stranger's captive bride, her face becalmed by hypothermia. But her children came to drag her home. Their muttering voices surged, soft at first, then angry. She tasted Holly's black-licorice breath and smelled Evan's wet wool socks. Meribeth said. *It's time, Mom. Get up.*

The children sat on the bed. Didi felt their weight, but never saw them. Tiny fingers pinched her legs like claws. Two little hands gripped her wrists and tugged. Six tight fists pressed hard: chest, ribcage, pelvis, throat.

The basin by the bed was full. It took all her strength and all her will to rise from this bed of death and go outside to piss in the snow. Her clamoring children had grown furiously still, unwilling to touch, unwilling to help. She ate pickled herrings from a tiny tin. They tasted terrible; they filled her up. She pulled Daniel Lute's wool pants over her own denim jeans and cinched them tight with his leather belt. Though the bearskin was heavy, she took it too, just in case she couldn't make it off the mountain, just in case she needed to lie down and sleep inside the animal.

She returned with gifts to appease her children: $309 in cash, two pounds of smoked salmon, a silver flask with a Celtic cross, still miraculously full of Daniel's brandy.

She came with a preposterous tale, the truth of sinking thigh-deep in the snow as she climbed down the ridge, the luck of finding the road around the lake before dark, the blessing of hitching a ride with an old woman driving herself to the hospital in Libby. Adela Odegard had crackers in the car, five hand-rolled cigarettes, half a thermos of coffee. *The gifts of God for the people of God: Body, Blood, Holy Ghost.* Didi ate and drank and smoked in humble gratitude.

Adela Odegard looked shriveled up dark as an old potato, a woman so yellow, so thin, Didi thought she might be dead already, but her wild, white hair glowed and made her weirdly beautiful.

In Libby, Adela delivered Didi to her nephew, Milo Kovash, and Didi slept on his couch that night. In the morning, Milo gave her ten dollars and dropped her at the truck stop diner. He knew a waitress there named Madrigal, and the waitress had a friend named Fawn who had a little brother named Gabriel, *Gabe Lofgren*, sixteen years old and glad to skip school to drive Didi Kinkaid down to Kalispell.

A story like that could turn the hard of heart into believers, or the most trusting souls into cynics.

V. HOME

DIDI'S CHILDREN CHOSE TO BELIEVE. *Mercy*, she thought, *who deserves it?* She smelled of creosote and pine, pickled herring, her own cold sweat gone rancid. She had Daniel's pants and belt as proof—so yes, some of what she remembered must have happened.

After her shower, Didi wore the bearskin around her naked self, his head above her head, and her children stroked her fur: their own mother, so soft everywhere. The Kodiak had a face like a dog's. He might be your best friend. *From a distance.*

Didi told her children that the cabin above the lake was dark as the inside of a bear's belly. *Swallowed alive*, she said, *but I had a silver fishing knife; I stole it from the trapper. She showed them the jagged blade. I cut myself out when the bear got sleepy.*

Now the Kodiak's skin was her skin, the gift of the father she never had, Daniel Lute: She could wear him like a coat, pin him to the wall, use him as her blanket.

Didi and her children drank Daniel's brandy, and the ones who wanted to forget almost did forget how they'd lived without her.

Two nights before Didi returned, little mother Meribeth, not yet thirteen, had made soup with ketchup and boiled water, crushed saltines and a shot of Tabasco. Every morning of the week, she got her ten-year-old brother and six-year-old sister to the bus on time—so nobody would know, so nobody would come to take them.

Though Evan might pull Holly from her swing, though Holly might bite him, though Meribeth might scold them both—*You little shits*, might cuss them down, *I'm so damn tired*—they belonged to one another in ways that children who live in real houses never belong to their brothers and sisters.

Only Holly stayed hard now, refusing to eat Daniel's fish, loving the pang of her hunger, the fishing knife stuck sharp in her belly. Brandy burned her throat and stomach, and she loved that too, the way it hurt at first, then soothed her. *Mother in a bottle, the slap before the kiss, the incredible peace that comes after.*

What do I know of Didi's grief? Who am I to judge her?

The day I became a twenty-two-year-old widow, the day my husband who was a fireman died by fire—not in a trailer or a house, not as a hero saving a child, but as a father driving home, as a husband who dozed, as a man too weary to the wheel—that day when my husband's silver truck skidded and rolled to the bottom of the gully—when three men came to my door to tell me there was no body for me to identify—only a man's teeth, only dental records—that impossibly blue October day, I began to understand why a woman might refuse to dress and forget to wash, how a mother might fail to rise, fail to love, fail to wake and feed her children.

Didi, I know what it means to melt away, to repent forever in dust and ashes. My daughters lived because my brother found us. My children ate because my brother in his bitter mercy stole them.

Lilla, Faye, Isabelle—most darling ones, most beloved—though I lay in my own bed, I deserted them in spirit.

In the days after the trailer burned, in the months after Didi Kinkaid went to prison, people said she got what she deserved. *But Didi, what about your children?*

One Friday night, as Didi lay rocking in the cradle of Daniel Lute's bed, Meribeth and Holly dressed up in her best clothes—a slinky green dress, a sparkly black sweater. The little girls teetered on their mother's spiked heels. Evan let Meribeth paint his nails pink and glossy. Holly rouged his cheeks and smeared his mouth red while he was sleeping. In the morning, the boy glimpsed the reflection of his own flushed face and soft lips, and before it occurred to him to be ashamed, he thought, *Look at me! I'm pretty.*

Didi, no matter what we deserved, our children deserved to stay together.

VI. MOTHER

AFTER HER NIGHTS UNDER THE BEARSKIN, Didi made a promise to

always get herself home before dawn, to never again let her children wake alone in daylight.

She vowed to love her work. That's where the trouble started. She'd spent the whole dark day hunched over her sewing machine, drinking and weeping like her own pitiful mother. *Oh, Daphne!* Seven years gone, ashes scattered to the wind from a high peak in Wyoming, and still, after all this time, she could blow through a crack under the door and make her daughter miserable.

They were ashamed together, mending clothes for the dead who can't complain and don't judge you. Didi saw Daphne's crippled hands, each joint twisted by arthritis. Mother needed her Whiskey Sours, her Winston Lights, her amber bottle of crushed pills—though the killers of pain made it hard to sew, and the smoke made her bad eyes blurry.

Seeing her mother like this made Didi wish for the father she didn't have. Murmuring beekeeper, Jehovah's Witness, busted-up rodeo rider with a broken clavicle—who was he?

Be kind, Daphne said, *any man you meet might be your daddy.*

Didi's real father was probably the hypnotist at Lola Fiori's eighteenth birthday party, the Amazing Quintero, who chose Daphne because, he said, *Pretty girls with red hair are the most susceptible.*

Under his spell, Daphne was an owl perched on a stool, a wolf on all fours, a skunk, a snake, a jackrabbit, a burro. She hooted and howled. Quintero made her ridiculous.

Alone, in Quintero's room, the hypnotist blindfolded her with a silky cloth, its violet so deep she felt it bleeding into her.

Didi imagined her mother on her hands and knees again, not hypnotized, the scarf tied around her head like a halter. If this was the night, if Quintero was the father, if her mother hooted and howled and bucked and brayed the night Didi was conceived, the whole world was horrible.

As Didi sewed, as Didi drank whiskey and water, as her own fingers ached, as her own seams grew crooked, she thought, *There you are, Mama. I'm just like you.*

At dusk, she delivered the pressed clothes to Devlin Slade's Funeral Home: a gray suit for a handsome young man and a white christening dress for a newborn baby.

She meant to drive straight home. Rain had turned to sleet, and all the dead were with her. She was almost to the Hollow, almost safe with her children in the trailer, and the sleet softly became snow, and she thought God must love her even now, despite her fear, despite her sorrow. In the beams of her headlights, He showed her the secret of snow: each flake illuminated.

Each one of them, each one of us, is precious.

Mesmerized by snow, Didi didn't see the deer until the animal leaped, with astonishing grace, as if to die on purpose. The doe bounced onto the hood and crumpled on the slick pavement, but she didn't die, and Didi stopped and got out of the truck and walked back down the road to witness the creature's suffering. The animal lay on her side, panting hard, legs still running. Frenzied, she tried to stand on fractured bones. They'd done this to each other.

A man appeared, walking out of the snow, a ghost at first, then human. He'd seen it all, before it happened. The stranger had a gun in his glove box to put Didi and the deer out of their misery. The blast of the bullet through the doe's skull made Didi's bones vibrate. She felt snowflakes melting on her cheeks and was amazed again: this mercy in the midst of sorrow.

The man dragged the limp animal toward the woods, then knelt to wipe his hands in the snow. She would have gone anywhere with him. That January night, Didi Kinkaid considered Daniel Lute her personal savior. *Heading to town,* he said. *Need some medicine.*

She ditched the Apache less than a mile from the trailer, and slid into Daniel's El Camino. She told him: *One drink, that's all, three kids home alone*; and Daniel said, *No problem.*

If Didi learned to work with love, nothing like this could ever happen again. She had small hands and a good eye for the eye of the needle, a mother's gifts, both curse and blessing. Self-pity led to betrayal. Any work done with dignity might become holy. Sometimes, as you sewed a frail woman into her favorite lavender dress, as you stitched the seams to fit close where she'd shrunken, you touched her skin and felt all the hands of all the people who had ever loved her.

After Didi Kinkaid came home to the children she'd abandoned, she saw every filthy, furious, half-starved stray who rose out of The Child Dump as her own. Their mothers had failed to love them enough, and now they hated themselves with bitter vengeance.

Mine, she thought, *each one. I was that careless.*

When she cut gum out of Holly's hair, or bandaged Meribeth's thin wrist, or touched the sharp blades of Evan's narrow shoulders, she couldn't believe she'd done what she had done; she didn't know how she'd survived one day without them. No man could save her now. No tub was deep enough to tempt her. She sewed with faith. She loved her children. She never stayed out till dawn. She kept these promises. She offered herself to the strays, and the ritual of love made her really love them.

VII. THE ROAD TO PRISON

BETWEEN MARCH 1989 AND EARLY APRIL 1990, Didi borrowed her cousin Harlan Dekker's white van three times to deliver bicycles to Beau Cryder who agreed to meet her just south of Evaro. For testimony against her, Beau walked free. *Flesh peddling,* the lawyers called it, not in court but to each other.

Nobody wanted Cryder, twenty-five and still a kid, a bad luck boy, out of work seven months, with a pregnant eighteen-year-old wife and a two-year-old son. Nobody wanted to trace the bikes to Liam Jolley, Beau's uncle, a once-upon-a-time hero in Vietnam and now just a crippled ex-cop in Missoula. Nobody ever wanted to hear how Liam's devoted daughter Gwyneth had ferried the bikes—sometimes whole and sometimes in pieces—to dealers in Butte, Boise, Anaconda, and Bozeman.

They were the victims of Didi's crimes. Her body could be exchanged for theirs, her breath for their freedom. Nobody in or out of court objected.

When Didi learned the value of Merle Tremble's bikes, she understood she'd been both betrayed and cheated. Beau paid two hundred for the set, three-twenty for the load: At the time, it seemed a fortune. Didi planned to stop in Kalispell on her way home. She wanted to buy her raggedy band of thieves two buckets of fried chicken and a tub of buttery mashed potatoes. They needed brushes and toothpaste, calamine for poison ivy, gauze to wrap their cuts and burns, arnica for bruises. She intended to bring gallons of ice cream: *Fudge Ecstasy, Banana Blast, Strawberry Heaven.* She wanted the children to know there was enough: They could eat themselves sick tonight and still eat again tomorrow. Sooner or later, she'd spend everything she'd earned on them. She didn't care about her profit.

Didi took Evan on her last trip, to help her load the bikes, to help her deal with Cryder. She promised to pay him fifty. *My best boyfriend,* she said, *my partner.* In truth, she'd made him her accomplice.

They might have gone free for lack of evidence, but Beau Cryder refused to take Angel Dormer's Dynamo and a cheap BMX with popped spokes and a bent axle. Didi headed back across reservation land, through Ravalli, Dixon, Perma. She thought she was safe here, outside whiteman's law, protected by the Kootenai and Salish. She planned to dump the bikes before she got to Elmo.

They stopped at Wild Horse Hot Springs, *to celebrate,* she said, and they left the bikes in the van while they soaked for an hour, naked together in one room, immersed in hot mineral water.

She never figured on a raid. Never contemplated the possibility that Travis Poole might become a snitch, might want to go home, might tell his father, who would tell the police, who would tip bounty hunters—two trackers who lived outside the laws of any nation, who were free to bust down the door of a private room and drag a kicking woman and her biting boy from sacred water. The men shoved Didi and Evan out the door barefoot and naked, wrapped them in stiff wool blankets, bound them, gagged them, and stuffed them face down in the backseat of their beat-to-hell black Cadillac.

At precisely 3:26, back on whiteman's time, the fearless hunters delivered two fugitives and their stolen bicycles to the proper authorities in Kalispell.

VIII. THE KINGDOM ON EARTH

DIDI NEVER CAUGHT A BREAK for good behavior. If a guard spit words, she spit back. She was disrespectful. She stashed contraband: twenty-seven unauthorized aspirin, ten nips of tequila, and one shiny gold tube of coral lamé lipstick. Lipstick inspired vanity and theft, dangerous trades and retribution. Twice denied parole, Didi Kinkaid served every minute of her 3,653-day sentence.

Now, four years free, she sews clothes for the living and the dead in Helena. She could start a new life with a new name and a grateful lover in Vermont or Texas. But she stays here, close enough to visit Evan once a week in Deer Lodge. Her boy lives in a cell, down for fifty-five, hard time, attempted murder.

Evan was twenty years old and out of the Pine Hills School for Boys just thirteen months when he hit the headlines. A weird tale: hunting with a forbidden friend, Gil Ransom, thirty-nine and on parole, a known felon— dusk, out of season—Gil's idea, *just a little adventure*. They fired from the windows of the car—dumb beyond dumb and highly illegal. Any shadow that moved was fair game: deer, dog, rat, chicken. They smoked some weed. They split a six-pack. Evan saw trees walk like men through the forest.

An off-duty cop who recognized the roar of Gil's Wrangler followed them up a logging road, bumped them into the ditch, and tried to arrest them. Gil shot Tobias Revell three times: *Just to slow him down, nothing serious*. They left him crawling in the snow, wounded in the leg and neck and shoulder. He could have bled to death. He could have died of shock or hypothermia. But he was too pissed off to die. He lived to speak. He lived to bring those men to justice.

Justice? Evan learned that it didn't matter who pulled the trigger. For the abandonment of Tobias Revell, for the failure to send someone out that night to save him, Evan Kinkaid shared Gil's crime: the gun, the hand, the thought, the bullets.

Meribeth does not visit her brother. She teaches in a three-room school and lives without husband or children in a two-room shack up a canyon west of Lolo. I picture her as she was: flat-chested and gangly. She speaks softly. She walks swiftly. She never looks anybody straight in the eyes, but she never looks away either. She seems humble and kind, dignified even when she wears a dress sewn from an old checkered tablecloth. Meribeth Kinkaid, a princess in rags, mysteriously moving among peasants who scorn her.

Meribeth's worst fear is that one day her mother and brother and sister will knock at the door of her secret cottage in the canyon. Meribeth's deepest desire is that Evan and Holly and Didi will one day sit at her table to share a meal of bread and fish and wine and olives, that they will all sleep that night and every night thereafter in one bed in the living room, on three mattresses laid out on the floor and pushed close together, breathing as one body breathes, heart inside of heart, holy and whole, miraculously healed.

Eight months after she was adopted, Holly Kinkaid escaped Reverend Cassolay and his good wife Alicia. She didn't want to be saved. She'd been baptized by fire. If she couldn't live with her brother and sister, if the trailer was burned to rubble and gone forever, Holly wanted to live alone in a junked car or a tree or a culvert.

I am a mother now, an orphan, and a widow.

Sometimes in the early dark of winter I feel Holly at my window watching my daughters and me as we eat our dinner. She won't come in. The cold no longer feels cold to her. The cold to her is familiar.

This morning—a deep gray November morning, woods full of damp snow, light drizzle falling—I followed the school bus to town, twenty-three miles. My daughters Lilla and Faye, nine and six, sat in the far backseat of the bus to flap their hands and wave furiously, to smash their lips and noses flat against smudged glass. Their terrible faces scared me.

Isabelle, my youngest, my baby, slept in her car seat. I heard every wet sound: wipers in the rain, melting snow, dripping trees, the murmuring woods closing around us.

I saw flowers in the rain: boys in blue and girls in yellow, a tiny child in a pink fur coat, and another dressed in bright red stockings—all the pretty children waiting for the bus in bright pairs and shimmering clusters. Sometimes a mother stood in the center to shelter them beneath her wide umbrella.

In this rain, in this dark becoming light, I began to see the ones who won't come out of the woods. *Griffin, Bix, Wanda, Wendy.* They wear olive green and brown and khaki, coats the color of fallen leaves, jeans stained with blood, boots always muddy. They steal the skins of wolves and wings of falcons. The red fur of the fox swirls down Tianna's spine and her teeth are long but broken.

Hansel, Heidi, Micah, LaFlora. They never grow up or old. They starve forever. Cleo Kruse who vanished without a trace, who could never be just one thing or another, has the body of a lynx and the eyes of a hoot owl, the legs of a mule deer, and the hands of a child.

Faith, Bliss, Trevor, Nova.

Vince Lavadour who betrayed Didi Kinkaid, who testified against her, has lost his arms and legs, has found instead his fins and tail. The boy slips free at last, a rainbow trout, gloriously striped and speckled.

Nate, Ray, Grace, Laurel.

Angel's skin bursts with thirty-thousand barbed quills. Bold in his new body, Angel says, *Only fire will kill me.*

Dustin, Rose, Lulu, Chloë—Georgia, Sheree, Travis, Devon.

Rooster knows that if he eats as the coyote eats, he will live forever. And so he does eat: snakes, eggs, plastic, rubber, sheep, tomatoes, rusted metal, dead horses by the road, dead salmon at the river.

Simone, Nuke, Duncan, Daisy.

Last summer, Sufi flung herself fifty feet into the air at twilight. Flying heart, vesper sparrow, she sang as if one ecstatic cry could save the world. Now she lies broken under dead leaves. She smells only of the woods—pine under snow, damp moss, a swirl of gold tamarack needles. Her wish comes true at last: She is one with God, one with mud and air and water. But if Didi called her name tonight, from death to life she might recover.

Naomi, Quinn, Madeleine, Skeeter—Rhonda, JoJo, Neville, Ezekiel—Finn, Scaria, Luke, Jewel.

How quickly the night comes!

I am home at dusk, so many hours later, my three girls safe this night in the house their father built before he left us. Birds cry from the yard, and I go to them, a mother alone in the gathering dark. A flock of crows whirls into the gray sky. *Didi, there must be ninety-nine, there must be three hundred dark birds rising on their dark wings.* When they land, the crows fill a single tree, every branch of a stripped maple.

Your children are my children. They are dangerous. They are in danger.

One by one, each black-eyed bird falls to the ground, brittle and breakable, terrible and human.

Oh, my children, all my little children, I knew you before you were in the womb. Love is the Kingdom on Earth. As we fall to earth this day, let us love, let us love one another.

Melanie Rae Thon's most recent book is the novel Sweet Hearts. *She is also the author of* Meteors in August *(Random House, 1990) and* Iona Moon *(Simon & Schuster, 1993) and the story collections* First, Body *and* Girls in the Grass. *She has just completed a collection of stories, entitled* Heavenly Creatures. *Her work has been included in* Best American Short Stories *in 1995 and 1996,* Pushcart Prize *anthologies in 2003 and 2005, and* O. Henry Prize Stories *in 2006. She is also a recipient of a Whiting Writers' Award, a fellowship from the National Endowment for the Arts, and a writer's residency from the Lannan Foundation. Originally from Montana, she now lives in migration between the Pacific Northwest, Arizona, and Salt Lake City, where she teaches at the University of Utah.*

✿ Sara Vogan

From *In Shelly's Leg*

S IT IN THE BLEACHERS AND watch the women practice. It is a roundhouse practice, the women fanned out in a rough star pattern. The man pacing the foul line wonders idly about the woman playing third. She has been with the team five years now and has always worn gold loops hanging through her earlobes. He has never seen her without them. He wonders if she wore those loops as a child, solid gold stuck through slits in her ears. Maybe she has hundreds of pairs of those same earrings. Sometimes they glint in the sun.

He looks out past third to the dark green firs covering the mountainsides, snow lingering around their tops, and over to the newly green leaves of the Lombardy poplars lining the left-field fence. This ballfield was once a homestead, the poplars imported as seedlings from France and carefully packed in wagons with tools and food and scrap quilts, essentials for a new life in these flat northern valleys of the West. Poplars were the first settlers' only lasting mark upon the land, tall plumes against the sky planted in rows fifty to one hundred years ago as a design to break the wind.

The man notices the wind stirring the leaves and looks back to his pitcher. She is working on her knuckleball, throwing it without a spin so the seams look parallel. The pitch dips and weaves through the air before it crosses the plate. It lands in the catcher's mitt lightly, not enough force to overcome the breeze. The catcher flips one of her black braids back over her shoulder before returning the pitch and signals for another knuckleball. The batter swings and misses. The ball sounds more solid in the catcher's glove and she nods her approval to the pitcher.

The batter steps back from the box and flexes her ringed fingers against the handle of the bat. She readjusts her stance. Once both hands are on the bat, the pitcher fires off another knuckleball. It passes the batter so quickly she merely turns her head to watch it go by. "Give me a break," the batter yells.

The pitch is another knuckleball and the batter connects, lining the ball out near second. The man waits for the shortstop to move, but hears her laugh instead. She is not in position to make the catch, standing too close to second and talking to a woman with her hair in rollers, bound by a scarf.

"Look alive there, ladies," comes a call from first base. "We're all supposed to be practicing. This ain't no hen session." The woman at first does a cartwheel, her gray sweatsuit flopping loosely around her body. "See!" she calls again. "I'm freezing my tits off 'cause I can't get no action from you broads." At second, the woman with her hair in rollers pounds her glove while the shortstop moves out to where the ball is lying in the grass. She fires it off to first and straightens the hem on her sweatshirt, making it even across her hips. It reads: A WOMAN'S PLACE IS IN THE HOUSE AND THE SENATE.

The next hit is a pop-up to the shortstop, who takes it easily and tosses it to first. "I don't need to practice this shit," the shortstop says.

"You need all you can get," the catcher calls. She turns to the batter. "Keep your head down and your ass in."

"Let me do the slider," the pitcher says.

"No," answers the catcher, flipping her braids back again. "Five Valleys pitches a lot of knuckles. Somebody on this team better be able to hit one."

The man on the foul line lets them go through six more knuckleballs before he blows his whistle and the star pattern begins to change. The pitcher and the catcher remain in the center while the other women move around them. He sees this game as dance; the women keep time to the positions they play and the whole field becomes a song.

The batter hands the bat to the woman with the gold loops and then moves out to replace the woman in the gray sweatsuit at first. The man watches as each woman swings one position to the left. He pays particular attention to the woman in curlers while she runs a windsprint out to center field. She is new this year and he studies her run, arms to the side, pumping.

"Let me do the slider," the pitcher asks and the catcher signals okay. The pitch comes across like a fastball but breaks and slides left underneath the swing of the bat.

"Crap," the woman with the gold loops says and the man notices her auburn hair is coming loose from her ponytails.

"That's a good one," the catcher calls. The next slider is too low and bounces on the plate. It is returned without comment. The batter rests the bat on her shoulder and touches at her earrings.

The pitcher runs a finger along the elastic line of her bra encircling her ribcage. She stamps at the mound with her toe for a moment before replacing her glove and winding up again. The slider comes across fast, drops to the right.

"Crap," the batter says as she swings and misses.

The next ten pitches are sliders; three bounce and the batter gets one hit, a dribbler that is picked up by the stocky woman with glasses now playing third. She throws it to first, hard. While the ball is returned to the pitcher, the woman at third looks around for the cigarette she has dropped and crushes it out with her foot.

The man at the sidelines blows his whistle again and the star pattern flows once more to the left. The stocky woman from third takes one of the lead donuts and limbers up with a few hard swings of the weighted bat. She sloughs off the donut and calls to the pitcher: "Let me work on the curve."

"No," says the catcher. "You can hit a curve clear to the trees. Try something new."

"Risers," calls the man from the sidelines.

The pitcher walks around the mound for a moment, playing with the straps on her bra again. Finally she sends off a wild pitch, the release coming too close to her ankle. It sails upward so high that the catcher jumps but cannot field it. The ball bounces off the top of the cyclone fenced backstop.

"Curves is easier," the stocky woman says as she takes a few more practice swings.

The catcher pulls the ball out of the mud and returns it without comment. The pitcher kicks at the mound a few more times and sends off another riser that passes the batter just below the waist and beneath the hard cut of the bat.

The stocky woman stamps in the box and pushes her glasses up her nose. "As soon as I hit one of these mothers I'm leaving," she says. She swings past two more pitches. For the third pitch she shifts, bending more at the knees, leaning left, her ass out behind her at a greater angle.

"You're so easy," the catcher says. "If this was a real game I'd signal up for your curve, just like you wanted."

"If this was a real game," the batter answers, "I wouldn't have to listen to your yapping "

The pitch is another riser. The batter swings hard and the metal bat rings as she connects solidly with the ball, lofting it over the head of the skinny left fielder and almost to the line of Lombardy poplars. She gets another hit to the same hole on the next pitch. The catcher stands and yells out to left field: "Look alive out there. Play her deep. Save you all that running."

"It's good for my figure," the left fielder calls as she moves back. "I can't get all my exercise in bed."

The batter swings hard on the next pitch, so hard the momentum of the swing spins her around until she ends up sitting on the plate, tailor fashion, with the bat lying behind her. The catcher laughs before sticking out her hand and helping the stocky woman up. "Don't bust your buns before the games," she says.

The batter lights another cigarette and begins to move off toward the parking lot. "I got to go get my kids," she says.

"Come on, Sullivan," the woman with her hair in rollers yells. "All this fresh air ain't good for my hairdo."

"I'm getting cramps," the catcher complains as she stretches and loosens the chest protector.

The pattern in the field begins to break, some of the women lighting cigarettes or unwrapping pieces of gum, scattering the burnt matches and shiny pieces of foil across the muddy grass.

Sullivan says nothing as he watches the women walk off. They look fat and sluggish but that will wear off them by June. "Go home," Sullivan says, although it is not necessary. "Maggie and Rita. You stay and work on those sliders."

There are shouts of 'Goodbye' and the slammings of car doors as Maggie, the pitcher, and Rita, the catcher, come over to Sullivan to complain.

"Don't you want me to go to work?" Rita asks as she unhooks the last strap of the chest protector and lets it slip to the ground. "Think of all the money you're going to lose if you make me stand out here to catch those dustballs of hers."

"Ten minutes," Sullivan says. He turns to Maggie. "They're coming off your wrist wrong." He demonstrates with his own hand how the ball should roll. Taking her hand in his, he turns it a few times, showing her the feel of the angle. Maggie goes back to the mound and Rita squats behind the plate, leaving the mask and chest protector lying near the backstop.

"Make no mistakes," Rita calls out to Maggie. "I've already had my nose busted once. A second time won't improve my looks."

"Trust me," Maggie says. "I never make mistakes."

Sullivan leaves the base line and goes to stand on the top tier of the bleachers. Overhead, three mallards are flying north, their silhouettes sharp against the snow on the mountaintops. Sullivan believes there is always snow on the mountaintops, except in August, just before the women's fastpitch softball state championship.

Sara Vogan, who lived in the Missoula area in the early 1970s, was known for her books portraying troubled people, ranging from Vietnam vets to burned-out flower children to AIDS victims. This selection, set in the Missoula area, was taken from In Shelly's Leg *(Knopf, 1981). Vogan published the novel* Loss of Flight *(Bantam Books, 1989) and a short story collection,* Scenes from Homefront *(Bantam Books, 1987). She taught creative writing at the University of Oregon. She died in San Francisco in 1991 at the age of forty-three.*

Patricia Goedicke

MONTANA PEARS

In the middle of Montana, eating.
What the man sliced for them, two pears on a plate
sprinkled with bottled lime juice
and sugar.

His fork. Then hers. Spearing up
naked, white-to-sour-green
chunks of moonless November's
cold orchards.

Tired, both of them.
On the thick, green
chemically textured part nylon
and wool sofa.

The man's comfortable
beige sweater bulges
next to the woman stuffed
into cheap stretch pants, a faded
apple red Tee shirt.

Eighty years old.
And sixty. Add or
subtract a few. What have they been doing
all those years?

You, out there in the dark,
don't be afraid.
See, they're all lit up for you, do you
know them? I don't,
and I'm stage manager here. In fact,
I'm one of the actors.

A tape purrs in the background.
As the man forks up
the last piece of pear and puts it
in the woman's mouth,

Mark Daterman's electric guitar wheedles
over Glen Moore's acoustic bass in
The Blimp Wars, two state-of-the-art
instruments plucking, twining around each other.

The next piece they play is named after William
Carlos Williams' *The Great Figure*, in gold
reedy overtones, crackling halos of twanged
glowing noise, but then Daterman

and Moore stop playing, the man
says something, the woman nods,
thanks the man for the pears, I think he
thanks her for the music.

Pleased, both of them
peer at their books again.
But even the smartest, new
chemical preservatives can't help:

crushed, folded in on themselves
like sausages,
all the orchards are dark now, cold
shadowy fruit lumped
in heaps on the bare ground.

Silence. Then she stretches,
tucks her stockinged feet
in his lap. He strokes them
without looking, pauses
every once in awhile to stare, rub his eyes
with the back of his hand. Well,

it's ten o'clock.
Soon they'll be going to bed.
Does the telephone ring? Doesn't anyone
recognize them? You, out there in the dark,
look in at the two of them,
glowing.

AT THE CENTER

Six feet by three feet patch
swells upward, slightly
greener toward the chest.

Plastic carnations, polka dots.

Behind, tall wheat,
some pines, a ragged fence.

And the occasional clink clunk
of the cow bells we hung here

once, when we came out
with Phoebe and Tobin, two blonde babies
tumbling, one still at the breast.

But now you are nowhere in evidence, down there
dressed in the green sweater I knitted for you
when we first met.

On the horizon, 350 degrees of raw mountains;
the passing brush of wind—
sunshine's glint.

At the center, a handful of whiskery
wild roses in a pot

and a clump of sunflowers that burns
like a yellow warning light, stuck, swinging
in the middle of a deserted intersection

surrounded by old ranch houses, faint flecks of snow
still visible on the mountains.

THE RIVER BASIN, THE RAPIDS

The moment you stepped away from me into your death
the lung waters within me ran dry I fell away from myself and you fell too
it was as if night had fallen had crashed
right from the sky no noon not even
a cup of water for the children the green banks cracked
inside there was nothing   bare as a whistle the sinks gurgled
flatly the pipes groaned the millpond disappeared
as if it had never been   behind the dam there was
caked sand the bathtub refused to bathe us   the whole world was sick
to its stomach   everywhere cells withered   it was black

                      so I kept putting on your smile
                    like a sweater   arms wide open
            at the front door but it only worked once in awhile
                 you were not behind me there was grit

in all the dishes there was stone in every gloved
handshake   the cherry wood pool of the dining table
was gravel and I shivered for you I wondered where you were
in the desert at night were you alone were you safe
in your tent was there a drop of water for your teeth   when
will you kiss me again with your firm
gardenia leaved lips your breath a wind
of thorn apples and roses   I know never

we both knew
is where all paths
all gardens end
in the high
rocky plains without water
only the arid crackle
of memory's joss sticks but listen

one day I woke to the sound of tides rushing away
that left us high and dry   but another day
because I did not die   because you wouldn't have wanted it
or anyone because it is ineluctable   grief permits itself to be forgotten
not life   that is what you believed   and you wanted us to live
as well as possible in a bare house
just as you said the news
wasn't exactly good   the river basin
didn't quite fill up but there was   water in it
once again slowly
painfully rising
and now over its thin   transparently
deceptive surfaces sunlight plays hide and
seek
with its shallows   its swift rippling   dark
shadows moving below   you said you worshiped

and light too   there are wild blackberries
bristling among the grasses
beside the river bank there are still things to be said
you told me   there will always be
in the riprap words go by   old ones
and new ones for carrying sadness
in its dripping sieve   so many drowned cars
still there   behind cracked windshields
staring up at the sky

as now in their brief sprint
stone flies flash   in the fast sliding away
of rapids in lace sheets over rocks
in quick   silvery glimpses
fish like dimes darting   first one place
then another I think I see you   I know you
and what you have become   everywhere   your flickering
almost invisible   face

THE GREAT SPHERES

The great spheres speak to us but we are deaf:
                              willfully or not, wind
        tugs at the sleeping house like a boat
                tied up at a rickety dock and knocking back at it,
                        some loose tool,

        hoe, maybe, or human hand
                        turning on itself,   white faces at the windows,
            the towers of Ilium toppling again and again,
                                    tents exploding in the desert
                    with wrecked fishing boats, wild children
            flailing, dragged out to sea —
                                        the raw hawser
                    of a black telephone wire creaks
                            at the end of its tether,   some
            long ago lost Connection,   giant umbilical
cord straining —

Patricia Goedicke authored eleven books of poetry, the most recent of which,
As Earth Begins to End *(Copper Canyon, 2000), was recognized by the
American Library Association as one of the top-ten poetry books of the year.
She taught for a number of years in the creative writing program at the
University of Montana–Missoula. She was the recipient of many awards for
her poetry, among them* Beloit Poetry Journal's Chad Walsh Poetry Prize for
2002. *Recent poems by Goedicke may be seen in the journals* Agni, Colorado
Review, Gettysburg Review, Hotel Amerika, Volt, *and* Contemporary
Northwest Poets. *She died on July 14, 2006.*

BIBLIOGRAPHY AND
PERMISSIONS ACKNOWLEDGMENTS

Alcosser, Sandra. "Mare Frigoris." *Sleeping Inside the Glacier*. San Diego: Brighton Press, 1997. "What Makes the Grizzlies Dance" and "Michael's Wine." *Except by Nature*, St. Paul, Minnestoa: Graywolf Press, 1998. "A Fish to Feed All Hunger." *A Fish to Feed All Hunger*. Ahsahta Press, 1993. Used by permission of the author.

Alderson, Nannie T. and Helena Huntington Smith. "Chapter IV." *A Bride Goes West*. New York: Farrar & Rinehart, Inc., 1942. Reprint. Lincoln, Nebraska: University of Nebraska Press, 1969. Used by permission of University of Nebraska Press.

Baumler, Ellen. "Dorothy's Rooms: Helena's Last, and Some Say Best, Place." *Roundup* (June 2002). Used by permission of the author.

Blew, Mary Clearman. "Paranoia." Used by permission of the author.

Blunt, Judy. "Salvage." *Breaking Clean*. New York: Alfred A. Knopf, 2002. Used by permission of the author.

Bower, B. M. "Cold Spring Ranch." *Lonesome Land*. Boston: Little, Brown and Company, 1912. Reprint, with an introduction by Pam Houston. Lincoln, Nebraska: University of Nebraska Press, 1997. Used by permission of University of Nebraska Press.

Coates, Grace Stone. "Hardness of Women." *Mead and Mangel-Wurzel*. Caldwell, Idaho: The Caxton Printers, Ltd., 1931. Reprint. *Grace Stone Coates: Honey-Wine and Hunger Root*, by Lee Rostad, Helena, Montana: Falcon Press, 1985. "Portulacas in the Wheat" and "The Cliff." *Portulacas in the Wheat.* Caldwell, Idaho: The Caxton Printers, Ltd., 1931. Used by permission of Lee Rostad.

Connolly, Geraldine. "Morel Hunting," "Lydia," and "Deep in the Barn." Used by permission of the author.

Custer, Elizabeth B. "Our Life's Last Chapter." *Boots and Saddles, Or Life in Dakota with General Custer.* New York: Harper & Brothers, 1885. Reprint. Norman, Oklahoma: University of Oklahoma Press, 1961.

DeFrees, Madeline. "Climbing the Sky Bridge Stair on my way to Suzzalo Library" and "The Poetry of Spiders." *Spectral Waves.* Seattle, Washington: Copper Canyon Press, 2006. "In the Hellgate Wind" and "The Shell." *Blue Dusk: New & Selected Poems,* 1951-2001. Seattle, Washington: Copper Canyon Press. Used by permission of the Copper Canyon Press.

Earling, Debra Magpie. "Bad Ways," "Winter Deeds," and "Old Ghosts." *Ploughshares,* 20:1 (Spring 1994). Used by permission of the author.

Fligelman, Frieda. "Narrow Streets I," "Solitude (Silence is Thought)," and "If I Were the Queen of Sheba." Used by permission of Alexandra Swaney.

Gadbow, Kate. "Buffalo Jump." *Epoch* 42:2 (Spring 1993). Used by permission of the author.

Goedicke, Patricia. "Montana Pears" and "At the Center." *The Hudson Review.* "The River Basin, the Rapids." *Hayden's Ferry Review.* "The Great Spheres." *NEO,* upcoming. Used by permission of the author.

Haaland, Tami. "The Dog," "First Trimester," "Scout Meeting at Mayflower Congregational," and "11:05." *Breath in Every Room.* Ashland, Oregon: Story Line Press, 2001. Used by permission of the author.

Haste, Gwendolen. "Ranch in the Coulee," "The Reason," and "The Solitary." *Young Land.* New York: Coward-McCann, 1930. Reprint. *The Selected Poems of Gwendolen Haste.* Boise, Idaho: Ahsahta Press, 1976.

Henley, Patricia. "The Secret of Cartwheels." *The Secret of Cartwheels.* St. Paul, Minnesota: Graywolf Press, 1992. Used by permission of the author.

Hugo, Ripley Schemm. Excerpt from Chapter 6, "The First Two Montana Novels." *Writing for Her Life: The Novelist Mildred Walker.* Lincoln, Nebraska: University of Nebraska Press, 2003. Used by permission of the University of Nebraska Press. "Lessons," "Retelling the Story," and "Building Fence." Used by permission of the author.

Johnson, Dorothy M. "Prairie Kid." *Indian Country.* New York: Ballantine Books, 1949. Used by permission of McIntosh and Otis.

Klink, Joanna. "Porch in Snow." *Smartish Pace* (April 2003). "Winter Field." *Boston Review* (2006). "Antelope" is forthcoming in *New Orleans Review.* Used by permission of the author.

Kuffel, Frances. "First Love." *Greensboro Review* (Summer 1995), number 58. Used by permission of the author.

Kwasny, Melissa. "Reading Novalis in Montana." *Willow Springs* 54 (2004). "Lepidoptera." *Poetry Northwest* 26:81. "Common Blue." *Ploughshares* (Spring 2000). Used by permission of the author.

MacLane, Mary. "February 3, [1901]." *The Story of Mary Maclane by Herself.* Chicago: Herbert S. Stone & Company, 1902. Reprint. Helena, Montana: Riverbend Press, 2002.

Maldonado, Bonnie Buckley. "Beneath the Northern Lights," "Blarney Castle Ranch," and "Annie's Bonfire." *From the Marias River to the North Pole.* Helena, Montana: Sweetgrass Press, 2006. Used by permission of the author.

McFadden, Cyra. "Chapter Two." *Rain or Shine: A Family Memoir.* New

York: Knopf, 1986. Reprint. Lincoln, Nebraska: University of Nebraska Press, 1998. Used by permission of University of Nebraska Press.

McLaughlin, Ruth. "Destiny" is part of a memoir, *Bound Like Grass*. Used by permission of the author.

McNamer, Deirdre. "Chapter Three," *One Sweet Quarrel*. New York: Harper Collins Publishers, 1994. Used by permission of the author.

Meloy, Maile. "Garrison Junction." *Half in Love*. New York: Scribner, 2002. Reprinted with the permission of Scribner, an imprint of Simon & Schuster Adult Publishing Group.

Noethe, Sheryl. "God's Riffling Touch," "Rural Poetry Workshop," and "The Sri Lanken's Golden Book of Death" Used by permission of the author.

Ronan, Mary. "The Jocko Valley." *Girl from the Gulches: The Story of Mary Ronan*. Reprinted, edited by Ellen Baumler. Helena, Montana: Montana Historical Society Press, 2003. Used by permission of the Montana Historical Society.

Rostad, Lee. "An Alien Land." *Grace Stone Coates: Her Life in Letters*. Helena, Montana: Riverbend Publishing, 2004. Used by permission of the author.

Schemm, Mildred Walker. "Rancher's Wife." *Junior League Magazine* (June 1940). Used by permission of Ripley Schemm.

Smith, Annick. "Virtue." *Ploughshares*. Used by permission of the author.

Smith, Diane. *Pictures from an Expedition*. New York: Penguin Group, Inc. Used by permission of the Penguin Group.

Smoker, M. L. "From the river's edge," "Winter again," and "Borrowing blue." *Another Attempt at Rescue*. New York: Hanging Loose Press, 2005. Used by permission of Hanging Loose Press.

Thon, Melanie Rae. "Heavenly Creatures." *Paris Review*, 2004. Used by permission of the Irene Skolnick Agency.

Vogan, Sara. *In Shelly's Leg*. New York: Alfred A. Knopf, 1980. Used by permission of Random House.

Vontver, May. "The Kiskis" in *The Frontier* at the University of Montana (March 1929). Used by permission of Dr. Louis Vontver.

Walker, Mildred. "Rancher's Wife." *Jumor League Magazine* (June 1940). Used by permission of Ripley Schemm Hugo.

Zupan, Janet. "Plunge," "Refugee," and "Prodigal Daughter." Used by permission of the author.